Scott Foresman · Addison Wesley
enVisionMATH 2.0 ★ 2.0

Volume 2 Topics 9-16

Authors

Randall I. Charles
Professor Emeritus
Department of Mathematics
San Jose State University
San Jose, California

Janet H. Caldwell
Professor of Mathematics
Rowan University
Glassboro, New Jersey

Juanita Copley
Professor Emerita, College of
Education
University of Houston
Houston, Texas

Warren Crown
Professor Emeritus of Mathematics
Education
Graduate School of Education
Rutgers University
New Brunswick, New Jersey

Francis (Skip) Fennell
L. Stanley Bowlsbey Professor
of Education and Graduate and
Professional Studies
McDaniel College
Westminster, Maryland

Stuart J. Murphy
Visual Learning Specialist
Boston, Massachusetts

Kay B. Sammons
Coordinator of Elementary
Mathematics
Howard County Public Schools
Ellicott City, Maryland

Jane F. Schielack
Professor of Mathematics
Associate Dean for Assessment
and Pre K-12 Education,
College of Science
Texas A&M University
College Station, Texas

Mathematicians

Roger Howe
Professor of Mathematics
Yale University
New Haven, Connecticut

Gary Lippman
Professor of Mathematics and
Computer Science
California State University East Bay
Hayward, California

PEARSON

Glenview, Illinois   Boston, Massachusetts   Chandler, Arizona   Upper Saddle River, New Jersey

Contributing Authors

Zachary Champagne
District Facilitator, Duval County
Public Schools
Florida Center for Research in
Science, Technology, Engineering,
and Mathematics (FCR-STEM)
Jacksonville, Florida

Jonathan A. Wray
Mathematics Instructional
Facilitator
Howard County Public Schools
Ellicott City, Maryland

ELL Consultants

Janice Corona
Retired Administrator
Dallas ISD, Multi-Lingual
Department
Dallas, Texas

Jim Cummins
Professor
The University of Toronto
Toronto, Canada

Texas Reviewers

Theresa Bathe
Teacher
Fort Bend ISD

Chrissy Beltran
School Wide Project Coordinator
Ysleta ISD

Renee Cutright
Teacher
Amarillo ISD

Sharon Grimm
Teacher
Houston ISD

Esmeralda Herrera
Teacher
San Antonio ISD

Sherry Johnson
Teacher
Round Rock ISD

Elvia Lopez
Teacher
Denton ISD

Antoinese Pride
Instructional Coach
Dallas ISD

Joanna Ratliff
Teacher
Keller ISD

Courtney Jo Ridehuber
Teacher
Mansfield ISD

Nannie D. Scurlock-McKnight
Mathematics Specialist
A.W. Brown Fellowship-Leadership
Academy
Dallas, TX

Brian Sinclair
Math Instructional Specialist
Fort Worth ISD

ISBN-13: 978-0-328-76730-4
ISBN-10: 0-328-76730-1

Digital Resources

Look for these digital resources in every lesson!

 Go to PearsonTexas.com

 Solve
Solve & Share problems plus math tools

 Learn
Visual Learning Animation Plus with animation, interaction, and math tools

 Glossary
Animated Glossary in English and Spanish

 Tools
Math Tools to help you understand

 Check
Quick Check for each lesson

 Games
Math Games to help you learn

eText
The pages in your book online

PearsonTexas.com
Everything you need for math anytime, anywhere

Key

Number and Operations
Algebraic Reasoning
Geometry and Measurement
Data Analysis
Personal Financial Literacy

Mathematical Process Standards are found in all lessons.

Digital Resources at PearsonTexas.com

Solve   Learn   Glossary
Check   Tools   Games

And remember, the pages in your book are also online!

Contents

🌟 Topics

VOLUME 1

TOPIC 1   **Place Value**

TOPIC 2   **Adding and Subtracting Whole Numbers and Decimals**

TOPIC 3   **Multiplying Whole Numbers and Decimals**

TOPIC 4   **Number Sense: Dividing by 2-Digit Divisors**

TOPIC 5   **Developing Proficiency: Dividing by 2-Digit Divisors**

TOPIC 6   **Dividing Decimals**

TOPIC 7   **Adding and Subtracting Fractions**

TOPIC 8   **Adding and Subtracting Mixed Numbers**

VOLUME 2

TOPIC 9   **Multiplying and Dividing Fractions**

TOPIC 10   **Expressions and Equations**

TOPIC 11   **Ordered Pairs and the Plane**

TOPIC 12   **Two-Dimensional Shapes**

TOPIC 13   **Perimeter, Area, and Volume**

TOPIC 14   **Measurement Units and Conversions**

TOPIC 15   **Data Analysis**

TOPIC 16   **Personal Financial Literacy**

TOPIC 1 — Place Value

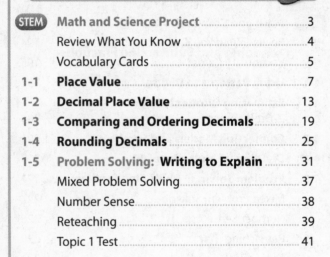

Hi, I'm Emily. This shows different ways to represent a decimal.

Standard Form: 0.245
Expanded Form: $0.2 + 0.04 + 0.005$
Word Form: two hundred forty-five thousandths

TEKS 5.1A, 5.1B, 5.1C, 5.1D, 5.1E, 5.1F, 5.1G, 5.2, 5.2A, 5.2B, 5.2C, 5.3B

STEM	Math and Science Project	3
	Review What You Know	4
	Vocabulary Cards	5
1-1	**Place Value**	7
1-2	**Decimal Place Value**	13
1-3	**Comparing and Ordering Decimals**	19
1-4	**Rounding Decimals**	25
1-5	**Problem Solving: Writing to Explain**	31
	Mixed Problem Solving	37
	Number Sense	38
	Reteaching	39
	Topic 1 Test	41

TOPIC 2 — Adding and Subtracting Whole Numbers and Decimals

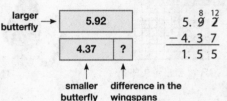

Hi, I'm Carlos. This shows how to regroup when subtracting decimals.

larger butterfly → 5.92

smaller butterfly — 4.37 — ?

difference in the wingspans

$$5.\overset{8}{9}\overset{12}{2}$$
$$-\,4.\,3\,7$$
$$\overline{1.\,5\,5}$$

TEKS 5.1A, 5.1B, 5.1C, 5.1D, 5.1E, 5.1F, 5.1G, 5.3, 5.3A, 5.3K

STEM	Math and Science Project	43
	Review What You Know	44
	Vocabulary Cards	45
2-1	**Mental Math**	47
2-2	**Estimating Sums and Differences**	53
2-3	**Adding and Subtracting Whole Numbers**	59
2-4	**Adding Decimals**	65
2-5	**Subtracting Decimals**	71
2-6	**Adding and Subtracting Decimals**	77
2-7	**Problem Solving: Multi-Step Problems**	83
	Mixed Problem Solving	89
	Number Sense	90
	Reteaching	91
	Topic 2 Test	93

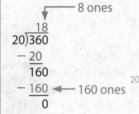

Volume 1

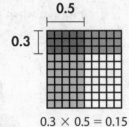

TOPIC 3 — Multiplying Whole Numbers and Decimals

Hi, I'm Jada. This shows how to multiply decimals using a grid.

0.5
0.3

$0.3 \times 0.5 = 0.15$

★ **TEKS** 5.1A, 5.1B, 5.1C, 5.1D, 5.1E, 5.1F, 5.1G, 5.2C, 5.3, 5.3A, 5.3B, 5.3D, 5.3E, 5.4B

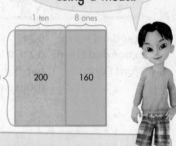

TOPIC 4 — Number Sense: Dividing by 2-Digit Divisors

Hi, I'm Daniel. This shows how to divide whole numbers using a model.

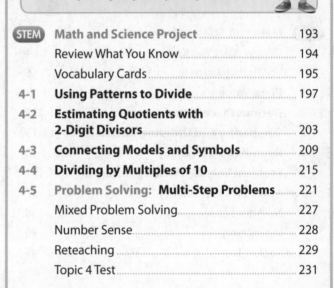

8 ones

$$\begin{array}{r} 18 \\ 20)\overline{360} \\ -\underline{20} \\ 160 \\ -\underline{160} \\ 0 \end{array}$$

← 160 ones

1 ten   8 ones
20   200   160

★ **TEKS** 5.1A, 5.1B, 5.1C, 5.1D, 5.1E, 5.1F, 5.1G, 5.3, 5.3A, 5.3C, 5.4B

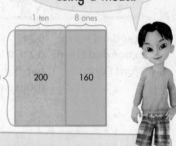

STEM Math and Science Project 95
Review What You Know 96
Vocabulary Cards 97
3-1 **Estimating Products** 99
3-2 **Multiplying 3-Digit by 2-Digit Numbers** 105
3-3 **Multiplying with Zeros** 111
3-4 **Multiplying Multi-Digit Numbers** 117
3-5 **Problem Solving: Use Reasoning** 123
3-6 **Multiplying Decimals by 10, 100, or 1,000** 129
3-7 **Estimating the Product of a Decimal and a Whole Number** 135
3-8 **Number Sense: Decimal Multiplication** 141
3-9 **Modeling Multiplying a Decimal by a Whole Number** 147
3-10 **Multiplying a Decimal by a Whole Number** 153
3-11 **Modeling Multiplying a Decimal by a Decimal** 159
3-12 **Multiplying Two Decimals** 165
3-13 **Multiplying with Money** 171
3-14 **Problem Solving: Draw a Strip Diagram and Write an Equation** 177
Mixed Problem Solving 183
Number Sense 184
Reteaching 185
Topic 3 Test 189

STEM Math and Science Project 193
Review What You Know 194
Vocabulary Cards 195
4-1 **Using Patterns to Divide** 197
4-2 **Estimating Quotients with 2-Digit Divisors** 203
4-3 **Connecting Models and Symbols** 209
4-4 **Dividing by Multiples of 10** 215
4-5 **Problem Solving: Multi-Step Problems** 221
Mixed Problem Solving 227
Number Sense 228
Reteaching 229
Topic 4 Test 231

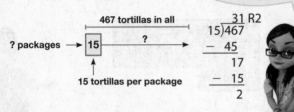

Volume 1

TOPIC 5 — Developing Proficiency: Dividing by 2-Digit Divisors

Hi, I'm Marta. This shows how to divide whole numbers with a remainder.

467 tortillas in all

? packages → 15 → ?

15 tortillas per package

```
      31 R2
15)467
   − 45
     17
   − 15
      2
```

⭐ TEKS 5.1, 5.1A, 5.1B, 5.1C, 5.1D, 5.1E, 5.1F, 5.1G, 5.3, 5.3C

STEM Math and Science Project 233
Review What You Know 234
5-1 **1-Digit Quotients** 235
5-2 **2-Digit Quotients** 241
5-3 **3-Digit Quotients** 247
5-4 **Dividing by 2-Digit Divisors** 253
5-5 **Problem Solving: Analyze Given Information** 259
Mixed Problem Solving 265
Number Sense 266
Reteaching 267
Topic 5 Test 269

TOPIC 6 — Dividing Decimals

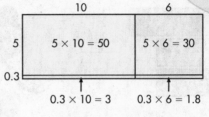

Hi, I'm Alex. This shows a model for dividing a decimal by a whole number.

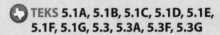

	10	6
5	5 × 10 = 50	5 × 6 = 30
0.3	0.3 × 10 = 3	0.3 × 6 = 1.8

50 + 30 + 3 + 1.8 = 84.8
16 × 5.3 = 84.8
84.8 ÷ 16 = 5.3

⭐ TEKS 5.1A, 5.1B, 5.1C, 5.1D, 5.1E, 5.1F, 5.1G, 5.3, 5.3A, 5.3F, 5.3G

STEM Math and Science Project 271
Review What You Know 272
6-1 **Patterns for Dividing with Decimals** 273
6-2 **Estimating Decimal Quotients** 279
6-3 **Models for Dividing by a 1-Digit Whole Number** 285
6-4 **Dividing by a 1-Digit Whole Number** ... 291
6-5 **Models for Dividing by a 2-Digit Whole Number** 297
6-6 **Dividing by a 2-Digit Whole Number** ... 303
6-7 **Problem Solving: Reasonableness** 309
Mixed Problem Solving 315
Number Sense 316
Reteaching 317
Topic 6 Test 319

Volume 1

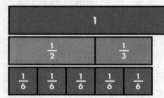

TOPIC 7 Adding and Subtracting Fractions

Hi, I'm Jada. This shows adding fractions with unlike denominators.

$$\frac{1}{2} = \frac{3}{6}$$
$$+ \frac{1}{3} = \frac{2}{6}$$
$$\frac{5}{6}$$

TEKS 5.1A, 5.1B, 5.1C, 5.1D, 5.1E, 5.1F, 5.1G, 5.3A, 5.3H, 5.3K, 5.4A

TOPIC 8 Adding and Subtracting Mixed Numbers

Hi, I'm Carlos. This shows subtracting mixed numbers with like denominators.

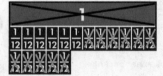

$$2\frac{5}{12} - 1\frac{11}{12} = \frac{6}{12}$$

TEKS 5.1A, 5.1B, 5.1C, 5.1D, 5.1E, 5.1F, 5.1G, 5.3A, 5.3H, 5.3K

STEM Math and Science Project		321
Review What You Know		322
Vocabulary Cards		323
7-1	Prime and Composite Numbers	325
7-2	Equivalent Fractions	331
7-3	Fractions in Simplest Form	337
7-4	Estimating Sums and Differences of Fractions	343
7-5	Finding Common Denominators	349
7-6	Adding Fractions with Unlike Denominators	355
7-7	Subtracting Fractions with Unlike Denominators	361
7-8	More Adding and Subtracting Fractions	367
7-9	Problem Solving: Draw a Strip Diagram and Write an Equation	373
Mixed Problem Solving		379
Number Sense		380
Reteaching		381
Topic 7 Test		383

STEM Math and Science Project		385
Review What You Know		386
Vocabulary Cards		387
8-1	Improper Fractions and Mixed Numbers	389
8-2	Estimating Sums and Differences of Mixed Numbers	395
8-3	Modeling Addition of Mixed Numbers	401
8-4	Adding Mixed Numbers	407
8-5	Modeling Subtraction of Mixed Numbers	413
8-6	Subtracting Mixed Numbers	419
8-7	More Adding and Subtracting Mixed Numbers	425
8-8	Problem Solving: Draw a Strip Diagram and Write an Equation	431
Mixed Problem Solving		437
Number Sense		438
Reteaching		439
Topic 8 Test		443

Glossary	G1

Volume 2

TOPIC 9 — Multiplying and Dividing Fractions

Hi, I'm Emily. This shows how to divide a whole number by a unit fraction using a model.

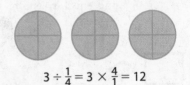

$$3 \div \frac{1}{4} = 3 \times \frac{4}{1} = 12$$

⭐ **TEKS** 5.1A, 5.1B, 5.1C, 5.1D, 5.1E, 5.1F, 5.1G, 5.3, 5.3I, 5.3J, 5.3L

STEM	Math and Science Project	447
	Review What You Know	448
	Vocabulary Cards	449
9-1	**Fractions as Multiples of Unit Fractions**	451
9-2	**Multiplying Fractions and Whole Numbers**	457
9-3	**More Multiplying Fractions and Whole Numbers**	463
9-4	**Dividing Whole Numbers by Unit Fractions**	469
9-5	**Dividing Unit Fractions by Non-Zero Whole Numbers**	475
9-6	**More Dividing with Whole Numbers and Unit Fractions**	481
9-7	**Problem Solving: Multi-Step Problems**	487
	Mixed Problem Solving	493
	Number Sense	494
	Reteaching	495
	Topic 9 Test	497

TOPIC 10 — Expressions and Equations

Hi, I'm Jackson. This shows how to evaluate an algebraic expression.

$23 + n$

$23 + 3 = 26$

DATA	n	$23 + n$
	3	$23 + 3$
	5	$23 + 5$
	7	$23 + 7$

⭐ **TEKS** 5.1A, 5.1B, 5.1C, 5.1D, 5.1E, 5.1F, 5.1G, 5.4, 5.4B, 5.4D, 5.4E, 5.4F

STEM	Math and Science Project	499
	Review What You Know	500
	Vocabulary Cards	501
10-1	**Order of Operations**	503
10-2	**Simplifying Expressions**	509
10-3	**Understanding Algebraic Expressions**	515
10-4	**Evaluating Algebraic Expressions**	521
10-5	**Addition and Subtraction Expressions**	527
10-6	**Multiplication and Division Expressions**	533
10-7	**Solving Equations**	539
10-8	**More Solving Equations**	545
10-9	**Problem Solving: Use Reasoning**	551
	Mixed Problem Solving	557
	Number Sense	558
	Reteaching	559
	Topic 10 Test	563

Volume 2

TOPIC 11 — Ordered Pairs and the Plane

Hi, I'm Marta. This graph shows a multiplicative pattern.

$y = 3x$

TEKS 5.1A, 5.1B, 5.1C, 5.1D, 5.1E, 5.1F, 5.1G, 5.4C, 5.4D, 5.8, 5.8A, 5.8B, 5.8C

STEM **Math and Science Project** 567
Review What You Know 568
Vocabulary Cards 569
11-1 **Ordered Pairs** 573
11-2 **Graphing Additive Patterns** 579
11-3 **Graphing Multiplicative Patterns** 585
11-4 **Graphing Equations** 591
11-5 **Recognizing Types of Patterns in Tables and Graphs** 597
11-6 **Problem Solving: Use Reasoning** 603
Mixed Problem Solving 609
Number Sense 610
Reteaching 611
Topic 11 Test 615

TOPIC 12 — Two-Dimensional Shapes

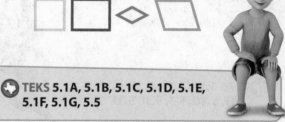

Hi, I'm Daniel. These shapes are all parallelograms because both pairs of opposite sides are parallel and equal in length.

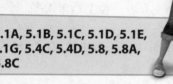

TEKS 5.1A, 5.1B, 5.1C, 5.1D, 5.1E, 5.1F, 5.1G, 5.5

STEM **Math and Science Project** 619
Review What You Know 620
Vocabulary Cards 621
12-1 **Polygons** 627
12-2 **Triangles** 633
12-3 **Properties of Quadrilaterals** 639
12-4 **Special Quadrilaterals** 645
12-5 **Classifying Quadrilaterals** 651
12-6 **Problem Solving: Use Reasoning** 657
Mixed Problem Solving 663
Number Sense 664
Reteaching 665
Topic 12 Test 667

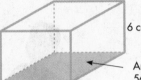

Volume 2

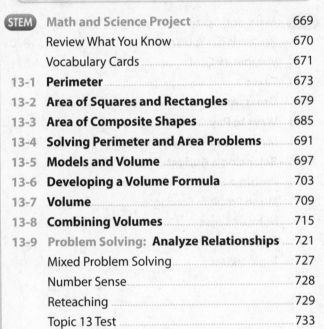

Hi, I'm Emily. This shows one way to find the volume of a rectangular prism.

$V = B \times h$
$V = 56 \times 6$
$V = 336$ cubic cm

6 cm

Area of base: 56 square cm

Hi, I'm Carlos. This shows how customary units of length are related.

1 foot (ft) = 12 inches (in.)
1 yard (yd) = 3 ft = 36 in.
1 mile (mi) = 1,760 yd = 5,280 ft

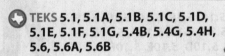

TEKS 5.1, 5.1A, 5.1B, 5.1C, 5.1D, 5.1E, 5.1F, 5.1G, 5.4B, 5.4G, 5.4H, 5.6, 5.6A, 5.6B

TEKS 5.1A, 5.1B, 5.1C, 5.1D, 5.1E, 5.1F, 5.1G, 5.4H, 5.7

STEM Math and Science Project	669	
Review What You Know	670	
Vocabulary Cards	671	
13-1 Perimeter	673	
13-2 Area of Squares and Rectangles	679	
13-3 Area of Composite Shapes	685	
13-4 Solving Perimeter and Area Problems	691	
13-5 Models and Volume	697	
13-6 Developing a Volume Formula	703	
13-7 Volume	709	
13-8 Combining Volumes	715	
13-9 Problem Solving: Analyze Relationships	721	
Mixed Problem Solving	727	
Number Sense	728	
Reteaching	729	
Topic 13 Test	733	

STEM Math and Science Project	737
Review What You Know	738
Vocabulary Cards	739
14-1 Converting Customary Units of Length	745
14-2 Converting Customary Units of Capacity	751
14-3 Converting Customary Units of Weight	757
14-4 Converting Metric Units of Length	763
14-5 Converting Metric Units of Capacity	769
14-6 Converting Metric Units of Mass	775
14-7 Problem Solving: Multi-Step Problems	781
Mixed Problem Solving	787
Number Sense	788
Reteaching	789
Topic 14 Test	791

Volume 2

TOPIC 15 — Data Analysis

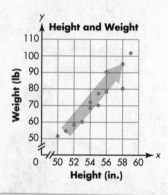

Height and Weight

Hi, I'm Jada. This shows how to identify a trend in a scatterplot.

TEKS 5.1A, 5.1B, 5.1C, 5.1D, 5.1E, 5.1F, 5.1G, 5.9, 5.9A, 5.9B, 5.9C

STEM	Math and Science Project	793
	Review What You Know	794
	Vocabulary Cards	795
15-1	**Reading Dot Plots**	799
15-2	**Making Dot Plots**	805
15-3	**Measurement Data**	811
15-4	**Reading Bar Graphs**	817
15-5	**Making Bar Graphs**	823
15-6	**Reading Stem-and-Leaf Plots**	829
15-7	**Making Stem-and-Leaf Plots**	835
15-8	**Reading Scatterplots**	841
15-9	**Making Scatterplots**	847
15-10	**Problem Solving: Use Representations**	853
	Mixed Problem Solving	859
	Number Sense	860
	Reteaching	861
	Topic 15 Test	865

TOPIC 16 — Personal Financial Literacy

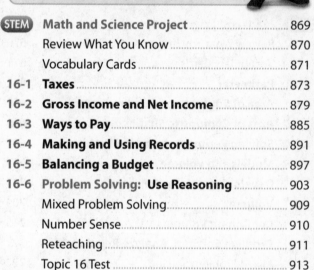

Drew's Budget

Income:
$24 dog walking
$16.75 raking leaves

Expenses:
$5 to charity
Save $10 for Summer trip
$12.95 for apps
Spend rest at fair.

Hi, I'm Carlos. This shows an example of a budget.

TEKS 5.1A, 5.1B, 5.1C, 5.1D, 5.1E, 5.1F, 5.1G, 5.10, 5.10A, 5.10B, 5.10C, 5.10D, 5.10E, 5.10F

STEM	Math and Science Project	869
	Review What You Know	870
	Vocabulary Cards	871
16-1	**Taxes**	873
16-2	**Gross Income and Net Income**	879
16-3	**Ways to Pay**	885
16-4	**Making and Using Records**	891
16-5	**Balancing a Budget**	897
16-6	**Problem Solving: Use Reasoning**	903
	Mixed Problem Solving	909
	Number Sense	910
	Reteaching	911
	Topic 16 Test	913

Volume 2

Step Up to Grade 6

These lessons help you prepare for Grade 6.

Have a great year!

TEKS **6.2B, 6.2C, 6.3A, 6.4C, 6.4E, 6.4G, 6.5A, 6.8B, 6.11**

	Table of Contents	915
	Grade 6 TEKS for Step-Up Lessons	916
1	**Understanding Integers**	917
2	**Comparing and Ordering Integers**	921
3	**Understanding Division of Fractions**	925
4	**Dividing a Whole Number by a Fraction**	929
5	**Understanding Ratios**	933
6	**Understanding Percents**	937
7	**Fractions, Decimals, and Percents**	941
8	**Rates and Unit Rates**	945
9	**Area of Parallelograms and Triangles**	949
10	**Graphing Points on a Coordinate Plane**	953

Glossary		G1

✪ Problem-Solving Handbook

Applying Math Processes

Analyze
- How does this problem connect to previous ones?
- What am I asked to find?
- What information do I know?

Plan
- What is my plan?
- What strategies can I use? (See the list of some helpful strategies.)
- How can I use tools?
- How can I organize and record information?

Solve
- How can I use number sense?
- How can I estimate?
- How can I communicate and represent my thinking?

Justify
- How can I explain my work?
- How can I justify my answer?

Evaluate
- Have I checked my work?
- Is my answer reasonable?

Use this Problem-Solving Handbook throughout the year to help you solve problems.

Some Helpful Strategies

- Represent the Problem
  - Draw a Picture or Strip Diagram
  - Write an Equation
  - Make a Table or List
- Look for a Pattern
- Use Reasoning
- Analyze Given Information
- Analyze Relationships

Problem-Solving Tools

Real Objects

$\frac{1}{6}$	$\frac{2}{6}$	$\frac{3}{6}$
$\frac{4}{6}$	$\frac{5}{6}$	$\frac{6}{6}$

Manipulatives

Distance swam

Bob	$\frac{5}{6}$ mile	
June	$\frac{7}{8}$ mile	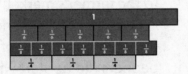
Tina	$\frac{3}{4}$ mile	

Paper and Pencil

$$\begin{array}{r} \$40.00 \\ -\ \$25.98 \\ \hline \$14.02 \end{array}$$

Technology

Problem-Solving Techniques

Mental Math

Sale!

T-shirt........$19.98
Jeans..........$48.50
Sweater.....$29.50

$19.98 + 48.50 + 29.50 = ?$
$20 + 50 + 30 = 100$
$100 - 2.02 = 97.98$

Estimation

The hummingbird's heart beats 597 times in a minute.

There are 60 minutes in an hour.
$597 \times 60 = ?$
About $600 \times 60 = 36{,}000$ heartbeats in an hour.

Number Sense

Soccer Attendance	
Game 1	550
Game 2	675
Game 3	642
Game 4	588

Each number is between 500 and 700. The total attendance will be between 2,000 and 2,800.

Strip Diagrams

You can draw a **strip diagram** to show how the quantities in a problem are related. Then you can write an equation to solve the problem.

Part-Part-Whole: Addition and Subtraction

Draw this **strip diagram** for situations that involve joining parts of a whole or separating a whole into parts.

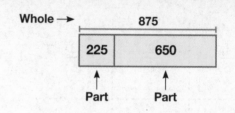

Whole → 875

| 225 | 650 |

↑ Part   ↑ Part

Problem 1

David saved $125.50. Then he spent $102.25 on a new bicycle. Now how much money does David have?

$125.50 → $125.50

| $102.25 | ? |

↑ $102.25 for bicycle   ↑ ? dollars left

$125.50 − $102.25 = ? or
$125.50 − ? = $102.25

He has $23.25 after buying the bicycle.

Problem 2

A farmer brought some peppers to the farmer's market. He sold 150 peppers. At the end of the day, he had 165 peppers left. How many peppers did he start with?

? peppers →   ?

| 150 | 165 |

↑ 150 peppers sold   ↑ 165 peppers left

150 + 165 = ? or ? − 150 = 165

He started with 315 peppers.

Comparison: Addition and Subtraction

Draw this **strip diagram** for comparison situations involving how much more one quantity is than another quantity.

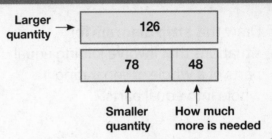

Larger quantity → 126

| 78 | 48 |

↑ Smaller quantity ↑ How much more is needed

Problem 1

Last year, 1,796 people attended the county fair. This year, 1,544 people attended. How many more people attended last year than this year?

1,796 people attended → | 1,796 |

| 1,544 | ? |

↑ 1,544 people attended   ↑ ? more people

$1,796 - 1,544 = ?$

Last year, 252 more people attended.

Problem 2

Ann's school raised $2,375 for charity. Brian's school raised $275 more than Ann's school. How much money did Brian's school raise?

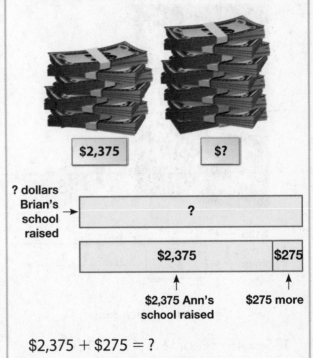

$2,375 $?

? dollars Brian's school raised → | ? |

| $2,375 | $275 |

↑ $2,375 Ann's school raised   ↑ $275 more

$\$2,375 + \$275 = ?$

Brian's school raised $2,650.

More Strip Diagrams

The **strip diagrams** on these pages can help you solve problems involving multiplication and division.

Equal Parts: Multiplication and Division

Draw this **strip diagram** for situations that involve joining equal parts of a whole or separating a whole into equal parts.

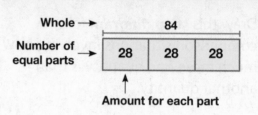

Whole → 84

Number of equal parts →

28	28	28

↑ Amount for each part

Problem 1

Tom spent $135 on some new video games. Each game cost the same. How many video games did he buy?

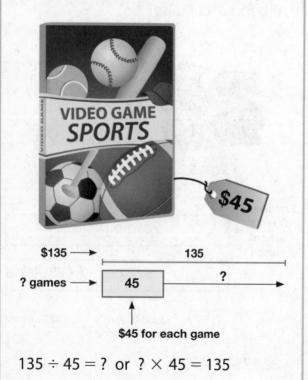

$45

$135 → 135

? games →

45	→ ?

↑ $45 for each game

$135 \div 45 = ?$ or $? \times 45 = 135$

Tom bought 3 video games.

Problem 2

Workers at an orchard sorted the apples they harvested. They put 120 apples into each of 4 containers. How many apples did they harvest?

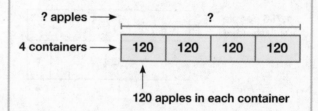

? apples → ?

4 containers →

120	120	120	120

↑ 120 apples in each container

$4 \times 120 = ?$ or $? \div 4 = 120$

They harvested 480 apples.

Multiplication and division are similar to addition and subtraction.

Comparison: Multiplication and Division

Draw this **strip diagram** for comparison situations involving how many times one quantity is of another quantity.

78			
Larger quantity →	26	26	26	3 times as many

Smaller quantity →	26

Problem 1

Joe buys a new tent and sleeping bag. The tent costs 4 times as much as the sleeping bag. How much does the sleeping bag cost?

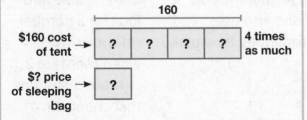

$160 \div 4 = ?$ or $4 \times ? = 160$

The sleeping bag costs $40.

Problem 2

Linda biked 175 miles last summer. Kendra biked 3 times as far as Linda. How many miles did Kendra bike?

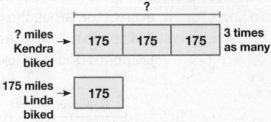

$3 \times 175 = ?$ or $? \div 3 = 175$

Kendra biked 525 miles.

Problem-Solving Handbook

More Problem-Solving Strategies

Creating a solution plan involves choosing and trying a strategy and then sometimes trying a different strategy.

Strategy	Example	When I Use It
Draw a Picture	Martin has a garden behind his house. The garden is 50 feet long and 20 feet wide. What is the perimeter of Martin's garden? 50 ft 20 ft 20 ft 50 ft The perimeter of Martin's garden is 140 feet.	A **representation** of the problem can help you visualize the facts and identify relationships.
Write an Equation	Monica made 144 ounces of punch for a party. If she pours the punch into 6-ounce glasses, how many glasses can she fill? Find $144 \div 6 = n$. $n = 24$, so Monica can fill 24 glasses.	You can **communicate ideas** by writing an equation to describe a situation involving an operation or operations.
Make a Table and Look for a Pattern	Barbara is making salsa at a restaurant. For every 3 tomatoes she uses, she also uses 2 jalapeños. If she uses 30 tomatoes, how many jalapeños does she use? <table><tr><td>Tomatoes</td><td>3</td><td>6</td><td>15</td><td>30</td></tr><tr><td>Jalapeños</td><td>2</td><td>4</td><td>10</td><td>20</td></tr></table> Barbara uses 20 jalapeños.	Make a table and look for a number **relationship** when there are 2 or more quantities that change in a predictable way.

xx

There's almost always more than one way to solve a problem.

Strategy	Example	When I Use It
Use Reasoning	Sue's train leaves at 7:30 A.M. She takes $\frac{1}{2}$ hour to get from home to the train station. She also takes an hour to get ready. She wants to arrive $\frac{1}{2}$ hour before the train leaves. What is the latest time she should get up? Time Sue needs to get up ← $1\frac{1}{2}$ hours — Time to arrive at station ← 30 minutes — Time train leaves **7:30** Sue should get up by 5:30 A.M.	**Reason** with the facts you know to find what actions cause the end result.
Analyze Given Information	Suzanne spent $8 on two items for lunch. What did she buy? $6.75 + $2.50 > $8 Too much $2.50 + $1.25 < $8 Not enough $6.75 + $1.25 = $8 Perfect! Suzanne bought a sandwich and a juice bottle.	**Analyze given information** to help find a solution. <table><tr><th>Item</th><th>Cost</th></tr><tr><td>Sandwich</td><td>$6.75</td></tr><tr><td>Chips</td><td>$2.50</td></tr><tr><td>Juice Bottle</td><td>$1.25</td></tr></table>
Analyze Relationships	A zoo has 75 animals. There are 25 mammals. The rest are reptiles and birds. There are 4 birds for every 1 reptile. How many birds and reptiles are there? There are 50 birds and reptiles in all. If there are 4 birds, then there will be 1 reptile. So, there are 40 birds and 10 reptiles: 40 + 10 = 50. There are 40 birds and 10 reptiles.	You can **analyze relationships** in information you are given to find unknown information.

Problem-Solving Recording Sheet

This sheet helps you organize your work and make sense of problems.

Name __Carlos__

Teaching Tool
1

Problem-Solving Recording Sheet

Problem:
A store sold 20 sweatshirts. Of these,
8 were red. Twice as many were green as yellow.
How many of each color sweatshirt did the store sell?

ANALYZE		PLAN
Need to Find	**Know**	**Strategies?**

ANALYZE

Need to Find

How many
sweatshirts
were sold in
each color?

Know

A total of
20 sweatshirts.
8 were red.
Twice as many
green sweatshirts
as yellow.

PLAN

Strategies?

☐ Represent the Problem
  ☐ Draw a Picture or Strip Diagram
  ☑ Write an Equation
  ☑ Make a Table or List

☐ Look for a Pattern
☐ Use Reasoning
☑ Analyze Given Information
☐ Analyze Relationships

SOLVE and JUSTIFY

Show Your Work and Answer.

20 – 8 = 12, so there are 12 green and
yellow sweatshirts.
If there are 2 green shirts, there
will be 1 yellow shirt.

green	yellow	total
2	1	3
4	2	6
6	3	9
8	4	12

So, there are 8 green sweatshirts
and 4 yellow sweatshirts.

EVALUATE

**Check Your Work.
Is Your Answer
Reasonable?**

I can add to
check my work.
8 red, 8 green, and
4 yellow sweatshirts.
8 + 8 + 4 = 20
There are
20 sweatshirts in all.

TT1

Multiplying and Dividing Fractions

Essential Questions: What does it mean to multiply and divide whole numbers and fractions? How can multiplication and division with whole numbers and fractions be shown using models and symbols?

Physical changes are reversible.

You can change a substance so that it looks and feels different, but it's still the same substance. The molecules haven't changed.

A substance can act differently because of a physical change. Here's a project about kitchen science.

Math and Science Project: Kitchen Chemistry

Do Research Use the Internet or other sources to learn about physical changes. Look for examples of physical changes that occur in the kitchen. When you condense, freeze, melt, vaporize, or whip air into a substance, you are making physical changes to that substance.

Journal: Write a Report Include what you found. Also in your report:

- Give examples of foods that are commonly condensed, frozen, melted, vaporized, or whipped.

- Write your favorite recipe that involves making physical changes to the food.

- Make up and solve multiplication and division problems with fractions.

Name _____

Review What You Know

Vocabulary

Choose the best term from the box. Write it on the blank.

> - compare
> - multiple
> - simplify
> - factor

1. When you _____ two numbers, you decide whether one is less than, greater than, or equal to the other number.

2. When you find an equivalent fraction by dividing both the numerator and the denominator by the same number, you _____ the fraction.

3. A _____ of a number is a product of the number and any nonzero whole number.

Multiply and Divide

Find each product or quotient.

4. 4×3 **5.** $42 \div 6$

6. 18×2 **7.** $27 \div 3$

8. 9×6 **9.** $60 \div 5$

Fractions

Write each fraction in simplest form.

10. $\frac{3}{9}$ **11.** $\frac{8}{12}$

12. $\frac{15}{18}$ **13.** $\frac{34}{52}$

14. Elena made two batches of food to put in a bird feeder. She used $\frac{1}{8}$ cup of cracked corn, $\frac{3}{4}$ cup of sunflower seeds, and $\frac{1}{4}$ cup of dried cranberries for each batch. Which of the following is the best estimate of the total amount of bird food she made?

A less than 1 cup
B less than 2 cups
C less than 3 cups
D less than 4 cups

15. At the library, Herb spent $\frac{1}{6}$ hour looking for a book, $\frac{1}{4}$ hour reading, and $\frac{1}{2}$ hour doing research on the computer. How many hours did Herb spend at the library? Write your answer as a fraction in simplest form.

Common Denominators

16. Writing to Explain Explain how you can find a common denominator for $\frac{3}{5}$ and $\frac{5}{8}$.

My Word Cards

Use the examples for each word on the front of the card to help complete the definitions on the back.

---

unit fraction

examples: $\frac{1}{4}, \frac{1}{3}, \frac{1}{2}$

reciprocal

$$\frac{2}{3} \times \frac{3}{2} = 1$$

So, $\frac{2}{3}$ and $\frac{3}{2}$ are reciprocals.

My Word Cards

A number is the _____ of a given number if the product of the numbers is 1.

A fraction with a numerator of 1 is called a _____.

Name _____

☆ ☆
Solve & Share

Kelly and Mara were working on their math homework. Kelly wrote $\frac{3}{4}$ as $\frac{1}{4} + \frac{1}{4} + \frac{1}{4}$. Mara looked at it and said, "I think you could use multiplication to rewrite that sum." Do you agree with Mara? *Show your work here and use digital tools to solve the problem.*

TEKS 5.3I Represent and solve multiplication of a whole number and a fraction that refers to the same whole using objects and pictorial models, including area models. Also, 5.3. Mathematical Process Standards 5.1A, 5.1C, 5.1D, 5.1E, 5.1G

Communicate You can use a drawing to explain your thinking. *Show your work!*

Digital Resources at PearsonTexas.com

 Solve Learn Glossary Check Tools Games

Look Back!

Number Sense How can you write $\frac{4}{5}$ using addition? using multiplication?

How Can You Describe a Fraction Using a Unit Fraction?

A unit fraction is a fraction that describes one part of the whole.

Unit fractions always have a numerator of 1.

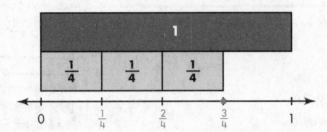

	1	
$\frac{1}{4}$	$\frac{1}{4}$	$\frac{1}{4}$

0     $\frac{1}{4}$ $\frac{2}{4}$ $\frac{3}{4}$ 1

B When a whole is divided into four equal parts, each part is described as $\frac{1}{4}$.

Three of those parts are described as $\frac{3}{4}$.

Multiplication and a unit fraction can also be used to describe $\frac{3}{4}$.

$\frac{3}{4} = 3 \times \frac{1}{4}$, or three $\frac{1}{4}$ parts.

$\frac{1}{4}$	$\frac{1}{4}$	$\frac{1}{4}$

0    $\frac{1}{4}$ $\frac{2}{4}$ $\frac{3}{4}$ 1

C Three $\frac{1}{4}$ parts make $\frac{3}{4}$.

$$\frac{3}{4} = 3 \times \frac{1}{4}$$

So, $\frac{3}{4}$ is a multiple of $\frac{1}{4}$.

A multiple is the result of multiplying a number by a whole number.

Can you think of another multiple of $\frac{1}{4}$?

Do You Understand?

Convince Me! Write $\frac{6}{4}$ as a multiple of a unit fraction.

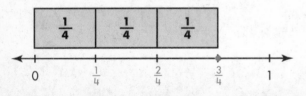

	1				1	
$\frac{1}{4}$	$\frac{1}{4}$	$\frac{1}{4}$	$\frac{1}{4}$	$\frac{1}{4}$	$\frac{1}{4}$

Name _____

Guided Practice

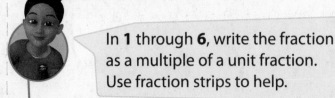

In **1** through **6**, write the fraction as a multiple of a unit fraction. Use fraction strips to help.

1. $\frac{2}{3} = \square \times \frac{1}{3}$

2. $\frac{5}{6} = 5 \times \frac{1}{\square}$

3. $\frac{3}{2} = \square \times \frac{\square}{\square}$

4. $\frac{6}{5} = \square \times \frac{\square}{\square}$

5. $\frac{2}{9} = \square \times \frac{\square}{\square}$

6. $\frac{10}{7} = \square \times \frac{\square}{\square}$

7. Tools Draw a picture to explain why $\frac{8}{5} = 8 \times \frac{1}{5}$.

8. Represent There are 5 people in Mark's family. Each family member ate $\frac{1}{6}$ of a pasta dish. What multiplication equation represents the part of the pasta dish the whole family ate?

Independent Practice

Leveled Practice In **9** through **24**, write the fraction as a multiple of a unit fraction. Use fraction strips to help.

9. $\frac{3}{4} = \square \times \frac{1}{4}$

10. $\frac{8}{12} = 8 \times \frac{1}{\square}$

11. $\frac{7}{10} = \square \times \frac{\square}{10}$

12. $\frac{6}{6} = 6 \times \frac{\square}{\square}$

13. $\frac{2}{5} = \square \times \frac{\square}{\square}$

14. $\frac{4}{9} = \square \times \frac{\square}{\square}$

15. $\frac{5}{2} = \square \times \frac{\square}{\square}$

16. $\frac{7}{3} = \square \times \frac{\square}{\square}$

17. $\frac{9}{9} = \square \times \frac{\square}{\square}$

18. $\frac{12}{10} = \square \times \frac{\square}{\square}$

19. $\frac{10}{7} = \square \times \frac{\square}{\square}$

20. $\frac{5}{11} = \square \times \frac{\square}{\square}$

21. $\frac{6}{4} = \square \times \frac{\square}{\square}$

22. $\frac{8}{5} = \square \times \frac{\square}{\square}$

23. $\frac{9}{8} = \square \times \frac{\square}{\square}$

24. $\frac{9}{4} = \square \times \frac{\square}{\square}$

Problem Solving

25. Represent Write an equation that describes the picture. Each pear part is $\frac{1}{2}$ of a pear. Show your answer as a multiplication equation with a unit fraction as a factor.

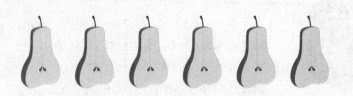

26. Connect Look at the picture. Write and solve a problem for it. Show your answer as a multiplication equation with $\frac{1}{2}$ as a factor.

27. Extend Your Thinking Each batch of cookies Celina is making uses $\frac{1}{8}$ pound of butter. Celina has $1\frac{3}{8}$ pounds of butter. How many batches of cookies can she make? Explain how you found your answer.

28. Nicole is 1.42 meters tall. She is 0.5 meter taller than her sister. How tall is her sister?

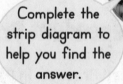

Complete the strip diagram to help you find the answer.

0.5	x

29. Kevin is making vegetable juice. If he makes 6 cups on Saturday and 8 cups on Sunday, what is the total amount of beets he will use?

A $\frac{2}{8}$ pound   C $\frac{14}{8}$ pounds

B $\frac{7}{8}$ pound   D $\frac{28}{8}$ pounds

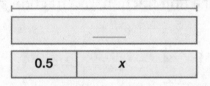

Vegetable Juice Recipe	
Type of Vegetable	**Amount Needed for 2 Cups**
Carrots	$\frac{3}{4}$ pound
Beets	$\frac{1}{8}$ pound
Celery	$\frac{3}{4}$ pound

30. How many pounds of carrots, beets, and celery does Kevin need in all to make 4 cups of vegetable juice?

Name _____

Another Look!

Evan eats $\frac{2}{3}$ of a sandwich. Write $\frac{2}{3}$ as a multiple of a unit fraction.

Remember that the numerator of a unit fraction is 1.

Evan's sandwich is divided into 3 equal parts. Each part is $\frac{1}{3}$.

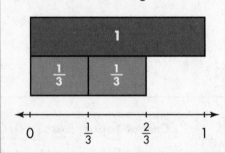

Two $\frac{1}{3}$ parts make $\frac{2}{3}$.

$$\frac{2}{3} = 2 \times \frac{1}{3}$$

In **1** through **14**, write the fraction as a multiple of a unit fraction. Use a number line or fraction strips to help.

1. $\frac{2}{5}$

The total number of equal parts is ___.

Each part is $\frac{\square}{\square}$.

$\frac{2}{5} = 2 \times \frac{\square}{\square}$

2. $\frac{2}{4}$

Each part is $\frac{\square}{\square}$.

$\frac{2}{4} = $ ___ $\times \frac{\square}{\square}$

3. $\frac{5}{9} = 5 \times \frac{1}{\square}$

4. $\frac{7}{15} = 7 \times \frac{1}{\square}$

5. $\frac{3}{6} = \square \times \frac{\square}{\square}$

6. $\frac{2}{2} = \square \times \frac{\square}{\square}$

7. $\frac{7}{12} = \square \times \frac{\square}{\square}$

8. $\frac{2}{10} = \square \times \frac{\square}{\square}$

9. $\frac{7}{20} = \square \times \frac{\square}{\square}$

10. $\frac{5}{18} = \square \times \frac{\square}{\square}$

11. $\frac{13}{9} = \square \times \frac{\square}{\square}$

12. $\frac{9}{10} = \square \times \frac{\square}{\square}$

13. $\frac{10}{3} = \square \times \frac{\square}{\square}$

14. $\frac{5}{21} = \square \times \frac{\square}{\square}$

15. **Communicate** How can you tell if a fraction is a unit fraction? Give two examples of unit fractions.

16. **Explain** Give two examples of multiples of $\frac{1}{6}$. Explain how to find multiples of a unit fraction.

17. **Connect** Mari is packing oranges into bags. She packs the same number of oranges in each bag. The table shows the number of oranges she packs for different numbers of bags. How many oranges does Mari need to pack 9 bags?

Number of Bags	3	5	7	9	11
Number of Oranges	9	15	21	■	33

18. Janice is making cereal yogurt bars. If she makes 32 bars in one batch and 48 bars in another batch, what is the total amount of honey she will use?

A $\frac{3}{8}$ cup   C $\frac{1}{40}$ cup

B $\frac{5}{8}$ cup   D $\frac{5}{40}$ cup

19. **Extend Your Thinking** Janice has a little more than 5 cups of flour. About how much flour will she have left after she makes the batches in Exercise 18?

Cereal Yogurt Bars	
Ingredient	Amount Needed for 16 Bars
Yogurt	1 cup
Bran cereal	2 cups
Applesauce	$\frac{1}{3}$ cup
Honey	$\frac{1}{8}$ cup
Flour	$\frac{3}{4}$ cup
Egg	1

20. William cut two whole tomatoes into fourths. What unit fraction describes each piece as part of a whole tomato? What multiplication equation represents the total number of fourths shown in the picture? Write the solution as a mixed number.

Name _____

Solve & Share

Brandon has 6 eggs. He needs $\frac{2}{3}$ of the eggs to make an omelet. How many eggs does he need?

⭐ TEKS 5.3I Represent and solve multiplication of a whole number and a fraction that refers to the same whole using objects and pictorial models, including area models. Also, 5.3. Mathematical Process Standards 5.1B, 5.1C, 5.1D, 5.1F, 5.1G

Select and Use Tools
Would a drawing help you picture the situation?

Digital Resources at PearsonTexas.com

Solve   Learn   Glossary   Check   Tools   Games

Look Back!

Number Sense Should your answer be less than or greater than 6? How do you know?

How Can You Multiply a Fraction and a Whole Number?

A rectangular flag has an area of 15 square feet. $\frac{4}{5}$ of the flag is red. $\frac{1}{5}$ of the flag is blue. What is the area of the red part of the flag?

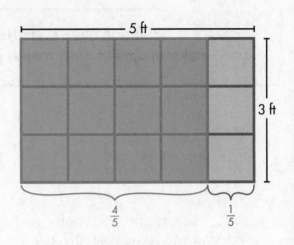

You can draw an area model to help you think through the problem.

The model shows that $\frac{1}{5}$ of 15 is 3.

B Step 1

$\frac{4}{5}$ of 15 means the same thing as $\frac{4}{5} \times 15$.

Multiply.

$\frac{4}{5} \times 15 = \frac{4 \times 15}{5} = \frac{60}{5}$

C Step 2

Then simplify the fraction.

$$\frac{60}{5} = 12$$

The area of the flag that is red is 12 square feet.

Do You Understand?

Convince Me! Here is how Lydia found the product $\frac{3}{4} \times 24$.

$\frac{3}{4} \times 24 = \frac{3 \times 24}{4} = \frac{72}{4} = 18$

Use the area model to show that Lydia's answer is correct.

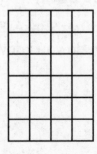

© Pearson Education, Inc. 5

Name _____

☆Guided Practice☆

In **1** through **3**, find each product.

1. $\frac{3}{4}$ of 8

$$\frac{3}{4} \times 8 = \frac{3 \times \square}{4} = \frac{\square}{\square} = $$

2. $\frac{2}{7}$ of 28

$$\frac{2}{7} \times 28 = \frac{2 \times \square}{7} = \frac{\square}{\square} = $$

3. $\frac{1}{6}$ of 42

$$\frac{1}{6} \times 42 = \frac{1 \times \square}{6} = \frac{\square}{\square} = $$

4. Construct Arguments Explain why $4 \times \frac{2}{3}$ is the same as adding $\frac{2}{3} + \frac{2}{3} + \frac{2}{3} + \frac{2}{3}$.

5. Communicate In the problem at the top of page 458, what is the area of the blue part of the flag? Show how you found your answer.

Independent Practice ☆

Leveled Practice In **6** through **16**, find each product.

6. $\frac{2}{3}$ of 30

$$\frac{2}{3} \times 30 = \frac{\square \times \square}{\square}$$
$$= \frac{\square}{\square} = \underline{\quad}$$

7. $\frac{1}{4}$ of 52

$$\frac{1}{4} \times 52 = \frac{\square \times \square}{\square}$$
$$= \frac{\square}{\square} = \underline{\quad}$$

8. $\frac{5}{8}$ of 104

$$\frac{5}{8} \times 104 = \frac{\square \times \square}{\square}$$
$$= \frac{\square}{\square} = \underline{\quad}$$

9. $\frac{3}{4}$ of 12

10. $\frac{2}{5}$ of 40

11. $\frac{6}{7}$ of 49

12. $\frac{5}{8}$ of 24

13. $\frac{8}{9}$ of 81

14. $\frac{1}{9}$ of 972

15. $\frac{3}{5}$ of 435

16. $\left(\frac{3}{4} - \frac{1}{4}\right) \times 24$

---

*For another example, see Set B on page 495.

Problem Solving

17. Construct Arguments Jo said that when you multiply a nonzero whole number by a fraction less than 1, the product is always less than the whole number. Do you agree?

18. Math and Science A scientist wants to find out how the properties of water change when salt is added to it. For every cup of water she has, she replaces $\frac{1}{8}$ of it with salt. If she has 24 cups of water, how many cups will she replace with salt?

19. Shanna attends school for 1 week ⭐ longer than $\frac{3}{4}$ of the year. How many weeks in a year does Shanna attend school?

   A 27 weeks
   B 38 weeks
   C 39 weeks
   D 40 weeks

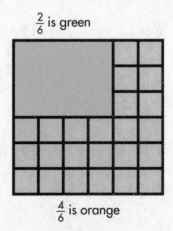

There are 52 weeks in a year.

20. Extend Your Thinking Gina has 48 stickers. $\frac{3}{8}$ of the stickers have pictures of flowers. $\frac{1}{8}$ of the stickers have pictures of plants. The rest of the stickers have pictures of people. How many stickers have pictures of people? Explain how you found your answer.

21. One CD costs $8.25. Two books cost $10. How much change will Stacy get if she buys two CDs and two books and gives the clerk two $20 bills?

Sale: CDs for $8.25 each

Sale: 2 books for $10.00

22. Analyze Information The wall tile has an area of 36 square inches. What is the area, in square inches, of the part of the wall tile that is green? Explain how you found your answer.

$\frac{2}{6}$ is green

$\frac{4}{6}$ is orange

Name _____

Another Look!

Tessa used $\frac{2}{3}$ of a 6-yard-long piece of fabric to make a dress. What was the length of fabric, in yards, that she used?

Remember: $\frac{2}{3}$ of 6 means $\frac{2}{3} \times 6$.

Step 1

Multiply to find $\frac{2}{3}$ of 6.

$$\frac{2}{3} \times 6$$

$$\frac{2 \times 6}{3} = \frac{12}{3}$$

Step 2

Simplify, if possible.

$$\frac{12}{3}$$

$$\frac{12 \div 3}{3 \div 3} = \frac{4}{1} = 4$$

So, Tessa used 4 yards of fabric.

Leveled Practice In **1** through **8**, find each product.

1. $\frac{2}{7}$ of 35

$\frac{2}{7} \times 35$

Multiply.

$$\frac{\square \times \square}{7} = \frac{\square}{7}$$

Simplify, if possible.

$$\frac{\square \div \square}{\square \div \square} = \frac{\square}{\square} = \underline{\quad}$$

2. $\frac{2}{9}$ of 27

$\frac{2}{9} \times 27$

$$\frac{2 \times \square}{9} = \frac{\square}{9} = \underline{\quad}$$

3. $15 \times \frac{3}{5}$

$$\frac{15 \times \square}{5} = \frac{\square}{\square} = \frac{\square}{\square} = \square$$

4. $\frac{5}{6}$ of 54

$$\frac{\square \times \square}{6} = \frac{\square}{6} = \frac{\square}{\square} = \underline{\quad}$$

5. $\frac{3}{5}$ of 45

6. $\frac{2}{3}$ of 333

7. $72 \times \frac{2}{9}$

8. $420 \times \left(\frac{1}{7} + \frac{3}{7} \right)$

9. **Communicate** Find the error in the work below. Then show the correct calculation.

$$\frac{8}{12} \times 6 = \frac{8}{12} \times \frac{6}{6} = \frac{48}{72} = \frac{2}{3}$$

10. A scientist measured the amount of rainfall during the afternoon. It rained 0.43 inch per hour. What was the total amount of rainfall in 6 hours?

---

11. **Connect** Theo's vegetable garden has an area of 40 square feet.

   a What is the area, in square feet, of the part of the garden that is planted with carrots?

   b What fraction, in simplest form, represents the part of the whole garden that is **NOT** planted with carrots?

$\frac{9}{20}$ of garden = carrots

---

12. **Analyze Information** A giraffe can run at a speed of 32 miles per hour. Which animal listed in the chart has a speed that is $\frac{15}{16}$ of the speed of a giraffe? Explain how you found your answer.

Animal	Speed (in miles per hour)
Cat	30
Cheetah	70
Jackal	35

---

13. Some frilled lizards grow to be 90 centimeters long. If $\frac{2}{3}$ of this length is its tail, how long is the tail?

   A $90\frac{2}{3}$ centimeters
   B 60 centimeters
   C 45 centimeters
   D 30 centimeters

14. **Extend Your Thinking** Eric has 240 coins in his collection. $\frac{11}{20}$ of the coins are pennies. $\frac{4}{20}$ of the coins are nickels. The rest of the coins are quarters. How many of the coins are quarters? Explain how you found your answer.

© Pearson Education, Inc. 5

Name _____

Solve & Share

Julie has 10 yards of ribbon. She divides the ribbon into 3 equal pieces and uses 2 of the pieces on gifts. How much ribbon does she use? *Solve this problem any way you choose.*

⭐ TEKS 5.3 Apply mathematical process standards to develop and use strategies and methods for positive rational number computations in order to solve problems with efficiency and accuracy. **Mathematical Process Standards 5.1B, 5.1C, 5.1D, 5.1E, 5.1G**

Digital Resources at PearsonTexas.com

Solve   Learn   Glossary   Check   Tools   Games

Create and Use Representations You can use words, pictures, and calculations to solve the problem. *Show your work in the space above!*

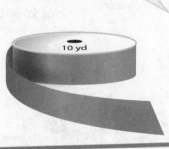

10 yd

Look Back!

Number Sense Should the answer be less than or greater than 5? How do you know?

How Can You Multiply a Fraction and Whole Number?

Hal spent $\frac{3}{4}$ hour reading each day for 7 days. In all, how much time did he spend reading?

I need to find $7 \times \frac{3}{4}$.

B One Way

Multiply to find the number of fourths.

$$7 \times \frac{3}{4} = \frac{7 \times 3}{4} = \frac{21}{4}$$

Rewrite the improper fraction as a mixed number.

$$\frac{21}{4} = 5\frac{1}{4}$$

Hal spent $5\frac{1}{4}$ hours reading.

To rename $\frac{21}{4}$, divide the numerator by the denominator.

C Another Way

Rename the whole number as a fraction. Multiply the numerators, multiply the denominators, and then write the quotient as a mixed number.

$$\frac{7}{1} \times \frac{3}{4} = \frac{7 \times 3}{1 \times 4} = \frac{21}{4} = 5\frac{1}{4}$$

Hal spent $5\frac{1}{4}$ hours reading.

Every whole number can be written as a fraction with a denominator of 1.

Do You Understand?

Convince Me! Find $6 \times \frac{4}{9}$. Then use repeated addition to justify your answer.

☆Guided Practice☆

In **1** through **3**, find each product. Write the product as a mixed number in simplest form.

1. $\frac{3}{8} \times 4 = \dfrac{\square \times \square}{\square} = \dfrac{\square}{\square} = \square\dfrac{\square}{\square} = \square\dfrac{\square}{\square}$

2. $8 \times \frac{5}{6} = \dfrac{\square \times \square}{\square} = \dfrac{\square}{\square} = \square\dfrac{\square}{\square} = \square\dfrac{\square}{\square}$

3. $5 \times \frac{4}{7} = \dfrac{\square \times \square}{\square} = \dfrac{\square}{\square} = \square\dfrac{\square}{\square}$

4. **Reason** In the example at the top of page 464, how can finding $\frac{1}{4}$ of 7 help you find $\frac{3}{4}$ of 7?

5. **Communicate** If Hal spent $\frac{2}{3}$ of an hour reading each day for 7 days, how much time, in all, did he spend reading? Show how you found your answer.

Independent Practice

Leveled Practice In **6** through **16**, find each product. Write each improper fraction as a mixed number.

6. $\frac{3}{4} \times 14 = \dfrac{\square \times \square}{\square} = \dfrac{\square}{\square} = \square\dfrac{\square}{\square} = \square\dfrac{\square}{\square}$

7. $27 \times \frac{2}{3} = \dfrac{\square \times \square}{\square} = \dfrac{\square}{\square} = \square$

8. $\frac{5}{9} \times 37 = \dfrac{\square \times \square}{\square} = \dfrac{\square}{\square} = \square\dfrac{\square}{\square}$

Remember:
Use division to rename an improper fraction as a mixed number.

9. $\frac{4}{5} \times 7$

10. $5 \times \frac{2}{3}$

11. $17 \times \frac{6}{8}$

12. $\frac{9}{10} \times 25$

13. $\frac{7}{8} \times 320$

14. $28 \times \frac{7}{12}$

15. $\frac{2}{3} \times 1,287$

16. $75 \times \frac{10}{11}$

Problem Solving

17. About $\frac{3}{5}$ of the human body is made up of water. If a person has a mass of 75 kilograms, what is the mass of the water in this person's body?

18. Mental Math How can you use mental math to find $25 \times \frac{3}{10}$?

19. During a nature walk, Jill identified 20 species of animals and plants.

  a Construct Arguments Jill said that $\frac{1}{3}$ of the species she identified were animals. Can this be correct? Explain.

  b If $\frac{3}{5}$ of the species Jill identified were animals, how many plants did Jill identify?

20. A rectangular painting is 2 feet long and $\frac{5}{6}$ foot wide. Which is the area of the painting?

  A $1\frac{2}{3}$ sq ft

  B $2\frac{5}{6}$ sq ft

  C $3\frac{1}{3}$ sq ft

  D $5\frac{2}{3}$ sq ft

21. Extend Your Thinking An art teacher makes a batch of purple paint by mixing $\frac{3}{4}$ cup red paint with $\frac{3}{4}$ cup blue paint. If she mixes 13 batches, how many cups of purple paint will she have?

22. Math and Science A water molecule is made up of 3 atoms. One third of the atoms are oxygen and the remaining atoms are hydrogen. If there are 114 water molecules, how many hydrogen atoms are there? Show your work.

For **23** and **24**, use the model.

23. The model is shaded to represent $1\frac{40}{100}$. Write two fractions that are equivalent to $1\frac{40}{100}$.

24. Write the decimal number that is represented by the model.

466

Name _____

Solve & Share

One ball of dough can be stretched into a circle to make a pizza. After the pizza is cooked, it is cut into 8 equal slices. How many slices of pizza can you make with 3 balls of dough? *Solve this problem any way you choose.*

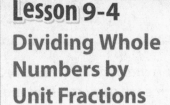

⭐ **TEKS 5.3J** Represent division of a unit fraction by a whole number and the division of a whole number by a unit fraction such as $\frac{1}{3} \div 7$ and $7 \div \frac{1}{3}$ using objects and pictorial models, including area models. Also, 5.3L.
Mathematical Process Standards 5.1A, 5.1C, 5.1D, 5.1E, 5.1F

Digital Resources at PearsonTexas.com

Solve   Learn   Glossary   Check   Tools   Games

You can **create and use a representation** to help you find the answer. *Show your work!*

Look Back!

Connect Ideas Into how many slices of pizza will each ball of dough be divided? What fraction of a whole pizza does 1 slice represent?

How Can You Divide by a Unit Fraction?

A

Joyce is making sushi rolls. She needs $\frac{1}{4}$ cup of rice for each sushi roll. How many sushi rolls can she make if she has 3 cups of rice?

You can use objects or draw a picture to find the solution.

Use objects.

B How many $\frac{1}{4}$s are in 3?

There are twelve $\frac{1}{4}$s in three whole cups. So, Joyce can make 12 sushi rolls.

You can also use a number line to find how many $\frac{1}{4}$s are in 3.

$3 \div \frac{1}{4} = 12.$

C Dividing by a fraction is the same as multiplying by its **reciprocal**.

Two fractions whose product is 1 are reciprocals.

For example, $\frac{1}{4} \times \frac{4}{1} = 1$, so $\frac{1}{4}$ and $\frac{4}{1}$ are reciprocals.

$$3 \div \frac{1}{4} = 12 \qquad 3 \times \frac{4}{1} = 12$$

So, Joyce can make 12 sushi rolls.

Do You Understand?

Convince Me! Use the diagram below to find $4 \div \frac{1}{3}$.

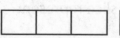
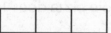

$4 \div \frac{1}{3} = $ _____

© Pearson Education, Inc. 5

☆ **Guided Practice**[*]

In **1** and **2**, use the picture below to find each quotient. Simplify, if possible.

1. How many $\frac{1}{3}$s are in 3?

$3 \div \frac{1}{3} = $ _____

2. How many $\frac{1}{3}$s are in 6?

$6 \div \frac{1}{3} = $ _____

3. In the example at the top of page 470, if Joyce had 4 cups of rice, how many rolls could she make?

4. In the example at the top of page 470, how does the number line help to show that $3 \div \frac{1}{4}$ is equal to 3×4?

☆ **Independent Practice** ☆

Leveled Practice In **5** and **6**, use the picture to find each quotient.

5. How many $\frac{1}{6}$s are in 1?

$1 \div \frac{1}{6} = $ _____

6. How many $\frac{1}{6}$s are in 5?

$5 \div \frac{1}{6} = $ _____

In **7** through **14**, draw a picture or use multiplication to find each quotient.

7. $4 \div \frac{1}{2}$

8. $2 \div \frac{1}{8}$

9. $2 \div \frac{1}{3}$

10. $6 \div \frac{1}{4}$

11. $8 \div \frac{1}{3}$

12. $3 \div \frac{1}{10}$

13. $9 \div \frac{1}{8}$

14. $15 \div \frac{1}{5}$

Problem Solving

15. Draw a Picture Dan has 4 cartons of juice. He pours $\frac{1}{8}$ carton for each person on a camping trip. How many people can he serve? Draw a picture to help you answer the question.

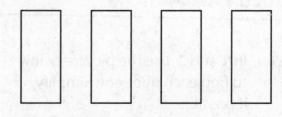

16. Reason When you divide a whole number by a fraction with a numerator of 1, explain how you can find the quotient.

17. Estimation The Nile River is 4,160 miles long. You want to spend three weeks traveling the entire length of the river. Estimate the number of miles you should travel each day.

18. Extend Your Thinking Maria used one bag of flour. She baked two loaves of bread. Then she used the remaining flour to make 48 muffins. How much flour was in the bag to begin with?

Recipe	Amount of Flour Needed
Bread	$2\frac{1}{4}$ cups per loaf
Muffins	$3\frac{1}{4}$ cups per 24 muffins
Pizza	$1\frac{1}{2}$ cups per pie

DATA

For **19** and **20**, use the table.

19. Deron is making light switch plates from pieces of wood. He starts with a board that is 6 yards long. How many light switch plates can he make?

A   9 light switch plates
B   24 light switch plates
C   27 light switch plates
D   54 light switch plates

Remember, 1 yard = 3 feet

Wood Projects	
Item	**Length Needed for Each**
Cabinet Shelf	$\frac{3}{4}$ foot
Light Switch Plate	$\frac{1}{3}$ foot
Shingle	$\frac{2}{3}$ foot

DATA

20. Which is longer, a cabinet shelf or a shingle? How much longer?

© Pearson Education, Inc. 5

Name _____

Another Look!

Ned has a 2-foot-long piece of rope. He cuts the rope into $\frac{1}{3}$-foot pieces. How many pieces of rope does Ned now have?

Think: How many $\frac{1}{3}$s are in 2? Use objects to help.

Draw a number line to model the problem.

Count how many $\frac{1}{3}$s there are in 2. There are three $\frac{1}{3}$s in 1, so there are six $\frac{1}{3}$s in 2.

You can use multiplication to check your answer.

$6 \times \frac{1}{3} = 2$

Ned now has 6 pieces of rope.

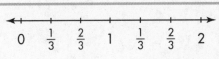

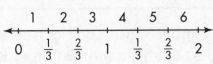

In **1** and **2**, use the picture to find each quotient.

1. How many $\frac{1}{5}$s are in 1? _____

$1 \div \frac{1}{5} =$ _____

2. How many $\frac{1}{5}$s are in 4? _____

$4 \div \frac{1}{5} =$ _____

In **3** through **10**, find each quotient. You may draw a picture or use objects to help.

3. $12 \div \frac{1}{2} =$

4. $9 \div \frac{1}{4} =$

5. $3 \div \frac{1}{7} =$

6. $10 \div \frac{1}{10} =$

7. $20 \div \frac{1}{3} =$

8. $7 \div \frac{1}{5} =$

9. $6 \div \frac{1}{6} =$

10. $15 \div \frac{1}{2} =$

11. Tools Use the number line. How many $\frac{1}{4}$-yard long pieces of pipe can be cut from two 1-yard-long pieces of pipe?

0   1   2

---

12. Built in 2005, the world's largest leather work boot is 16 feet tall. A typical men's work boot is $\frac{1}{2}$ foot tall. How many times as tall as a typical work boot is the largest boot?

13. Communicate Write a word problem that can be solved by dividing 10 by $\frac{1}{3}$. Find the answer to the problem.

---

14. Number Sense Look for a pattern in the table. Find the missing addends and sums. Write each sum in simplest form.

Addends	$\frac{1}{8} + \frac{1}{4}$	$\frac{1}{4} + \frac{1}{4}$	$\frac{3}{8} + \frac{1}{4}$	
Sum	$\frac{3}{8}$	$\frac{1}{2}$		

---

15. Extend Your Thinking Omar had 5 cups of cornmeal. He made 24 corn muffins. How many cups of cornmeal did he have left? Explain how you found your answer.

Cornmeal Recipes

Item	Amount Needed
Cornbread	$\frac{3}{4}$ cup per loaf
Corn Muffins	$\frac{1}{2}$ cup for 6 muffins
Hush Puppies	$\frac{5}{8}$ cup per batch

---

16. David made a dot plot of how many ⭐ miles he biked each day for two weeks. How many miles did he bike in all?

A $12\frac{1}{2}$ miles

B $145\frac{1}{2}$ miles

C 158 miles

D 168 miles

Miles Biked Each Day

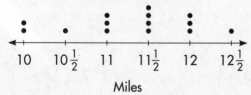

10    $10\frac{1}{2}$ 11 $11\frac{1}{2}$ 12 $12\frac{1}{2}$

Miles

Name _____

Solve & Share

Yesterday, the cooking club made a pan of lasagna. They left half of the lasagna for four members of the photography club to share equally. What fraction of the pan of lasagna did each photography club member get? *Solve this problem any way you choose.*

⭐ TEKS 5.3J Represent division of a unit fraction by a whole number and the division of a whole number by a unit fraction such as $\frac{1}{3} \div 7$ and $7 \div \frac{1}{3}$ using objects and pictorial models, including area models. Also, 5.3L.
Mathematical Process Standards 5.1A, 5.1B, 5.1C, 5.1D, 5.1E, 5.1G

Digital Resources at PearsonTexas.com

Solve   Learn   Glossary   Check   Tools   Games

You can **create and use a representation** to show how to divide what is left. *Show your work!*

Look Back!

Communicate What number sentence can you write to show how you solved this problem?

How Can You Model Dividing a Unit Fraction by a Whole Number?

Half of a pan of cornbread is left over. Ann, Beth, and Chuck are sharing the leftovers equally. What fraction of the original cornbread does each person get?

You can make a drawing to show $\frac{1}{2}$ of the cornbread.

B One Way

Use a model. Divide $\frac{1}{2}$ into 3 equal parts.

$\frac{1}{2} \div 3$

Each part contains $\frac{1}{6}$ of the whole.

$\frac{1}{2} \div 3 = \frac{1}{6}$

Each person gets $\frac{1}{6}$ of the cornbread.

C Another Way

Use a number line. Shade $\frac{1}{2}$ on the number line. Divide $\frac{1}{2}$ into 3 equal parts.

$\frac{1}{2} \div 3$

Each part is $\frac{1}{6}$.

$\frac{1}{2} \div 3 = \frac{1}{6}$

Each person gets $\frac{1}{6}$ of the cornbread.

Do You Understand?

Convince Me! In the example above, how is dividing by 3 the same as multiplying by $\frac{1}{3}$?

☆ **Guided Practice** *

In **1** through **4**, use the picture or objects to help find each quotient.

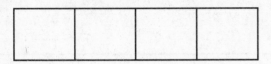

1. $\frac{1}{4} \div 2$ **2.** $\frac{1}{4} \div 4$

3. $\frac{1}{2} \div 2$ **4.** $\frac{1}{2} \div 4$

5. Draw a Picture In the example at the top of page 476, suppose that 4 people were sharing half of the cornbread equally. What fraction of the original cornbread would each person get? Draw a picture or use objects to help.

6. Check for Reasonableness When you divide a unit fraction by a whole number greater than 1, will the quotient be greater than or less than the unit fraction?

☆ **Independent Practice** ☆

Leveled Practice In **7** and **8**, find each quotient. Use a picture or objects to help.

7. $\frac{1}{2} \div 5$

Pictures and objects can help when dividing fractions by a whole number.

8. $\frac{1}{5} \div 2$ 0 $\frac{1}{5}$ $\frac{2}{5}$ $\frac{3}{5}$ $\frac{4}{5}$ 1

In **9** through **14**, find the quotient.

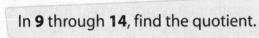

9. $\frac{1}{2} \div 7$

10. $\frac{1}{4} \div 3$

11. $\frac{1}{6} \div 2$

12. $\frac{1}{3} \div 4$

13. $\frac{1}{4} \div 5$

14. $\frac{1}{5} \div 3$

*For another example, see Set D on page 496.

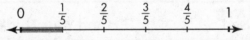

Problem Solving

15. Draw a Picture Vin, Corrie, Alexa, and Joe equally shared one-fourth of a submarine sandwich. What fraction of the original sandwich did each friend get? Use the number line to help you find the answer.

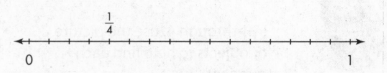

$\frac{1}{4}$

0   1

---

16. Sue has $\frac{1}{2}$ gallon of milk to share evenly among four people. How much milk, in gallons, should she give each person?

17. Construct Arguments Taryn says that $\frac{1}{4}$ of a cereal bar is larger than $\frac{1}{3}$ of the cereal bar. Is she correct? Explain.

---

18. Analyze Information Use the table. It shows distances run in miles. Who ran farther from Monday to Friday, Amir or Janie? How much farther?

DATA	Mon	Tues	Wed	Thurs	Fri
Amir	$2\frac{1}{2}$	$1\frac{1}{2}$	$3\frac{1}{4}$	$1\frac{3}{4}$	$2\frac{1}{2}$
Janie	$2\frac{3}{4}$	$2\frac{1}{2}$	$3\frac{3}{4}$	$2\frac{1}{4}$	$1\frac{1}{2}$

---

19. ⭐ Jamie cut a rope into thirds. He used two of the pieces to make a swing. He used equal lengths of the leftover rope on four picture frames. What fraction of the original rope did he use for each picture frame?

A $\frac{1}{4}$ C $\frac{1}{16}$

B $\frac{1}{12}$ D $\frac{3}{4}$

20. Extend Your Thinking Five friends equally shared half of one large pizza and $\frac{1}{4}$ of another large pizza. What fraction of each pizza did each friend get? How do the two amounts compare to each other?

Name _____

Another Look!

Sal has $\frac{1}{3}$ of a sheet of poster board. Four friends are sharing the $\frac{1}{3}$ sheet equally. What fraction of the original sheet does each friend get?

How can you divide $\frac{1}{3}$ into 4 equal parts?

Step 1

Use a drawing.

Divide 1 whole sheet into 3 equal parts.

Shade to show Sal's $\frac{1}{3}$.

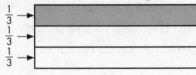

Step 2

Next, divide each third into 4 equal parts.

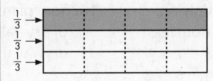

Step 3

Count the total number of parts. The total is the denominator.

$\frac{1}{12}$ ← each friend's part
← total number of parts

So, each friend gets $\frac{1}{12}$ of the original sheet.

In **1** through **11**, find each quotient. Draw a picture to help.

1. $\frac{1}{2} \div 4$

2. $\frac{1}{3} \div 2$

3. $\frac{1}{3} \div 5$

4. $\frac{1}{5} \div 3$

5. $\frac{1}{2} \div 5$

6. $\frac{1}{8} \div 2$

7. $\frac{1}{5} \div 4$

8. $\frac{1}{5} \div 2$

9. $\frac{1}{6} \div 4$

10. $\frac{1}{4} \div 3$

11. $\frac{1}{8} \div 2$

12. Draw a Picture Marge and Kimo equally shared one-fourth of a pie that was left over. What fraction of the original pie did each friend get? Use the picture to help you find the solution.

---

13. Connect Steven has $\frac{1}{3}$ of a package of biscuit mix left. He will use equal parts of the leftover mix to make three batches of biscuits. What fraction of the original package will he use for each batch?

14. Estimation What are two decimals whose product is close to 10?

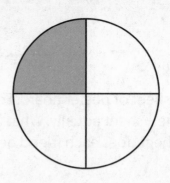

Use compatible numbers to help you find a product.

---

15. Number Sense Without multiplying, order the following products from least to greatest.

$2 \times \frac{3}{5}$ $\frac{1}{4} \times \frac{3}{5}$ $1\frac{2}{5} \times \frac{3}{5}$ $\frac{6}{6} \times \frac{3}{5}$

16. Tom plans to replace a rectangular piece of drywall. Find the area of the piece of drywall that Tom needs to replace.

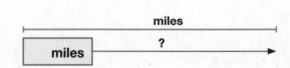

$\frac{3}{4}$ foot   16 feet

---

17. Use a Strip Diagram Linda wants to ride 288 miles to train for a bicycle race. If she rides 24 miles each day, how many days will it take her to complete her training? Complete the strip diagram to help you solve the problem.

miles

miles   ?

---

18. Mrs. Sims cut a melon into fifths. She gave 1 piece to each of her four children. She used equal amounts of the leftover melon to make three fruit cups. What fraction of the original melon did she use to make each fruit cup?

A $\frac{1}{4}$ C $\frac{1}{15}$

B $\frac{1}{12}$ D $\frac{1}{20}$

19. Extend Your Thinking Kim and Gerard each have $\frac{1}{2}$ of a poster to paint. Kim divided her half into 6 equal sections. She painted one section blue. Gerard divided his half into 5 equal sections. He painted one section blue. Whose blue section is larger? Explain.

Name _____

☆ ☆
Solve & Share

The Brown family is planting $\frac{1}{3}$ of their garden with flowers, $\frac{1}{3}$ with berries, and $\frac{1}{3}$ with vegetables. The vegetable section has equal parts of carrots, onions, peppers, and tomatoes. What fraction of the garden is planted with carrots?

🔷 TEKS 5.3L Divide whole numbers by unit fractions and unit fractions by whole numbers. Also, 5.3J.
Mathematical Process Standards 5.1A, 5.1C, 5.1D, 5.1E, 5.1F

Digital Resources at PearsonTexas.com

Solve   Learn   Glossary   Check   Tools   Games

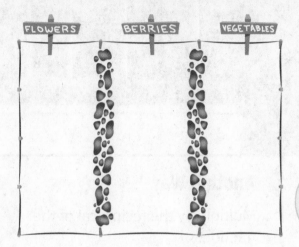

FLOWERS   BERRIES   VEGETABLES

Draw a Picture
How can you show an equal share of each vegetable?

Look Back!

Analyze Relationships Write an equation that models this problem. Explain your reasoning.

How Can You Divide with Unit Fractions and Whole Numbers?

A-Z

A utility company is planning to install wind turbines on 4 square miles of land. Each turbine requires $\frac{1}{6}$ square mile of land. How many turbines can be installed?

> You can find $4 \div \frac{1}{6}$ to find the number of turbines that will fit on the land.

B One Way

Use an area model to show 4 square miles. Divide each square mile into 6 equal parts to represent $\frac{1}{6}$ square mile.

1 mi   1 mi

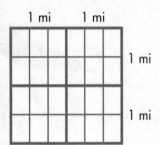

1 mi

1 mi

There are 24 parts.
So, 24 wind turbines will fit on the land.

C Another Way

Multiply by the reciprocal of the fraction.

> Dividing by a number is the same as multiplying by its reciprocal.

$$4 \div \frac{1}{6} = 4 \times \frac{6}{1}$$

$$= \frac{4 \times 6}{1}$$

$$= 24$$

24 wind turbines will fit on the land.

Do You Understand?

Convince Me! Use an area model to find $2 \div \frac{1}{4}$. Then find the quotient by multiplying by the reciprocal of the fraction.

Name _____

Another Look!

Find $8 \div \frac{1}{4}$.

You can use an area model to solve the problem.

First, draw a rectangle and divide it into 8 equal parts to represent 8 wholes.

Then use another color to divide each of the 8 parts into fourths and count the total number of fraction parts.

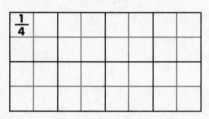

There are 32 squares, so you know that $8 \div \frac{1}{4} = 32$.

Find $\frac{1}{4} \div 8$.

You can also divide unit fractions by whole numbers.

First, rename the whole number 8 as the improper fraction $\frac{8}{1}$.

Then multiply $\frac{1}{4}$ by the reciprocal of $\frac{8}{1}$.

$\frac{1}{4} \times \frac{1}{8} = \frac{1}{32}$

So, you know that $\frac{1}{4} \div 8 = \frac{1}{32}$.

In **1** through **9**, find each quotient. Use a picture to help.

1. $6 \div \frac{1}{2}$

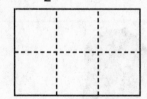

2. $4 \div \frac{1}{4}$

3. $5 \div \frac{1}{3}$

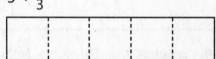

4. $\frac{1}{2} \div 6$

5. $\frac{1}{5} \div 2$

6. $\frac{1}{8} \div 3$

7. $\frac{1}{7} \div 8$

8. $5 \div \frac{1}{5}$

9. $\frac{1}{3} \div 9$

10. Draw a Picture Cynthia has a piece of wood that is 6 feet long. She cuts it into $\frac{1}{2}$-foot pieces. How many pieces does she have? Use the number line to help you solve the problem.

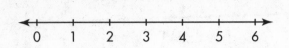

11. Connect Gregg has a coin collection album with 275 pages. Each coin is displayed on $\frac{1}{6}$ of a page.

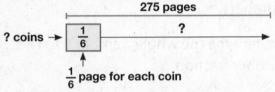

How many coins will fit in the album?

12. Josie has an 18-square-foot rug and a 24-square-foot rug. Her floor is covered in $\frac{1}{3}$-square-foot tiles. How many tiles will the two rugs cover?

A 126 tiles
B 84 tiles
C 42 tiles
D 14 tiles

13. Meredith modeled a division problem on the number line. What division problem did she model? Find the quotient.

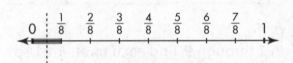

14. Extend Your Thinking Millie has 5 yards of blue fabric and 7 yards of pink fabric. How many quilt squares can she make with the fabric she has if both colors are needed to make one square? Explain your reasoning.

DATA

Amount of Fabric Needed for One Quilt Square	
Fabric Color	**Amount Needed**
Blue	$\frac{1}{4}$ yard
Pink	$\frac{1}{3}$ yard

Name _____

Solve & Share

Organizers of an architectural tour need to set up information tables every $\frac{1}{8}$ mile along the 6-mile tour, beginning $\frac{1}{8}$ mile from the start of the tour. Each table needs 2 signs. How many signs do the organizers need? *Solve this problem any way you choose.*

TEKS 5.1A Apply mathematics to problems arising in everyday life, society, and the workplace. Also, 5.3I, 5.3L. Mathematical Process Standards 5.1B, 5.1C, 5.1D, 5.1E, 5.1F

Digital Resources at PearsonTexas.com

Solve   Learn   Glossary   Check   Tools   Games

Formulate a Plan Can you find any hidden questions? *Show your work!*

Look Back!

Connect Ideas How many signs would the organizers need if they use only 1 sign at each table?

What Information Do You Need to Know to Solve a Multi-Step Problem?

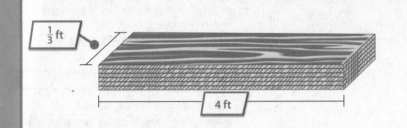

John plans to buy sheets of plywood like the one shown to make boxes with lids. Each box is a cube that has $\frac{1}{3}$-foot edges. How many sheets of plywood does John need in order to make 5 boxes with lids?

$\frac{1}{3}$ ft

4 ft

Remember, a cube has 6 identical faces.

B Plan

What do you know?
Six pieces of plywood are needed for each of the 5 boxes.

Boxes are $\frac{1}{3}$-foot cubes.

Each sheet of plywood is $\frac{1}{3}$ foot wide and 4 feet long.

What are you asked to find?
The number of sheets of plywood John needs to buy

C Solve

Find and answer all of the questions.

1. How many pieces of plywood are needed for 5 boxes with lids?

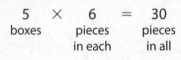

5	×	6	=	30
boxes		pieces in each		pieces in all

2. How many pieces can be cut from 1 sheet of plywood?

    $4 \div \frac{1}{3} = 12$

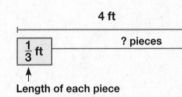

Length of each piece

3. How many sheets of plywood does John need for 5 boxes with lids?

    $30 \div 12 = 2\ R6$

    John needs 3 sheets of plywood.

Do You Understand?

Convince Me! Write a real-world problem that can be solved by first adding 24 and 36 and then dividing by $\frac{1}{4}$. Find the solution to your problem and explain your answer.

 **Guided Practice***

Solve.

1. Tamara needs tiles to make a border for her bathroom wall. The border will be 9 feet long and $\frac{1}{3}$ foot wide. Each tile measures $\frac{1}{3}$ foot by $\frac{1}{3}$ foot. Each box of tiles contains 6 tiles. How many boxes of tiles does Tamara need?

2. Two waiters in a restaurant share $\frac{1}{4}$ of their tips with the host. On Saturday, one waiter earned $60 in tips and the other waiter earned $80 in tips. What was the host's share of their tips?

3. What question do you need to answer in Problem 1 before you can solve the problem?

4. **Represent** What are two equations that can be used to solve Problem 2?

Remember, to find $\frac{1}{4}$ of their tips means to multiply by $\frac{1}{4}$.

Independent Practice

Write the hidden question or questions. Then solve.

5. Robert needs to earn $450 to buy books for college. He plans to work only during the summer, which is $\frac{1}{4}$ year. If he tutors during the summer, will he earn enough money to buy books?

Questions: _____

_____

_____

Answers: _____

_____

_____

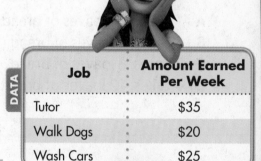

DATA	Job	Amount Earned Per Week
	Tutor	$35
	Walk Dogs	$20
	Wash Cars	$25

Problem Solving

6. **Formulate a Plan** Sandra is making vegetable soup. If she makes 12 cups of soup, how many cups of onions does she need? Write the hidden question or questions. Then solve.

Vegetable Soup Recipe	
Vegetable	**Amount Needed for 3 Cups of Soup**
Carrots	$\frac{1}{3}$ cup
Onions	$\frac{1}{8}$ cup
Peas	$\frac{1}{4}$ cup

DATA

7. Emily needs to buy fabric to make curtain panels for her windows. Each panel will be 4 feet long and $\frac{1}{2}$ foot wide. Each piece of fabric that she can buy is 4 feet long and 2 feet wide. How many panels can she make from 1 piece of fabric?

8. **Personal Financial Literacy** Barry buys a package of pasta for $2.39 and a jar of tomato sauce for $3.09. He uses a $0.75 coupon and a $0.50 coupon. What is the total cost of Barry's purchase?

9. Sophia uses $\frac{1}{2}$ pound of white flour to make one loaf of bread and $\frac{1}{4}$ pound of cake flour to make one cake. Which shows how many cakes and loaves of bread Sophia can make with the amount of flour that she has?

Flour in Pantry	
Kind of Flour	**Amount**
Cake	3 pounds
White	2 pounds
Whole Wheat	4 pounds

DATA

A 12 cakes, 4 loaves of bread
B 6 cakes, 8 loaves of bread
C 8 cakes, 6 loaves of bread
D 4 cakes, 12 loaves of bread

How many steps do you need to solve the problem?

10. **Extend Your Thinking** Mr. Moss had 4 gallons of paint. He painted 8 doors. How many benches can he paint with the paint that is left? Show your work.

Amount of Paint Needed	
Door	$\frac{1}{2}$ gallon per 2 doors
Bench	$\frac{1}{3}$ gallon per bench

Another Look!

Nell participated in a 3-day charity walk. She raised $0.50 for each $\frac{1}{3}$ mile that she walked. The first day, Nell walked 12 miles. The second day, she walked 8 miles. The third day, she walked 16 miles. How much money did Nell raise?

What information do you need to answer all of the questions?

What do you know?	What do you need to find?	Write and solve all of the questions.
Nell walked 12 miles, 8 miles, and 16 miles. She raised $0.50 for each $\frac{1}{3}$ mile she walked.	How much money Nell raised	**a** What is the total number of miles Nell walked? Nell walked $12 + 8 + 16$, or 36 miles. **b** How many $\frac{1}{3}$ miles did Nell walk? Nell walked $36 \div \frac{1}{3} = 36 \times \frac{3}{1}$, or 108 one-third miles. **c** How much money did Nell raise? Nell raised $108 \times \$0.50$, or $54.

Write and then answer all of the questions.

1. Anna's garden has an area of 48 square feet. She plants peas in $\frac{3}{8}$ of the garden and herbs in $\frac{1}{4}$ of it. The rest of her garden is planted with peppers. How many square feet of the garden are planted with peppers?

Questions: _____

_____

Answers: _____

_____

2. Benjamin is making bow ties. How many $\frac{1}{2}$-yard-long bow ties can he make if he has 18 feet of fabric?

3. Connect Ms. James has a 6-square-foot bulletin board and a 12-square-foot bulletin board. She wants to cover both boards with index cards without gaps or overlaps. Each index card has an area of $\frac{1}{4}$ square foot. How many index cards does she need?

4. Formulate a Plan One batch of fruit punch contains $\frac{1}{4}$ quart grape juice and $\frac{1}{2}$ quart apple juice. Colby makes 9 batches of fruit punch. Which of the following questions does **NOT** need to be answered to find how many cups of fruit punch Colby made?

A How much grape juice did he use for 9 batches?

B How much apple juice did he use for 9 batches?

C How many $\frac{1}{4}$-quarts and $\frac{1}{2}$-quarts are in 9 quarts?

D How many cups are in 1 quart?

5. Debbie cut a cord into sixths. She used five of the pieces to make necklaces. She used equal lengths of the remaining cord for each of four bracelets. What fraction of the original cord did Debbie use for each bracelet?

A $\frac{1}{6}$

B $\frac{1}{12}$

C $\frac{1}{16}$

D $\frac{1}{24}$

You can draw a picture to help.

6. Number Sense Craig has 36 ounces of flour left in one bag and 64 ounces of flour in another bag. Use the Baking Flour Equivalents table to find how many cups of flour Craig has in all.

7. Extend Your Thinking Doris uses 8 square pieces of fabric to make one scarf. Each side of a square piece of fabric is $\frac{1}{4}$ foot in length. Doris can buy large pieces of fabric that are $\frac{1}{4}$ foot long and 2 feet wide. How many large pieces of fabric should she buy to make 7 scarves? Show your work.

Baking Flour Equivalents	
Number of Ounces	**Number of Cups**
16	3.6
10	2.3
8	1.8

DATA

Name _____

1. Charles has $5\frac{3}{4}$ acres of land. He planted fruit trees on $2\frac{2}{5}$ acres of the land. How many acres of the land were **NOT** planted with fruit trees?

Applying Math Processes
- How does this problem connect to previous ones?
- What is my plan?
- How can I use tools?
- How can I use number sense?
- How can I communicate and represent my thinking?
- How can I organize and record information?
- How can I explain my work?
- How can I justify my answer?

2. **Personal Financial Literacy** Cathy saves $\frac{4}{5}$ of the money she earns from her part-time job. How much does she save when she earns $140?

3. **Explain** Use the table. Savannah plans to sew a baby dress. How many yards of lace trim and ruffle trim does she need in all?

Baby Dress	
Material	**Amount Needed**
Cotton Fabric	1 yard
Lace Trim	$\frac{1}{4}$ yard
Ruffle Trim	$\frac{1}{6}$ yard

4. **Extend Your Thinking** Mr. Casey needs to drive 278 miles in 7 hours. He estimates that he should drive at a speed of 50 miles per hour. Is his estimate greater than or less than the actual speed at which he should travel? Explain.

5. For an experiment, Kelly poured equal amounts of distilled water into each of 30 beakers. She used a total of 4.2 liters of distilled water. How many liters did she pour into each beaker?

6. A total of 359 children from Westboro and 417 children from Eastboro signed up for the county recreation program. Martha divided the children into groups of 97 so that each group could have its own time slot at the gym. The time slots were divided evenly between Saturday and Sunday. How many time slots were there on each day?

   A 4 time slots   C 16 time slots
   B 8 time slots   D 40 time slots

Error Search

Is the answer *correct* or *incorrect*? If it is incorrect, rewrite the problem so it is correct.

1.
$$\frac{5}{6} = \frac{8}{12}$$
$$-\frac{1}{2} = \frac{6}{12}$$
$$\frac{2}{12} = \frac{1}{6}$$

2.
$$\frac{2}{3} = \frac{8}{12}$$
$$+\frac{1}{4} = \frac{4}{12}$$
$$\frac{12}{12}$$

3.
$$\frac{1}{5} = \frac{4}{20}$$
$$+\frac{11}{20} = \frac{11}{20}$$
$$\frac{15}{20} = \frac{3}{4}$$

4.
$$\frac{7}{10} = \frac{12}{15}$$
$$-\frac{8}{15} = \frac{8}{15}$$
$$\frac{4}{15}$$

Reasoning

Tell whether each statement is *true* or *false*. If a statement is false, rewrite it so that it is true.

5. A good estimate of $\frac{1}{8} + \frac{9}{10}$ is $0 + \frac{1}{2}$, or $\frac{1}{2}$.

6. A good estimate of $\frac{7}{9} - \frac{5}{11}$ is $1 - \frac{1}{2}$, or $\frac{1}{2}$.

7. A hair clip is $1\frac{4}{7}$ inches long. A paper clip is $\frac{5}{6}$ inch long. The two items are about the same length.

8. A good estimate of $1\frac{3}{4} + 2\frac{15}{16}$ is $2 + 3$, or 5.

9. A good estimate of $6\frac{1}{4} - 4\frac{2}{3}$ is $7 - 5$, or 2.

Name _____

Set A pages 451–456

A fraction can be written as the product of a whole number and a unit fraction. Consider the model shown below.

Each fraction strip represents the unit fraction $\frac{1}{8}$.

There are 5 fraction strips in all.

So, the model represents $5 \times \frac{1}{8}$, or $\frac{5}{8}$.

Select a digital tool to solve the problems in Set A.

Remember that a unit fraction has a numerator of 1.

Reteaching

Write a multiplication equation with a unit fraction that describes the fraction shown. Use fraction strips to help.

1.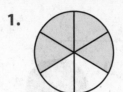

2. | $\frac{1}{4}$ | $\frac{1}{4}$ |
   |---|---|

3. $\frac{4}{5} = \square \times \dfrac{\square}{\square}$

4. $\frac{7}{12} = \square \times \dfrac{\square}{\square}$

Set B pages 457–462, 463–468

Find $\frac{2}{3}$ of 6.

One Way

$\frac{1}{3}$ of 6 is 2.

$\frac{2}{3}$ is twice as much as $\frac{1}{3}$.

So, $\frac{2}{3}$ of 6 is 4.

Another Way

Multiply first and then divide.

$\frac{2}{3} \times 6 = \frac{12}{3} = 4$

Remember that the word *of* often means to multiply.

Find each product. Simplify, if possible.

1. $4 \times \frac{1}{2}$

2. $\frac{3}{4}$ of 16

3. $24 \times \frac{1}{8}$

4. $\frac{4}{7}$ of 28

5. $\frac{4}{5} \times 37$

6. $\frac{7}{8} \times 219$

Set C pages 469–474

A 4-foot board is cut into pieces that are $\frac{1}{2}$ foot in length. How many pieces are there?

length of board ⟶ 4 feet

$\frac{1}{2}$ ft   x pieces ⟶

↑ length of each piece

$4 \div \frac{1}{2} = 4 \times \frac{2}{1} = \frac{8}{1} = 8$

There are 8 pieces.

Remember that you can draw a picture or use objects such as fraction strips to help you understand the problem.

1. A 12-foot-long playground is marked off into $\frac{1}{5}$-foot-long sections for a game. How many sections are there?

2. A 4-pound package of peanuts is divided into $\frac{1}{4}$-pound packages. How many $\frac{1}{4}$-pound packages will there be?

pages 475–480, 481–486

Find $\frac{1}{2} \div 4$.

Use multiplication.
Multiply by the reciprocal of the divisor.

$$\frac{1}{2} \div 4 = \frac{1}{2} \times \frac{1}{4}$$
$$= \frac{1}{8}$$

Remember,
you can use objects or a number line to help you divide.

Remember that to write the reciprocal of a fraction, switch the numerator and denominator.

Find each quotient.

1. $\frac{1}{3} \div 2$ **2.** $\frac{1}{7} \div 7$

3. $\frac{1}{2} \div 8$ **4.** $\frac{1}{8} \div 2$

5. $7 \div \frac{1}{2}$ **6.** $25 \div \frac{1}{6}$

7. Mr. Holms had $\frac{1}{5}$ of a carton of orange juice left. He used equal amounts of the leftover juice for two servings. What fraction of the whole carton of juice did he use for each serving?

pages 487–492

Helen has $97 in quarters and half-dollars combined. She has $13 in quarters. How many half-dollars does she have?

What is the hidden question or questions?

How much does Helen have in half-dollars?

$97

$13	?

$$\$97 - \$13 = \$84$$

How many $\frac{1}{2}$ dollars are in $84?

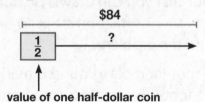

value of one half-dollar coin

$$\$84 \div \frac{1}{2} = 84 \times \frac{2}{1} = 168$$

Helen has 168 half-dollars.

Remember to answer the hidden question or questions first.

1. Ana was in a charity walk. She raised $0.25 for each $\frac{1}{2}$ mile that she walked. The first day, Ana walked 11 miles. The second day, she walked 14 miles. How much money did Ana raise?

2. In Problem 1, write and solve any hidden question or questions that you need to answer first.

3. Leo has a store coupon for $0.40 off and another coupon for $0.75 off. He buys a carton of juice for $4.19 and a carton of milk for $2.89. What is his total cost after using the coupons?

1. If the diameter of a tree trunk is growing $\frac{1}{4}$ inch each year, how many years will it take for the diameter to grow 8 inches?

   A 2 years

   B 8 years

   C 24 years

   D 32 years

2. Samantha wrote three products equal to $\frac{7}{8}$. Which of the following did she **NOT** write?

   A $\frac{6}{8} \times 1$

   B $\frac{7}{8} \times 1$

   C $7 \times \frac{1}{8}$

   D $21 \times \frac{1}{24}$

3. Mrs. Webster wants to divide 6 pints of milk into $\frac{1}{3}$-pint-size servings. How many servings will she have?

4. One-half of a cantaloupe was shared equally among 3 people. What fraction of the whole cantaloupe did each person get?

   A $\frac{1}{6}$ cantaloupe

   B $\frac{1}{5}$ cantaloupe

   C $\frac{1}{3}$ cantaloupe

   D $\frac{1}{2}$ cantaloupe

5. Raven is making pillows. Each pillow requires $\frac{1}{5}$ yard of fabric. Raven has 6 yards of fabric. Use the model to find the number of pillows Raven can make.

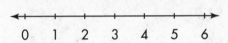

   A $\frac{1}{30}$ pillow

   B $\frac{7}{5}$ pillows

   C 11 pillows

   D 30 pillows

6. A farmer owns 24 acres of land. He plans to use 6 acres for an entrance into the farm and divide the remaining land into $\frac{1}{3}$-acre lots. How many $\frac{1}{3}$-acre lots will he have?

   A 6 lots

   B 18 lots

   C 54 lots

   D 72 lots

7. Jason spends $\frac{1}{3}$ of each day sleeping. What is the total number of days that Jason spends awake in 1 week?

8. Gus bought $\frac{2}{3}$ pound of turkey and $\frac{1}{4}$ pound of ham. The turkey cost $9 per pound, and the ham cost $7 per pound. In all, how much did Gus spend?

A $1.75   **C** $7.75

B $6   **D** $16

9. Tracy took a quiz containing 12 items. If she answered $\frac{5}{6}$ of the items correctly, how many items did she answer correctly?

10. Which number sentence is represented by the model that Jesse drew?

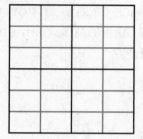

A $\frac{1}{6} \div 4 = \frac{1}{24}$ **C** $4 \div \frac{1}{4} = 16$

B $\frac{1}{24} \div 4 = \frac{1}{96}$ **D** $4 \div \frac{1}{6} = 24$

11. Three-quarters of a veggie pizza is left over. Mariah, Nick, and Kathryn are sharing the leftover pizza equally. What fraction of the original pizza does each person get?

A $\frac{1}{8}$ pizza   **C** $\frac{1}{2}$ pizza

B $\frac{1}{4}$ pizza   **D** Not here

12. The Marks family has two orchards. The orchard by the river is 6 acres in size. The orchard on the hill is 9 acres in size. If $\frac{2}{3}$ of the river orchard has apple trees and $\frac{1}{3}$ of the hill orchard has apple trees, how many total acres are planted with apple trees?

Expressions and Equations

Essential Question: How are the values of an algebraic expression and a numerical expression found?

A *food chain* shows a path of energy moving through an ecosystem.

For example, plants capture the Sun's energy and convert it to food energy. Cows eat plants.

So when I eat a hamburger, I am part of that food chain. Yum! Here's a project on food chains and food webs.

Math and Science Project: Food Chains and Food Webs

Do Research Use the Internet or other sources to find out more about food chains and food webs. Investigate the roles of producers, consumers, and decomposers. Explain how energy from sunlight is transferred to consumers.

Journal: Write a Report Include what you found. Also in your report:

- Draw a food web from an ecosystem near your home.

- Draw arrows on your food web to show how energy moves. Explain why the order is important.

- On one food chain of your food web, label each organism as a producer, consumer, or decomposer.

Review What You Know

Vocabulary

Choose the best term from the box. Write it on the blank.

> • sum
>
> • difference
>
> • product
>
> • quotient

1. The answer to a division problem is the _____.

2. The _____ of 5 and 7 is 12.

3. To find the _____ between 16 and 4, you subtract.

Mixed Review

Find each answer.

4. $32 \div 4$

5. 35×100

6. $47 + 92$

7. $\frac{1}{4} + \frac{2}{4}$

8. $3.4 - 2.7$

9. $1.9 + 7$

10. A baker has 15 pounds of flour. She divides the flour equally among 3 recipes. How many pounds of flour does each recipe use?

   A 3 pounds   C 6 pounds

   B 5 pounds   D 12 pounds

Mixed Review

Find each answer.

11. $3 + \frac{1}{2}$

12. $75 \div 5$

13. $\$3.75 + \$2.49$

14. $8\frac{5}{8} - 1\frac{2}{8}$

15. Jackson bought 2 tickets to the state fair. Each ticket cost $12. He spent $15 on rides and $8.50 on food. How much did Jackson spend in all?

Division

16. Use objects such as pieces of paper to divide.
   $\frac{1}{3} \div 2$

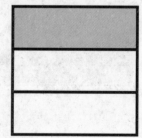

17. Use objects such as pieces of paper to find $2 \div \frac{1}{4}$.

My Word Cards

Use the examples for each word on the front of the card to help complete the definitions on the back.

A-Z

---

order of operations

$$6 \times 5 + 12 \div 3$$

$$30 \quad + \quad 4$$

$$34$$

---

brackets

$$3[(15 - 7) \div 2]$$

---

parentheses

$$3(15 - 7)$$

---

equation

$$x - 7 = 15$$

---

numerical expression

$$15 - 7$$

---

unknown

$$x - 7 = 15$$

$$\uparrow$$

unknown

---

algebraic expression

$$x - 7$$

My Word Cards

Complete the definition. Extend learning by writing your own definitions.

A square symbol used in mathematical expressions and equations to group numbers or variables together

is called _____.

The _____ tells the rule for which calculations to do before others. First, do the work inside parentheses and brackets. Then do multiplication and division in order from left to right. Finally, do addition and subtraction in order from left to right.

A mathematical sentence that uses an equal sign to show that two expressions have the same value is called an

_____.

Curved mathematical symbols used in expressions and equations to group numbers or variables together are

called _____.

A letter, such as x, that represents a number in an expression or an equation

is called an _____.

A _____ is a mathematical phrase that contains numbers and at least one operation.

A mathematical phrase involving a variable or variables, numbers, and operations is called an

_____.

© Pearson Education, Inc. 5

Name _____

Solve & Share
Two students evaluated the expression $15 + 12 \div 3 + 5$ and got two different answers. Neither student made a mistake in the calculations, so how did they get different results? *Solve this problem any way you choose.*

$$15 + 12 \div 3 + 5$$

TEKS 5.4E Describe the meaning of parentheses and brackets in a numeric expression. Also, 5.4F.
Mathematical Process Standards 5.1A, 5.1B, 5.1C, 5.1D, 5.1E, 5.1G

Digital Resources at PearsonTexas.com

Solve Learn Glossary Check Tools Games

Reason You can use the order of operations to evaluate expressions that have more than one operation. *Show your work!*

Look Back!
Communicate Why is it important to use the order of operations when evaluating an expression?

How Can You Evaluate a Numerical Expression with More Than One Operation?

Two students evaluated the same numerical expression but got different answers. To avoid getting more than one answer, use the order of operations. Rebecca used the correct order.

Rebecca's Way

$36 + 9 \div 3 \times 5$

$36 + 3 \times 5$

$36 + 15$

51

Juan's Way

$36 + 9 \div 3 \times 5$

$45 \div 3 \times 5$

15×5

75

You can find the value of $12 \div 4 + (9 - 2) \times (3 + 5)$ by using the order of operations.

B ## Step 1

In using order of operations, do the operations inside parentheses first.

$12 \div 4 + (9 - 2) \times (3 + 5)$

$\downarrow \quad \downarrow \quad \downarrow \quad \downarrow$

$12 \div 4 + \quad 7 \quad \times \quad 8$

Remember to rewrite the operations not yet performed.

C ## Step 2

Then, multiply and divide in order from left to right.

$12 \div 4 + 7 \times 8$

$\downarrow \quad \downarrow$

$3 \quad + \quad 56$

D ## Step 3

Finally, add and subtract in order from left to right.

$3 + 56$

$\downarrow$

59

Do You Understand?

Convince Me! In the first example, why was Juan's answer incorrect?

Name _____

Another Look!

Evaluate $8 \div 2 + 3 \times 6 - (1 \times 5)$.

If you do not use the correct order of operations, you will not get the correct answer.

Step 1	**Step 2**	**Step 3**
Do the operations inside the parentheses.	Multiply and divide in order from left to right.	Add and subtract in order from left to right.
$(1 \times 5) = 5$	$8 \div 2 = 4$ and $3 \times 6 = 18$	$4 + 18 = 22$ and $22 - 5 = 17$
$8 \div 2 + 3 \times 6 - 5$	$4 + 18 - 5$	So, $8 \div 2 + 3 \times 6 - (1 \times 5) = 17$

For **1** through **12**, use the order of operations to find the value of each expression.

1. $6 \times (3 + 2) \div 10$

2. $12 - (3 \times 3) + 11$

3. $(10 - 4) \times (16 - 8)$

4. $(8 \div 4) \times (4 - 2)$

5. $5 + 10 \times 3 - 6$

6. $18 - (8 \div 2) + 25$

7. $12 \div 3 + 4 \times 5$

8. $50 - (5 \times 5) + 13$

9. $(14 - 8) \times (15 - 4)$

10. $85 - 10 \div 2 + 3$

11. $20 - 12 + 8 \times 5$

12. $31 - (75 \div 3) \div 5$

For **13** through **18**, insert parentheses to make each statement true.

13. $15 - 3 \times 4 + 9 = 12$

14. $21 - 8 - 6 = 7$

15. $18 \div 3 - 5 + 1 = 2$

16. $15 - 3 \times 4 + 9 = 57$

17. $21 - 8 - 6 = 19$

18. $18 \div 3 - 5 + 1 = 0$

19. Dion bought 3 pounds of oranges and 2 pounds of grapefruit. Write an expression to represent the amount of money Dion spent on the fruit. Then evaluate the expression. How much did Dion spend?

DATA

Fruit Prices	
Fruit	Cost (per pound)
Lemons	$0.79
Oranges	$0.99
Limes	$1.09
Grapefruit	$1.59

20. Dion paid with a $20 bill. How much change did she get?

---

21. Patty made $34 babysitting on each of 3 weekends. If she spent $50 on gifts for her family, how much money does she have left?

22. Extend Your Thinking Carlos evaluated $20 - (2 \times 6) + 8 \div 4$ and got 29. Is his answer correct? If not, explain what Carlos did wrong and find the correct answer.

---

23. What is the value of the expression $(25 - 7) \times 2 \div 4 + 2$?

A 18
B 11
C 6
D 5

24. Insert parentheses in the expression $6 + 10 \times 2$ so that

a the expression equals 32.

b the expression equals $(12 + 1) \times 2$.

---

25. Estimation The highest point in Colorado is Mount Elbert, at 14,433 feet. About how many miles is that?

26. Connect Susan is 50 inches tall. Myra is 3 inches taller than Elaine, who is 2 inches shorter than Susan. How tall is Myra?

Remember, there are 5,280 feet in 1 mile.

Name _____

Solve & Share

Evaluate the expression $3 + (6 - 2) \times 4$.
Solve this problem using the order of operations.

TEKS 5.4F Simplify numerical expressions that do not involve exponents, including up to two levels of grouping. Also, 5.4E.
Mathematical Process Standards 5.1B, 5.1C, 5.1G

Digital Resources at PearsonTexas.com

 Solve   Learn   Glossary   Check   Tools   Games

You can use **number sense** to evaluate expressions with more than one operation. *Show your work!*

Look Back!

Justify Are parentheses needed in the expression $(8 \times 5) - 9 + 6$? Explain your answer.

What Order Should You Use When You Simplify an Expression?

Jack evaluated
$[(7 \times 2) - 3] + 8 \div 2 \times 3.$

To avoid getting more than one answer, he used the order of operations given at the right.

You can use the order of operations any time you are evaluating an expression with more than one operation.

Order of Operations

1. Evaluate inside parentheses and brackets.

2. Multiply and divide from left to right.

3. Add and subtract from left to right.

B   Step 1

First, do the operations inside the parentheses.

$[(7 \times 2) - 3] + 8 \div 2 \times 3$

$[14 - 3] + 8 \div 2 \times 3$

Then, evaluate any terms inside brackets.

$[14 - 3] + 8 \div 2 \times 3$

$11 + 8 \div 2 \times 3$

C   Step 2

Next, multiply and divide in order from left to right.

$11 + 8 \div 2 \times 3$

$11 + 4 \times 3$

$11 + 12$

D   Step 3

Finally, add and subtract in order from left to right.

$11 + 12 = 23$

So, the value of the expression is 23.

Do You Understand?

Convince Me! Would the value of $(15 - 3) \div 3 + 1$ change if the parentheses were removed? Explain.

Name _____

For **1** through **5**, use the order of operations to simplify the expression.

1. $8 + 14 \div 2 - (3 - 1)$

2. $[7 \times (6 - 1)] + 100$

3. $17 + 4 \times 3$

4. $(8 + 1) + 9 \times 7$

5. $(4 \times 3) \div 2 + 1 + 2 \times 6$

6. Communicate Explain the steps involved in simplifying the expression $(4 + 2) - 1 \times 3$.

7. Which is greater, $1 \times 5 + 4$ or $1 + 5 \times 4$?

8. Would the value of $(12 - 4) \div 4 + 1$ change if the parentheses were removed?

☆ Independent Practice ☆

Leveled Practice In **9** through **23**, use the order of operations to simplify the expression.

Remember to evaluate inside parentheses and brackets first.

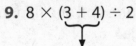

9. $8 \times (3 + 4) \div 2$

$8 \times \underline{\quad} \div 2$

$\underline{\quad} \div 2 = 28$

10. $39 + 6 \div 2$

$39 + \underline{\quad} = 42$

11. $12 \div 6 + 10 \times 2$

$\underline{\quad} + \underline{\quad} = \underline{\quad}$

12. $5 \div 5 + 4 \times 12$

13. $[6 - (3 \times 2)] + 4$

14. $(4 \times 8) \div 2 + 8$

15. $(18 + 7) \times (11 - 7)$

16. $2 + 3 \times 4 + 5 \times 6$

17. $(9 + 11) \div (5 + 4 + 1)$

18. $90 - 5 \times 5 \times 2$

19. $120 - 40 \div 4 \times 6$

20. $22 + (96 - 40) \div 8$

21. $8 \times 9 + (20 - 6) \div 2$

22. $32 \div (12 - 4) + 7$

23. $(77 + 3) \div 10 \times 4$

Problem Solving

24. Dan and his 4 friends want to share the cost of a meal equally. They order 2 large pizzas and 5 small drinks. If they leave a tip of $6.30, how much does each person pay?

Menu	
Small pizza	$8.00
Large pizza	$12.00
Small drink	$1.50
Large drink	$2.25

DATA

25. **Construct Arguments** Use the operation signs $+$, $-$, $\times$, and $\div$ once each in the expression below to make the number sentence true.

   6 ☐ (3 ☐ 1) ☐ 5 ☐ 1 = 17

26. Using order of operations, which operation should you perform last to evaluate this expression?

   $(1 \times 2.5) + (52 \div 13) + (6.7 - 5) - (98 + 8)$

   A Addition
   B Subtraction
   C Multiplication
   D Division

27. Theresa bought three containers of tennis balls at $2.98 each. She had a coupon for $1 off. Her mom paid for half of the remaining cost. How much did Theresa pay? Evaluate the expression $[(3 \times 2.98) - 1] \div 2$.

Simplify the expression in the parentheses first. Then subtract inside the brackets.

28. **Extend Your Thinking** Laurel buys 3 balls of yarn. Each ball of yarn costs $4.75. She also buys 2 pairs of knitting needles. Each pair costs $5.75. She pays for her purchase with two 20-dollar bills. Explain how to find the amount of change she receives. Then write an expression and find the amount of change.

29. **Analyze Information** Carlotta needs $12\frac{1}{2}$ yards of ribbon for a project. She has $5\frac{1}{4}$ yards of ribbon on one spool and $2\frac{1}{2}$ yards on another spool. How much more ribbon does she need?

30. **Math and Science** Giraffes are *herbivores*, or plant eaters. A giraffe can eat up to 75 pounds of leaves each day. Write and evaluate an expression to find how many pounds of leaves 5 giraffes can eat in a 7-day week.

Name _____

Another Look!

When an expression contains more than one operation, **parentheses ( )** can be used to show which operation should be done first.

Parentheses are one type of **grouping symbol**.

Do the operation inside the parentheses first.

> Operations in grouping symbols are always done first.

Evaluate $(2 + 8) \times 3$.

$$10 \quad \times 3 = 30$$

Evaluate $2 + (8 \times 3)$.

$$2 + \quad 24 = 26$$

Brackets are another type of **grouping symbol**. Evaluate terms inside brackets after doing operations within parentheses.

Evaluate $\quad [(4 + 9) - (30 \div 5)] \times 10$

$$[13 \quad - \quad 6] \times 10$$

$$7 \times 10 = 70$$

> Use the order of operations to choose which calculation to do next. Multiply and divide from left to right. Add and subtract from left to right.

In **1** through **12**, simplify the expression.

1. $(16 + 4) \div 10$

$$\underline{\hspace{1cm}} \div 10 = \underline{\hspace{1cm}}$$

2. $60 \div (3 \times 4)$

$$60 \div \underline{\hspace{1cm}} = \underline{\hspace{1cm}}$$

3. $(16 \div 4) + (10 - 3)$

4. $64 \div (2 \times 4)$

5. $27 - (5 \times 3)$

6. $(4 \times 6) \div 6 + 6$

7. $(5 + 2) \times (14 - 9)$

8. $5 + (2 \times 14) - 9$

9. $(52 + 48) \div (8 + 17)$

10. $[52 + (48 \div 8)] + 17$

11. $(80 + 16) \div (4 + 12) =$

12. $80 + 16 \div 4 + 12 =$

Use the table for **13** and **14**.

13. Write an expression to show how much Gretchen paid for drama, action, and comedy videos if she paid $4 for each at a sale. Evaluate the expression.

DATA	Gretchen's Video Purchases	
	Mystery	6
	Action	3
	Comedy	5
	Drama	2
	Romance	2

14. How much did Gretchen spend in all on videos?

15. Rewrite using parentheses to make each expression true.

a $42 + 12 \div 6 = 9$

b $33 - 14 + 4 = 15$

c $32 \div 8 \times 2 = 2$

16. Communicate Evaluate the expression $7 + (32 \div 16) \times 4 - 6$. What steps did you use to find the answer?

17. Keisha bought a new pair of skis for $450. She put $120 down and got a student discount of $45. Her mother paid $\frac{1}{2}$ of the balance. Which of the following expressions could be used to find the amount Keisha has left to pay?

A $450 - 120 + 45 \div 2$
B $[450 - (120 - 45) \div 2]$
C $450 - [(120 - 45) \div 2]$
D $[450 - (120 + 45)] \div 2$

18. Analyze Information Ellen is $5\frac{1}{2}$ feet tall. Her sister is $\frac{3}{4}$ foot shorter than Ellen. How tall is Ellen's sister? Write your answer as an improper fraction and as a mixed number.

19. Extend Your Thinking Milton makes trail mix for his hiking group. He mixes $1\frac{1}{4}$ pound of peanuts, 14 ounces of raisins, 12 ounces of walnuts, and 10 ounces of chocolate chips. If Milton divides the trail mix equally among the 8 hikers in the group, how many ounces of trail mix does each hiker receive?

Remember: There are 16 ounces in 1 pound.

Name _____

☆ ☆ ☆
Solve & Share

Every year for the past five years, the Hawks have won 2 more games than the Metros. Complete the table to show how many games the Hawks won based on the number of games the Metros won. **Solve this problem any way you choose.**

 TEKS 5.4 The student applies mathematical process standards to develop concepts of expressions and equations. Mathematical Process Standards 5.1D, 5.1E, 5.1F, 5.1G

Communicate You can write an algebraic expression to help you solve the given problem. **Show your work!**

Digital Resources

Solve Learn Glossary Check Tools Games

No. of Games Metros Won	No. of Games Hawks Won
1	
3	
6	
8	
10	

Look Back!

Analyze Relationships In each of the past five years, the Wildcats won 3 more games than the Hawks. How many games did the Wildcats win each year?

How Can You Write an Algebraic Expression?

A

Donnie bought DVDs for $10 each. How can you represent the total cost of the DVDs?

Variables help you translate word phrases into algebraic expressions.

A variable is a quantity that can change. It is often represented with a letter.

DATA

Number of DVDs	Total Cost
1	$10 × 1
2	$10 × 2
3	$10 × 3

An algebraic expression is a mathematical phrase that has at least one variable and one operation. The total cost of *n* DVDs is represented by:

$$\$10 \times n$$

B

The table shows algebraic expressions for given situations.

Word Phrase	Operation	Algebraic Expression
three dollars more than cost *c*	addition	$c + 3$
twelve pencils decreased by a number *n*	subtraction	$12 - n$
five times a distance *d*	multiplication	$5 \times d$ or $5d$
a apples divided by four	division	$a \div 4$ or $\frac{a}{4}$
five less than three times an amount *x*	multiplication and subtraction	$3x - 5$

Do You Understand?

Convince Me! There were 5 chaperones assigned to go with students on a field trip. What algebraic expression represents the total number of students and chaperones who went on the field trip?

Use the letter *n* to represent the number of students on the field trip.

DATA

Field Trip Participants

Number of Students (*n*)	Number of Chaperones
10	5
15	5
20	5
25	5

Name _____

☆ **Guided Practice** *

In **1** through **4**, write an algebraic expression for each situation.

1. the difference of a number *t* and 22

2. *m* bicycles added to 18 bicycles

3. 11 times a number *z*

4. 4 less than 5 times a number *g*

5. In the example at the top of page 516, what does the variable *n* represent?

6. Reason Identify the variable and the operation in the algebraic expression 8*y*.

7. Represent Write an algebraic expression for this situation: *n* more students than the 8 students sitting in each of the 3 rows.

☆ **Independent Practice** ☆

For **8** through **15**, write algebraic expressions.

8. A number *p* increased by 22

9. 15 divided by a number *r*

10. 12 more than 8 times a number *p*

11. 6 less than 7 times a number *b*

12. 5 more than the product of *x* and 9

13. 7 times the difference of *y* and 4

14. 3 less than the quotient of 24 ÷ *a*

15. 7 times a number *s* added to 16

Problem Solving

16. Reason The distance around a closed shape can be expressed as 3 times the length of side *s*, or 3*s*. Draw an example of this geometric shape.

17. Manuel sold *a* cartons of apple juice and *r* cartons of raisins. Write an algebraic expression to represent how many cartons of apple juice and raisins Manuel sold in all.

18. Represent One float for the Tournament of Roses parade uses as many flowers as a florist usually sells in 5 years. If *x* is the number of flowers a florist sells in 1 year, write an algebraic expression for the number of flowers used for one float.

19. Extend Your Thinking Devin's DVD case has 3 rows of slots, but 5 slots are broken. If *x* equals the number of slots in a row, explain how the expression $3x - 5$ relates to Devin's DVD case.

20. Use the diagram. Betty wants to put fencing around the perimeter of her vegetable garden. How many feet of fencing will she need?

21. What is the area of the vegetable garden?

Betty's Vegetable Garden

15 ft

40 ft

22. Connect Farmer John has hens, geese, ducks, and 2 goats. The number of hens equals the number of geese and ducks combined. There are 5 fewer geese than ducks. If the total number of animals is 40, how many are ducks?

23. Which expression shows a quantity of rolls, *r*, added to 8 bagels?

A $8 - r$

B $8r$

C $8 + r$

D $r \div 8$

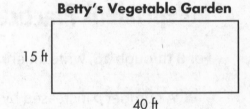

Read the problem and look for words or phrases that tell what operation to use.

Name _____

Another Look!

A variable represents a quantity that can change. To write an algebraic expression for a situation, decide which operation is appropriate. Look at the examples below.

> First, identify the variables.
> Then, identify the operations.

Word phrase	Variable	Operation	Algebraic Expression
ten **more than** a number b the **sum** of 8 and a number c	b c	Addition	$b + 10$ $8 + c$
five **less than** a number d 15 **decreased by** a number e	d e	Subtraction	$d - 5$ $15 - e$
the **product** of 8 and a number f 19 **times** a number g	f g	Multiplication	$8f$ $19g$
a number h **divided by** 2 50 divided into i equal parts	h i	Division	$h \div 2$ $50 \div i$

In **1** through **8**, write an algebraic expression.

1. a number k **divided by** 6

2. 8 **less than** a number t

3. the **sum** of 8 and a number q

4. 5 **times** a number b

5. a number j **divided by** 3

6. 7 **less than** a number d

7. n fewer carrots than 12

8. w lunches at $9 each

9. Use the table. In the first quarter, the Hawks scored *t* touchdowns and *f* field goals.

DATA		
Touchdown	:	6 points
Extra Point	:	1 point
Field Goal	:	3 points
Safety	:	2 points

Write an algebraic expression to represent the number of points the Hawks scored.

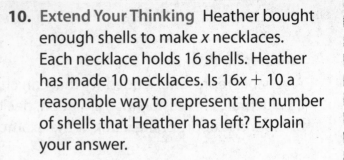

An algebraic expression has at least one variable and one operation.

10. Extend Your Thinking Heather bought enough shells to make *x* necklaces. Each necklace holds 16 shells. Heather has made 10 necklaces. Is $16x + 10$ a reasonable way to represent the number of shells that Heather has left? Explain your answer.

11. Cassie uses 1 quart cranberry juice, $\frac{1}{2}$ gallon ginger ale, and $1\frac{1}{2}$ pints orange juice to make fruit punch. How many 6-ounce servings can she make?

Remember:
1 gallon = 4 quarts,
1 quart = 2 pints,
1 pint = 2 cups, and
1 cup = 8 fluid ounces.

12. Represent Write an algebraic expression to represent the following situation.

Some children share 6 oranges equally.

Explain how the expression relates to the situation.

13. A theater has main floor and box seating. The main floor can seat 14 people in each row. Another 20 people can sit in the box seats. Which expression shows how many people can be seated in the theater?

A $20f - 14$

B $20f + 14$

C $14f - 20$

D $14f + 20$

14. John walked 2.5 miles on Monday, 1.75 miles on Tuesday, and 0.5 miles on Wednesday. How many fewer miles did John walk on Tuesday, than on Monday and Wednesday combined?

Name _____

☆ **Solve & Share** ☆

Every day after school Hector spends *d* minutes walking his dog. How long might he spend walking his dog in a month? *Solve this problem any way you choose.*

TEKS 5.4 The student applies mathematical process standards to develop concepts of expressions and equations. Mathematical Process Standards 5.1A, 5.1C, 5.1D, 5.1G

Digital Resources at PearsonTexas.com

Solve   Learn   Glossary   Check   Tools   Games

Communicate You can use an algebraic expression to find possible solutions to a problem. *Show your work!*

Look Back!

Connect Can you think of a real-world situation when you would use an algebraic expression to solve a problem?

A

A Tae Kwon Do class has 23 people. If *n* more people sign up, how many people will be taking the class?

A variable is a symbol that stands for a number.

n	23 + *n*
3	
5	
7	

B What You Show

Use the expression 23 + *n* to find the unknown numbers.

23 + *n*
↓
23 + 3 = 26

n	23 + *n*
3	23 + 3
5	23 + 5
7	23 + 7

C What You Write

If 3 more people sign up, there will be 26 people in the class.

If 5 more people sign up, there will be 28 people in the class.

If 7 more people sign up, there will be 30 people in the class.

Do You Understand?

Convince Me! Marlene has 3 times as much money as Nicole.

1. *n* represents the amount of money Nicole has. Use *n* to write an algebraic expression that shows the amount of money Marlene has.

Nicole
n

Marlene
m

2. *m* represents the amount of money Marlene has. Use *m* to write an algebraic expression that shows the amount of money Nicole has.

© Pearson Education, Inc. 5

Name _____

☆ Guided Practice *

In **1** through **3**, complete the table.

	c	c + 8
1.	4	
2.	9	
3.	13	

4. **Explain** Could you use the variable *k* instead of *n* to represent more students signing up for the Tae Kwon Do class?

5. Look back at page 522. If *n* is 12, how many people will be taking the Tae Kwon Do class?

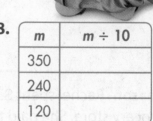

Use the algebraic expression to complete the table of values.

☆ Independent Practice ☆

For **6** through **8**, complete each table.

6.

d	d + 30
3	
7	
12	

7.

g	5g
6	
9	
15	

8.

m	m ÷ 10
350	
240	
120	

For **9** through **12**, fill in the unknown numbers.

9.

z	24	56	72	88
z ÷ 8	3		9	11

10.

t	43	134	245	339
t + 47	90	181		386

11.

y	387	201	65	26
y − 13	374	188		

12.

x	5	7	10	20
12x	60	84		

*For another example, see Set C on page 560.

Problem Solving

13. A Ferris wheel has 12 cars. Complete the table to show how many people can ride if each car holds 4 people.

Number of filled cars	Number of people
6	
8	
10	

DATA

14. Which expression represents how many seconds are in *m* minutes?

A $m + 60$
B $m \div 60$
C $60m$
D $m - 60$

15. Write an expression to represent the cost of parking a car for *n* hours in a lot that charges $7.00 per hour. Find the cost of parking the car for 3 hours.

16. **Extend Your Thinking** Edgar used 10*d* to represent the number of pennies in *d* dollars. Is this reasonable? Explain

17. Stan takes 1.5 hours to paint one door. Write the expression to represent the number of hours it takes him to paint *d* doors.

18. A ticket to a sporting event costs $9.25. Write the expression to represent the cost for *t* number of tickets. Find the cost for 23 tickets.

19. **Reason** Rachel spent $36.32 in the grocery store. She paid the exact amount and used exactly 4 bills and 4 coins. What bills and coins did Rachel use?

20. The year 2036 will be the fifth leap year after 2016. Name the years from 2016 to 2036 that are leap years. What pattern did you use?

A leap year occurs every 4 years.

Name _____

Another Look!

How do you evaluate algebraic expressions?

To evaluate an expression with a variable, replace the variable with a value and compute.

Evaluate $36 + n$ for $n = 6$.

Substitute 6 for n. Then add. $36 + 6 = 42$

Find an unknown number.

First substitute a value for the variable. Then simplify the numerical expression.

t	$t - 15$
28	13
41	26
35	
19	4

$28 - 15 = 13$

$41 - 15 = 26$

Substitute 35 for t. $35 - 15 = 20$.

$19 - 15 = 4$.

In **1** through **6**, complete each table.

w	$w + 16$
6	$6 + 16 =$
9	$9 + 16 =$
14	$+ 16 = 30$

1.
2.
3.

a	$26 - a$
5	
7	
18	

4.
5.
6.

In **7** through **10**, find the unknown number in each table.

7.

e	16	22	26	31
$3e$	48	66	78	

8.

g	100	72	56	12
$g \div 2$	50		28	6

9.

z	1	18	25	33
$100 - 3z$	97		25	1

10.

p	2	5	10	25
$100 \div 2p$	25	10		2

11. Communicate Explain how you could show five less than a number using an algebraic expression.

12. Number Sense Does the expression $d - 12$ have a greater value when $d = 42$ or when $d = 46$? Explain, without computing.

13. Use the table. Anton buys two posters and a mug online. He uses a coupon for $2 off and pays $4.95 for shipping.

DATA	Item	Cost
	Poster	$10.75
	Mouse pad	$9.95
	Mug	$5.75

What is Anton's total cost, including shipping?

14. Extend Your Thinking Matt says the expressions $12 \div p$ and $p \div 12$ are equivalent. Darla says they are not equivalent. Who is correct? Explain.

15. Brian worked for $7\frac{2}{3}$ hours yesterday and $6\frac{3}{4}$ hours today. How many hours in all did he work yesterday and today? Give your answer as a mixed number in simplest form.

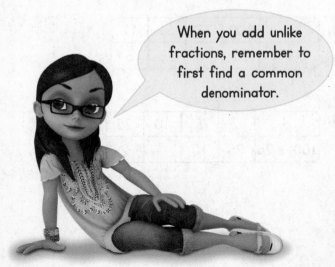

When you add unlike fractions, remember to first find a common denominator.

16. Jane is making lunch for 12 people. She is serving hot dogs and plans on each person eating 2 hot dogs. Hot dog buns are sold in packages of 8. Which expression can be used to find the number of packages she needs to buy?

A $(12 \div 2) \div 8$

B $(12 \times 2) \div 8$

C $(12 \div 2) \times 8$

D $(12 \times 2) \times 8$

Name _____

Solve & Share

A marching band plays at halftime during a football game. The percussion section follows the brass section as they march onto the field from the end zone. The table shows the yard line where the musicians are positioned. What rule can be used for the position of the brass and percussion musicians? *Solve this problem any way you choose.*

⭐ **TEKS 5.4D** Recognize the difference between additive and multiplicative numerical patterns given in a table or graph. Also, 5.4.
Mathematical Process Standards 5.1C, 5.1D, 5.1E, 5.1F

Digital Resources at PearsonTexas.com

Solve | Learn | Glossary | Check | Tools | Games

DATA	Instrument	Yard Line			
	Brass	17	20	25	32
	Percussion	13	16	21	28

You can **analyze relationships** between numbers given in a data table. *Show your work!*

Look Back!

Number Sense The brass section stops at the 50-yard line. Can you write an algebraic expression to represent where the percussion section would be when the brass section is at the 50-yard line?

How Can You Find a Rule and Write an Expression?

A

Everett made a table to record the regular and sale prices of store items. What is a rule for the table? How can you use a rule to write an expression and find the sale price when the regular price is $18?

> You can let *p* stand for the regular price.

Regular price (p)	$21	$20	$19	$18
Sale price	$16	$15	$14	☐

B Subtract to find the sale price.

For a regular price of $21:

21 − 5 = 16

For a regular price of $20:

20 − 5 = 15

For a regular price of $19:

19 − 5 = 14

A rule is subtract 5.
So, the expression is $p - 5$.

C Use the expression $p - 5$ to find the missing value when $p = 18$.

$p - 5 = 18 - 5$

Regular price (p)	$21	$20	$19	$18
Sale price	$16	$15	$14	$18 − 5

When the regular price is $18, the sale price is $13.

Do You Understand?

Convince Me! A certain city charges a fixed amount on top of any hotel bill to pay for new city buses. Write an algebraic expression that shows the total hotel charge including the fixed amount. How much is the fixed amount? How did you decide?

Hotel Bill (n)	$85.75	$132.50	$150.09	$203.06
Total Hotel Charge	$100.75	$147.50	$165.09	$218.06

528

© Pearson Education, Inc. 5

☆ **Guided Practice** *

For **1** and **2**, use the table.

Total number of test questions (q)	20	30	40	50
Number of multiple-choice questions	10	20	30	☐

1. What is a rule for the table in words? in symbols?

2. How many multiple-choice questions would be on a 50-question test?

3. Tools How could you use tools to find a rule in the table to the left?

4. In the example at the top of page 528, what is the sale price when the regular price is $30?

5. Roxanne makes a table. She labels the top row w and writes 4, 8, 12, and 16 in order from left to right. In the bottom row, she writes the rule w − 3. What numbers should she write in the bottom row, in order from left to right?

☆ **Independent Practice** ☆

Leveled Practice For **6** through **9**, find a rule.

6.

r	24	28	31	36
	11	15	18	23

24 is _____ than 11, so rule out _____.

24 is _____ more than 11, so the rule involves

_____. The rule is _____

7.

n	3	4	5
n + ☐	7	8	9

8.

x	18	21	26
x − ☐	5	8	13

9.

q	0	2	8
q + ☐	15	17	23

For **10** and **11**, complete each table, and find a rule.

10.

n	15	18	20	27
n + ☐	58	61	63	☐

11.

u	212	199	190	188
u − ☐	177	164	155	☐

Problem Solving

For 12 and 13, use the table.

12. Tools The United States Congress includes 2 senators from each state, plus members of the House of Representatives. If *r* represents the number of representatives from each state, which rule represents the total number of members each state has in Congress?

A 2r   **C** r − 2

B r ÷ 2   **D** r + 2

13. How many members in Congress does each state in the table have?

Number of Members in the United States Congress

State	House	Senate
Florida	25	2
Missouri	9	2
Hawaii	2	2
New York	29	2

14. Number Sense Hakim wrote an equation to represent the number of meters he would run for each kilometer, *k*, in a long distance race. What is the value of *k* if 1,000k = 0?

15. Chang has driven 1,372 miles. If the total mileage for his trip is 2,800 miles, how many miles does Chang have left to drive? Explain.

16. Donna makes $10.50 each hour she works at her job. How much money does she make for 15.75 hours of work? Round your answer to the nearest cent.

17. Lance has 24 pretzels. He keeps one-half of the pretzels for himself and gives the remaining pretzels to 3 of his friends. If each friend gets the same number of pretzels, how many does each friend get?

A 3 pretzels   **C** 6 pretzels

B 4 pretzels   **D** 12 pretzels

18. Extend Your Thinking A plumber charges an hourly rate as well as a fixed amount for a service call. Write an algebraic expression that shows the total charge including the fixed amount. How much is the fixed amount? How did you decide?

Hourly Bill Amount (h)	Total Charge
$91.50	$156.50
$122.00	$187.00
$152.50	$217.50
$183.00	$248.00

530   © Pearson Education, Inc. 5

Name _____

Another Look!

To find a rule and write an expression, compare pairs of numbers. What is a rule for this table?

v	57	28	10
	50	21	3

↑   ↑   ↑

Compare the numbers in each column of the table.

The top numbers are greater than the bottom numbers, so try subtraction.

Compare each pair of numbers. Each top number is 7 more than the bottom number.

The rule is subtract 7, so the expression is $v - 7$.

Make sure your rule works for all the pairs of numbers in a table.

In **1** through **4**, find a rule and complete each table.

1.

c	31	54	60	64
c − ☐	5	28	34	☐

2.

a	589	485	400	362
a − ☐	575	471	386	☐

3.

f	17	41	86	93
	21	45	90	97

4.

c	7	10	15	19
	32	35	40	44

In **5** and **6**, find a rule and write the missing number for each table.

5.

h	52	47	40	36
	44	39		28

6.

m	68	72	77	82
	25		34	39

---

7. Represent Tony earns $7 and saves $2. When he earns $10, he saves $5. When he earns $49, he saves $44. Write an expression for the amount Tony saves each time he earns money.

You can make a table to help you find a rule.

8. Extend Your Thinking Emily takes different routes when she rides her bike to school each day. Going home, she always takes the same 4-mile route. Write an algebraic expression to represent the total distance Emily travels each day. Explain how you chose the variable and what the variable represents.

9. Which expression stands for "32 more than a number *d*"?

A 32*d*

B 32 − *d*

C 32 + *d*

D 32 ÷ *d*

10. Number Sense Kevin orders 2 tacos with beans and rice and a drink for lunch. One taco costs $1.69. Write the cost of the taco in word form.

11. Use a Strip Diagram The month of April has 30 days. Corey's iguana eats $2\frac{1}{2}$ ounces of peas a day. How many ounces of peas will Corey's iguana eat during the month of April?

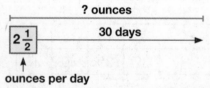

? ounces

30 days

$2\frac{1}{2}$

ounces per day

12. Darcy's house is 6 times as far from school as her friend's house. If her friend's house is $\frac{3}{4}$ mile from school, how many miles from school is Darcy's house?

13. Hannah practices her guitar for 40 minutes on Monday. On Tuesday she practices for $\frac{5}{8}$ of the time she practiced on Monday. On Wednesday she practices for $\frac{4}{5}$ of the time she practiced on Tuesday. How many minutes did Hannah practice on Wednesday?

A 20 minutes   C 30 minutes

B 25 minutes   D 40 minutes

14. Laura bought 28 juice boxes and 18 bags of pretzels for her bowling league. How much did she spend in all?

DATA	Bowling Alley Snacks	
	Snack	Cost
	Juice Box	$0.75
	Cookies	$1.89
	Pretzels	$1.29

Name _____

☆ ☆
Solve & Share

Sheena is making her famous spaghetti sauce. The table shows the number of ounces of pasta needed for each number of servings. What rule works for the table? *Solve this problem any way you choose.*

⊕ **TEKS 5.4D** Recognize the difference between additive and multiplicative numerical patterns given in a table or graph. Also, 5.4.
Mathematical Process Standards 5.1A, 5.1B, 5.1C, 5.1D, 5.1E

You can **create and use a representation** to model multiplication and division patterns. *Show your work!*

Digital Resources at PearsonTexas.com

Solve   Learn   Glossary   Check   Tools   Games

DATA					
Number of Servings	6	12	14	20
Ounces of Pasta	18	36	42	60

Look Back!

Connect Describe a situation in which a quantity is always multiplied or divided by the same number.

How Can You Find a Rule and Write an Expression?

What is a rule for the table? How can Josie use a rule to write an expression and find the number of cards in 4 boxes?

You can let *b* stand for the number of boxes.

DATA	Number of boxes (*b*)	1	2	3	4
	Number of note cards	15	30	45	☐

B Multiply to find the number of cards.

For 1 box:
$1 \times 15 = 15$

For 2 boxes:
$2 \times 15 = 30$

For 3 boxes:
$3 \times 15 = 45$

A rule is multiply by 15.
So, the expression is $b \times 15$.

C Use the expression $b \times 15$ to find the missing value when $b = 4$.

$b \times 15 = 4 \times 15$

DATA	Number of boxes (*b*)	1	2	3	4
	Number of note cards	15	30	45	4×15

There are 60 note cards in 4 boxes.

Do You Understand?

Convince Me! In the example given, how many note cards are in 13 boxes?

How many boxes would there be if there were 150 note cards? Tell how you decided.

Name _____

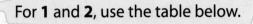

For **1** and **2**, use the table below.

Number of tickets (t)	2	4	6	8
Total price	$60	$120	$180	

1. What is a rule for the table in words? In symbols?

2. How much would 8 tickets cost?

3. Communicate How could you use tools to describe a rule in the table to the left?

4. Reason How could you find the price of 1 ticket using the information from Exercises 1 and 2?

☆ Independent Practice ☆

For **5** through **7**, find a rule.

5.

n	3	8	10
n × ☐	18	48	60

6.

p	2	4	8
p ÷ ☐	1	2	4

7.

t	2	3	4
☐ × t	16	24	32

For **8** through **11**, complete each table, and find a rule.

8.

e	4	8	12	16
e ÷ ☐	1	2	3	☐

9.

i	4	9	10	16
☐ × i	28	63	70	☐

10.

w	5	7	8	10
☐ × w	45	63	72	☐

11.

s	20	35	40	45
s ÷ ☐	4	7	8	☐

Problem Solving

12. Estimation There are 60 minutes in one hour, 24 hours in 1 day, and 7 days in one week. About how many minutes are in one week? Explain how you found your estimate.

13. Cami bought two books for $12 each and two journals for $4 each. How much change would she get if she paid with two $20 bills?

A $2   C $32

B $8   D $40

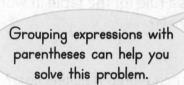

Grouping expressions with parentheses can help you solve this problem.

14. Math and Science In a food chain, producers turn the Sun's energy into chemical energy. Plants use about $\frac{9}{10}$ of the Sun's energy to stay alive. The rest of the energy is stored in the plant's tissue. A primary consumer, such as a cow, eats plants and grass for energy. What part of the Sun's energy is passed on to a cow?

15. Communicate Is the rule for the table an addition expression or a multiplication expression? Explain. Find the rule.

q	2	3	4	5
	14	21	28	35

For **16** and **17**, use the table.

Extend Your Thinking Three students are playing a math game. Each student gives a value for the variable in the expression and then evaluates the expression. The student with the greatest value wins the round. The students' variable values are given in the table.

Student	Value
Bobby	6
Hannah	2
Carlos	4

16. The first expression is $(3 + 7) \times (10 - n \div 2)$. Who wins the round? What is the value of each expression?

17. The next expression is $(2 \times n + 2) \div 2$. Who wins the round? What is the value of each expression?

© Pearson Education, Inc. 5

Name _____

Homework 10-6
Multiplication and Division Expressions

Another Look!

To find a rule and write an expression using multiplication and division, compare pairs of numbers.

What is a rule for this table?

b	3	6	8
	24	48	64

Remember, 8 × b means 8b.

Compare the numbers in each column of the table.

The bottom numbers are greater than the top numbers, so try multiplication.

Compare each pair of numbers.
Each bottom number is 8 times as great as the top number.

A rule is multiply by 8, so the expression is 8 × b.

In **1** and **2**, find a rule for each table.

1.

a	48	56	64	72
	6	7	8	9

2.

u	8	11	13	16
	32	44	52	64

In **3** through **6**, find a rule and write the missing number for each table.

3.

k	18	14	12	8
	9	7		4

4.

e	2	4	6	7
	6	12	18	

5.

p	4	6	10	17
	20		50	85

6.

q	48	42	30	24
	8		5	4

7. **Represent** Draw lines on the picture of the $1 bill to represent dimes. Write an expression for the number of dimes in *d* dollars.

8. **Reason** Katie says the expression $18 \times y$ is equivalent to the expression $y \times 18$. Is she correct? Explain.

9. **Analyze Information** The length of the Oregon Trail was about 2,000 miles. This route would take settlers 4 months to travel. Use *n*, the number of miles traveled per month, to write a multiplication expression that represents the total distance traveled. How can you find the value of *n* given what you know about the length of the Oregon Trail?

10. Lisa wants to use an expression to represent "3 times a number *h*". Which expression could she use?

    A $3 \times h$
    B $3 - h$
    C $3 + h$
    D $3 \div h$

11. **Extend Your Thinking** Find a rule and write the missing number in the table. How could you change the table so that the new rule uses a different operation?

e	5	7	9	11
		42	54	66

12. ★ Sherri is making 15 bags of party favors. Each bag contains between 6 and 9 items. Which is a reasonable estimate for the total number of items in all the bags?

    A 8 items
    B 75 items
    C 105 items
    D 150 items

    Remember to check that your estimate is reasonable.

Name _____

☆ ✦ ☆
Solve & Share

Write and solve a problem using the equation shown. Tell how you solved it.

$$8,000 = 20 \times n$$

⭐ TEKS 5.4B Represent and solve multi-step problems involving the four operations with whole numbers using equations with a letter standing for the unknown quantity. Also, 5.4. Mathematical Process Standard 5.1B, 5.1C, 5.1D

Digital Resources at PearsonTexas.com

| Solve | Learn | Glossary | Check | Tools | Games |

You can **formulate a plan** to solve the problem.

Look Back!

Check for Reasonableness How can you check that your answer is reasonable?

How Can You Solve an Equation?

Jared loves sharks. He writes equations to find how many tons an adult shark weighs and how many pounds a young shark needs to gain to weigh the same as the adult. Solve each equation.

Jared's Equations:

$t \times 2,000 = 10,000$

$1,400 + p = 10,000$

An equation is a number sentence that uses an equal sign to show that two expressions have the same value.

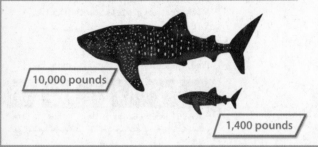

10,000 pounds

1,400 pounds

You need to solve for the unknown, or variable, in each equation.

B How many tons, *t*, does an adult shark weigh?

Solve $t \times 2,000 = 10,000$.

$5 \times 2 = 10$

$5 \times 20 = 100$

$5 \times 200 = 1,000$

$5 \times 2,000 = 10,000$. So $t = 5$.

The adult shark weighs 5 tons.

To solve, think: what number times 2,000 equals 10,000?

C How many pounds, *p*, does a young shark need to gain?

Solve $1,400 + p = 10,000$.

$1,400 + 600 = 2,000$

$2,000 + 8,000 = 10,000$

I added $600 + 8,000 = 8,600$.

$1,400 + 8,600 = 10,000$. So $p = 8,600$.

The young shark needs to gain 8,600 pounds.

To solve, think: what number can I add to 1,400 to get 10,000?

Do You Understand?

Convince Me! How would you solve the following equation?

$5,400 \div n = 60$

Guided Practice*

In **1** through **4**, solve each equation.

1. $n + 500 = 2{,}000$

2. $x - 2 = 18$

3. $2{,}000 \times y = 14{,}000$

4. $16{,}000 \div z = 80$

You can substitute the value of the variable into the equation to check your answer.

5. What question can you answer to help solve the equation in Exercise 1?

6. What could you ask yourself to help you solve the equation in Exercise 4?

Use compatible numbers to help you.

Independent Practice

Leveled Practice In **7** and **8**, enter the missing numbers to solve each equation.

7. $v + 550 = 8{,}000$

_____ $+ 550 = 600$

_____ $+ 600 = 8{,}000$

_____ $+ 550 = 8{,}000$

So, $v =$ _____.

8. $4{,}200 \div n = 70$

$4{,}200 \div$ _____ $= 700$

$4{,}200 \div$ _____ $= 70$

So, $n =$ _____.

In **9** through **17**, solve each equation.

9. $b + 1{,}600 = 5{,}000$

10. $500 \times r = 25{,}000$

11. $18 \div a = 6$

12. $400 + x = 6{,}800$

13. $90 \times r = 810$

14. $x - 4{,}200 = 8{,}000$

15. $4{,}000 \div z = 500$

16. $x - 80 = 440$

17. $3{,}000 \times y = 27{,}000$

Problem Solving

For **18** through **20**, use the table.

18. **Math and Science** The rings of Saturn are made of chunks and particles of ice and rocks, all orbiting the planet. How many kilometers longer is the distance of the B ring from Saturn than the distance of the C ring?

Rings of Saturn	Distance from Planet
A	122,200 km
B	92,000 km
C	74,500 km
D	66,900 km

19. A spacecraft flies from the D ring of Saturn to the A ring. How many kilometers does it travel?

20. How much farther away from Saturn is ring A than ring B?

21. **Reason** Kelly paid a $2.10 fine for returning a library book d days late. The library charges $0.15 per day for late returns. Write an equation which describes how many days she was charged for late fees.

22. **Communicate** Explain how to solve the equation below.
$$x + 1,500,000 = 4,000,000$$

23. ⭐ Pat saved 2,500 pennies. He wants to put the pennies into piles of 50. How many piles will he have?

    A 5   **C** 125

    B 50   **D** 500

24. **Extend Your Thinking** Without solving, determine whether the solution to the equation $32,531 \div y = 160$ is greater than or less than 200. Explain.

25. Kara sold 134 pizza kits for a fundraiser. Fifty-six of the kits were cheese pizza kits and the rest were pepperoni pizza kits. How much money did Kara raise in all?

Pizza Kits for Sale

Cheese $9.75

Pepperoni $12.50

Name _____

Another Look!

Celia wants to buy a digital camera that costs $125. So far, she has saved $60. How much more money does she need to save? Let *d* be the amount of money she still needs to save. Solve the equation $60 + d = 125$.

You can use a strip diagram to help you solve the problem.

Think: 60 plus what number equals $125?

$60 + 40 = 100$

$100 + 25 = 125$

So, $40 + 25 = 65$ and $d = 65$.

Celia needs to save $65 to have enough money to buy the camera.

	$125	
$60		*d*

A strip diagram gives you a visual representation of the problem.

In **1** and **2**, draw a strip diagram to model each equation. Then solve.

1. $x + 65 = 92$

2. $5 \times y = 95$

	x

x =

In **3** through **14**, solve each equation.

3. $q - 75 = 50$

4. $15 \times r = 3,000$

5. $a + 300 = 4,000$

6. $p \div 7 = 15$

7. $a \times 300 = 1,800$

8. $970 - f = 880$

9. $s + 18 = 70$

10. $120 \div q = 40$

11. $23 \times m = 460$

12. $5,000 \div x = 250$

13. $p + 75 = 800$

14. $2,100 \times c = 63,000$

For **15** and **16**, use the table.

15. A pilot flies from New York to Los Angeles. Then he flies from Los Angeles to Honolulu. How many miles does the pilot fly in all?

Distances Between Cities	
Cities	**Distance (miles)**
New York to Los Angeles	2,450
New York to Chicago	715
Los Angeles to San Francisco	340
Los Angeles to Honolulu	2,550

16. Jolene travels Los Angeles to San Francisco round-trip. How many miles does Jolene travel in all?

---

17. Selma bakes 36 granola bars. After 3 days there are 27 granola bars left. Write an equation to solve the problem. How many of the granola bars were eaten?

18. Jake is driving 370 miles to an amusement park. So far, he has driven 124 miles. How many miles does he have left to drive?

---

19. Extend Your Thinking Use the strip diagram.

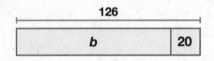

Write two equations that the strip diagram could model. Explain your reasoning.

20. Tomika saved $25. She bought a DVD for $9.50. Then she saved $15 more. She gave $5 to a local animal shelter and spent $8.75 for a movie. How much money does Tomika have left?

A $40.00
B $28.75
C $21.75
D $16.75

---

21. Personal Financial Literacy Julius wants to save $2,390 in 12 months. About how much does he need to save each month? Tell how to estimate to solve.

22. Number Sense Evaluate the expression $[3 \times (12.4 + 2.1)] - 14 + 7.9$. Which operation did you do first?

Eric has $24. He buys 3 identical notebooks and has $18 left. How much did each notebook cost?

You can **create and use representations** to solve. You can write an equation by thinking about what operations can be used to describe the situation.

⭐ TEKS 5.4B Represent and solve multi-step problems involving the four operations with whole numbers using equations with a letter standing for the unknown quantity. Also, 5.4. Mathematical Process Standards 5.1B, 5.1C, 5.1D, 5.1E

Digital Resources at PearsonTexas.com

Solve   Learn   Glossary   Check   Tools   Games

Look Back!

Check for Reasonableness How can you check that your answer is reasonable?

How Can You Solve an Equation with More Than One Operation?

Suzy and her brother Tim are putting their leaf collections into scrapbooks. Suzy has 175 leaves. Tim has 125 leaves. How many pages, like the one shown, do they need if they combine their collections? Use a strip diagram and write an equation to solve.

Let p = the number of pages.

175	125

10 ────────────────────────────▶
p times

$175 + 125 = p \times 10$

Step 1
B

First, find the total number of leaves by adding 175 and 125.

$$175 + 125 = p \times 10$$

$$300 = p \times 10$$

Step 2
C

Then solve for the number of pages.

$$300 = p \times 10$$
$$300 \div 10 = p$$
$$30 = p$$

Suzy and Tim need 30 pages.

Do You Understand?

Convince Me! What is the first step to solving the following equation? What is the second step?

$$n \times 100 = 25 + 275$$

Name _____

☆ Guided Practice *

In **1** through **5**, solve each equation.

1. $18 + 34 = 2 \times n$

2. $3 \times y = 8 + 10$

3. $r \div 2 = 32 - 16$

4. $90 + 50 = 10 \times a$

5. $175 - 75 = 400 \div z$

6. What is the first step to solve the equation in Exercise 1?

7. What is the simpler equation you solved in Exercise 1?

Remember to substitute the value of the variable into the equation to check your work!

Independent Practice ☆

In **8** through **19**, solve each equation.

8. $4 + 8 = 3 \times n$

9. $5 \times y = 10 + 10$

10. $8 \times p = 64 - 8$

11. $v \div 10 = 125 + 25$

12. $18 + 18 = z \times 6$

13. $8 + 28 = 4 \times w$

14. $30 \times d = 300 + 600$

15. $60 \times s = 158 + 82$

16. $9 + 2 = u \div 2$

17. $m \div 5 = 23 - 3$

18. $164 + 16 = n \times 30$

19. $4 \times a = 63 + 37$

Problem Solving

20. Seven times a number gives the same result as subtracting 1441 from 2001. What is the number? Write an equation and solve.

21. Don and his friend decide to share the cost of a meal equally. Don's dinner cost $9 and his friend's dinner cost $11. Which equation best describes the amount each person pays, which is represented by s?

    A $9 + 11 = 2 \times s$

    B $11 - 9 = 2 \times s$

    C $9 + 11 = s \div 2$

    D $11 \times 9 = 2 + s$

22. Erica has 166 video games. She buys 14 more and now has 20 times as many as Joe. How many video games does Joe have? Write an equation and solve.

23. **Reason** What is the first step in solving the equation $3 \times t = 200 - 18$?

24. Duncan wants to put a fence around his garden. He has 50 feet of fencing. Does he have enough fencing to enclose his garden? Explain.

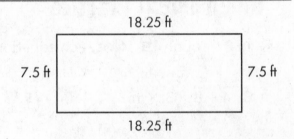

18.25 ft

7.5 ft   7.5 ft

18.25 ft

25. **Estimation** The table shows the baseball game attendance for three consecutive nights. About how many people attended the three games?

DATA	Baseball Game Attendance	
	Day	**Attendance**
	Monday	52,104
	Tuesday	48,899
	Wednesday	49,023

26. **Extend Your Thinking** Jerry saved $219. He bought a book for $15 and now has 3 times as much money as his brother. How much money does his brother have? Write an equation to solve. Explain how you can check your solution.

27. **Math and Science** Vietnamese pot-bellied pigs are popular as pets. A pot-bellied pig eats 1.5 cups of food a day for every 25 pounds it weighs. Germaine's pot-bellied pig weighs 75 pounds. About how many cups of food does her pig eat in one week?

Name _____

Another Look!

Dana is 4 years old. Tanya is 6 years old. The sum of their ages is twice Carolyn's age. How old is Carolyn?

You can use tools to model and solve the problem.

Step 1

Add Dana's age and Tanya's age.

Dana's age   Tanya's age

Step 2

The sum, 10, is twice Carolyn's age. So, divide 10 by 2.

$10 \div 2 = 5$

Carolyn is 5 years old.

Draw a picture or diagram to help solve the equation.

1. $6 + 9 = 3 \times c$ Model the sum:

$6 + 9 =$ ____.

Divide the sum by 3 to find c: ____ $\div 3 =$ ____.

So, $c =$ ____.

In **2** through **10**, solve each equation.

2. $t \times 12 = 10 + 2$ **3.** $128 - 24 = 2 \times n$ **4.** $3 \times p = 6 + 15$

5. $r \div 3 = 6 + 1$ **6.** $600 + 700 = 13 \times a$ **7.** $12 - 8 = z \div 5$

8. $5 + 3 = s \times 2$ **9.** $n \div 3 = 7 - 5$ **10.** $25 \times 3 = a - 29$

11. Cody is selling popcorn for his scout troop. His goal is to raise $350. So far, Cody has raised $284. How much more does Cody need to raise to meet his goal? Write and solve an equation to find the answer.

12. Paul and Dina are in a 17-kilometer race. Paul has completed 5 kilometers. Dina has completed one-half the distance Paul has left to complete. Which of the following equations can be used to find how many kilometers, k, of the race Dina has completed?

    A $17 - 5 = k \div 2$
    B $17 - 5 = 2 \times k$
    C $17 + 5 = k \div 2$
    D $17 + 5 = 2 \times k$

13. **Extend Your Thinking** Caryn drew a strip diagram and wrote an equation to represent the following problem.

A zoo has 19 more species of fish than birds. There are 152 species of fish at the zoo. How many species of birds does the zoo have? Is Caryn correct? Explain your answer.

$$b$$
| 19 | 152 |

$$b - 19 = 152$$

14. **Personal Financial Literacy** Rachel deposited $261 of her babysitting money into her bank account. She had $79 left. How much money did Rachel earn from babysitting? Write an equation and solve.

15. Ramon paid $8 for a T-shirt. Juan paid $7 for a T-shirt. The total that Ramon and Juan paid together is one-half of the amount Dennis paid for a T-shirt. How much did Dennis pay?

16. **Number Sense** The land area of the United States is 3,676,487 square miles. What is the land area rounded to the nearest thousand?

17. Darien's kitten weighs 2.25 pounds. Her dog weighs 10 times the weight of the kitten. How much does her dog weigh?

Name _____

Solve & Share

A store sold 20 sweatshirts. Of these, 8 were red. Twice as many were green as were yellow. How many of each color sweatshirt did the store sell? *Solve this problem any way you choose.*

Connect Ideas You can use what you know to evaluate and solve this problem. *Show your work!*

TEKS 5.1D Communicate mathematical ideas, reasoning, and their implications using multiple representations, including symbols, diagrams, graphs, and language as appropriate.
Mathematical Process Standards 5.1B, 5.1C, 5.1E, 5.1F

Digital Resources at PearsonTexas.com

Solve   Learn   Glossary   Check   Tools   Games

Look Back!

Reason What information in the problem posed above was not given? How were you able to use reasoning to solve the problem?

A Analyze

How Can You Use a Strip Diagram to Find Missing Information?

A children's zoo displays birds in 3 different cages. The zoo has three kinds of birds. There are 36 birds in all. How many of each type of bird are in the zoo?

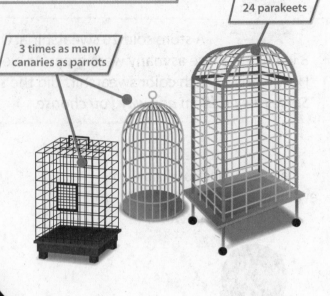

24 parakeets

3 times as many canaries as parrots

You can use a strip diagram to show the number of birds and then use reasoning to solve the problem.

B Plan

Use a strip diagram to show what you know. You already know there are 36 birds in all.

You can use reasoning to make conclusions.

36 birds

24 parakeets	

12 canaries and parrots

C Solve

Let p equal the number of parrots. Use the strip diagram to write an equation:
$12 = 3p + p$, or $12 = 4p$.

12 canaries and parrots

3 times as many canaries →

c	c	c	p

$12 = 4p$, so the value of p is 3. There are 3 parrots and 9 canaries.

$24 + 9 + 3 = 36$, so the answer is correct.

Do You Understand?

Convince Me! Tracey has daisies, roses, and irises. Use the clues to find how many of each kind of flower Tracey has. Write the number of each kind.

Clues: 18 flowers in all
             2 irises
             3 times as many daisies as roses

Daisies _____

Roses _____

Irises _____

☆ Guided Practice ☆

Use a strip diagram to solve the problem.

1. The Rodriquez family is donating 25 baseball caps to a charity auction. There are 11 blue caps. There are 2 more white caps than green caps. How many of each color cap are they donating?

2. **Reason** Write a real-world problem that can be solved by drawing a strip diagram and using reasoning.

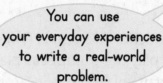
You can use your everyday experiences to write a real-world problem.

Independent Practice ☆

In **3** and **4**, use a strip diagram and reasoning to solve each problem.

3. Mr. Niles has a box of accessories for clarinets. He has a total of 42 objects. He has 12 mouthpieces. He has four times as many reeds as neck straps. How many of each object does he have?

4. Sylvia has a jewelry collection of bracelets, necklaces, and earrings. She has 16 bracelets. The number of earrings is 2 times the number of necklaces.

   a Write an expression that shows how many pieces of jewelry she has in all.

   b How many necklaces does she have if she has 43 pieces of jewelry in all?

Problem Solving

For **5** through **7**, use the table.

5. **Tools** In Group 1, there are 8 students who play the tuba. There are $\frac{1}{2}$ as many students playing the clarinet as the flute. Write an expression that shows how to find the number of students who play each instrument. How many students play the clarinet?

6. There are 41 students in Group 2. Twice as many students play the trumpet as play the trombone. How many students in Group 2 play each instrument?

Instrument	Number of Students
Group 1	44
Tuba	8
Clarinet	
Flute	
Group 2	41
Saxophone	8
Trumpet	
Trombone	

7. **Extend Your Thinking** An additional 7 students joined Group 2, but 1 student left Group 2 to join Group 1. Now 20 students play trombone and 7 more students play the trumpet than play the saxophone. How many students play each instrument in Group 2?

8. Jane worked 1.5 hours on Monday, 3 hours on Tuesday, and 4.5 hours on Wednesday. If the pattern continues, how many hours will she work on Friday?

   A 5 hours

   B 7.5 hours

   C 8 hours

   D 9.5 hours

9. **Represent** The Garden Theater presented a play. A total of 179 people attended in 3 days. The first day, 58 people attended. On the second day, 47 people attended. How many attended on the third day?

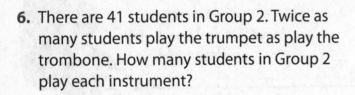

58 people	47 people	x

    ↑ 1st day   ↑ 2nd day   ↑ 3rd day

Name _____

Another Look!

Of 23 students, 14 students have brown hair.
Two times as many students have blond hair
as have red hair.

How many students have each hair color?

Draw a diagram to show what you know.

You can use 2-color counters and reasoning to solve the problem.

There are 9 students left. Make a table. Try
different numbers to see which pair
fits the problem.

23 students total

14 students with brown hair

	red	× 2	blond	Do the numbers add up to 9?
DATA	1	1 × 2 =	2	does not equal 9
	2	2 × 2 =	4	does not equal 9
	3	3 × 2 =	6	equals 9

Since 2 × 3 = 6 and 3 + 6 = 9, the number pair, 3 and 6,
is the correct answer.

So, 14 students have brown hair, 6 have blond hair,
and 3 have red hair.

---

1. Jacobson Animal Shelter has 48 animals, of which 30 animals
   are dogs. There are half as many rabbits as there are cats. If
   only dogs, cats, and rabbits are housed at the shelter, how
   many of each animal are at the shelter?

   48 animals in all − 30 dogs = _____ cats and rabbits

cats	× $\frac{1}{2}$	rabbits	Do the numbers add up to 18?
8	8 × $\frac{1}{2}$		equal 18
10	10 × $\frac{1}{2}$		equal 18
12	12 × $\frac{1}{2}$		equal 18

You can also use mental math to help you solve this problem.

There are _____ dogs, _____ cats, and _____ rabbits
at the shelter.

2. Represent Reggie earned $360 in the summer. If he earned $40 per week, how many weeks did he work?

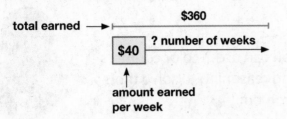

total earned → $360

$40

? number of weeks

amount earned per week

3. Extend Your Thinking Summer's mother gave her $20 to share with her 3 brothers equally. Explain how you can write an equation to solve the problem. How much did each person get?

4. Christina collects stamps. She has 47 stamps in all. She has 20 stamps from Europe. The number of African stamps is 2 times the number of Asian stamps. How many stamps from each of these three continents does she have?

5. Use a Strip Diagram A public pool opened for the summer. A total of 246 people came to swim over the first 3 days it was open. On the first day, 79 came to swim. On the second day, 104 people swam. How many people swam on the third day?

246 people

| 79 people | 104 people | x |

1st day   2nd day   3rd day

6. Marissa earned $560 in the summer. She earned $40 each week for part of the summer and $60 each week for the rest. If she earned $40 each week twice as often as she earned $60, how many weeks did she earn $40?

A 4 weeks
B 6 weeks
C 8 weeks
D 12 weeks

7. Deanna biked 45 miles on Monday, Tuesday, and Wednesday. She biked 9 miles on Monday. She biked 2 times as many miles on Wednesday as she biked on Tuesday. How many miles did she bike on Tuesday? On Wednesday?

8. Math and Science Doctors recommend that school-age children get beween 8.5 and 11 hours of sleep each night. According to the dot plot of 32 fifth-graders, what was the number of hours of sleep reported most frequently?

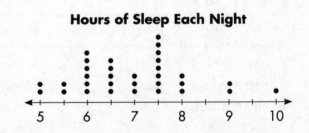

Hours of Sleep Each Night

5   6   7   8   9   10

Name _____

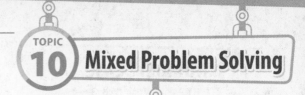
1. **Tools** Solve by using a strip diagram. Tricia ran 5 times as far as Ali. Ali ran 375 meters. How far did Tricia run?

_____

2. **Estimation** Ms. Walker has a new motorcycle that gets 40 miles per gallon. About how many miles can Ms. Walker drive on 8.9 gallons of gas?

Applying Math Processes

- How does this problem connect to previous ones?
- What is my plan?
- How can I use tools?
- How can I use number sense?
- How can I communicate and represent my thinking?
- How can I organize and record information?
- How can I explain my work?
- How can I justify my answer?

3. Daria measured the length of 3 ants in science class. They were $\frac{2}{3}$ inch, $\frac{3}{5}$ inch, and $\frac{1}{4}$ inch long. Which ant is the longest?

4. Which operation would you perform first to solve the equation $34 + 22 = 3 \times y$?

   A subtract 22 from 34
   B multiply 22 by 3
   C divide 22 by 3
   D add 34 and 22

5. A sequoia tree called General Grant is 273 feet tall. A typical red oak tree is about 70 feet tall. Which equation can be used to estimate how many times as tall as a typical red oak tree General Grant is?

   A $x \div 70 = 280$
   B $280 - x = 70$
   C $x + 70 = 280$
   D $70 \times x = 280$

6. **Extend Your Thinking** Why will the equations $f + 120 = 350$ and $f - 120 = 350$ have different solutions for f?

Error Search

Find each problem that is not correct. Change what is wrong and rewrite the answer so it is correct.

1. $2 \times n = 16; n = 14$

2. $1,720 + a = 7,000; a = 5,280$

3. $24 + 32 = 7 \times v; v = 8$

4. $x - 460 = 320; x = 140$

5. $3,500 \div d = 500; d = 3,000$

6. $f \div 2 = 78 + 62; f = 70.$

7. $q + 1,200,000 = 2,400,000;$ $q = 3,600,000$

8. $6 \times z = 9,600; z = 160$

9. $84 = d - 22; d = 106$

Target Number

Mental Math Using any numbers from the box and one variable, write as many equations whose solutions are equal to the Target Number as you can. Numbers in the boxes may be used more than once.

10.

28

2	3	4	8	9
12	14	24	36	56

11.

30

5	6	10	15	30	35
60	100	150	200	300	900

12.

25

2	3	5	15	25
50	75	150	250	275

Name _____

10

Set A pages 503–508 and 509–514

Use the order of operations to evaluate expressions with brackets.

Order of Operations

1. Calculate inside parentheses and brackets.

2. Multiply and divide from left to right.

3. Add and subtract from left to right.

Step 1

Perform the operations inside the parentheses.

$(8 + 2) \times (3 + 7) + 50 = 10 \times 10 + 50$

Step 2

Multiply and divide in order from left to right.

$10 \times 10 + 50 = 100 + 50$

Step 3

Add and subtract in order from left to right.

$100 + 50 = 150$

Remember that you can think of brackets as outside parentheses and evaluate the inside parentheses first.

Evaluate each expression.

1. $(78 + 47) \div 25$

2. $4 + 8 \times 6 \div 2 + 3$

3. $[(8 \times 25) \div 5] + 120$

4. $312 \times (40 + 60) \div 60$

5. $(87 - 32) \div 5$

6. $80 - (4 + 2) \times 10$

7. $(18 - 3) \div 5 + 4$

8. $8 \times 5 + 7 \times 3 - (10 - 5)$

Set B pages 515–520

Variables represent values that can change.

The expression $24 + n$ means "the sum of 24 and a number." The unknown number is a variable that is expressed by a letter, n.

Operation Terms

Addition → Sum

Subtraction → Difference

Multiplication → Product

Division → Quotient

Remember that you can use any letter as a variable to represent an unknown value.

Write the phrases as algebraic expressions.

1. 22 fewer forks than a number, f

2. 48 times a number of game markers, g

3. a number of eggs, e, divided by 12

4. 3 times the number of milk cartons, m, used by the 5th grade class

Topic 10 | Reteaching   **559**

Set C pages 521–526

Each car on a ride holds 8 children. For c children, $c \div 8$ cars will be full on the ride. How many cars will be full if there are 16, 24, or 40 children?

Find the value of $c \div 8$ for each value of c.

c	$c \div 8$
16	2
24	3
40	5

If there are 16 children, 2 cars will be full.

If there are 24 children, 3 cars will be full.

If there are 40 children, 5 cars will be full.

Remember to find unknown values, you replace the variable with known values.

1.
e	16	25	36
$20 + e$			

2.
h	14	16	18
$h \times 4$			

3.
n	112	56	28
$n - 14$			

4.
f	18	36	42
$f \div 6$			

Set D pages 527–532 and 533–538

Look at the table below. Start with the number in the first column. What rule tells you how to find the number in the second column?

Regular price (p)	Sale price	
$43	$41	$43 - 2 = 41$
$45	$43	$45 - 2 = 43$
$46	$44	$46 - 2 = 44$
$47		

The rule is subtract 2, or $p - 2$.

Use this rule to find the missing number in the table.

$47 - 2 = 45$

The sale price is $45.

Remember to ask "What is a rule?"

Complete each table and find a rule.

1.
n	$n -$
18	3
20	5
25	10
37	

2.
x	$x +$
34	100
0	66
8	74
13	

3.
n	2	6	8	9
$\times n$	6	18	24	

4.
s	45	40	35	15
$s \div$	9	8		3

Name _____

Set E | pages 539–544

An equation is a number sentence that uses an equal sign to show that two expressions have the same value.

A flower shop needs 500 flowers. They already have 250 flowers. How many more flowers are needed?

Solve the equation.

f = the number of flowers needed

$250 + f = 500$

$250 + 50 = 300$
$300 + 200 = 500$
$50 + 200 = 250$

So, $f = 250$.

A flower shop has 200 flowers arranged equally among 10 vases. How many flowers are in each vase?

Solve the equation.

n = the number of flowers in each vase

$n \times 10 = 200$
$20 \times 1 = 20$
$20 \times 10 = 200$

So, $n = 20$.

You can double check your work by using inverse operations. So, if $n \times 10 = 200$; then, $n = 200 \div 10$. Substitute 20 for n. It works in both equations!

Remember to use reasoning to solve an equation.

Write and solve an equation.

1. The 5 members of the Wyler family paid $112.50 for admission to a water park. What was the price, p, of each ticket?

2. Tom and his sister earned money by doing yard work. He collected the money after each job and gave his sister $54 and kept $54. There was $42 left, which they gave to their family. How much money, m, did Tom collect for all their yard work?

3. Darlene saved $300 that she earned by working in the school cafeteria. She spent $175 to buy textbooks and then paid $45 of her cell phone bill. How much money does Darlene have left?

4. Katie's horse eats 3 bales of hay each week. Find the number of weeks, w, that 36 bales of hay will feed her horse.

5. The math club is selling pencil cases to raise money for a field trip. The field trip costs $508, of which they already have $76. How many p pencil cases for $2 each do they need to sell to raise enough money?

Reteaching
Continued

Austin has 145 pictures from his trip to visit his grandparents and 125 pictures from his trip to the ocean. He wants to put the pictures in a photo album. If each page of the album holds 6 pictures, how many pages does he need for all of his pictures?

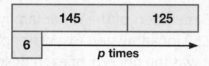

| 145 | 125 |

6 → p times

$145 + 125 = p \times 6$

Step 1

First, find the total number of pictures.

$145 + 125 = 270$

$270 = p \times 6$

Step 2

Then solve for p to find the number of pages needed.

$270 = p \times 6$
$270 \div 6 = p$
$p = 45$

Austin needs 45 pages.

Remember you can use a strip diagram and write an equation to help you solve the problem.

1. Sylvia has 120 mystery books and 130 science fiction books. She wants to put the books in a bookcase. If each shelf holds 25 books, how many shelves, s, does she need for all of her books?

2. John is 15 and his sister is 9. Their aunt is twice the sum of their ages. How old is their aunt?

3. Carolina has 55 guppies in her fish tank. She gives 28 guppies to her friend. The number of guppies remaining is three times the number of tetra fish in her tank. How many tetra fish, t, are in her fish tank?

A pet shop has a total of 19 dogs, cats, and ferrets. There are 4 ferrets, and twice as many cats as dogs. How many of each kind of pet are in the shop?

Use 19 cubes and let 4 of them represent the ferrets. That leaves 15 cubes to represent the cats and dogs. Since there are twice as many cats as dogs, there must be 10 cats and 5 dogs.

Remember that objects can help you reason through a problem.

1. Kerry has 12 paperweights in her collection. She has twice as many glass paperweights as metal, and 3 are wood. How many of each type of paperweight does she have?

Name _____

1. Which expression can be used to represent the phrase "three times the amount of money"?

A $3 + m$

B $3 - m$

C $3 \times m$

D $3 \div m$

2. If Lisa travels an average of 65 miles per hour for 8 hours, she will travel 8×65 miles. Which of the following is **NOT** equal to 8×65?

A $(8 + 60) \times (8 + 5)$

B $(60 \times 8) + (5 \times 8)$

C $(8 \times 60) + (8 \times 5)$

D $(8 \times 50) + (8 \times 15)$

3. Ryan had 18 more shots on goal during the soccer season than Peyton, who had 36. Charlie had a third of the number of shots on goal that Ryan had. Two of Charlie's shots on goal went out of bounds. What is the value of the expression for Charlie's shots, $(36 + 18) \div 3 - 2$?

A 9

B 16

C 40

D 54

4. There are 24 dancers in Joy's recital. If n represents the number of dancers who leave the stage, and $24 - n$ represents the number of dancers remaining, what is the value of the expression if 9 dancers leave the stage?

A 9   **C** 33

B 15   **D** 16

5. Which expression gives the rule for the table to find the discount price when the regular price is p?

	Small	Medium	Large	X-large
Sweater Price (p)	$28	$32	$45	$52
After Discount	$19	$23	$36	

A $p + 9$ **C** $p \times 19$

B $p - 9$ **D** $p \div 19$

6. What is the first step in evaluating the expression shown below?

$8 - 7 + 12 \div (3 + 1)$

A Add 3 and 1.

B Divide 12 by 3.

C Add 7 and 12.

D Subtract 7 from 8.

7. James has 435 large and small rocks combined. There are 159 large rocks. James puts 12 small rocks into each egg carton. How many egg cartons does he need for the small rocks?

A   23 egg cartons

B   50 egg cartons

C   276 egg cartons

D   3,312 egg cartons

8. Last month, Maya read 9 books and her sister Tess read 3. Their teacher read twice as many books as Maya and Tess. How many books did their teacher read? Write an equation.

9. The cost for *n* students to attend a workshop is 7*n* + 12 dollars. What is the cost, in dollars, for 6 students to attend?

10. Math books are being shipped to a school in cartons. The school ordered 56 books. How many cartons will the school receive when the number of books, *b*, is 56?

Number of Books (*b*)	14	28	42	56
Number of Cartons	1	2	3	

A   3 cartons

B   4 cartons

C   5 cartons

D   6 cartons

11. Marci made 16 kites. There are 3 times as many diamond kites as box kites, and 4 are stunt kites that look like small parachutes. How many of each type of kite did she make?

12. Janice wrote the following expression. What is the value of the expression?
$6 + (13 - 1) \div 4 + 2$

© Pearson Education, Inc. 5

13. Which expression represents the phrase "*n* students separated into equal groups of 6?"

A $n - 6$

B $n \div 6$

C $6 \times n$

D Not here

14. Nick wrote the expression $[7 + (3 \times 4)] - 2$. What is the value of this expression?

A 38

B 20

C 17

D 12

15. Hannah purchased flowers to plant in her garden. She planted 2 flowers in each of her garden beds. If *t* represents the number of garden beds, which expression represents the total number of flowers she planted?

A $t \div 2$

B $2 \times t$

C $t + 2$

D $t - 2$

16. A factory shipped 100 boxes with 15 skateboards in each box and 10 boxes with 15 pairs of in-line skates in each box. They wrote an expression to show the total number of items they shipped. What is the value of the expression?

$15 \times 100 + 15 \times 10$

A 1,650

C 3,750

B 2,350

D 15,150

Mr. Honig wrote an expression on the board. Use the expression to answer **17** and **18**.

$6 \times (24 - 4) + 8 \div 2$

17. Which step do you perform first in evaluating this expression?

A Add 4 and 8.

B Divide 8 by 2.

C Multiply 6 by 24.

D Subtract 4 from 24.

18. Which is the value of the expression?

A 32

B 64

C 74

D 124

19. The table shows the cost to board Lucy's dog at a kennel. Lucy boarded her dog for 7 days.

Number of Days	Total Cost
3	$36
4	$48
5	$60

What was the total cost for boarding her dog? Look for a pattern to find a rule.

A $204   C $84

B $132   D $78

---

20. Each pod at the Trotter School holds 12 classrooms. For c classrooms, $c \div 12$ is the number of pods. The school has 60 classrooms. How many pods are there?

---

21. Jerome needs to save $1,260 for a trip to visit colleges next year. He will save the same amount each month for 20 months. He uses the equation $\$1,260 \div m = 20$, where m equals the amount he will save each month. What is the value, in dollars, of m?

			.		
⓪	⓪	⓪		⓪	⓪
①	①	①		①	①
②	②	②		②	②
③	③	③		③	③
④	④	④		④	④
⑤	⑤	⑤		⑤	⑤
⑥	⑥	⑥		⑥	⑥
⑦	⑦	⑦		⑦	⑦
⑧	⑧	⑧		⑧	⑧
⑨	⑨	⑨		⑨	⑨

---

22. Use the rule. Which number completes the table?

w	72	60	48	42
w ÷ 6	12	10		7

A 8

B 9

C 42

D 288

---

23. A group of students planted 225 flowers around their school. Each student planted 15 flowers. How many students were in the group? Write an equation then solve.

---

24. Milton School has 285 sixth graders and 259 fifth graders. Students in both grades will attend an assembly in the auditorium. Each row in the auditorium can hold 16 students. How many rows will the students fill?

Solve $r \times 16 = 285 + 259$.

		.		
⓪	⓪	⓪	⓪	⓪
①	①	①	①	①
②	②	②	②	②
③	③	③	③	③
④	④	④	④	④
⑤	⑤	⑤	⑤	⑤
⑥	⑥	⑥	⑥	⑥
⑦	⑦	⑦	⑦	⑦
⑧	⑧	⑧	⑧	⑧
⑨	⑨	⑨	⑨	⑨

Ordered Pairs and the Plane

Essential Questions: How are points plotted? How are equations graphed?

Day and night are caused by Earth spinning.

The imaginary line through Earth's center is Earth's *axis*. The spinning of Earth on its axis is called *rotation*.

I'm getting dizzy thinking about it! Here's a project about Earth's rotation.

Math and Science Project: Earth's Rotation

Do Research Use the Internet or other sources to find out more about Earth's rotation. Investigate why it appears that the Sun is moving across the sky. Design a model to explain Earth's day/night cycle. Compare Earth's rotation to another planet's.

Write a Report: Journal Include what you found. Also in your report:

- Write a step-by-step procedure of how to use a ball and a flashlight to represent the day/night cycle.

- Explain what happens if the ball rotates slowly. What happens if the ball rotates quickly?

- Make up and solve problems for plotting points and graphing equations.

Review What You Know

Vocabulary

Choose the best term from the box. Write it on the blank.

- equation
- evaluation
- expression
- variable

1. An algebraic _____ is a mathematical phrase that has at least one variable and one operation.

2. A number sentence that uses an equal sign to show that two expressions have the same value is called a(n) _____.

3. The letter n in $\$10 \times n$ is called a(n) _____ and is a quantity that can change.

Expressions

Write an algebraic expression for each word phrase.

4. p number of papers shared equally by seven students

5. four times a distance d

6. three less than two times an amount a

7. six dollars more than a cost c

Solving Equations

Solve each equation.

8. $7,200 + x = 13,000$

9. $6,000 = 20 \times g$

10. $105 + 45 = w \times 3$

11. $38 + 42 = 480 \div b$

12. Janine has 85 hockey cards in one book and 105 hockey cards in another book. The hockey cards come in packages of 5 cards. If Janine bought all of her hockey cards in packages, how many packages did she buy?

A 21 packages
B 38 packages
C 190 packages
D 195 packages

Find Rules and Writing Expressions

13. **Writing to Explain** Explain how to write an expression to find the sale price when the regular price is $11. Let r stand for the regular price.

Regular price (r)	$9	$10	$11	$12
Sale price	$5	$6	■	$8

My Word Cards

Use the examples for each word on the front of the card to help complete the definitions on the back.

A-Z

coordinate grid

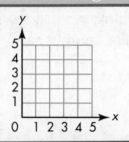

x-axis

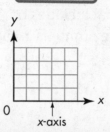

y-axis

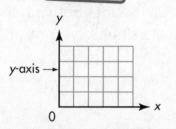

origin

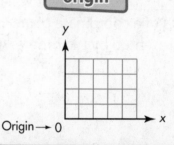

ordered pair

(4, 2)

x-coordinate

(4, 2)

↑

x-coordinate

y-coordinate

(4, 2)

↑

y-coordinate

additive pattern

3 + 2 = 5

5 + 2 = 7

6 + 2 = 8

Pattern: Add 2

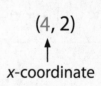

My Word Cards

Complete the definition. Extend learning by writing your own definitions.

✂

A horizontal line passing through the origin that includes both positive and negative numbers is called the _____.

A _____ is used to locate points in a plane using an ordered pair of numbers.

The _____ is the point where the two axes of a coordinate plane intersect. It is represented by the ordered pair (0, 0).

A vertical line passing through the origin that includes both positive and negative numbers is called the _____.

The first number in an ordered pair, which names the distance to the right or left from the origin along the x-axis, is called the _____.

An _____ is pair of numbers used to locate a point on a coordinate grid.

An _____ is when corresponding values are related by addition.

The second number in an ordered pair, which names the distance up or down from the origin along the y-axis, is called the _____.

570

My Word Cards

Use the examples for each word on the front of the card to help complete the definitions on the back.

A-Z

---

input-output table

INPUT	0	1	2	3
OUTPUT	5	6	7	8

---

multiplicative pattern

$3 \times 2 = 6$

$5 \times 2 = 10$

$6 \times 2 = 12$

Pattern: Multiply by 2

My Word Cards

Complete the definition. Extend learning by writing your own definitions.

A _____
is when corresponding values are related
by multiplication.

An _____
is a table of related values.

Name _____

Solve & Share

On the first grid, plot a point where two lines intersect. Name the location of the point. Plot and name another point. Take turns describing the locations of the points on your grids. Without looking at each other's grids, plot the points your partner describes on your second grid. Compare your first grid with your partner's second grid to see if they match. **Work with a partner and use the grids below to solve this problem.**

🧭 TEKS 5.8A Describe the key attributes of the coordinate plane, including perpendicular number lines (axes) ... the x-coordinate, ... and the y-coordinate....
🧭 TEKS 5.8B Describe the process for graphing ordered pairs of numbers in the first quadrant of the coordinate plane. Also, 5.8. Mathematical Process Standards 5.1A, 5.1C, 5.1D, 5.1G

Digital Resources at PearsonTexas.com

Solve   Learn   Glossary   Check   Tools   Games

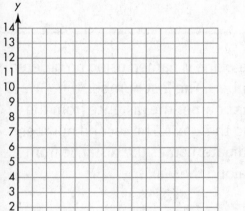

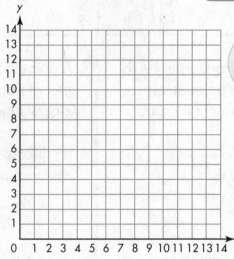

Select and Use Tools You can use grid paper to graph ordered pairs. *Show your work!*

Look Back!

Justify Why does the order of the numbers inside the parentheses matter? Explain your thinking.

A

How Do You Name a Point on a Coordinate Grid?

A map shows the locations of landmarks and has guides for finding them. In a similar way, a coordinate grid is used to graph and name the locations of points in a plane.

You can use ordered pairs to locate points on a coordinate grid.

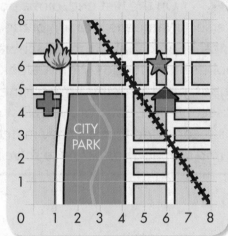

B A coordinate grid has a horizontal *x*-axis and a vertical *y*-axis. The point at which the *x*-axis and *y*-axis intersect is called the origin.

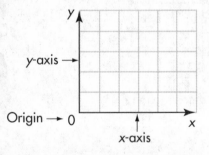

C A point in a plane is named using an ordered pair of numbers. The first number, the *x*-coordinate, names the distance from the origin along the *x*-axis. The second number, the *y*-coordinate, names the distance from the origin along the *y*-axis.

A (1, 3)

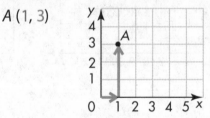

Do You Understand?

Convince Me! In the example above, name the ordered pair for Point *B* if it is 3 units to the right of Point *A*. Tell how you decided.

Name _____

In **1** and **2**, write the ordered pair for the point. Use the grid.

1. B

2. A

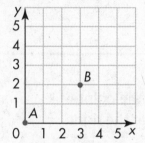

In **3** and **4**, graph and label each point on the grid above.

3. C (1, 4)   **4.** D (5, 3)

5. Explain You are graphing Point E at (0, 5). Do you move right zero units, or up zero units? Explain.

6. What ordered pair names the origin of any coordinate grid?

7. Communicate Describe how to graph Point K at (5, 4).

☆ **Independent Practice** ☆

In **8** through **13**, write the ordered pair for the point. Use the grid.

8. T   **9.** X

10. Y   **11.** W

12. Z   **13.** S

In **14** through **18**, graph and label the point for each ordered pair on the grid above.

14. L (2, 2)   **15.** M (0, 3)   **16.** N (1, 5)   **17.** O (5, 4)   **18.** P (4, 0)

Problem Solving

19. Communicate Describe to a friend how to find and name the ordered pair for Point *R* on the grid.

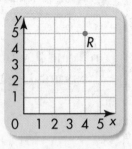

Tools For **20** through **24**, complete the table. List the point and ordered pair for each vertex of the pentagon at the right.

	Point	Ordered Pair
20.		
21.		
22.		
23.		
24.		

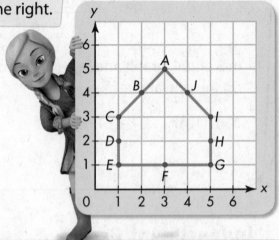

---

25. Explain Why is the order important when naming or graphing the coordinates of a point?

26. Shawna took a test that had a total of 20 items. She got $\frac{4}{5}$ of the items correct. How many items did she get correct?

For **27** and **28**, use the graph.

27. Dina's family will visit the place located at (4, 1) on the city map. Which of the following places is located at (4, 1)?

   A Ace Sports Arena   **C** Bay Bridge

   B Art Museum   **D** Pond Park

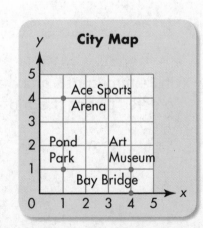

28. Extend Your Thinking After visiting the place located at (4, 1), Dina's family will walk to Pond Park. If one unit on the city map represents one block, how many blocks will they walk? Explain how you would get to Pond Park.

Name _____

Another Look!

The ordered pair (4, 3) gives the location of the playground. Graph this point on the coordinate grid. Label the point *P*.

Step 1

Start at 0. Move 4 units to the right along the *x*-axis.

Move 3 units up.

Step 2

Draw Point *P* at (4, 3).

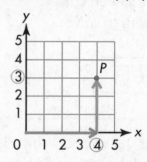

In **1** through **6**, graph and label the point for each ordered pair on the grid.

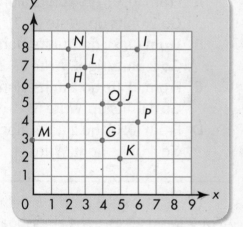

1. *A* (8, 4)   **2.** *B* (1, 4)   **3.** C (0, 8)

4. *D* (2, 1)   **5.** *E* (7, 1)   **6.** *F* (7, 6)

In **7** through **16**, name the point that is located at each ordered pair.

7. (4, 3) Point _____

8. (3, 7) Point _____

9. (0, 3) Point _____

10. (5, 2) Point _____

11. (6, 8) Point _____

12. (6, 4) Point _____

13. (4, 5) Point _____ **14.** (2, 8) Point _____ **15.** (5, 5) Point _____ **16.** (2, 6) Point _____

17. Communicate Describe to a friend how to graph a point at (2, 5).

18. Explain How are the locations on a coordinate grid different for the ordered pairs (7, 0) and (0, 7)?

19. To make the parts needed for an electric circuit, Steven cut a wire into 5 equal pieces. He started with a wire that was 6.8 meters long. How many meters long was each piece that Steven cut? Complete the strip diagram to solve.

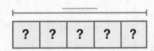

| ? | ? | ? | ? | ? |

20. Connect The streets of many cities are laid out like a coordinate grid. How is this helpful when using a map to find locations in a city such as Houston, Texas?

21. ⭐ Jeremy wants to visit the Duck Pond. Which is a correct description of how to find the ordered pair for the Duck Pond?

A From (0, 0), go 4 units along the x-axis. Go 2 units up. Write (4, 2).

B From (0, 2), go 2 units along the y-axis. Go 2 units right. Write (2, 2).

C From (0, 0), go 2 units along the x-axis. Go 4 units up. Write (2, 4).

D From (0, 0), go 2 units along the y-axis. Go 4 units right. Write (4, 2).

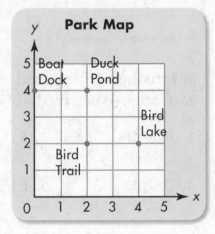

For **22** and **23**, use the chessboard.

22. Extend Your Thinking A chessboard is similar to a coordinate grid. The pieces that look like horses are knights. What letter-number combinations name the locations of the white knights?

23. Andre moves the pawn located at (e, 7) down 2 units. What letter-number combination names the pawn's new location? Explain.

Name _____

Solve & Share

Joan has a bucket under her leaky sink. There are 3 inches of water in the bucket today, and the water rises 1 inch each day. Extend and complete the table to find ordered pairs. Draw a graph showing the height of the water in the bucket each day through Day 10.

TEKS 5.8C Graph in the first quadrant of the coordinate plane ordered pairs of numbers arising from mathematical and real-world problems, including those generated by number patterns or found in an input-output table. Also, 5.8A, 5.8B. Mathematical Process Standards 5.1C, 5.1D, 5.1F, 5.1G

Analyze Relationships
The graph will show the relationship between the number of days and the height of water in the bucket.

Day	Height (in.)
0 (today)	3
1	
2	

Digital Resources at PearsonTexas.com

 Solve   Learn   Glossary   Check   Tools   Games

3 in.

Look Back!

Construct Arguments Joan said the bucket had 10 inches of water in it after 10 days. Is she correct? Explain.

How Can You Use Coordinate Grids to Solve Problems Involving Additive Patterns?

A-Z

When you add the same amount to a given number and to a sequence of related values, you form an additive pattern. Samir's puppy, Belle, weighs 2 pounds. If she gains 1 pound each week, how much will Belle weigh after 6 weeks? A coordinate grid can be used to record the puppy's growth pattern.

You can extend the input-output table to find more ordered pairs.

An input-output table is a table of related values.

DATA	Week	Weight (lb)
	0	2
	1	3
	2	4

B Label the axes on a coordinate grid. Let x be the number of weeks. Show 6 weeks. Let y be Belle's weight measured in pounds.

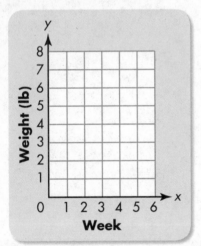

C Graph the ordered pairs. Draw a line to show the pattern.

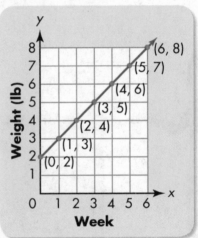

The point at (6, 8) means that after 6 weeks, Belle's weight will be 8 pounds.

Do You Understand?

Convince Me! How could you set up the axes to graph a pattern involving a plant that is 5 inches tall and grows 1 inch each week? Give an ordered pair that would be on the graph. What does the ordered pair represent?

☆ Guided Practice*

In **1** and **2**, suppose a graph shows that Jenny started with $3 and saved $2 each day.

1. What would the point (5, 13) represent?

2. List two other ordered pairs that show this relationship.

3. **Make a Graph** How would you set up the axes to graph Exercise 1?

4. **Reason** How can you find the data for a point that is off a graph?

Independent Practice ☆

In **5** and **7**, use the input-output table to make a coordinate graph.

5.

Grass Growth	
Week	**Height (in.)**
0	2
1	3
2	4
3	5

7.

Food Scraps Eaten in Worm Compost	
Day	**Amount (lb)**
0	1
1	2
2	3
3	4

6. In Exercise 5, tell what the ordered pair (3, 5) represents.

8. In Exercise 7, tell what the ordered pair (2, 3) represents.

Problem Solving

For **9** through **11**, use the table.

9. **Tools** Luis has 5 pages of a science report typed. He plans to type 1 page each hour. Fill in the values that are missing in the input-output table.

Science Report						
Time (h)	0	1	2	3	4	5
Pages Typed	5	6	7			10	11

10. **Make a Graph** Use the input-output table to make a graph. Label the axes and ordered pairs on a coordinate grid. Then draw a line.

11. **Reason** If Luis continues the pattern, how many pages will he have typed in $8\frac{1}{2}$ hours?

12. How do you know if a line on a graph shows an additive pattern?

13. Mrs. James has a jug that contains 16 cups of juice. She wants to pour equal servings that are $\frac{1}{3}$ cup each. How many servings can she pour?

For **14** and **15**, use the Child's Hair Growth graph.

14. **Extend Your Thinking** What is the missing y-coordinate for the red point in the graph? Explain what the ordered pair for that point represents.

15. If the pattern continues, how would the line and graph look when it is extended?

16. For a science experiment, Zack heated water at a low heat. The temperature of the water started at 4° Celsius. The temperature of the water increased by 1° Celsius every minute. What was the temperature of the water at 7 minutes?

   A 5°C
   B 7°C
   C 10°C
   D 11°C

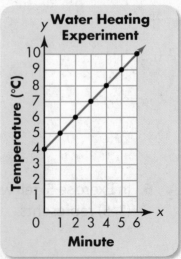

Name _____

Another Look!

Cara started with $2. She will earn $1 each day for doing chores. What will her total earnings be on Day 5?

Step 1

Make an input-output table.

Cara's Earnings

Day	Total ($)
0	2
1	3
2	4
3	

Step 2

Graph each point and draw a line to show the pattern.

Cara has $7 on Day 5.

For **1** through **4**, use the input-output table to make a graph.

1.

Worm Growth

Month	Length (cm)
0	1
1	2
2	3
3	4

2.

Sofia's Savings

Week	Total ($)
0	3
5	8
10	13
15	18

3.

Phone Activity

Minute	Number of Text Messages
0	5
1	6
2	7
3	8

4.

Bamboo Growth

Day	Height (in.)
0	4
1	5
2	6
3	7

For **5** through **7**, use the table.

5. **Tools** To set prices for her rings, Taylor increased the profit by $1 each time it cost her $1 more to make a ring. She sells rings that cost her $6 or less at no profit. Complete the input-output table.

Pricing for Rings						
Cost ($)	6	7	8	9	10	11
Profit ($)	0	1	2			5

6. **Make a Graph** Use the input-output table to make a graph that shows the relationship between the cost and profit for Taylor's rings.

7. **Reason** What would be Taylor's profit on a ring that costs her $13.50 to make? What would be the price of the ring?

8. Rupert made a banner by sewing together a piece of green fabric that was $4\frac{1}{8}$ feet long and a piece of blue fabric that was $2\frac{3}{12}$ feet long. Complete the strip diagram to find the total length of the banner.

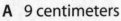

$4\frac{1}{8}$

For **9** and **10**, use the Scarf Knitting Project graph.

9. What is the missing y-coordinate for the red point in the graph? Explain what this ordered pair represents.

10. **Extend Your Thinking** Write a word problem that has a solution that would be on the line, but is not shown on the graph.

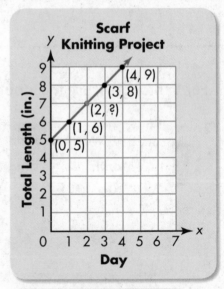

11. Alexa's bucket contained 3 centimeters of rainwater from last night. For the next 6 hours, it rained the same amount each hour. What was the total amount of rain in the bucket at Hour 6?

   A 9 centimeters
   B 8 centimeters
   C 7 centimeters
   D 6 centimeters

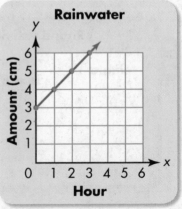

Name _____

Solve & Share

Sally measured the height of her bean plant and recorded the following results: Day 1 = 2 cm, Day 2 = 4 cm, Day 5 = 10 cm, Day 7 = 14 cm. How can you show the growth of Sally's bean plant on a graph? *Make a graph to plot each point.*

★ **TEKS 5.8C** Graph in the first quadrant of the coordinate plane ordered pairs of numbers arising from mathematical and real-world problems, including those generated by number patterns or found in an input-output table. Also, 5.8A, 5.8B. **Mathematical Process Standards** 5.1C, 5.1D, 5.1G

Digital Resources at PearsonTexas.com

Solve   Learn   Glossary   Check   Tools   Games

DAY 7 = 14 cm

DAY 5 = 10 cm

DAY 2 = 4 cm

DAY 1 = 2 cm

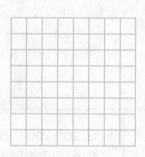

Create and Use Representations You can create and use a coordinate grid to represent a problem. *Show your work!*

Look Back!

Reason Can you predict how tall Sally's bean plant will be on Day 10? Graph the point and explain your reasoning.

How Do You Use Coordinate Grids to Solve Problems?

Carla makes friendship bracelets and sells them at a craft fair on the weekend. She earns $2 for each bracelet she sells. Can you find how much she earns if she sells 6 bracelets?

Use the table to make a graph and find the answer.

The formula $y = 2x$ helps you find the ordered pairs.

DATA

y = 2x		
x	y	(x, y)
1	2	(1, 2)
3	6	(3, 6)
6	12	(6, 12)

B Label the axes on a coordinate grid.

Let x be the number of bracelets Carla sells. Show 6 bracelets.

Let y be the amount Carla earns on each bracelet. Each interval can be 2 dollars.

C Graph the ordered pairs. Draw a line to show the multiplicative pattern that is created by charging $2 for each bracelet.

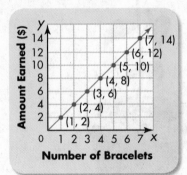

So, Carla earns $12 if she sells 6 bracelets.

Do You Understand?

Convince Me! In the example above, how much money would Carla earn if she sold 8 bracelets? How did you decide?

© Pearson Education, Inc. 5

Name _____

In **1** and **2**, a graph shows the speed of an object rolling down a ramp and records the speeds in meters per second. The speed of the object is four times as great as each meter the ramp is raised.

1. What would the point (3, 12) represent?

2. List two other ordered pairs that show this relationship.

3. Make a Graph How would you set up the axes to graph Exercise 1?

4. Reason How can you find the data for a point that is off a graph?

Independent Practice ☆

In **5** and **6**, use the table to make a graph on the coordinate grid.

5.

y = 5x		
Time in Seconds (x)	Total Distance Crawled in Centimeters (y)	(x, y)
1	5	(1, 5)
2	10	(2, 10)
3	15	(3, 15)
4	20	(4, 20)

6.

y = 6x		
Number of Yards of Fabric (x)	Cost in Dollars (y)	(x, y)
1	6	(1, 6)
2	12	(2, 12)
3	18	(3, 18)

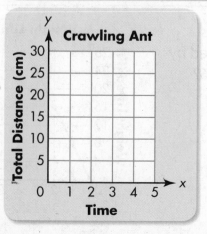

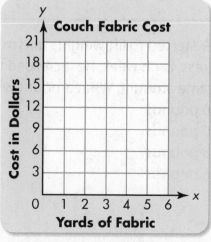

Problem Solving

For **7** through **9**, use the table.

7. **Tools** Janna reads 20 pages of a book each hour. Fill in the values that are missing in the table.

8. **Make a Graph** Use the table to make a graph. Label the points with ordered pairs and draw a line through the points.

9. **Reason** If Janna continues the pattern, how many pages will she read in 7 hours?

y = 20x		
Time in Hours (x)	Total Number of Pages Read (y)	(x, y)
1	20	(1, 20)
2	40	(2, 40)
3		
4		
5	100	(5, 100)
	120	(6, 120)

10. **Explain** What do the graphs of multiplicative patterns have in common?

11. Harold spends $\frac{1}{6}$ of the year on his aunt's farm. He has done this for the last 8 years. What is the total amount of years, in simplest form, that Harold has spent on his aunt's farm?

12. **Extend Your Thinking** What is the missing y-coordinate for the red point in the graph? Explain what the ordered pair for that point represents. If the pattern continues, how would the line and graph look when it is extended?

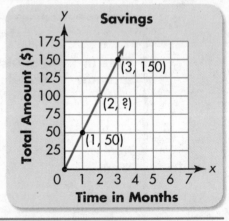

13. Roger started to lift weights and made a graph of his progress. Each week, he increased the weight he lifted by the same amount. What amount will he lift in Week 6?

   A 36 pounds
   B 40 pounds
   C 48 pounds
   D 56 pounds

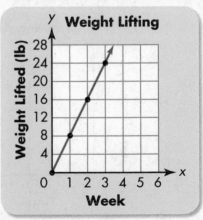

Name _____

Another Look!

Ira earns $4 for each dog that he walks. What will be his total earnings for walking 7 dogs? Make a graph.

Let x be the number of dogs walked. Let y be the amount earned.

Step 1

Make a table to find the ordered pairs.

$y = 4x$		
x	y	(x, y)
1	4	$(1, 4)$
2	8	$(2, 8)$
4		$(4, \quad)$
7		

Step 2

Graph the points and draw a line.

Ira earns $28 for walking 7 dogs.

For **1** and **2**, use the table to make a graph.

1.

$y = 8x$	
Time in Days (x)	Total Water Drank (y)
1	8
2	16
3	24
4	32

2.

$y = 12x$	
Number of Egg Cartons (x)	Total Number of Eggs (y)
1	12
2	24
3	36
4	48

3. **Tools** Kimo planted 12 seedlings in each row of his garden. Fill in the values that are missing in the table.

4. **Make a Graph** Graph the information in the table on a coordinate grid. Label the points with ordered pairs and draw a line through the points.

5. **Reason** If Kimo continues the pattern, what is the total number of seedlings he will plant in 7 rows? in 8 rows?

$y = 12x$		
Number of Rows (x)	Total Number of Seedlings (y)	(x, y)
1	12	(1, 12)
2	24	(2, 24)
4		
5		
7		
	120	(10, 120)

6. A recipe for bread uses $5\frac{3}{4}$ cups of white flour and $3\frac{1}{3}$ cups of wheat flour. How many more cups of white flour than wheat flour are used in the recipe? Complete the strip diagram to solve.

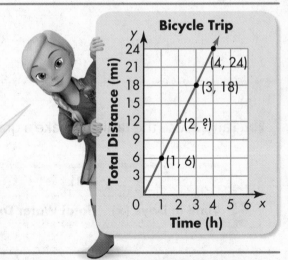

cups
_____

cups	c
_____	

7. **Extend Your Thinking** What is the missing y-coordinate for the red point in the graph? Explain what the ordered pair for that point on the line represents.

How many miles are traveled for each hour of the trip?

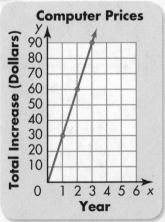

Bicycle Trip

(4, 24)
(3, 18)
(2, ?)
(1, 6)

Total Distance (mi)
Time (h)

8. Clare studied the price of computers over several years. She saw a pattern in how much the price increased each year. If the pattern continues, what would be the total increase in price in Year 5?

A $90

B $110

C $120

D $150

Computer Prices

Total Increase (Dollars)
Year

Name _____

Solve & Share

The equation $y = x + 2$ is a linear equation. Complete the table of values for this equation and graph the point represented by each pair of numbers. **Work with a partner to solve.**

⬆ TEKS 5.4C Generate a numerical pattern when given a rule in the form $y = ax$ or $y = x + a$ and graph. Also, 5.8, 5.8C. Mathematical Process Standards 5.1A, 5.1C, 5.1D, 5.1E, 5.1G

Digital Resources at PearsonTexas.com

 Solve   Learn   Glossary   Check   Tools   Games

Select and Use Tools You can show how an equation is graphed on a coordinate grid. **Show your work!**

$y = x + 2$		
x	y	(x, y)
1		
4		
8		

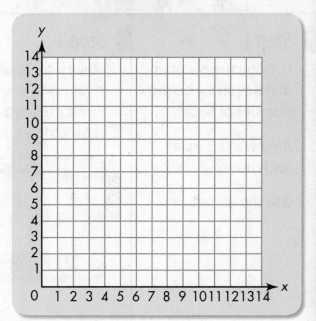

Look Back!

Communicate What do you notice about the line you graphed from this equation? Can you tell where the point would be on the graph when $x = 104$? Explain how you know.

How Do You Graph an Equation on a Coordinate Grid?

A

Amy walks 3 miles in 1 hour. At that speed, how far would she walk in 7 hours?

An equation whose graph is a straight line is called a linear equation.

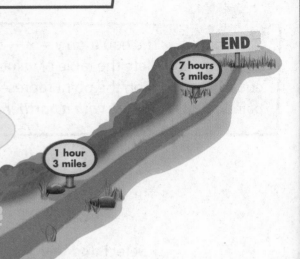

END
7 hours
? miles

1 hour
3 miles

START

B ## Step 1

Let *y* be the number of miles and *x* be the number of hours.

Amy walks 3 miles each hour.

Use the equation:

$$y = 3x$$

C ## Step 2

Make a table of *x*- and *y*-values to show how *x* and *y* relate and satisfy the equation.

DATA

y = 3x		
x	**y**	**(x, y)**
1	3	(1, 3)
3	9	(3, 9)
5	15	(5, 15)

D ## Step 3

Label the axes on a coordinate grid. Graph the ordered pairs and connect the points to graph the equation.

Extend the *y*-axis. The *y*-value, when *x* = 7, shows that Amy would walk 21 miles.

Do You Understand?

Convince Me! A certain orange drink calls for 2 cans of water for every 1 can of orange concentrate.

x is the number of cans of orange concentrate.

y is the number of cans of water.

$$y = 2x$$

Complete the table of values. Use the table of values to complete the graph.

y = 2x		
x	**y**	**(x, y)**
1	2	
2	4	
3	6	

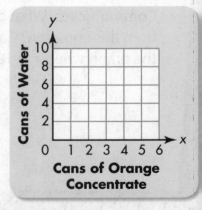

☆ Guided Practice*

For **1**, write the equation. Then complete the table.

1. Robby earns $4 each hour.

Total earned = $____ × number of hours

    ↑   ↑

    y x

Equation: $y = 4$ _____

$y =$ _____		
x	y	(x, y)
1	4	(1, 4)
2	8	(2, 8)
4		
7		

2. **Explain** How can you use the graph on page 592 to find how far Amy would walk in 8 hours?

3. A giant tortoise is about 6 times as fast as a garden snail. Using the equation $y = 6x$, explain how you would record and graph this relationship.

☆ Independent Practice ☆

In **4**, write an equation. Make a table of x- and y-values. Then graph the equation.

4. Coby is 2 years older than Jamal.
   Coby's age = Jamal's age + _____

    ↑   ↑

    y x

Equation: $y = x +$ _____

$y = x +$ _____		
x	y	(x, y)
1	3	(1, 3)
2	4	(2, 4)
3		
7		

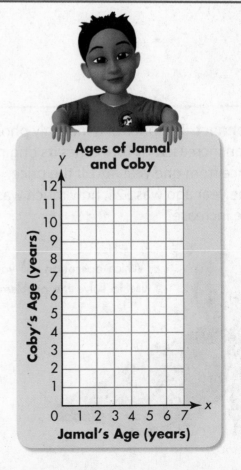

Ages of Jamal and Coby

Coby's Age (years) / Jamal's Age (years)

Problem Solving

For **5** through **7**, use the table and grid.

5. **Represent** Mr. Shay lost 3 pounds each month. He continued losing pounds in this pattern. Let *y* be the total number of pounds lost. Let *x* be the number of months. Write an equation that shows how *x* and *y* relate. Complete the table.

$y = \underline{\quad\quad}$		
x	**y**	**(x, y)**
1	3	(1, 3)
2	6	(2, 6)
3		
7		
9		

6. **Make a Graph** Complete the coordinate grid using the ordered pairs from the table. Connect the points to graph the equation.

Mr. Shay's Weight Loss

7. **Extend Your Thinking** If Mr. Shay continues this pattern, how many pounds will he lose in 14 months? Explain how you found your answer.

---

8. **Connect** The price of a monthly phone plan increased by 0.14 times its original price from one year ago. If the price one year ago was $26, how much was the increase?

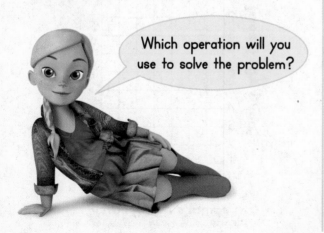

Which operation will you use to solve the problem?

9. The height of the average person is four times the width of the person's shoulders. Which of the following equations represents the relationship?

A $y = x + 4$

B $y = x - 4$

C $y = 4x$

D $y = 4 \div x$

Name _____

Another Look!

Sabrina's dog, Fido, is 2 years older than her other dog, Spot. What is each dog's age at different years?

Step 1

Use an equation to complete the table.

y = x + 2		
x	y	(x, y)
1	3	(1, 3)
2	4	(2, 4)
3		(3,)
4		

Step 2

Graph the points and draw a line.

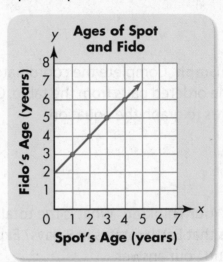

In **1** and **2**, fill in the missing information and complete the tables. Then graph the equations.

1. Ron earns $7 for each hour he works.

Total earned = $____ × number of hours

↑ _y_   ↑ _x_

Equation: y = ____x

y = ____ x		
x	y	(x, y)
1	7	(1, 7)
2	14	(2, 14)
3	____	(3, __, __)
4	____	(____, ____)

2. Mark is 4 years older than Nate.

Mark's age = Nate's age + ____

↑ _y_   ↑ _x_

Equation: y = x + ____

y = x + ____		
x	y	(x, y)
1	5	(1, 5)
2	6	(2, 6)
3	____	(3, ____)
4	____	(____, ____)

For **3** through **5**, use the table and grid.

3. **Math and Science** It takes 24 hours for Earth to complete one rotation about its axis. Let *y* be the number of hours. Let *x* be the number of days. Complete the table.

$y = 24x$		
x	**y**	**(x, y)**
1	24	(1, 24)
2	48	(2, 48)
3		
5		
7		

4. **Make a Graph** Complete the coordinate grid using the ordered pairs from the table. Connect the points to graph the equation.

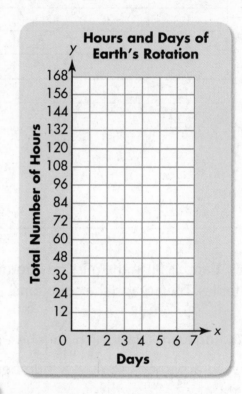

Hours and Days of Earth's Rotation

5. **Extend Your Thinking** What is the total number of hours that Earth rotates in 8 days? Explain how you found your answer.

On which axis can you find the total number of hours?

6. **Personal Financial Literacy** Marsha's new refrigerator costs $1,872. She will pay for it in equal payments over 12 months. What will be the monthly cost?

7. Elsie is 14 years older than her youngest cousin. Let *y* be Elsie's age in years. Let *x* be her youngest cousin's age in years. Which equation represents this relationship?

A $y = x + 14$
B $y = x - 14$
C $y = 14x$
D $y = x \div 14$

Name _____

☆ ☆
Solve & Share

José starts with no money and saves $4 each week. Mary has $5 and saves $1 each week. Make a table to show how much money each has from 0 to 4 weeks. How are the two patterns different?

TEKS 5.4D Recognize the difference between additive and multiplicative numerical patterns given in a table or graph. Also, 5.4C. **Mathematical Process Standards** 5.1C, 5.1D, 5.1G

Digital Resources at PearsonTexas.com

Solve   Learn   Glossary   Check   Tools   Games

You can **create and use representations** by writing a rule for each pattern.

Look Back!

Construct Arguments Is it easier to use a graph or a table to identify a numerical pattern as one that grows by adding or multiplying? Explain.

How Can You Tell an Additive Pattern From a Multiplicative Pattern?

A-Z

Make a table and graph each equation. How can you tell the additive pattern from the multiplicative pattern in a table and in a graph?

$$y = x + 4$$
$$y = 3x$$

Increase the x-values by 1. Then, look at how the y-values change.

B Make a table and graph for $y = x + 4$.

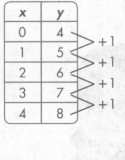

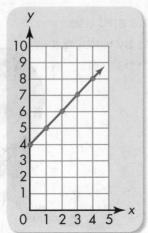

In the additive pattern, the y-values do not start at zero and they increase by 1 in both the table and the graph.

C Make a table and graph for $y = 3x$.

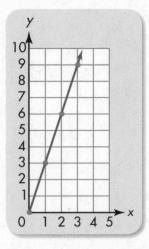

In the multiplicative pattern, the y-values start at zero and they increase by multiples of 3 in both the table and the graph.

Do You Understand?

Convince Me! Does the graph show an additive or a multiplicative pattern? Explain.

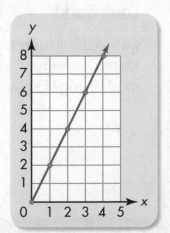

☆ Guided Practice *

In **1** and **2**, does the table or graph show an additive or a multiplicative pattern? Explain.

1.

x	y
0	0
1	9
2	18
3	27

2.

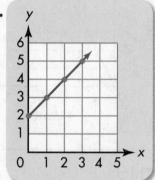

3. **Tools** In the table and graph for $y = x + 4$ on page 598, what are the y-values for the next 5 values of x?

4. **Number Sense** In **1**, what multiplication facts can help you find values for y?

5. In **2**, explain how you can use the graph to find the value of y when $x = 7$.

> Remember, the x-axis goes across and the y-axis goes up and down.

☆ Independent Practice ☆

In **6** and **7**, does the table or graph show an additive or a multiplicative pattern? Explain.

6.

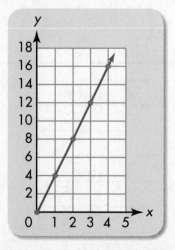

7.

x	y
0	6
1	7
2	8
3	9

Problem Solving

8. **Explain** What do the ordered pairs (2, 5) and (3, 6) represent in the graph? Is the pattern in the graph additive or multiplicative? Explain.

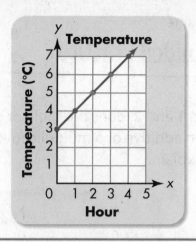

9. **Communicate** List the ordered pairs for Month 4 and Month 5 on the graph. What do these ordered pairs represent? Is the pattern in the graph an additive pattern or a multiplicative pattern? Explain.

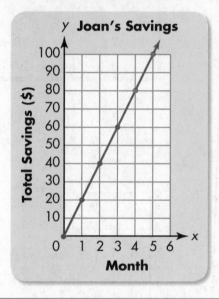

10. Pedro, Maya, Rick, and Leslie shared $\frac{1}{2}$ of a hero sandwich. They each received 1 equal part. What fraction of the original sandwich did each friend get?

11. **Extend Your Thinking** Melanie says she can tell whether the graph of a line shows an additive or multiplicative pattern simply by looking where the line crosses the y-axis. Is she correct? Explain.

12. Which ordered pair represents the missing x and y values in the table?

    A (2, 15)
    B (3, 14)
    C (3, 15)
    D (4, 15)

x	y
0	12
1	13
2	14
4	16

Name _____

Another Look!

Kate has 3 necklaces. She makes 1 new necklace each day. How many total necklaces will she have in 4 days? Find and use a pattern.

Use the equation $y = x + 3$.

Make a table.

Number of Days x	Total Necklaces y
0	3
1	4
2	5
3	6
4	7

DATA

The pattern is additive.

Kate will have 7 necklaces in 4 days.

Make a graph.

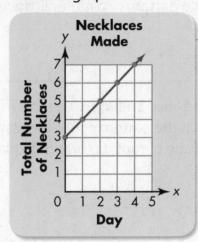

Necklaces Made

In **1** and **2**, does the table or graph show an additive or a multiplicative pattern? Explain.

1.

x	y
0	13
1	14
2	15
3	16
4	17

2.

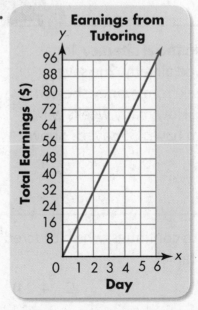

Earnings from Tutoring

For 3 through 5, use the Plant Growth graph.

3. What are the ordered pairs for Month 7 and Month 8 in the graph?

4. What do these ordered pairs represent?

5. **Communicate** Is the pattern in the graph an additive pattern or a multiplicative pattern? Explain.

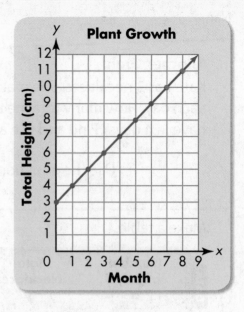

6. **Extend Your Thinking** Use the Truck Delivery Trip graph. If the pattern continues, can the ordered pair (4, 165) be part of the graph? Explain.

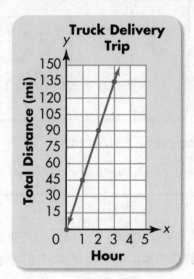

How can you tell what the *y*-value will be when *x* is 4?

7. **Personal Financial Literacy** Irina has $15 saved already. She saves $4 each week from money she earns babysitting. How many weeks will it take her to have $55 saved? Show your work.

8. **Reason** In a graph titled Alisa's Savings, the ordered pair for Day 0 is (0, 6). Why do you think the *y*-value does not begin at 0?

9. If the pattern continues, which ordered pair comes next in the table?

   A (3, 24)   C (4, 24)

   B (3, 28)   D (4, 28)

x	y
0	0
1	7
2	14
3	21

Solve & Share

Ben agrees to meet his friends at the ballpark for a 7:30 P.M. game. Trains leave the station near his home at 6:30, 6:50, 7:10, and 7:30 P.M. The train ride takes 30 minutes. It takes Ben 10 minutes to walk from his home to the train station and 5 minutes to walk from the train station to the ballpark. Which is the latest train that Ben can take without being late for the game? *Solve this problem any way you choose.*

⭐ **TEKS 5.1D** Communicate mathematical ideas, reasoning, and their implications using multiple representations, including symbols, diagrams, graphs, and language as appropriate. Also, 5.8C.
Mathematical Process Standards 5.1B, 5.1C, 5.1F

Digital Resources at PearsonTexas.com

Solve   Learn   Glossary   Check   Tools   Games

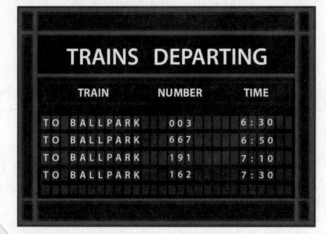

TRAINS DEPARTING

TRAIN	NUMBER	TIME
TO BALLPARK	003	6:30
TO BALLPARK	667	6:50
TO BALLPARK	191	7:10
TO BALLPARK	162	7:30

Formulate a Plan
You can work backward to solve a problem. *Show your work!*

Look Back!

Connect Ideas What time does Ben have to leave his house to make the train on time and not be late to meet his friends at the ballpark?

How Can You Work Backward to Solve a Problem?

A Analyze

Stan walked 5 blocks to the right from his house. He turned left and walked 3 blocks. He turned left again and walked another 4 blocks. Can you use a coordinate grid to find where he walked?

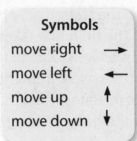

Symbols

move right →

move left ←

move up ↑

move down ↓

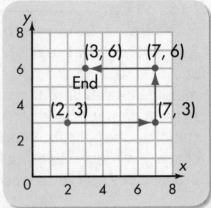

Symbols can show movement on a coordinate grid.

Starting Position   (2, 3)

5 units   →   (7, 3)

3 units   ↑   (7, 6)

4 units   ←   (3, 6) **Ending Position**

B Plan

Can you find the starting position?

If you know the ending position and the motions used, you can work backward to find the starting position.

Starting (x, y)

5 units   →   (7, 3)

3 units   ↑   (7, 6)

4 units   ←   (3, 6) **Ending**

C Solve

Begin at the ending position. Do the opposite motions and work backward.

Ending (3, 6)

4 units   →   (7, 6)

3 units   ↓   (7, 3)

5 units   ←   (2, 3) **Starting**

The starting position is (2, 3).

Do You Understand?

Convince Me! A soccer team needs $500 for a trip. The team account had some money. The team spent $50 on new uniforms. After they received donations of $240 and raised another $190, they had exactly enough money for the trip. How much money was in the account to begin with?

☆ Guided Practice *

For **1** and **2**, use a coordinate grid and work backward to find the starting position.

1.   **Starting** (x, y)

3 units → (4, 6)

5 units ↓ (4, 1)

2 units → (6, 1) **Ending**

2.   **Starting** (x, y)

3 units ↑ (7, 11)

5 units ← (2, 11)

7 units ↓ (2, 4) **Ending**

3. **Check for Reasonableness** How can you check the answer for the starting position in the example at the top of page 604?

4. **Tools** Write a problem involving movement on a coordinate grid that can be solved by working backward.

Independent Practice ☆

In **5** and **6**, find the starting position.

5.   **Starting** (x, y)

4 units ←

6 units ↑

2 units ↓

3 units → (3, 9) **Ending**

6.   **Starting** (x, y)

2 units ↓

7 units →

2 units ↑

14 units → (21, 2) **Ending**

How can you use reasoning to check that your answer is correct?

In **7** and **8**, use reasoning to solve.

7. Five friends are comparing their heights. Sam is taller than Don. Mei is shorter than Naomi, but taller than Sam. Carol is shorter than Don. Who is the tallest?

8. Pat used some flour to bake biscuits. Then she used $3\frac{3}{4}$ cups of flour to make bread and $1\frac{1}{4}$ cups of flour to make pretzels. If Pat used a total of $7\frac{1}{4}$ cups of flour for all her baking, how much flour did she use to make biscuits?

Problem Solving

9. Philip wants to take the quickest train from Elgin to Chicago. Some trains make more stops than others. Which train should he take?

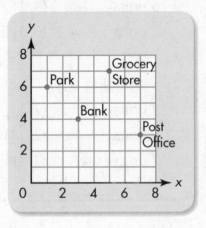

Train Schedule

Train	Leave from Elgin	Arrive in Chicago
A	8:45 A.M.	9:55 A.M.
B	2:35 P.M.	3:50 P.M.
C	3:55 P.M.	5:00 P.M.

10. **Extend Your Thinking** Mrs. Bale is at the park. She walked there from the post office. Draw a way to walk back from the park to the post office. Use only vertical or horizontal lines on the grid. Then write directions to get from the post office to the park. Name any ordered pair when you make a turn.

11. **Mental Math** The Tigers scored 20 points during a basketball game. The team scored 6 points during the fourth quarter, 4 points during the third quarter, and the same number of points in both the second and first quarters. How many points did the Tigers score in the first quarter of the game? the second quarter?

12. **Reason** Heather is thinking of a solid that has 5 faces. One of the faces is a polygon that has sides of equal length. The other 4 faces are polygons that have three sides. What is the name of Heather's solid?

13. Emma wants to complete errands on her walk home from the library. She uses the grid to plan her route. From the library, go down 1 block to the pet store. Next, go right 2 blocks to the post office. Then go 4 blocks up to buy milk at the market. Home is 5 blocks to the left. Which ordered pair is the location of the library?

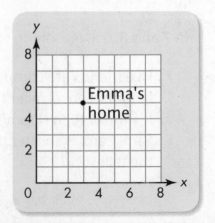

A (0, 8)   C (6, 2)

B (4, 2)   D (6, 8)

Name _____

Another Look!
What is the starting position?

Starting (*x*, *y*)

1 unit	←	☐1
3 units	↓	☐2
3 units	←	☐3
2 units	↑	(3, 4) **Ending** ☐4

Number the steps.
Do the opposite
motion and work
backward.

4: 2 units ↓   **3:** 3 units →   **2:** 3 units ↑   **1:** 1 unit →

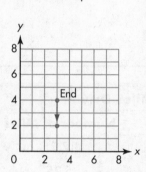 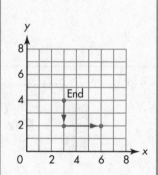 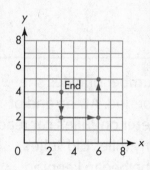 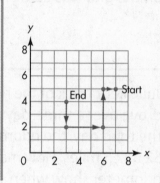

The starting position is (7, 5).

In **1**, and **2**, find the starting position.

1.   **Starting** (*x*, *y*)

9 units	↓	
4 units	←	
3 units	↑	
3 units	→	(12, 8) **Ending**

2.   **Starting** (*x*, *y*)

4 units	↑	
1 unit	→	
3 units	←	
12 units	↑	(6, 19) **Ending**

In **3** and **4**, use reasoning to solve.

3. Cheryl had some money at the beginning
of the month, so she bought a coat for $69.
Then she earned $110 from babysitting and
$27 from tutoring. At the end of the month,
Cheryl had $159. How much money did
Cheryl have at the beginning of the month?

4. Adam, Derrin, Sid, Spencer, and Naji are
waiting in line to buy tickets to a movie.
Derrin is in front of Spencer and behind
Sid. Adam is between Sid and Derrin. Naji
is behind Spencer. Who is first in line?

5. **Math and Science** Earth completes one revolution around the Sun in 365 days. Earth moves around the Sun in a counterclockwise direction. Its path around the Sun is called its orbit. Suppose Earth's position today is at (1, 4). Name the ordered pairs for two other positions in Earth's orbit.

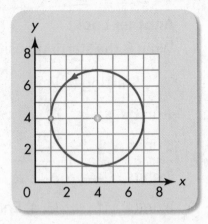

6. **Extend Your Thinking** Suppose Earth took 91 days to get from Point (4, 7) to where it is today. At which ordered pair on the grid was Earth 182 days ago?

7. Julie kept track of the number of miles she drove over a three-day period. At the end of the third day, the odometer on Julie's car read 52,607.5 miles. How many miles did Julie's odometer show when she began keeping track of her mileage?

Miles Driven	
Day	Number of Miles
1	17.25
2	5.25
3	24

8. Kori arrived at school on time, at exactly 8:30 A.M. Before that, he walked to school, ate breakfast, got dressed, and woke up. What time did he wake up this morning?

Time Needed in Morning	
Activity	Number of Minutes
Walk to School	15
Eat Breakfast	10
Get Dressed	18

   A 7:37 A.M.   **C** 7:57 A.M.

   B 7:47 A.M.   **D** 8:07 A.M.

9. **Use a Strip Diagram** An art teacher buys 126 paintbrushes for her students. The brushes come in packs of 18. Each pack costs $19.75. What is the total cost of the brushes before tax? Complete the strip diagram to help you solve.

brushes

n

Name _____

1. **Communicate** Describe the process for graphing the ordered pair (10, 12) in the first quadrant of the coordinate plane.

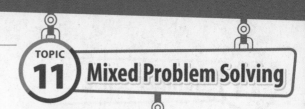

Applying Math Processes

- How does this problem connect to previous ones?
- What is my plan?
- How can I use tools?
- How can I use number sense?
- How can I communicate and represent my thinking?
- How can I organize and record information?
- How can I explain my work?
- How can I justify my answer?

2. **Represent** Lev had 112 marbles. He gave 31 of the marbles to his sister. He shared the rest of the marbles equally between himself and 2 friends. How many marbles did each friend get? Write an equation with more than one operation to represent the information. Solve.

3. **Extend Your Thinking** Keiko swam a race in 61.2 seconds. Lisa took 0.36 second longer than Keiko. If Keiko estimates that Lisa swam the race in 61.3 seconds, is her estimate greater or less than Lisa's actual time? Explain.

4. **Reason** Ellen sees that each tile in a package is square-shaped. What is the area of the tile?

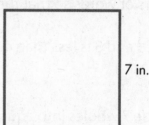

7 in.

5. Jeb baked a bread loaf, bread rolls, and a pizza. If Jeb used a total of $8\frac{1}{4}$ cups of flour for all the baking, how much flour did he use to make bread rolls?

A $2\frac{1}{4}$ cups

B $2\frac{3}{4}$ cups

C $3\frac{1}{2}$ cups

D $3\frac{3}{4}$ cups

Flour Needed	
Recipe	**Amount in Cups**
Bread Loaf	$3\frac{3}{4}$
Ravioli	$2\frac{1}{4}$
Pizza	$1\frac{3}{4}$

DATA

Error Search

Find each problem that is not correct. Circle what is wrong and rewrite the problem so it is correct.

1. $12 \times \frac{3}{4} = \frac{12}{12} \times \frac{3}{4} = \frac{36}{48} = \frac{3}{4}$

2. $\frac{1}{6} \div 5 = \frac{1}{6} \times \frac{1}{5} = \frac{1}{30}$

3. $\frac{5}{7} \times 14 = \frac{5}{7} \times \frac{14}{7} = \frac{70}{49} = 1\frac{21}{49} = 1\frac{3}{7}$

4. $9 \div \frac{1}{3} = 9 \times \frac{1}{3} = \frac{9}{3} = 3$

Reasoning

Write whether each statement is true or false. If you write false, change the numbers or words so that the statement is true.

5. The product of $\frac{3}{4}$ and 8 is less than 4.

_____

6. When you divide 7 wholes into equal $\frac{1}{4}$ pieces, the quotient is less than 1.

_____

7. When you combine $\frac{7}{12}$ of a whole with $\frac{5}{12}$ of the same whole, the total is equal to the whole.

_____

8. When you divide $\frac{1}{2}$ into 3 equal pieces, the quotient is less than 1.

_____

9. When you multiply 17 and $\frac{5}{8}$, the product is greater than 17.

_____

10. To divide a whole number by a fraction, you can divide by the reciprocal of the fraction.

_____

Set A pages 573–578

What ordered pair names Point A?

Start at the origin. The x-coordinate is the horizontal distance along the x-axis. The y-coordinate is the vertical distance along the y-axis.

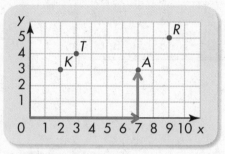

Point A is at (7, 3).

Remember to first find the x-coordinate. Then find the y-coordinate. Write the coordinates in (x, y) order.

Use the grid to answer the questions.

1. Which point is located at (9, 5)?

2. Which point is located at (2, 3)?

3. What ordered pair names Point T?

4. What is the ordered pair for the origin?

Set B pages 579–584

Mary has 4 dollars. She will save 1 dollar each week. How much money will Mary have after 3 weeks?

Make an input-output table to show pairs of values. The input is the week number. The output is the total savings.

Use the table to graph the ordered pairs. Then draw a line to show the pattern.

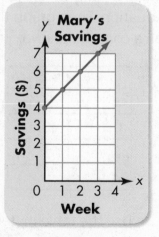

So, Mary will have $7 after 3 weeks.

Remember that the first point does not need to begin at (0, 0).

1. Find the missing value in the table. Use the ordered pairs in the table to make a graph. If the pattern continues, how tall will the plant be after 4 months?

Month	Plant Height (cm)
0	3
1	4
2	5
3	6
4	

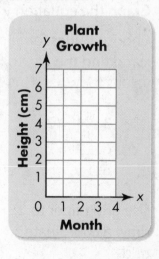

Each package has 3 juice boxes. Show this multiplicative pattern in a table and graph.

y = 3x		
Number of Packages (x)	Total Juice Boxes (y)	(x, y)
1	3	(1, 3)
2	6	(2, 6)
3	9	(3, 9)

Use the ordered pairs from the table. Graph the ordered pairs. Then draw a line to show the pattern.

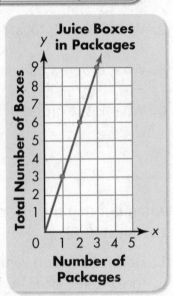

Remember that the x-values go across, and the y-values go up.

1. Use the table to graph the ordered pairs.

y = 2x		
x	y	(x, y)
1	2	(1, 2)
2	4	(2, 4)
3	6	(3, 6)

Graph the equation y = x + 2.

Choose values for x and find the values for y.

3 = 1 + 2
6 = 4 + 2
9 = 7 + 2

y = x + 2		
x	y	(x, y)
1	3	(1, 3)
4	6	(4, 6)
7	9	(7, 9)

Use grid paper to draw a coordinate grid.

Label and number the axes.

Graph the ordered pairs and connect the points.

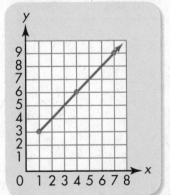

Remember to check that your ordered pairs fit the equation.

Make a table of values for each equation. Then graph the equation on a coordinate grid.

1.

y = x + 5		
x	y	(x, y)
0		(0,)
3		
4		

2.

y = 8x		
x	y	(x, y)
0		(0,)
1		
2		

3. Use the table in Item 2. A choir meets 8 times in 1 month. If the pattern continues, write the ordered pair that shows how many times the choir would meet in 14 months.

© Pearson Education, Inc. 5

An additive pattern in a graph has *y*-values that increase by 1.

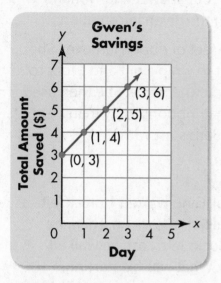

A multiplicative pattern in a graph has *y*-values that increase by a number greater than 1.

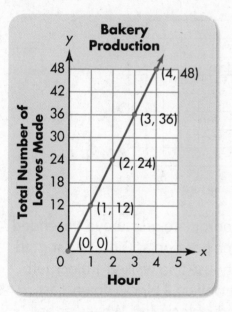

Remember: A multiplicative pattern starts at (0, 0), the origin, in a graph.

Remember to compare the *y*-coordinates to find if the pattern is additive or multiplicative.

Tell whether each table or graph shows an additive or a multiplicative pattern. Tell how you know.

1.

DATA

x	y
4	15
5	16
6	17
7	18

2.

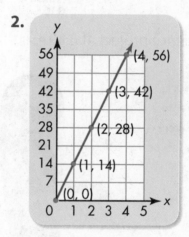

3.

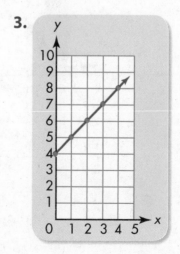

Rocio worked on her science fair project for 35 minutes. Then she spent 20 minutes on her math homework. After that, Rocio spent 45 minutes on the computer. If she logged off the computer at 8:10 P.M., what time did Rocio begin working on her science fair project?

You can draw a picture to help you work backward.

Use inverse operations for each change.

| Start | −35 min | −20 min | −45 min | Finish |
| 6:30 P.M. | | 7:05 | 7:25 | 8:10 P.M. |

Rocio began her science project at 6:30 P.M.

To organize your work, list the steps or events in a problem. Then work backward through the steps one at a time.

Remember to check your solution by beginning with your answer and working forward through the given information.

1. Barb has $3\frac{1}{4}$ feet of ribbon left over. She used $2\frac{1}{4}$ feet to wrap a gift and $\frac{3}{4}$ foot to decorate a picture frame. She then used $1\frac{3}{4}$ feet for hair ribbons. How many feet of ribbon did Barb start with?

2. From school, Gino walked 1 block left. Next, he walked 1 block up. Then, he walked 4 blocks left. Last, he walked 2 blocks up. What was his starting position?

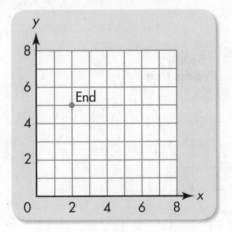

3. Use the coordinate grid above. Val ended at the same position as Gino. She started from her house and walked 1 block left. Then, she walked 2 blocks down. Last, she walked 3 blocks left. What was her starting position?

Name _____

1. Adele graphed points *W, X, Y,* and *Z* on the coordinate grid. What is the ordered pair for Point *Y*?

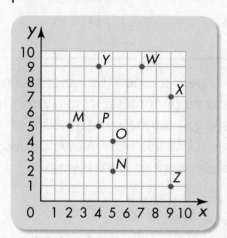

A (7, 9)   **C** (9, 1)

B (9, 7)   **D** (4, 9)

2. Use the grid above. Mark graphed a point at (5, 2). Which point did he graph?

A Point *M*   **C** Point *O*

B Point *N*   **D** Point *P*

3. Blake was graphing the multiplicative pattern shown below when he stopped to eat dinner. What is the missing *y*-coordinate for the red point in his graph?

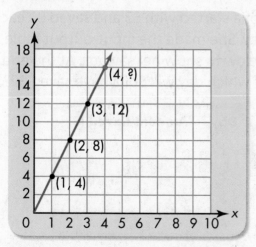

A 4   **C** 16

B 6   **D** 18

4. Marci writes 3 songs each day. She graphed the line $y = 3x$ to show this relationship. Which ordered pair is a point on the line $y = 3x$?

A (2, 1)   **C** (2, 5)

B (2, 2)   **D** (2, 6)

5. There are 10 millimeters in every centimeter. Let *x* be the number of centimeters and *y* be the number of millimeters. Which equation represents the relationship between millimeters and centimeters?

A $y = 10x$ **C** $y = x + 10$

B $x = 10y$ **D** $x = y + 10$

6. A charity collected $615 in donations and raised another $135. They now have $1,735. How much did they have to begin with?

			.		
⓪	⓪	⓪		⓪	⓪
①	①	①		①	①
②	②	②		②	②
③	③	③		③	③
④	④	④		④	④
⑤	⑤	⑤		⑤	⑤
⑥	⑥	⑥		⑥	⑥
⑦	⑦	⑦		⑦	⑦
⑧	⑧	⑧		⑧	⑧
⑨	⑨	⑨		⑨	⑨

7. Esperanza made a table to find the ordered pairs on the graph of $y = 4x$. What number is the missing y-value in her table?

y = 4x		
x	y	(x, y)
1	4	(1, 4)
2	8	(2, 8)
7		(7,)

8. Morgan graphed the equation $y = 5x$. If the pattern continues, which ordered pair is **NOT** on the graph of this equation?

A (2, 10)   **C** (5, 25)

B (4, 16)   **D** (8, 40)

9. Mr. Halladay tracked and graphed the production of cars at a factory each hour. Which of the following equations does the graph represent?

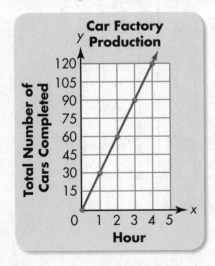

A $y = x + 30$ **C** $y = 15x$

B $y = x + 15$ **D** $y = 30x$

10. Sara bought a bamboo plant that was 4 inches tall. It grew 1 inch each day. What will be the height of the plant after Day 3?

A 5 in.   **C** 7 in.

B 6 in.   **D** 8 in.

11. A zookeeper recorded the weight gain of a baby elephant after it was born. The elephant gained the same amount of weight each week. How many pounds did the elephant gain each week?

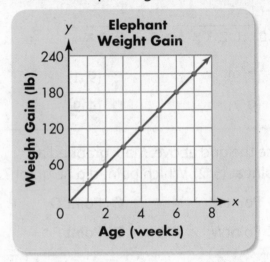

A 20 lb   **C** 60 lb

B 30 lb   **D** 90 lb

12. Sofia started with $3 and saved $1 each day. She made the input-output table below to show her savings. At the end of which day will Sofia have saved $9?

Day	Amount Saved ($)
1	4
2	5
3	6
4	7

A Day 3   **C** Day 5

B Day 4   **D** Not here

13. The graph shows the distance Trudy's small jet car travels. How far has the jet car traveled after 5 seconds?

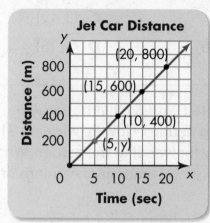

A 400 m
C 100 m
B 200 m
D 5 m

14. Use the graph above. How many meters does the jet car travel in 1 second?

A 40 m
C 100 m
B 60 m
D 200 m

15. Each year, Genny recorded the height of a tree growing in her front yard. She graphed her results. What was the height of the tree after the first year?

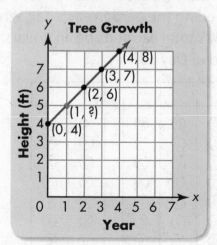

16. Chip gives his dog 3 treats. Now, he gives his dog a treat only when he does a trick. He made the table below to keep track of the number of treats the dog eats. Is this pattern additive or multiplicative?

Number of Tricks	Total Number of Treats Eaten
0	3
1	4
2	5
3	6
4	7

17. Use the table above. If Chip's dog eats 10 treats, how many tricks did the dog perform?

A 5 tricks
C 7 tricks
B 6 tricks
D 8 tricks

18. It takes Earth approximately 1 year, or 365 days, to orbit the Sun. Let x represent the number of years and y represent the number of days. Which equation shows the relationship?

A $y = x + 365$
C $y = 365x$
B $x = y + 365$
D $x = 365y$

19. Les drew a rectangle and graphed some points on a coordinate grid. Write the ordered pair for a point on the grid that is **NOT** a vertex of the rectangle.

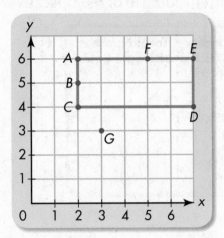

20. Use the graph above. Which point did Les graph at (7, 4)?

A Point *A*

C Point *C*

B Point *B*

D Point *D*

21. Every 2 years of a coin program, more states received a new design on a quarter. Let *y* = the total number of states with a quarter design. Let *x* = the year number of the program. What is the missing number in the table of ordered pairs for *y* = 5*x*?

y = 5x		
x Years	**y** States	**(x, y)**
0	0	(0, 0)
2	10	(2, 10)
4		(4,)
6	30	(6, 30)

A 5

C 40

B 20

D 60

22. Charles graphed the equation $y = x + 9$. Which of the following ordered pairs is on the graph?

A (1, 9)   **C** (3, 12)

B (2, 12)   **D** (5, 15)

23. Billy started with $3 that he earned trimming hedges. Now he will earn $1 each day for weeding the garden. What will be his total amount of earnings on Day 8?

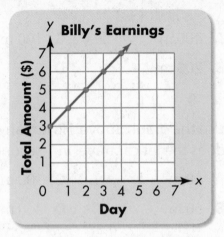

A $4   **C** $11

B $8   **D** $12

24. Use the graph above. After Day 8, Billy will earn twice as much money for weeding the garden each day. What will Billy's total earnings be, in dollars, at the end of Day 10?

			•		
⓪	⓪	⓪		⓪	⓪
①	①	①		①	①
②	②	②		②	②
③	③	③		③	③
④	④	④		④	④
⑤	⑤	⑤		⑤	⑤
⑥	⑥	⑥		⑥	⑥
⑦	⑦	⑦		⑦	⑦
⑧	⑧	⑧		⑧	⑧
⑨	⑨	⑨		⑨	⑨

TOPIC 12

Two-Dimensional Shapes

Essential Questions: How can angles be classified? How can polygons, triangles, and quadrilaterals be described, classified, and named?

Prickly pears, coyotes, scorpions, sand, and rocks are all part of the desert ecosystem of the Guadalupe Mountains.

An *ecosystem* is an interaction of all living organisms in a particular environment.

Hey, did you ever think of school as a kind of ecosystem? Here's a project about ecosystems.

Math and Science Project: Ecosystems

Do Research Use the Internet or other sources to learn more about ecosystems. Look for examples of changes that living organisms might cause. List three different ecosystems and describe any changes that humans might have made to each one.

Journal: Write a Report Include what you found. Also in your report:
- Compare two ecosystems. List 10 living things and 5 non-living things you might find in each one.
- Evaluate changes that can occur in an ecosystem. Are they positive changes or negative? Why?
- Use two-dimensional shapes to make a map or diagram of an ecosystem.

Name _____

Review What You Know

Vocabulary

Choose the best term from the box. Write it on the blank.

> • algebraic expression
>
> • equation
>
> • variable

1. $3x = 15$ is a(n) _____ .

2. $3x$ is a(n) _____ .

Writing Rules

Find the missing value and write a rule for the table.

3.

r	22	25	31	48
$r +$ ☐	30	33	39	☐

4.

x	16	28	36	40
$x \div$ ☐	4	7	9	☐

Fractions

Find each product or quotient. Simplify if possible.

5. $3 \times \frac{1}{2}$ **6.** $5 \div \frac{1}{5}$

7. $\frac{7}{8} \times 3$ **8.** $14 \div \frac{1}{7}$

9. If 3 out of 4 bananas are green, what fraction names the bananas that are **NOT** green?

A $\frac{1}{4}$

B $\frac{1}{3}$

C $\frac{1}{2}$

D $\frac{3}{4}$

Coordinate Plane

Find each answer.

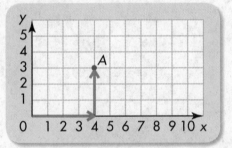

10. What is the x-coordinate of Point A?

11. Describe the x-coordinate in an ordered pair.

12. What is the y-coordinate of Point A?

13. Describe the y-coordinate in an ordered pair.

© Pearson Education, Inc. 5

My Word Cards

Use the examples for each word on the front of the card to help complete the definitions on the back.

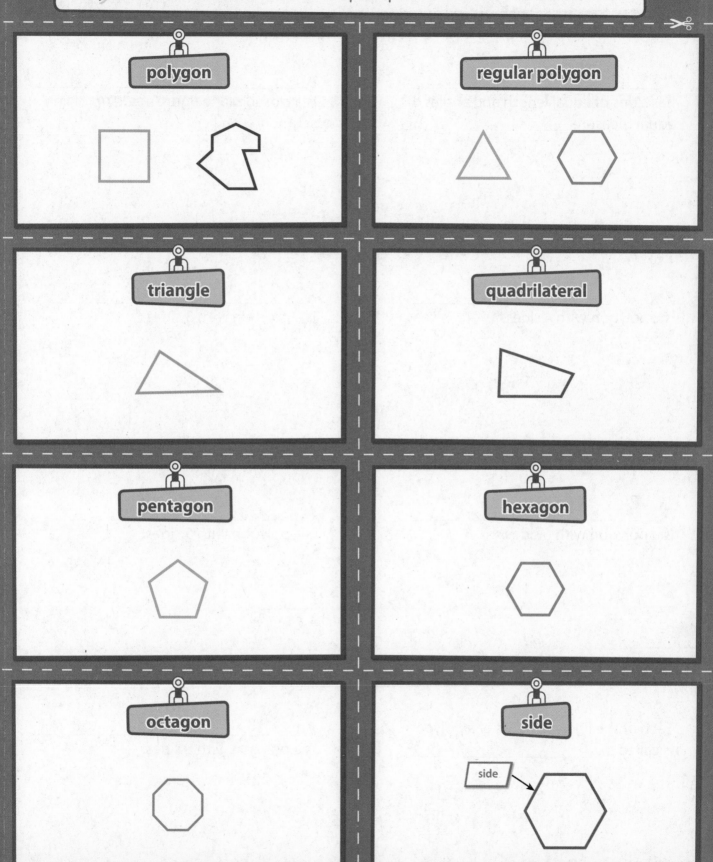

polygon

regular polygon

triangle

quadrilateral

pentagon

hexagon

octagon

side

side

My Word Cards

Complete the definition. Extend learning by writing your own definitions.

A _____
has sides of equal length and angles of equal measure.

A _____
is a closed plane figure made up of line segments.

A _____
is a polygon with 4 sides.

A _____
is a polygon with 3 sides.

A _____
is a polygon with 6 sides.

A _____
is a polygon with 5 sides.

Each of the line segments of a polygon is called a _____.

An _____
is a polygon with 8 sides.

My Word Cards

Use the examples for each word on the front of the card to help complete the definitions on the back.

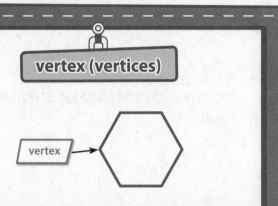

vertex (vertices)

vertex →

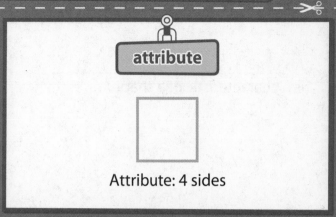

attribute

Attribute: 4 sides

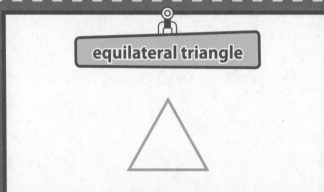

equilateral triangle

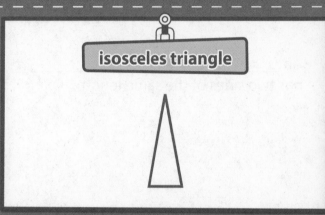

isosceles triangle

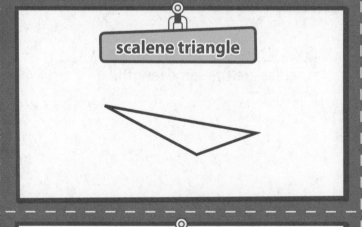

scalene triangle

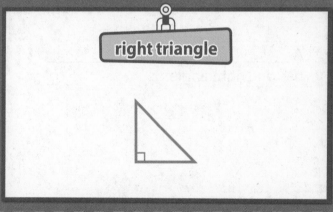

right triangle

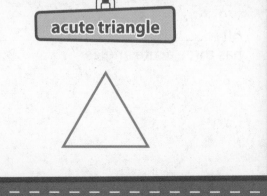

acute triangle

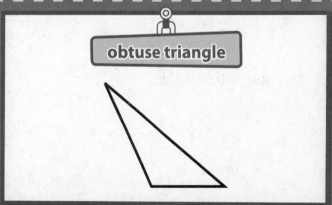

obtuse triangle

My Word Cards

Complete the definition. Extend learning by writing your own definitions.

An _____
is a characteristic of a shape.

A _____
is a point where the sides of a polygon
meet.

An _____
has two sides of the same length.

In an _____,
all sides are the same length.

A _____
has one right angle.

In a _____,
no sides are the same length.

An _____
has one obtuse angle.

An _____
has three acute angles.

My Word Cards

Use the examples for each word on the front of the card to help complete the definitions on the back.

parallelogram

trapezoid

parallel sides

1 and 2 are parallel sides.

rectangle

rhombus

square

My Word Cards

Complete the definition. Extend learning by writing your own definitions.

A _____
is a quadrilateral that has exactly one pair of parallel sides.

A _____
is a quadrilateral with both pairs of opposite sides parallel and equal in length.

A _____
is a parallelogram with four right angles.

A polygon has _____
if the sides are the same distance apart at every point.

A _____
is a rectangle with all sides the same length.

A _____
is a parallelogram with all sides the same length.

Name _____

Solve & Share

Renee wants to design a play area for her puppies. On paper, how many different shapes for the play area can you create? All the shapes must have straight lines that connect at each end. Draw as many shapes as you can and label the number of sides for each shape. *Solve this problem any way you choose.*

⭐ TEKS 5.5 Classify two-dimensional figures by attributes and properties. Classify two-dimensional figures in a hierarchy of sets and subsets using graphic organizers based on their attributes and properties. Mathematical Process Standards 5.1C, 5.1E, 5.1F, 5.1G

Digital Resources at PearsonTexas.com

| Solve | Learn | Glossary | Check | Tools | Games |

Create and Use Representations You can create different shapes by connecting line segments. *Show your work!*

Look Back!

Justify Which of the shapes you created are regular polygons? Tell how you know.

How Do You Name a Polygon?

A polygon is a closed plane figure made up of line segments. A regular polygon has sides of equal length and angles of equal measure. Polygons can be described by their attributes, such as the number of sides or vertices they have.

Can you see any polygons in the real world?

B Polygons

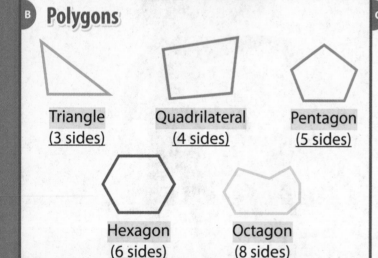

Triangle
(3 sides)

Quadrilateral
(4 sides)

Pentagon
(5 sides)

Hexagon
(6 sides)

Octagon
(8 sides)

C Not Polygons

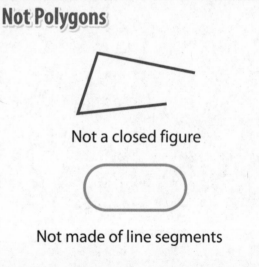

Not a closed figure

Not made of line segments

Do You Understand?

Convince Me! Which of the polygons above appears **NOT** to be a regular polygon? Redraw it so that it appears to be a regular polygon.

Guided Practice

In **1** and **2**, name the polygon and classify it as regular or irregular.

1.

2.

3. How many sides and how many vertices does a pentagon have? a hexagon?

4. What type of polygon does each road sign in the example at the top of page 628 appear to be? Which one is a regular polygon?

How can you tell if a figure is a regular polygon?

Independent Practice

In **5** through **8**, name each polygon. Then write *yes* or *no* to tell if it is regular.

5.

6.

7.

8.

In **9** through **12**, write *yes* or *no* to tell if the figure is a polygon. If not, explain why.

9.

10.

11.

12.

Problem Solving

13. Kathleen draws a regular hexagon with six angles that are all equal. If the total measure of the angles is 720°, how many degrees is each angle of the hexagon?

    A 40°   **C** 60°

    B 90°   **D** 120°

14. Number Sense Marco wrote the equation $k \div 12 = 4$. What is the value of k in this equation?

    A $k = 3$ **C** $k = 60$

    B $k = 48$ **D** $k = 72$

---

15. If each side of a regular pentagon equals 4 feet, what is its perimeter?

The perimeter of a figure is the distance around the figure.

16. Tools Divide a square in half by connecting two opposite vertices. What types of polygons are formed? Are they regular or irregular? Explain.

---

17. Connect Juanita's car gets 28 miles per gallon. Which expression shows how many gallons it will take to drive 720 miles?

    A 720×28

    B $720 \div 28$

    C $720 + 28$

    D $720 - 28$

18. While driving, Shania saw a No Passing Zone sign and an Interstate Highway sign. Are these polygons? If so, are they regular?

---

19. Each cell from a wasps' hive has 6 sides. What is the name of this polygon?

20. Extend Your Thinking Shakira sorted shapes into two different groups. Use geometric terms to describe how she sorted the shapes.

Group A	Group B
V ⬠ ▯	⌂ ▭ ⬡

Name _____

Another Look!

A polygon is a closed plane figure made up of line segments. Common polygons have names that tell the number of sides the polygon has.

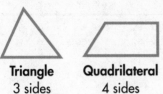

Triangle
3 sides

Quadrilateral
4 sides

Pentagon
5 sides

Hexagon
6 sides

Octagon
8 sides

Open Figure

A **regular polygon** has sides of equal length and angles of equal measure.

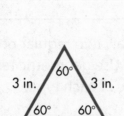

Open figures are never polygons. Some polygons are regular and some are not.

Each side is 3 inches long.
Each angle is 60°.

In **1** through **4**, name each polygon. Then write *yes* or *no* to tell if it is regular.

1.

2.

3.

4.

In **5** through **8**, write *yes* or *no* to tell if the figure is a polygon. If not, explain why.

5.

6.

7.

8.

For **9** and **10**, use the polygon.

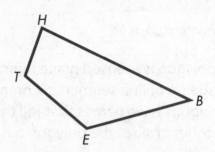

9. Lisa drew this polygon. Name her polygon.

10. Name the vertices of the polygon.

---

11. **Extend Your Thinking** Draw two regular polygons and two that are irregular. Use geometric terms to describe one characteristic of each type.

---

12. Cam drew a pentagon, a triangle, an ⭐ octagon, a hexagon, and a quadrilateral. Which of these polygons has eight sides?

   A Quadrilateral
   B Pentagon
   C Hexagon
   D Octagon

13. Patricia drew the figures shown below. ⭐ Which figure is **NOT** a regular polygon?

  A   **B**

  C   **D**

---

14. **Number Sense** Peter has 18 dimes. He uses 12 dimes to buy a drink. The number of dimes he has left is one-half the number of pennies he has. How many pennies does Peter have? Write an equation to solve the problem.

15. Carlos owns an orchard. His apple trees produced 315 bushels of apples. Each bushel of apples weighs about 48 pounds. There are about 3 apples in each pound. About how many apples did Carlos' apple trees produce?

> Should the answer be an estimate or an exact answer?

Name _____

Solve & Share

Draw six different triangles with different properties. Next to each triangle list the properties. For example, 2 equal sides, 1 right angle, 3 acute angles, and so on. *Work with a partner to solve this problem.*

TEKS 5.5 Classify two-dimensional figures by attributes and properties. Classify two-dimensional figures in a hierarchy of sets and subsets using graphic organizers based on their attributes and properties. Mathematical Process Standards 5.1F, 5.1G

Construct Arguments
How can you tell which properties describe a triangle? *Show your work!*

Digital Resources at PearsonTexas.com

Solve Learn Glossary Check Tools Games

Look Back!

Connect Ideas Can you classify the triangles you created based on their properties? Do some triangles have more than one classification? Tell how you know.

How Can You Classify Triangles?

 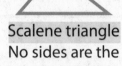

A

Triangles can be classified by the lengths of their sides.

Equilateral triangle
All sides are the
same length.

Isosceles triangle
Two sides are the
same length.

Scalene triangle
No sides are the
same length.

Can you tell if the
sides of a triangle are the same
without measuring them?

The total measure
of all the angles in a triangle
is 180°.

B Triangles can also be classified by the
measures of their angles.

Right triangle
One angle is a right angle.

Acute triangle
All three angles are
acute angles.

Obtuse triangle
One angle is an
obtuse angle.

Do You Understand?

Convince Me! Can you draw an equilateral
right triangle? Explain using precise
mathematical language.

To justify a mathematical
argument, you must use
precise mathematical
language and ideas to
explain your thinking.

634

© Pearson Education, Inc. 5

Name _____

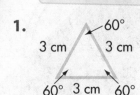

In **1** and **2**, classify each triangle by its sides and then by its angles.

1.

60°
3 cm   3 cm
60° 3 cm 60°

2.

9.9 in.   7 in.
7 in.

3. Construct Arguments Can a right triangle have an obtuse angle in it? Why or why not?

4. Can an equilateral triangle have only two sides of equal length? Why or why not?

Independent Practice *

In **5** through **10**, classify each triangle by its sides and then by its angles.

5.

30°
6 in.   6 in.
75°   75°
3.1 in.

6.

9 yd   12 yd
15 yd

7.

11 cm /60°\ 11 cm
60° 60°
11 cm

8.

15.1 m
9.2 m
110°
9.2 m

9.

6 m   10 m

8 m

10.

70°
40°
70°

Think about what you need to compare to classify the triangle correctly.

Problem Solving

For **11,** use the picture.

11. The Louvre Pyramid serves as an entrance to the Louvre Museum in Paris. The base of the pyramid is 35 meters long and the sides are 32 meters long. Classify the triangle on the front of the Louvre Pyramid by the lengths of its sides and the measures of its angles.

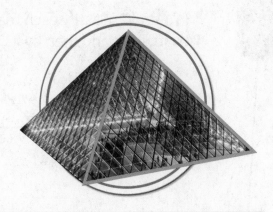

12. Extend Your Thinking The measures of two angles of a triangle are 23° and 67°. Is the triangle acute, right, or obtuse? Use geometric terms in your explanation.

13. Connect During a sale at the bookstore, books sold for $3 and magazines sold for $2.50. Jan spent $16 and bought a total of 6 books and magazines. How many of each did she buy?

14. A pizza is divided into twelve equal slices. Glenn and Ben each ate $\frac{1}{6}$ of the pizza on Monday. The next day Ben ate $\frac{1}{2}$ of the pizza that was leftover. How many slices of the original pizza remain?

   A 2 slices
   B 3 slices
   C 4 slices
   D 6 slices

15. An animal shelter houses dogs, cats, and rabbits. There are 126 animals at the shelter. Of the animals, $\frac{1}{3}$ are cats. Three fourths of the remaining animals are dogs. How many of the animals are rabbits?

16. Justify Two sides of a triangle measure 5 inches and 6 inches. Jason says the triangle must be scalene. Is Jason correct? Explain.

A scalene triangle has no sides that are the same length.

© Pearson Education, Inc. 5

Name _____

Solve & Share

Draw as many different quadrilaterals as you can by changing the side lengths and relationships as well as the angles. *Work with a partner to solve this problem.*

TEKS 5.5 Classify two-dimensional figures by attributes and properties. Classify two-dimensional figures in a hierarchy of sets and subsets using graphic organizers based on their attributes and properties.
Mathematical Process Standards 5.1D, 5.1F, 5.1G

Digital Resources at PearsonTexas.com

Solve   Learn   Glossary   Check   Tools   Games

You can use **reason** to draw quadrilaterals with more than one property. *Show your work!*

Look Back!

Analyze Relationships How many different ways can you describe the quadrilaterals on your paper? Classify the quadrilaterals and tell how you know.

How Can You Recognize a Quadrilateral?

A quadrilateral is any polygon with 4 sides. Quadrilaterals can be classified by their angles or pairs of sides.

Can you find any quadrilaterals in everyday life?

Parallelogram
both pairs of opposite sides are parallel and equal in length

Trapezoid
only one pair of parallel sides

B

The total measure of all the angles in a quadrilateral is 360°.

Rectangle
a parallelogram with four right angles

Rhombus
a parallelogram with all sides the same length

Square
a rectangle with all sides the same length

A square can also be called a rhombus.

Do You Understand?

Convince Me! Is a square also a parallelogram? Explain using precise mathematical language.

To justify a mathematical argument, you must use precise mathematical language and ideas to explain your thinking.

Name _____

In **1** through **4**, name each quadrilateral.

1.

2.

3.

4.

5. Communicate A square and a rhombus both have four sides that are equal in length. How can you tell the difference between the two quadrilaterals?

6. Construct Arguments Why can a rectangle also be called a parallelogram?

☆ **Independent Practice** ☆

In **7** through **10**, classify each quadrilateral. Be as specific as possible.

Remember to compare side lengths and angles to classify each figure correctly.

7.

8.
9 ft
9 ft [ ] 9 ft
9 ft

9.
6 m
9 m [ ] 9 m
6 m

10.
3 ft
3 ft [ ] 3 ft
3 ft

In **11** through **16**, the angle measures of a quadrilateral are given in order. Draw the quadrilateral and name the figure.

11. 54°, 126°, 126°, 54°

12. 150°, 30°, 30°, 150°

13. 54°, 126°, 54°, 126°

14. 90°, 90°, 90°, 90°

15. 60°, 120°, 60°, 120°

16. 90°, 90°, 35°, 145°

Problem Solving

17. Construct Arguments Which quadrilateral cannot have 4 sides of the same length?

A Square
B Trapezoid
C Rectangle
D Rhombus

18. Draw a quadrilateral that is **NOT** a parallelogram.

How many pairs of parallel sides does a parallelogram have?

---

19. Extend Your Thinking Draw rectangle *ABCD*. Then draw a diagonal line connecting points *B* and *D*. If triangle *BCD* is a right isosceles triangle, what do you know about rectangle *ABCD*?

20. Hot dog buns come in packages of 12. Which of the following is **NOT** needed to find out how much you will spend on hot dog buns?

A The cost of one pack of buns
B The cost of the hot dogs
C The number of buns you need
D All of the information is necessary.

---

21. The perimeter of a polygon is 24 inches. Each side of the polygon is 3 inches long. What is the name of the polygon?

22. Pilar rode her bike $3\frac{3}{5}$ miles to school. What improper fraction is equivalent to $3\frac{3}{5}$?

---

23. Use a Strip Diagram For a food drive, Tony's class collected 108 cans of soup. If one box holds 18 cans, how many boxes will be needed to hold all of the cans?

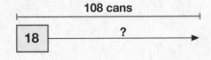

108 cans

18   ?

24. A restaurant can seat 100 diners. Four of the tables can each seat 6 people. The rest of the tables can each seat 4 people. How many tables does the restaurant have in all?

Name _____

Another Look!

Quadrilateral	Definition	Example
Parallelogram	A quadrilateral with both pairs of opposite sides parallel and equal in length	
Rectangle	A parallelogram with four right angles	
Rhombus	A parallelogram with all sides the same length	
Square	A rectangle with all sides the same length	
Trapezoid	A quadrilateral with only one pair of parallel sides	

Remember that the sum of the measures of the angles in a quadrilateral is 360°.

In **1** through **4**, classify each quadrilateral. Be as specific as possible.

1.
6 ft
3 ft   3 ft
6 ft

2.
4 in.
4 in.   4 in.
4 in.

3.
9 m
6 m   7 m
3 m

4.
4 cm
7 cm   7 cm
4 cm

In **5** through **8**, the angle measures of a quadrilateral are given in order. Draw the quadrilateral and name the figure.

5. 75°, 105°, 75°, 105°   **6.** 90°, 90°, 90°, 90°   **7.** 45°, 135°, 45°, 135°   **8.** 160°, 20°, 20°, 160°

9. How is a rectangle similar to a square? How is it different?

10. What is the name of the figure shown?

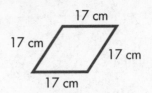

17 cm
17 cm
17 cm
17 cm

A Square   C Rhombus
B Rectangle   D Trapezoid

11. Extend Your Thinking The angles of a quadrilateral measure 80°, 100°, 100°, and 80° in that order. What kind of quadrilateral is it? How do you know?

12. Communicate Can a trapezoid have four obtuse angles? Explain.

13. Rhoda drew the quadrilateral below.

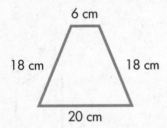

6 cm
18 cm   18 cm
20 cm

What is the most specific name for Rhoda's quadrilateral?

14. The bottom of a small box has the dimensions shown in the figure.

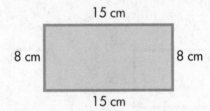

15 cm
8 cm   8 cm
15 cm

What is the area?

15. Kim drew the figures below. Which of the figures appear to have exactly 2 obtuse angles?

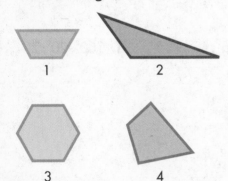

1   2
3   4

A 2, 3, and 4   C 1, 3, and 4
B 2 and 3   D 1 and 4

16. Connect A section of seats at a stadium has 12 rows with 14 seats in each row and 8 rows with 12 seats in each row. If 272 band members purchase all the seats in the section, will there be enough seats for everyone? Explain.

644

Name _____

☆ ☆
Solve & Share

In the space below, draw any size line segment that will fit on the page. The line can go in any direction but it must be straight. Draw another line segment of any length that is parallel to your first line. Connect the ends of each line with another line segment so it makes a closed four-sided figure. What does your shape look like? Can you classify it? *Discuss your thoughts with a partner.*

Lesson 12-4
Special Quadrilaterals

TEKS 5.5 Classify two-dimensional figures by attributes and properties. Classify two-dimensional figures in a hierarchy of sets and subsets using graphic organizers based on their attributes and properties. **Mathematical Process Standards** 5.1C, 5.1D, 5.1F, 5.1G

Digital Resources at PearsonTexas.com

Solve   Learn   Glossary   Check   Tools   Games

You can **communicate** the differences and similarities of properties when classifying quadrilaterals. *Show your work!*

Look Back!

Connect Ideas How can you draw a quadrilateral different than the one above? Describe what you can change and why it changes the quadrilateral.

Which Shapes Are Special Cases of Another Shape?

Groups of quadrilaterals are classified by their properties.

Think about the questions below when you are classifying quadrilaterals.

- How many pairs of opposite sides are parallel?

- Which sides have equal lengths?

- How many right angles are there?

B

A trapezoid has exactly one pair of parallel sides.

A parallelogram has two pairs of opposite sides parallel and equal in length.

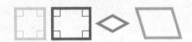

C

A rectangle has four right angles.

A rhombus has all sides the same length.

D

A square has all sides the same length.

A square has four right angles.

Do You Understand?

Convince Me! How is a parallelogram different from a rhombus? How are they similar?

☆ **Guided Practice** *

In **1** through **4**, use as many names as possible to identify each polygon. Tell which name is most specific.

1.

2.

3.

4.

5. How are a square and a rhombus alike?

6. How is a trapezoid different from a parallelogram?

Use the questions at the top of page 646 to help you classify the quadrilaterals.

☆ **Independent Practice** *

7. Identify the polygon using as many names as possible.

8. Identify the polygon using as many names as possible.

9. Why is a square also a rectangle?

10. Which special quadrilateral is both a rectangle and a rhombus? Explain how you know.

Problem Solving

11. Each time Sophie makes a cut to a polygon, she can make a new type of polygon. What kind of polygon appears to be formed by cutting the top off the isosceles triangle shown?

12. **Estimate** Donald's car gets about 30 miles per gallon. About how many miles can Donald drive on 9.2 gallons of gas? At $3.15 a gallon, about how much would that amount of gas cost?

13. **Reason** Is it possible to draw a quadrilateral that is not a rectangle but has at least one right angle? Explain.

14. What properties help you classify a quadrilateral as a parallelogram, but not a rhombus?

15. Which shows one way of listing the side lengths of a parallelogram?

  A 5 m, 5 m, 5 m, 1 m
  B 1 m, 5 m, 1 m, 5 m
  C 4 m, 1 m, 1 m, 1 m
  D 1 m, 1 m, 1 m, 5 m

16. The area of a quadrilateral is 8.4 square feet. Find two decimals that give a product close to 8.4.

17. Suppose you cut a square into two identical triangles. What type of triangles will you make?

18. **Extend Your Thinking** A parallelogram has four sides that are the same length. Is it a square? Explain how you know.

What do you know about the sides of a parallelogram?

Name _____

Homework 12-4
Special Quadrilaterals

Another Look!

Some **quadrilaterals** have special properties.

A **trapezoid** has exactly one pair of parallel sides.

A **parallelogram** has two pairs of opposite sides parallel and equal.

A **rectangle** is a parallelogram with 4 right angles.

A **rhombus** is a parallelogram with 4 equal sides.

A **square** is a parallelogram with 4 right angles and 4 equal sides.

In **1** through **6**, identify each polygon. Describe each polygon by as many names as possible.

1.

2.

3.

4.

5.

6.

7. **Communicate** A parallelogram has one side that is 4 centimeters long and one side that is 6 centimeters long. What is the perimeter of the parallelogram? Explain how you found your answer.

How can you find the perimeter of a parallelogram?

8. For Howard's science experiment he needs 69 blocks that each have a mass of 0.5 kilogram. Is the total mass of the blocks 3.45 kilograms, 34.5 kilograms, or 345 kilograms? Explain how you found your answer.

9. **Extend Your Thinking** Marvin says that all rhombuses are squares. Aretha says that all squares are rhombuses. Who is correct? Explain.

10. **Explain** What characteristics help you tell the difference between a rhombus and a rectangle? Explain.

11. Which of the following statements is **NOT** true?

   A A trapezoid is a rectangle.
   B A square is also a rectangle.
   C A rectangle is a quadrilateral.
   D A square is also a rhombus.

12. **Personal Financial Literacy** Lilly saves $\frac{2}{9}$ of her allowance. Her allowance is $18 per week. How much does she save each week?

13. **Math and Science** Bella is putting 576 cicadas into 8 different terrariums. The same number of cicadas will be put in each one. How many cicadas will be in each terrarium?

576 cicadas

| ? | ? | ? | ? | ? | ? | ? | ? |

14. A store has caps on display. Five of the caps are red. There are 4 more blue caps than green caps. There are 3 fewer yellow caps than green caps. If there are 24 caps in all, how many caps are there of each color?

Name _____

Solve & Share

Look at the quadrilaterals below. In the table, write the letters for all the figures that are trapezoids. Then do the same with each of the other quadrilaterals. *Work with a partner to solve this problem.*

TEKS 5.5 Classify two-dimensional figures by attributes and properties. Classify two-dimensional figures in a hierarchy of sets and subsets using graphic organizers based on their attributes and properties. **Mathematical Process Standards 5.1C, 5.1D, 5.1F, 5.1G**

Digital Resources at PearsonTexas.com

| Solve | Learn | Glossary | Check | Tools | Games |

G

M

R

L

S

Q

O

N

V

U

Connect Ideas
You can classify quadrilaterals that have more than one property. *Show your work!*

List the letter of each figure in each group.

Trapezoids	
Parallelograms	
Rectangles	
Squares	
Rhombuses	

Look Back!

Justify Which quadrilateral had the most figures listed? Can you explain why this group had the most? Justify your answer.

How Are Special Quadrilaterals Related to Each Other?

A

This "family tree" shows how special quadrilaterals are related to each other.

You can classify quadrilaterals using a "tree".

Quadrilaterals

Parallelogram   Trapezoid

Rectangle   Rhombus

Square

B Each branch of the tree shows a subgroup of the figure above.

A square is a type of rectangle. All rectangles are parallelograms.

So, each group can have more than one subgroup.

Each figure shares all of the properties of the figures above it.

A square and a rectangle have four right angles.

C All of the figures below the parallelogram have two pairs of parallel opposite sides.

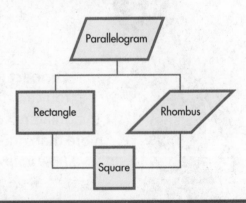

Do You Understand?

Convince Me! When can a rectangle be a rhombus? Can a rhombus be a rectangle? Explain using examples.

Name _____

In **1** through **4**, tell whether each statement is true or false.

1. All rectangles are squares.

2. Every rhombus is a parallelogram.

3. Parallelograms are special rectangles.

4. A trapezoid can be square.

5. Explain how the family tree diagram on page 652 shows that every square is a rectangle.

6. How are a rectangle and a rhombus alike?

Independent Practice

In **7** through **10**, write whether each statement is true or false.

7. All rhombuses are rectangles.

8. Every trapezoid is a quadrilateral.

9. Rhombuses are special parallelograms.

10. All rectangles are quadrilaterals.

11. What properties does the shape have? Why is it not a parallelogram?

12. Why is a square also a rhombus?

Problem Solving

13. Construct Arguments Draw a quadrilateral with one pair of parallel sides and two right angles. Explain why this figure is a trapezoid.

14. Tools A reflecting pool is shaped like a rhombus with a side length of 6 meters. What is the perimeter of the pool? Explain how you found your answer.

> Think about the properties of a rhombus to help you solve.

15. A bakery sold 73 bagels in the first hour of business. If the bakery had 246 bagels to start with, how many bagels were left after the first hour?

246 bagels	
73	?

16. Extend Your Thinking Ann says the figure below is a square. Pablo says that it is a parallelogram. Felix says that it is a rectangle. Can they all be right? Explain.

17. Kudzu is the world's fastest growing weed. The table below shows the growth rate of kudzu.

Day (d)	1	2	3	4	5	6
Inches	12	24	■	■	■	72

Which is a rule for the table?

A $d + 11$
B $d - 11$
C $d \div 12$
D $d \times 12$

18. All parallelograms have opposite sides parallel. Are squares and other rectangles parallelograms? Explain.

> Make sure your answer is simple, complete, and easy to understand.

Name _____

Solve & Share

The area of a rug measures 36 square feet. Carla thinks the rug is a square. Sam thinks the rug is a rectangle. Can they both be correct? Explain your thinking. **Solve this problem any way you choose.**

You can use **number sense** to analyze a problem. *Show your work!*

Problem Solving

Lesson 12-6
Use Reasoning

TEKS 5.1D Communicate mathematical ideas, reasoning, and their implications using multiple representations, including symbols, diagrams, graphs, and language as appropriate. Also, 5.5.
Mathematical Process Standards 5.1A, 5.1B, 5.1C

Digital Resources at PearsonTexas.com

Solve   Learn   Glossary   Check   Tools   Games

Look Back!

Connect Can you give another example of something that can be described in several different ways?

How Can You Use Information to Draw Conclusions?

A Analyze

You can analyze information to come to a conclusion about a problem.

Test this statement:
A rectangle can be cut in half diagonally to make two identical triangles.

> Test your idea on some rectangles!

B Plan

Test the statement.
Draw a rectangle with the length at the base.

> You can move one triangle onto the other to see if they're identical.

C Plan and Solve

Test again if possible.
Draw a different rectangle. Cut this rectangle diagonally to make two identical triangles.

D Justify and Evaluate

Conclusion
To prove your statement is incorrect you need an example of when the test shows it is incorrect.

Based on the results of the test, the statement appears to be correct.

Do You Understand?

Convince Me! Can all trapezoids be folded in half such that one side folds exactly on top of the other? Explain.

Name _____

☆ Guided Practice *

In **1** and **2**, analyze the information and draw a conclusion about each statement. Is the statement correct or incorrect? If incorrect, give an example to support why.

1. All right triangles are scalene triangles.

2. Two equilateral triangles with equal side lengths can be joined to make a rhombus.

3. **Reason** In the exercise on page 658, how was the conclusion reached?

4. What is another statement you can make and test about rectangles?

5. Write a real-world problem that can be solved by testing a statement and drawing a conclusion.

☆ Independent Practice ☆

In **6** through **12**, test the statement and tell whether it appears to be correct or incorrect. If incorrect, give an example to support why.

6. The sum of the angles of any triangle is 180°.

7. Parallel lines never intersect.

8. All rectangles have four congruent sides.

9. All even numbers are composite.

> What does it mean for a number to be composite?

10. All triangles have at least two acute angles.

11. The sum of the angles of any quadrilateral is 360°.

12. Two angles in a parallelogram each measure 75°. The other two angles each measure 120°.

*For another example, see Set F on page 666.

Topic 12 | Lesson 12-6   **659**

Problem Solving

13. **Reason** What do all of these polygons have in common?

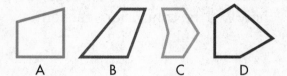

A   B   C   D

14. **Reason** Emma says that the following statement is incorrect.

All quadrilaterals can be divided into two triangles.

Is Emma correct? Explain.

15. **Estimate** Inez drew the picture below and shaded part of it.

What is the best estimate of the shaded portion of the picture?

16. Mike weighs 24 pounds more than Mark. Together they weigh 250 pounds. How much does Mike weigh?

A 113 pounds
B 137 pounds
C 162 pounds
D 226 pounds

17. Ron walks dogs every day. He made a table to keep track of his earnings.

Days (d)	1	2	4	7
Dollars	$8	$16	$32	

Write a rule for the table. How much will Ron earn in 7 days?

18. **Extend Your Thinking** How many whole numbers have exactly two digits? Explain how you found your answer.

19. Lucy buys 2.8 pounds of apples at $1.69 per pound and 3.5 pounds of bananas at $0.79 per pound. She also buys 6 oranges for $3. About how much does Lucy spend on apples and bananas?

20. Coach Peterson is making teams of players. Use the table.

Teams (t)	1	2	4	9
Players	5	10	20	

Write a rule for the table. How many players are needed to make 9 teams?

Another Look!

Test the statement: Any square can be cut in half by a diagonal. The result is always two isosceles right triangles.

Test the statement:

1. Draw a diagonal.

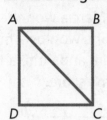

2. Inspect the triangles.

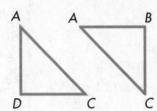

3. Analyze the results.

- $AB = BC$
- $CD = DA$
- Angle $B = 90°$
- Angle $D = 90°$

Conclusion: The statement is true for the square *ABCD*.

Test other squares. If the conclusion is the same, the statement appears to be correct.

In **1** through **6**, test the statement and tell whether it appears to be correct or incorrect. If incorrect, give an example to support why.

1. A square can be cut in half vertically to make two identical rectangles.

2. A parallelogram can be cut in half horizontally to make two identical rectangles.

3. A cut can be made between the two parallel sides of an isosceles trapezoid to make two isosceles trapezoids.

4. A rhombus can be cut in half by a diagonal to make two isosceles triangles.

5. A rhombus is different from a parallelogram because there is only one pair of parallel opposite sides.

6. If one angle of a triangle measures 54° and the other angle measures 36°, the other angle has to be an acute angle.

7. One pint of blueberries contains about 80 berries. Lee's fruit salad recipe calls for 20 blueberries per serving. She has all of the other fruit necessary for the salad, but only 1 quart of blueberries. How many servings of the fruit salad can Lee prepare?

8. Which statement is correct?

⭐

A All triangles have right angles.

B Any two triangles can be joined to make a rhombus.

C All rectangles can be cut in half horizontally to make two identical rectangles.

D All squares can be cut in half vertically to make two identical squares.

9. Extend Your Thinking Determine whether the statement is correct or incorrect. Explain your answer.

A square can be a rhombus, and Figure X is a rhombus, so Figure X must be a square.

10. Use a Strip Diagram Marcia and Tim played ping-pong. Marcia won the game with a score of 21. She won by 7 points. Use the strip diagram and write an equation to find Tim's score.

21	
s	7

11. Estimate Mr. Walker has a new motorcycle that gets 40 miles per gallon. About how many miles can Mr. Walker drive on 8.9 gallons of gas?

Think about which operation you need to use.

12. Tools Anil is growing tomatoes and lettuce. He collected the information in the table.

Row	1	2	3	4	5
Tomato Plants	2	4	6	8	10
Lettuce Plants	4	8	12	16	

Find the number of lettuce plants in Row 5. What is the relationship between the number of lettuce plants and the number of tomato plants in each row?

1. Deborah has two cats, Duncan and Cleo. The cats eat a total of $1\frac{1}{6}$ cups of cat food each day. Duncan eats $\frac{1}{3}$ cup of food twice a day. If Cleo eats twice a day, how many cups of food does she get at each meal?

A $\frac{1}{4}$ cup   **C** $\frac{1}{2}$ cup

B $\frac{1}{3}$ cup   **D** $\frac{2}{3}$ cup

Applying Math Processes

- How does this problem connect to previous ones?
- What is my plan?
- How can I use tools?
- How can I use number sense?
- How can I communicate and represent my thinking?
- How can I organize and record information?
- How can I explain my work?
- How can I justify my answer?

2. Estimate Jasmine sells ladybugs to gardeners. Each bag contains 500 ladybugs. If she sells 32 bags on Monday and 19 bags on Tuesday, about how many ladybugs did she sell in all?

3. Formulate a Plan A rectangle has a perimeter of 66 meters. The length of the rectangle is twice the width. Find the length and width of the rectangle.

4. Which operation would you perform first to evaluate the expression?

$$22 + 15 \div 3 \times 2 - 1$$

A $22 + 15$ **C** 3×2

B $15 \div 3$ **D** $2 - 1$

5. Which of the figures shown does **NOT** appear to have a right angle?

A

B

C

D

6. Extend Your Thinking Dave drew the quadrilateral family tree shown. Did Dave show the relationships correctly? If not, what errors did he make?

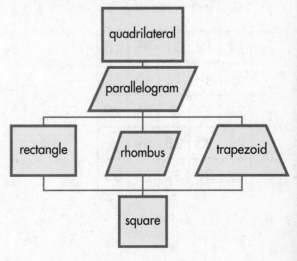

TOPIC 12 Number Sense

Error Search

Find each expression that is not correctly evaluated. If an expression is incorrectly evaluated, use the order of operations to find the correct value.

1. $4 + 8 \times 7$
evaluates to 64

2. $15 \div 3 \times 2 - 1$
evaluates to 9

3. $(22 + 8) \div 2 - 4$
evaluates to 22

4. $120 + 5 \div 5$
evaluates to 121

5. $9 + 5 + 3 - 2 \times 4$
evaluates to 60

6. $44 \div 2 + (17 + 3) \div 4$
evaluates to 27

7. $8.4 + 12.5 \times 2.1 + 4.5$
evaluates to 48.39

8. $(18 \times 10) +$
$(15 + 200) - 8 \div 2$
evaluates to 391

9. $(3.5 + 11.5) \times 8 + 17.5$
evaluates to 19.375

Compatible Numbers

Mental Math Draw loops around two or more numbers next to each other, across or down, with a sum of 60 or 100. Look for compatible numbers (numbers that are easy to compute with mentally).

10. Find sums of 60.

17	12	31	45	18
8	44	16	15	14
29	27	9	24	28
11	23	28	54	6
12	37	32	25	35

11. Find sums of 100.

25	18	54	12	16
75	54	46	85	15
33	73	27	7	14
45	62	19	68	2
22	38	81	25	84

Name _____

Set A | pages 627–632

Name the polygon and state whether it is regular or irregular.

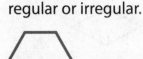

The polygon has six sides that are all equal in length and angles that are equal in measure. It is a regular hexagon.

Remember that a regular polygon has sides of equal length and angles of equal measure.

Name the polygon and state whether it is regular or irregular.

1.   **2.**

Set B | pages 633–638

Classify the triangle by the measures of its angles and the lengths of its sides.

Since one of the angles is right, this is a right triangle. Since two of the sides are the same length, this is an isosceles triangle.

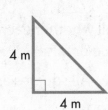

4 m

4 m

It is a right, isosceles triangle.

Remember that right, obtuse, and acute describe the angles of a triangle. Equilateral, scalene, and isosceles describe the sides of a triangle.

Classify each triangle by the measures of its angles and the lengths of its sides.

1.
60°
60° 60°

2.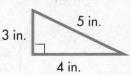
5 in.
3 in.
4 in.

Set C | pages 639–644

Classify the quadrilateral. Then find the missing angle measure.

The quadrilateral has two pairs of parallel sides with all sides the same length. It is a rhombus.

4 cm
? 60°
4 cm   4 cm
60° 120°
4 cm

The sum of the measures of the angles in a quadrilateral is 360°.

$360° - (60° + 60° + 120°) = 120°$

So, the missing angle measure is 120°.

Remember that the sum of the angles of a quadrilateral is 360°.

Classify the quadrilateral. Then find the missing angle measure.

1.
3 cm
110°   ?
70°   110°
6 cm

2.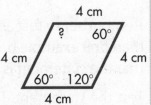
4 ft
?
5.7 ft   4 ft
45°
8 ft

Set D | pages 645–650

Many special **quadrilaterals** have special **properties**.

A **trapezoid** has exactly one pair of parallel sides.

A **parallelogram** has two pairs of equal parallel sides.

A **rectangle** is a parallelogram with 4 right angles.

A **rhombus** is a parallelogram with 4 equal sides.

A **square** is a parallelogram with 4 right angles and 4 equal sides.

Identify each quadrilateral. Describe each quadrilateral by as many names as possible.

1. 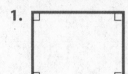   2.

3.   4.

Set E | pages 651–656

This family tree diagram shows how special quadrilaterals are related to each other.

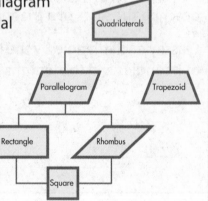

Tell whether each statement is true or false.

1. All squares are rectangles.

2. Every parallelogram is a rectangle.

3. Rhombuses are special parallelograms.

4. All trapezoids are quadrilaterals.

Set F | pages 657–662

Test if the following statement appears to be correct or incorrect. If incorrect, give an example why.

Statement The sum of the angle measures in any rectangle is 180°.

Test the Statement
Draw a rectangle. Find the sum of the angle measures. $90° + 90° + 90° + 90° = 360°$

Conclusion
The statement is incorrect.

Remember to test a statement using more than one example before drawing a conclusion that the statement is correct.

Test the statement. Tell if it appears to be correct or incorrect. If incorrect, give an example to support why.

1. The sum of two prime numbers equals a prime number.

Name _____

1. Harry drew the triangles shown. Which of the following correctly describes the triangles?

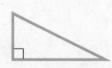

A Both triangles have a right angle.

B Only one triangle has an acute angle.

C Both triangles have at least two obtuse angles.

D Both triangles have at least two acute angles.

2. A right triangle has an angle whose measure is 35°. What is the measure of the third angle in the triangle?

A 35°

B 55°

C 72.5°

D 145°

3. Sabra's glasses have lenses that are the shape shown in the picture below. Which of the following could **NOT** be used to describe the lenses?

A Quadrilateral

B Regular polygon

C Hexagon

D Opposite sides parallel

4. The necklace charm shown has one pair of parallel sides. What type of quadrilateral is the charm?

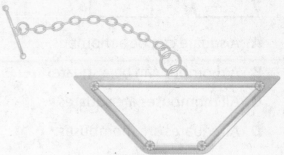

5. Which of the following can be used to describe the square below?

A Opposite sides are perpendicular.

B All angles are obtuse.

C Adjacent sides are parallel.

D All sides are the same length.

6. Nat says that a square is a rectangle because it has 4 right angles. Amy says that a square is a rhombus because it has 4 equal sides. Who is correct? Explain.

7. Pika drew the rhombuses shown. Which statement is incorrect, based on these figures?

A A square can be a rhombus.

B A rhombus can be a square.

C All rhombuses are squares.

D All squares are rhombuses.

8. This quadrilateral has one pair of parallel sides. What is it?

A Square

C Rhombus

B Trapezoid

D Rectangle

9. Steve drew a regular octagon. How many equal sides does his figure have?

⓪	⓪	⓪	•	⓪	⓪
①	①	①		①	①
②	②	②		②	②
③	③	③		③	③
④	④	④		④	④
⑤	⑤	⑤		⑤	⑤
⑥	⑥	⑥		⑥	⑥
⑦	⑦	⑦		⑦	⑦
⑧	⑧	⑧		⑧	⑧
⑨	⑨	⑨		⑨	⑨

10. A sail on a sailboat is a triangle with two sides perpendicular and each side is a different length. What are the two terms that could be used to describe the triangular sail?

A Isosceles, right

B Isosceles, acute

C Scalene, right

D Scalene, obtuse

11. Two angles of a parallelogram each measure 115°. What is the degree measure of each of the other two angles?

A 65°   **C** 115°

B 90°   **D** Not here

12. Triangle *HJK* is an isosceles triangle. The measures of angles *J* and *K* are equal. The measure of angle *H* is 100°. What is the degree measure of angle *J*?

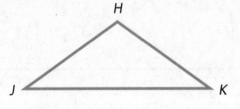

⓪	⓪	⓪	•	⓪	⓪
①	①	①		①	①
②	②	②		②	②
③	③	③		③	③
④	④	④		④	④
⑤	⑤	⑤		⑤	⑤
⑥	⑥	⑥		⑥	⑥
⑦	⑦	⑦		⑦	⑦
⑧	⑧	⑧		⑧	⑧
⑨	⑨	⑨		⑨	⑨

TOPIC 13

Perimeter, Area, and Volume

Essential Questions: How can area and perimeter of rectangles and composite shapes be found? What is the meaning of volume of a solid? How can the volume of a rectangular prism be found?

You use energy 24-7, from getting out of bed in the morning to texting your friends late at night!

Chemical energy from food transforms to mechanical energy to get you out of bed.

That's powerful! And, chemical and mechanical energy moves the bus that takes me to school. Here's a project about everyday energy.

Math and Science Project: Everyday Energy

Do Research Use the Internet and other sources to learn more about these five types of energy: electrical, light, mechanical, sound, and thermal. Make a table of the various types of energy you use every day. Include at least one example of how you use each type of energy.

Journal: Write a Report Include what you found. Also in your report:

- Draw a diagram of your classroom and label where and how 3 types of energy are used.

- Estimate how far your desk is from a light energy source and add this dimension to your sketch.

- Use your diagram to make up and solve problems involving the perimeter, area, and volume of your classroom.

Review What You Know

Vocabulary

Choose the best term from the box.
Write it on the blank.

> • cube
> • perimeter
> • rectangle
> • square

1. A quadrilateral with 4 right angles that does not have 4 sides of equal length is called a _____ .

2. A solid figure with exactly 6 square-shaped faces is called a _____ .

3. The total distance around a picture frame is called its _____ .

Area

Find the area of each figure.

4.
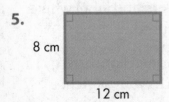
6 ft

10 ft

5.

8 cm

12 cm

Operations

Find each product or quotient.

6. 16 × 6   7. 3 × 42

8. 216 ÷ 3   9. 128 ÷ 4

10. (5 × 6) × 3   11. (6 × 6) × 6

12. Joanie has two 12-inch-long wood pieces and two 16-inch-long wood pieces. What is the combined length of the wood pieces?

   A 28 inches
   B 32 inches
   C 56 inches
   D 192 inches

Finding Area

13. Writing to Explain Niko used square tiles to make a rectangle with 2 rows and 7 tiles in each row. Explain how you can find the area of the rectangle.

My Word Cards

Use the examples for each word on the front of the card to help complete the definitions on the back.

perimeter

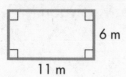

6 m

11 m

Add the side lengths:
Perimeter = 11 + 6 + 11 + 6 = 34 m

formula

formula for perimeter of a rectangle:
$$P = (2 \times \ell) + (2 \times w)$$

P = perimeter
ℓ = length
w = width

area

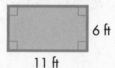

6 ft

11 ft

Multiply length by width:
Area = 11 × 6 = 66 square feet

composite shape

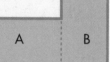

A   B

This composite shape is made up of rectangle A and rectangle B.

volume

Multiply length by width by height:
Volume = 4 × 2 × 2 = 16 cubic units

cubic unit

1 unit   1 unit

1 unit

The volume of the cube is 1 cubic unit.

cube

rectangular prism

My Word Cards

Complete the definition. Extend learning by writing your own definitions.

A _____ is a rule that uses symbols.

_____ is the distance around the outside of any polygon.

A figure that is made up of two or more shapes is called a _____.

_____ is the number of square units needed to cover a surface or figure.

A _____ is the volume of a cube that measures 1 unit on each side.

_____ is the number of cubic units needed to fill a solid figure.

A _____ is a solid figure with six rectangular faces.

A _____ is a solid figure with six identical squares as its faces.

672

Name _____

Solve & Share

A rectangular playground is 4 units long and 2 units wide. Use the grid to find the number of units of fence needed to enclose the shape. *Solve this problem any way you choose.*

⊙ TEKS 5.4H Represent and solve problems related to perimeter and/or area and related to volume. Also, 5.4B. Mathematical Process Standards 5.1A, 5.1C, 5.1D, 5.1F, 5.1G

Connect You can use a grid to find the distance around a real-world figure. *Show your work!*

Digital Resources at PearsonTexas.com

Solve   Learn   Glossary   Check   Tools   Games

Look Back!

Connect Ideas Would the perimeter of the playground change if it was 2 units long and 4 units wide? Tell how you know.

How Can You Find the Distance Around a Polygon?

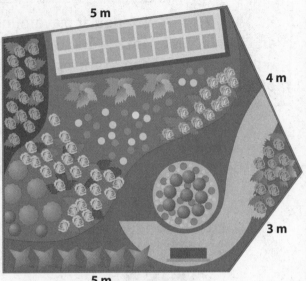

The city wants to build a new fence around the rose garden in the town square. Perimeter is the distance around the outside of any polygon. Use the picture to help you solve the problem.

You can use addition to find the perimeter of a polygon.

B

Can you find the total length of the new fence needed?

Perimeter is equal to the sum of the side lengths of a polygon.

Add the lengths of the sides.

$$P = 5 + 5 + 4 + 3 + 5$$
$$P = 22 \text{ m}$$

The perimeter of the rose garden is 22 m.

C Since the longest side lengths are the same, multiplication can be used in the equation.

$$P = 5 + 5 + 4 + 3 + 5$$
$$P = (3 \times 5) + 4 + 3$$
$$P = 15 + 7$$
$$P = 22 \text{ m}$$

So, the perimeter of the rose garden is 22 m.

Do You Understand?

Convince Me! In the example, the side lengths were added in the order they appear on the drawing of the garden. To find perimeter, do the side lengths have to be added in the order they are shown? Explain.

Another Example

A formula is a rule that uses symbols.

Use a formula to find the perimeter of a square.

Perimeter = 4 × side

$P = 4 \times s$

$P = 4 \times 29 = 116$ cm

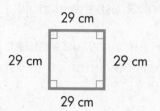

29 cm

29 cm   29 cm

29 cm

☆ Guided Practice *

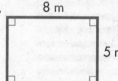

In **1**, find the perimeter of the figure.

1.
8 m

5 m

Tip: The opposite sides of a rectangle are the same length.

What operations might you use?

2. Look at the dimensions of the garden at the top of page 674. If the longest sides of the garden were 9 meters, how long would the fence need to be?

3. **Reason** How can you apply what you have found in Exercise 1 about perimeter to other rectangles?

☆ Independent Practice ☆

In **4** through **6**, find the perimeter of each figure.

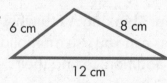

4.
6 cm   8 cm

12 cm

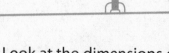

5.
12 m

12 m   12 m

12 m

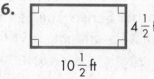

6.
$4\frac{1}{2}$ ft

$10\frac{1}{2}$ ft

Problem Solving

In **7** through **9**, use the triangle.

7. Justify Alfonso said that the perimeter of this triangle is 66 centimeters. What was his error?

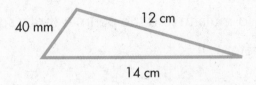

40 mm

12 cm

14 cm

8. What is the perimeter of the triangle? Show your work.

9. Classify the triangle by the lengths of its sides and by the measures of its angles.

10. Connect What is the perimeter of this United States flag?

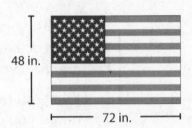

48 in.

72 in.

11. Reason Maria says her pencil is 1.7 meters long. Is this measurement reasonable? Explain.

Is a meter a customary or metric unit of measurement?

12. Stan has $2\frac{3}{4}$ pounds of oranges, $1\frac{1}{3}$ pounds of lemons, and $1\frac{3}{4}$ pounds of limes. How many pounds of fruit does Stan have in all?

13. Number Sense The perimeter of an equilateral triangle is 51 feet. What is the length of each of its sides?

A 13 ft

B 15 ft

C 17 ft

D 21 ft

14. Extend Your Thinking With what kinds of polygons can you use multiplication, instead of addition, to find their perimeters? Explain.

Name _____

Homework 13-1
Perimeter

Another Look!

> Here are two ways to find perimeter, the distance around a figure.

You can add.

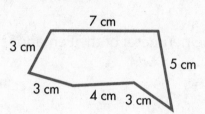

$3 + 3 + 7 + 5 + 3 + 4 = 25$

So, the perimeter of the figure is 25 cm.

You can use a formula.

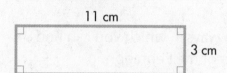

$P = (2 \times \ell) + (2 \times w)$
$P = (2 \times 11) + (2 \times 3)$
$P = 22 + 6 = 28$ cm

So, the perimeter of the rectangle is 28 cm.

In **1** through **9**, find the perimeter of each figure.

1.

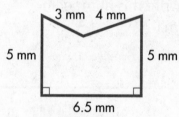

2.

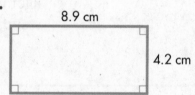

3.

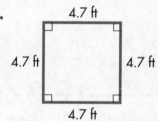

4.

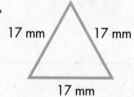

5.

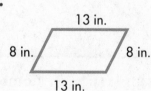

6.

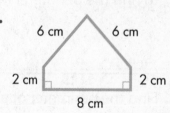

7.

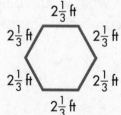

8.

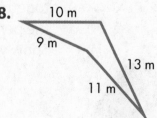

9.

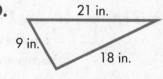

Digital Resources at PearsonTexas.com   **Topic 13** | Lesson 13-1   **677**

In **10** through **12**, use the picture.

10. Is the Pentagon near Washington, D.C., a regular pentagon? Explain.

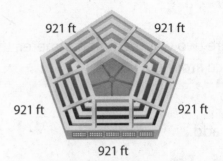

921 ft   921 ft

921 ft   921 ft

921 ft

11. Describe two ways in which you can find the perimeter of the Pentagon.

12. What is the perimeter of the Pentagon?

13. It takes Neptune about 165 Earth years to complete one orbit around the Sun. How many Earth months does it take Neptune to orbit the Sun once?

14. The planet Neptune was discovered in 1846. Neptune's average distance from the Sun is four billion, four hundred ninety-eight million, two hundred fifty-two thousand, nine hundred kilometers. Write this number in standard form.

15. Extend Your Thinking Suppose you cut a square shape in half, as shown. What formula can you write to find the perimeter of one part of the figure?

16. Find the perimeter of a parallelogram with sides measuring $3\frac{3}{10}$ meters, $8\frac{5}{10}$ meters, $3\frac{3}{10}$ meters, and $8\frac{5}{10}$ meters.

A $23\frac{8}{10}$ m

B $23\frac{3}{5}$ m

C $24\frac{6}{10}$ m

D 24 m

You can draw a picture to help you solve this problem!

17. Communicate Suppose you have two squares, each with a side length of 18 inches. If you put the two squares together side-by-side, what would be the perimeter of the combined figure? Show your work.

678

Name _____

Solve & Share

Use grid paper to draw a 10-by-4 rectangle. How can you find the area of this rectangle? *Use grid paper to solve this problem.*

🔹 TEKS 5.4H Represent and solve problems related to perimeter and/or area and related to volume.
Mathematical Process Standards 5.1C, 5.1D, 5.1E, 5.1F, 5.1G

Digital Resources at PearsonTexas.com

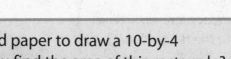

Solve   Learn   Glossary   Check   Tools   Games

Select and Use Tools
You can use a grid to find the area of a figure. *Show your work!*

Look Back!

Justify Count the number of squares in the figure. Can you tell why square units are used to measure area? Justify your answer.

How Can a Formula Be Used to Find Area?

A-Z

The area of a figure is the amount of surface it covers. What are the areas of the baseball infield and the tennis court?

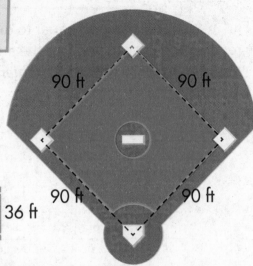

90 ft 90 ft

90 ft 90 ft

Can you tell the shape of each figure?

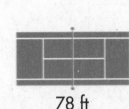

36 ft

78 ft

B The infield is a square because all of its sides are equal and the sides meet at right angles.

Use the formula below to find the area of a square.

Area is measured in square units.

Area = side × side
$A = s \times s$
$A = 90 \text{ ft} \times 90 \text{ ft}$
$A = 8{,}100$ square feet

s

s

The area of the infield is 8,100 square feet.

C The tennis court is a rectangle because its opposite sides are equal.

Use the formula below to find the area of a rectangle.

Area = length × width
$A = \ell \times w$
$A = 78 \text{ ft} \times 36 \text{ ft}$
$A = 2{,}808$ square feet

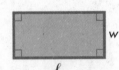

w

ℓ

The area of the tennis court is 2,808 square feet.

Do You Understand?

Convince Me! In the example above, how can you decide which figure has the greater area, without using the formula?

680

© Pearson Education, Inc. 5

☆ Guided Practice *

In **1** and **2**, find the area of each figure.

1. Find the area of a square with a side that measures 34 centimeters.

2. Find the area of a rectangle with length 21 meters and width 9 meters.

3. Which two dimensions are multiplied when finding the area of a rectangle?

4. **Connect** What is the perimeter of the tennis court in the problem at the top of page 680? How is finding the perimeter different from finding the area?

☆ Independent Practice ☆

In **5** through **10**, find the area of each figure.

5.

11 in.
17 in.

6.

14 ft
14 ft

7.
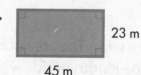
23 m
45 m

8. A square with a side that measures 25 centimeters

9. A rectangle with length 245 inches and width 67 inches

10. A square with a side that measures 31 yards

Problem Solving

In **11** and **12**, use the picture.

11. The East Room of the White House is 79 feet long by 36 feet wide. What is the area of the room?

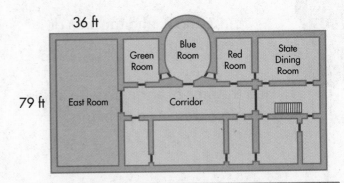

36 ft

79 ft

12. What is the perimeter of the East Room?

---

13. **Connect** What is the perimeter and area of a square with a side that measures 15 meters?

14. **Number Sense** A set of four postcards costs $1.00. Single postcards cost $0.50. What is the least amount of money you can spend to buy exactly 15 postcards?

In **15** and **16**, use the picture.

15. **Explain** How can you find the length of side w if you are given the area of the rectangle?

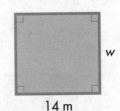

w

14 m

16. **Reason** The area of a playground is 182 square meters. What is the length of side w?

---

17. Ben's mom wants to buy new carpet for the family room that measures 12 feet by 11 feet. She can purchase the carpet on sale for $6 per square foot including installation. How much will Ben's mom spend to carpet the family room?

A $132
B $791
C $792
D $794

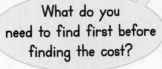

What do you need to find first before finding the cost?

18. **Extend Your Thinking** Which has the greater area: a square with a side that measures 7 meters, or a 6-meter by 8-meter rectangle? How much more area does that figure have? Show your work.

Name _____

Another Look!

You can use square units to find the amount of surface area that a figure covers.

You can use a formula to find the area of rectangles.

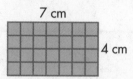

7 cm

4 cm

$A = \ell \times w$
$A = 7 \text{ cm} \times 4 \text{ cm}$
$A = 28$ square cm or 28 sq cm

You can use a formula to find the area of squares.

5 ft

5 ft

$A = s \times s$
$A = 5 \text{ ft} \times 5 \text{ ft}$
$A = 25$ square ft or 25 sq ft

In **1** through **9**, find the area of each figure.

1.   58 ft

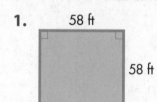

58 ft

2.   5.5 in.

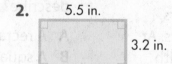

3.2 in.

3.

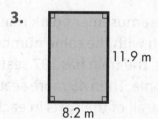

11.9 m

8.2 m

4.

12.3 cm   12.3 cm

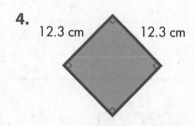

5.

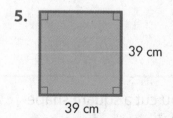

39 cm

39 cm

6.   2 in.

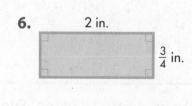

$\frac{3}{4}$ in.

7. A rectangle with length 42 meters and width 30 meters

8. A rectangle with length 17 feet and width 22 feet

9. A square with sides that each measure 2.7 centimeters

For **10** through **12**, use the information in the picture.

10. What is the perimeter of an Olympic-size swimming pool?

11. What is the area of the swimming pool?

12. What is the perimeter of each lane?

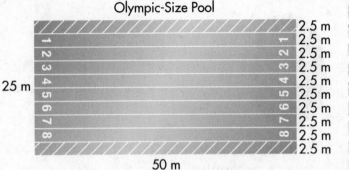

Olympic-Size Pool

2.5 m
2.5 m
2.5 m
2.5 m
2.5 m
2.5 m
2.5 m
2.5 m
2.5 m
2.5 m

25 m

50 m

---

13. Explain Find the area of the rectangle. What units did you use to find the area? Explain.

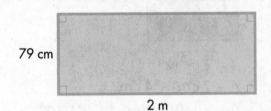

79 cm

2 m

---

14. Represent Write an equation with more than one operation to represent the information. Then solve.

One amusement park ride has 4 cars, each with the same number of seats. At first, the train has 107 seats filled with people. Then 45 more seats are filled. Now all of the seats in each car are filled. How many people are seated in each car?

15. A polygon has a perimeter of 36 inches. ⭐ Each side is exactly 6 inches long. Which of the following figures does this describe?

A   A rectangle
B   A square
C   A regular octagon
D   A regular hexagon

---

16. Extend Your Thinking Suppose you cut a square shape in half, as shown. How can you find the area of one part of the figure?

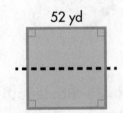

52 yd

Name _____

Solve & Share

The figure shown is a design for a patio. What is the area of the patio? **Solve this problem any way you choose.**

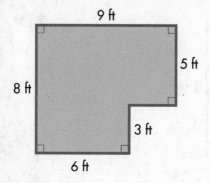

9 ft

5 ft

8 ft

3 ft

6 ft

TEKS 5.4H Represent and solve problems related to perimeter and/or area and related to volume.
Mathematical Process Standards 5.1C, 5.1D, 5.1E, 5.1F, 5.1G

Digital Resources at PearsonTexas.com

 Solve   Learn   A-Z Glossary   Check   Tools   Games

Connect Ideas You can find the area of composite shapes by breaking them into smaller shapes. **Show your work!**

Look Back!

Communicate How does breaking up a composite figure into parts help to find the area of the whole figure?

How Can You Use Area Formulas to Solve Problems?

A

A garden has the shape and size shown here. Mr. White wants to find the area of the garden to know how much fertilizer he will need to buy. What is the area of the garden?

You can use the area formulas to find the area of the whole garden.

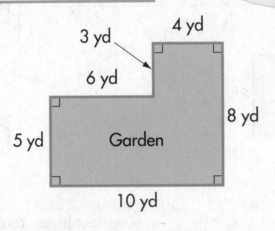

3 yd
4 yd
6 yd
8 yd
5 yd
Garden
10 yd

B

You can separate the composite shape into two rectangles.

Identify the length and width of each rectangle.

3 yd
4 yd
6 yd
B
8 yd
5 yd
A
10 yd

C Use the formula $A = \ell \times w$ to find the area of each rectangle.

Area of Rectangle A

$A = \ell \times w$
$= 6 \times 5$
$= 30$ square yards

Area of Rectangle B

$A = \ell \times w$
$= 4 \times 8$
$= 32$ square yards

Add to find the total area.

$30 + 32 = 62$ square yards.

The area of the garden is 62 square yards.

Do You Understand?

Convince Me! Show a different way to break apart the garden. Is the total area the same? Explain.

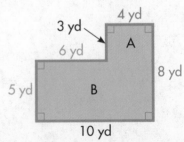

3 yd
4 yd
A
6 yd
8 yd
5 yd
B
10 yd

Name _____

☆Guided Practice*

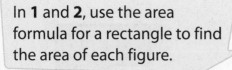

In **1** and **2**, use the area formula for a rectangle to find the area of each figure.

1.

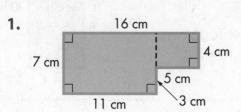

16 cm
7 cm
4 cm
5 cm
11 cm
3 cm

2.

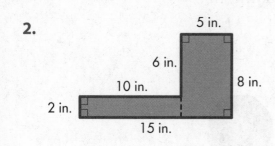

5 in.
6 in.
10 in.
8 in.
2 in.
15 in.

3. In the example at the top of page 686, how did separating the figure into two rectangles make it possible to find the area of the garden?

4. Connect What is the perimeter of the figure in the problem at the top of page 686? How is finding the perimeter of this figure different from finding the perimeter of a rectangle?

☆ Independent Practice ☆

In **5** through **7**, find the area of each figure.

5.

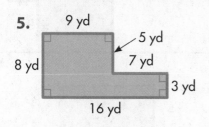

9 yd
5 yd
8 yd
7 yd
3 yd
16 yd

6.

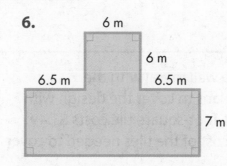

6 m
6 m
6.5 m
6.5 m
7 m

7.

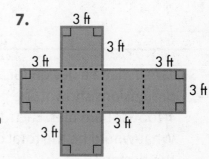

3 ft
3 ft
3 ft
3 ft
3 ft
3 ft
3 ft

Problem Solving

In **8** and **9**, use the diagram of the City Park.

8. It will cost $2 per square foot to plant grass in the park. What will be the total cost, in dollars, of planting the grass?

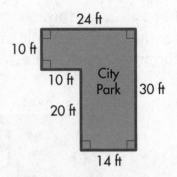

9. The cost of installing iron fencing with gates is $12 per foot. What will be the total cost of installing a fence with gates around the entire perimeter of the park?

10. **Number Sense** The largest breed of rabbit is the White Flemish Giant, which can have a mass of up to 8 kilograms. In a report, Rebecca said that the mass of this kind of rabbit could be up to 800 grams. Was Rebecca's report correct? Explain.

11. Kevin drew a 180° angle and classified it as obtuse. Is Kevin correct? Explain why or why not.

What does it mean for an angle to be obtuse?

12. **Extend Your Thinking** How can you separate the building floor plan into 3 parts to find the total area of the building floor? Show your work.

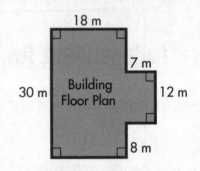

13. Janell made a design for a wall mural with the dimensions shown. She plans to cover the design with 1-foot-square tiles. Each 1-foot-square tile costs $1.49. What would be the total cost of the tiles needed to cover the design?

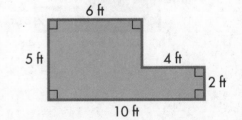

   A $38.00
   B $39.49
   C $40.23
   D $56.62

Name _____

Another Look!

What is the area of the figure?

Think: It is not a familiar figure. So, what smaller figures can help?

Step 1

Separate the figure into two rectangles.

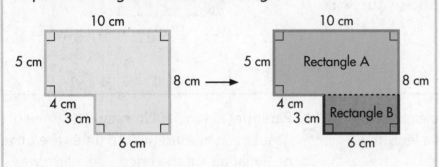

Step 2

Find the area of each rectangle. Add the areas.

Rectangle A:

$A = 10 \times 5 = 50$ sq cm

Rectangle B:

$A = 6 \times 3 = 18$ sq cm

The total area is
$50 + 18 = 68$ sq cm.

In **1** through **6**, find the area of each figure.

1.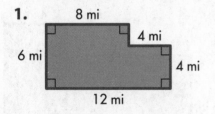
8 mi, 4 mi, 6 mi, 4 mi, 12 mi

2.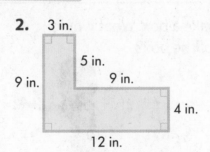
3 in., 5 in., 9 in., 9 in., 4 in., 12 in.

3.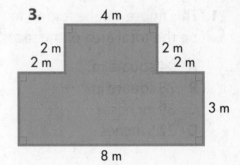
4 m, 2 m, 2 m, 2 m, 2 m, 3 m, 8 m

4.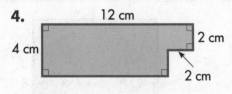
12 cm, 2 cm, 4 cm, 2 cm

5.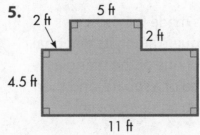
5 ft, 2 ft, 2 ft, 4.5 ft, 11 ft

6.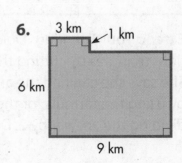
3 km, 1 km, 6 km, 9 km

In **7** and **8**, use the diagram of the Animal Reserve.

7. **Explain** Is it possible to separate the Animal Reserve area into only 2 rectangles to find the total area of the Animal Reserve? Explain.

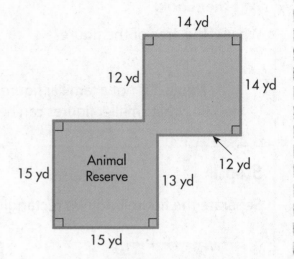

14 yd

12 yd

14 yd

15 yd

Animal Reserve

13 yd

12 yd

15 yd

8. **Extend Your Thinking** How can you separate the Animal Reserve area into 3 parts to find the total area of the reserve? Show your work.

---

9. **Represent** Write an algebraic expression for the word phrase: six times a length *w*.

10. **Personal Financial Literacy** The price of gasoline increased by 0.16 times the price of 1 year ago. If the price 1 year ago was $3, how much was the increase?

---

11. This figure can be folded to make a box. What would be the total area of the faces of the box?

   A 94 square in.
   B 78 square in.
   C 39 inches
   D 22.5 inches

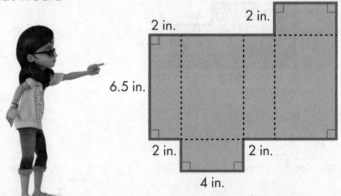

4 in.

2 in.

2 in.

6.5 in.

2 in.

2 in.

4 in.

---

12. **Extend Your Thinking** Dolores made two isosceles right triangles by cutting the square along its diagonal. She says she can find the area of one of the triangles by using the formula for the area of a square, and then dividing the answer by 2. Do you agree? Explain.

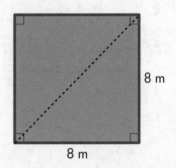

8 m

8 m

Name _____

☆ ☆
Solve & Share

A can of paint will cover 225 square feet of wall. What is the maximum length in feet of an 8-foot high wall that can be covered with one can of this paint? If tape were placed around the sides of this wall before painting, how much tape would you need? *Solve this problem any way you choose.*

TEKS 5.4H Represent and solve problems related to perimeter and/or area and related to volume. **Mathematical Process Standards 5.1A, 5.1B, 5.1C, 5.1D, 5.1E**

Digital Resources at PearsonTexas.com

Solve   Learn   Glossary   Check   Tools   Games

Connect You can use area and perimeter to find solutions to real-world problems. *Show your work!*

Look Back!

Reason How do you know your answer is correct? Tell why there is a maximum length for the wall.

How Can You Use Perimeter and Area to Solve Problems?

Perimeter is the distance around a figure.
Area is the amount of surface a figure covers.
What is the area of the new state park?

How can you find the area if you are only given the perimeter?

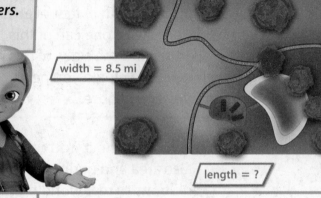

Perimeter = 40 mi

width = 8.5 mi

length = ?

Step 1

Answer the hidden question.

You know the perimeter and the width. Can you find the length?

$8.5 + 8.5 = 17$ Add the two known sides.
$40 - 17 = 23$ Subtract the sum of the two known sides from the perimeter to find the sum of the two unknown sides.
$23 \div 2 = 11.5$ Find the length of one side.

The length of the park is 11.5 miles.

Step 2

Use the answer to the hidden question to answer the original question.

Area = length × width
$\ell = 11.5$ miles
$w = 8.5$ miles

$A = \ell \times w$
$\quad = 11.5 \times 8.5$
$\quad = 97.75$

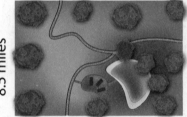

8.5 miles

11.5 miles

The area of the park is 97.75 square miles.

Do You Understand?

Convince Me! The area of the park below is 10 square miles. What is the perimeter? Tell how you decided.

4 miles

692

© Pearson Education, Inc. 5

Guided Practice

In **1** and **2**, find the missing dimension or dimensions.

1.

Area = 216 sq in.   8 in.

x

2.   32 in.

y   y

x

Perimeter = 94 in.

3. A mural is shaped like a rectangle. Its area is 48 square feet. The side lengths are whole numbers. What are possible dimensions of this mural?

4. **Estimation** The length of a rectangular-shaped playground is 25 feet. The area is greater than 200 square feet but less than 300 square feet. What must the width of the playground be, in a whole number of feet?

Independent Practice

In **5** through **8**, find the area or perimeter.

Use the perimeter or area formula to help you solve these problems.

5. What is the perimeter of the rectangle?

Area = 60 sq ft

6 ft

ℓ

6. What is the area of the rectangle?

Perimeter = 30 in.

5 in.

ℓ

7. What is the area of the rectangle?

Perimeter = 84 yd

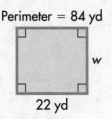

w

22 yd

8. What is the perimeter of the square?

Area = 81 sq mi

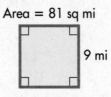

9 mi

For another example, see Set D on page 730.   **Topic 13** | Lesson 13-4   **693**

Problem Solving

9. Greg built a picture frame with a perimeter of 50 inches. How wide is the picture frame?

You can write an equation to help you!

14 in.

10. **Draw a Picture** Julie planted a rectangular garden that is 20 feet long. She placed 56 feet of fencing around her garden. Draw and label a sketch of her garden. What is the width of her garden? What is the area?

11. **Personal Financial Literacy** Wilbur spends $\frac{2}{3}$ of his income, shares $\frac{1}{12}$, and saves the rest. What part of his income does he save? Give the answer in simplest form.

12. A park has an area of 12.5 square miles and a width of 5 miles. What is the perimeter of the park?

   A 35 miles   **C** 14.5 miles

   B 15 miles   **D** 10 miles

13. **Represent** Thelma served five pieces of a pie. The pie was cut into eighths. What fraction of the pie did she serve? Write a multiplication equation using a unit fraction to represent the information.

14. **Extend Your Thinking** Nancy wove the potholder shown. The lengths and widths of the sides are whole numbers. List all of the possible dimensions for the area given. Which dimensions make the most sense for a potholder? Explain.

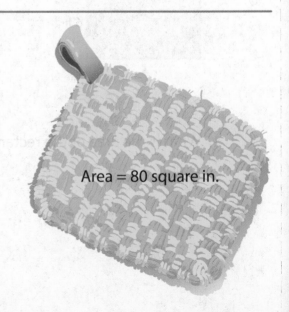

Area = 80 square in.

Name _____

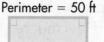
Another Look!

Mrs. Adams is building a sandbox. What is the area of the sandbox?

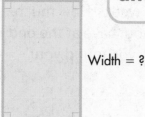

Perimeter = 50 ft

Width = ?

Length = 10 ft

> You know the perimeter. You need to find the area.

Step 1

To find the width, w, you can use the perimeter and length information.

Think: What number times 2 is equal to $50 - 10 - 10$?

$2 \times 15 = 30$

So, $w = 15$.

Step 2

Now that you have found w, use the area formula.

$A = \ell \times w$
$A = 10 \times 15$
$A = 150$ square ft

So, the area of the sandbox is 150 square feet.

In **1** through **6**, find the area or perimeter.

1. What is the area of the rectangle?

Perimeter = 40 in.

w

12 in.

2. What is the perimeter of the rectangle?

Area = 33 sq m

3 m

ℓ

3. What is the perimeter of the square?

Area = 361 sq cm

19 cm

4. What is the area of the square?

Perimeter = 108 mi

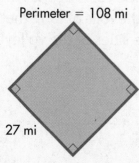

27 mi

5. What is the perimeter of the square?

Area = 1,681 sq cm

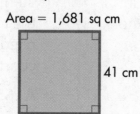

41 cm

6. What is the area of the rectangle?

Perimeter = 70 ft

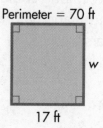

w

17 ft

7. Personal Financial Literacy Raoul saves $14.50 each month for 3 months. He puts his money in the bank and earns $0.33 interest. Hector puts $3.60 each week in his piggy bank for 12 weeks. How much more money does Raoul have at the end than Hector? Tell how you found your answer.

8. Check for Reasonableness Tony measures a drum stick and gets a length of 31 centimeters. Kate converts Tony's measurement to meters and gets 3.1 meters. Is her answer reasonable? Tell how you know.

9. Formulate a Plan Mr. Chen is putting tile down in his kitchen. The kitchen has a perimeter of 48 feet. The tile costs $5 per square foot. How much will it cost Mr. Chen to tile his kitchen?

8 ft

For **10** and **11**, use the poster.

10. Ellen separated the area of a poster into four equal sections. The perimeter of the poster is 120 inches. What is the area of each section of the poster?

11. Connect If Ellen divides each fourth of the poster into 4 equal parts, what fraction of the original poster is each equal part?

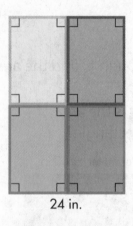

24 in.

12. Extend Your Thinking An art class is planning to paint a rectangular mural with an area of 60 square feet. It has to be at least 4 feet but no more than 6 feet high. How long could the mural be if the length and height have to be whole numbers?

13. Jeff is using tape on the gym floor to mark the sides of a rectangular volleyball court. The court is 18 meters long. It has an area of 162 square meters. Each 20-meter roll of tape costs $2.79. What is the total cost for the rolls of tape that Jeff needs to mark the sides of the volleyball court?

  A $5.58
  B $8.37
  C $11.16
  D $13.95

Name _____

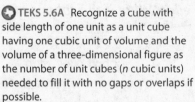

☆ ✫ ☆
Solve & Share

Gina is building a rectangular prism out of sugar cubes for her art class project. She started by drawing a diagram of the rectangular prism that is 4 cubes high and 4 cubes wide. How many cubes does she use to make the prism? *Solve this problem any way you choose.*

Create and Use Representations You can draw a picture to find the number of cubes in a rectangular prism.
Show your work!

◉ TEKS 5.6A Recognize a cube with side length of one unit as a unit cube having one cubic unit of volume and the volume of a three-dimensional figure as the number of unit cubes (*n* cubic units) needed to fill it with no gaps or overlaps if possible.
◉ TEKS 5.6B Determine the volume of a rectangular prism with whole number side lengths in problems related to the number of layers times the number of unit cubes in the area of the base. Also, 5.6. Mathematical Process Standards 5.1A, 5.1C, 5.1D, 5.1F

Digital Resources at PearsonTexas.com

 Solve Learn Glossary Check Tools Games

Side View   Front View

   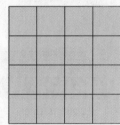

Top View

Look Back!

Connect Ideas Gina decided to change her art project and build a rectangular prism that is 4 cubes long, 3 cubes wide, and 2 cubes high. Use the picture to determine the number of cubes she used.

How Can You Measure Space Inside a Solid Figure?

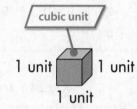

A

Volume is the number of cubic units needed to fill a solid figure. A cubic unit is the volume of a cube measuring 1 unit on each edge. What is the volume of this rectangular prism?

Each cube of a solid figure represents 1 cubic unit.

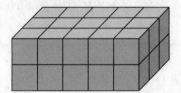

cubic unit

1 unit   1 unit

1 unit

B Use unit cubes to make a model.

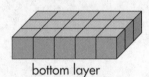

bottom layer

Count the number of cubes.

There are 15 cubes in the bottom layer.

C There are two layers.

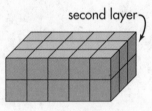

second layer

Multiply the volume of the bottom layer by 2.

The volume of the prism is 2 × 15 or 30 cubic units.

Do You Understand?

Convince Me! What is the volume of the solid shown below? How did you decide?

698

☆ Guided Practice*

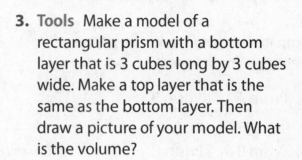

In **1** and **2**, use unit cubes to make a model of each rectangular prism. Find the volume.

1.

2.

3. **Tools** Make a model of a rectangular prism with a bottom layer that is 3 cubes long by 3 cubes wide. Make a top layer that is the same as the bottom layer. Then draw a picture of your model. What is the volume?

4. If you add another layer to the top of the prism in Exercise 1, what would the new volume be in cubic units?

☆ Independent Practice ☆

In **5** through **13**, find the volume of each solid. Use unit cubes to help.

5.

6.

7.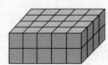

8.

9.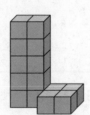

10.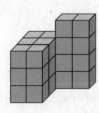

11.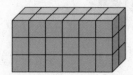

12.

13.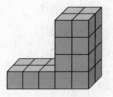

Problem Solving

For **14** through **18**, use the table.

Compare the volumes of the prisms.
Write >, <, or = for each ◯.

14. Prism A ◯ Prism B

15. Prism B ◯ Prism C

16. Prism C ◯ Prism A

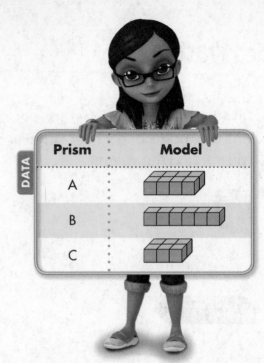

Prism	Model
A	
B	
C	

17. If you added another layer of unit cubes on top of Prism A, what would its volume be in cubic units?

18. If you put Prism C on top of Prism A, what would the volume of the new solid be in cubic units?

19. Connect In an election, 4,713 people voted. Candidate B received $\frac{2}{3}$ of the votes. How many votes did Candidate B receive?

20. Extend Your Thinking Ms. Kellson's storage closet is 3 feet long, 3 feet wide, and 7 feet high. Can she fit 67 boxes that each have a volume of 1 cubic foot in her closet? Explain your answer.

21. Tools Natalie's younger brother made the solid shown using unit cubes. What is the volume of the solid?

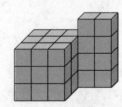

    A 17 cubic units

    B 26 cubic units

    C 35 cubic units

    D 44 cubic units

Name _____

Homework 13-5
Models and Volume

Another Look!

Volume is the measure of space inside a solid figure.

> Volume is measured in cubic units.

Find the volume of this solid by counting the number of unit cubes.

There are 8 cubes in the bottom layer and there are 4 layers. The total number of unit cubes is 32.

So, the volume is 32 cubic units.

In **1** through **9**, find the volume of each solid.

1.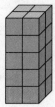

2.

3.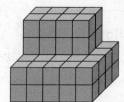

4.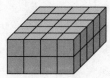

5.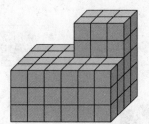

6.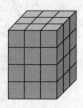

7.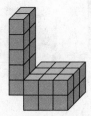

8.

9.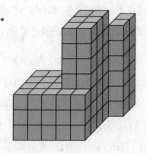

For **10** through **12**, use the table.

10. **Extend Your Thinking** Complete the table. Show some different ways that a rectangular prism can have a volume of 12 cubic units.

11. **Reason** Look across each row of the table. What pattern do you see?

12. **Tools** Use the table to help. How many cubic units are needed to make a model of a rectangular prism that is 4 units long, 3 units wide, and 2 units tall?

Number of Cubes Long 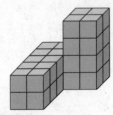	Number of Cubes Wide	Number of Cubes Tall
1	1	12
2	2	3
2	3	
2		1
3	1	
3	2	
3		1
4	1	
6		1

13. A building is 509 feet tall. Each floor is about 14 feet tall. About how many floors does the building have?

Do you need an estimate or an exact answer?

14. Velma and Bruce combined their model buildings to make one building. How can they change each building part to make the parts equal in volume?

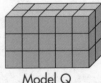

15. Both of the models shown are made up of 1-inch cubes. Which statement about these models is true?

Model Q   Model R

   A Model Q and Model R have the same volume.
   B Model R has a greater volume than Model Q.
   C The volume of Model Q is 7 cubic inches greater than the volume of Model R.
   D The volume of Model Q and Model R combined is 54 cubic inches.

Name _____

☆ ☆
Solve & Share

Rachel built a rectangular prism that is 4 cubes long, 2 cubes wide, and 3 cubes high. Can you find the number of cubes that make up this prism? **Solve this problem any way you choose.**

🔵 **TEKS 5.4G** Use concrete objects and pictorial models to develop the formulas for the volume of a rectangular prism, including the special form for a cube ($V = \ell \times w \times h$, $V = s \times s \times s$, and $V = Bh$). Also, 5.6.
Mathematical Process Standards 5.1A, 5.1C, 5.1D, 5.1E, 5.1F

Digital Resources at PearsonTexas.com

Solve   Learn   Glossary   Check   Tools   Games

You can **create and use a representation** to find the volume of a solid figure. **Show your work!**

Look Back!

Analyze Relationships How many more cubes would be added to make the above rectangular prism 4 cubes high?

How Can You Find the Volume of a Rectangular Prism When the Area of the Base Is Given?

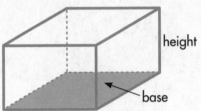

Carrie needs to know how much sand will fill a rectangular prism for her science project. The rectangular prism has a base area of 56 square centimeters and a height of 6 centimeters.

Volume = B × h, where B is the base area.

You can find the base area of the rectangular prism by using $A = \ell \times w$.

height

base

Find the volume of the rectangular prism with a base area of 56 square centimeters and a height of 6 centimeters.

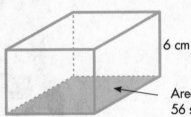

6 cm

Area of base: 56 square cm

$V = B \times h$
$V = 56 \times 6$
$V = 336$ cubic cm

So, the volume of the rectangular prism is 336 cubic cm.

Do You Understand?

Convince Me! In the example above, what are possible length and width dimensions of the base of the rectangular prism? Explain.

Name _____

☆Guided Practice☆

In **1** and **2**, find the volume of each rectangular prism.

1.

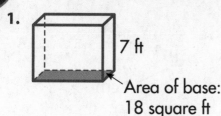

7 ft

Area of base:
18 square ft

2.

9 yd

Area of base:
24 square yd

3. In the example at the top of page 704, what is the shape of the base of the rectangular prism? How do you find the area of that kind of shape?

4. **Represent** A cereal box measures 6 inches long, 2 inches wide, and 10 inches tall. The area of the base is 12 square inches. Draw and label a rectangular prism to represent the box. What is the volume of the figure you drew?

☆Independent Practice ☆

In **5** through **10**, find the volume of each rectangular prism.

5.
2 yd
16 square yd

6.
3 m
52 square m

7.
5 in.
70 square in.

8.
4 cm
64 square cm

9.
11 yd
90 square yd

10.
7 ft
153 square ft

Problem Solving

11. Connect Use the diagram of the ice cube tray. Each small ice cube section has a base with an area of 20 square centimeters. What is the volume of all the ice cube sections in the tray?

What operation(s) do you need to use to solve this problem?

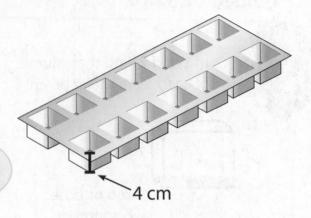

4 cm

12. Extend Your Thinking Two ovens have measurements as shown. Which oven has a greater volume? How much greater is its volume?

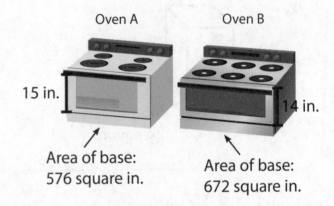

Oven A   Oven B

15 in.

14 in.

Area of base: 576 square in.   Area of base: 672 square in.

13. Only $\frac{1}{3}$ of the students who run in each event win medals at the track meet. If 9 students are running the mile, how many of them will win a medal?

14. Mental Math Harry is in line at the store. He has 3 items that cost $5.95, $4.25, and $1.05. Explain how Harry can add the cost of the items mentally before he pays for them.

15. Which expression can be used to find the ⭐ volume of the carton?

A $(12 \times 12) + 308$
B $12 \times 12 \times 308$
C $308 + 12 + 308 + 12$
D 308×12

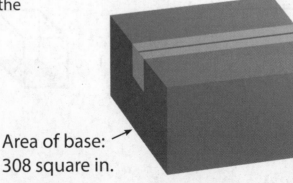

12 in.

Area of base: 308 square in.

Name _____

Another Look!

What is the volume of the rectangular prism? Use cubes to help.

$V = B \times h$

   B = the area of the base
   h = height

What is the area of the base?

$A = \ell \times w$
$A = 4 \times 2$
$A = 8$ sq units

base →

What is the height, h?

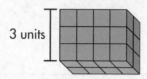

3 units

The prism is 3 units tall.

Use the values to complete the formula.

$V = B \times h$
$V = 8 \times 3$
$V = 24$ cubic units

In **1** through **6**, find the volume of each rectangular prism.

1.

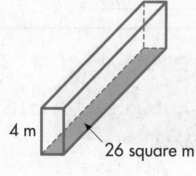

4 m

26 square m

2.

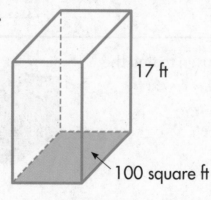

17 ft

100 square ft

3.

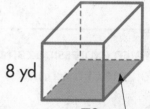

8 yd

72 square yd

4.

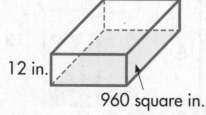

12 in.

960 square in.

5.

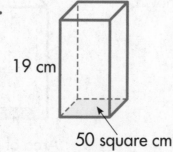

19 cm

50 square cm

6.

6 m

144 square m

---

7. **Math and Science** If two objects are pushed by the same amount of force, the one with the greater mass will move more slowly. For a science project, Kendra used cube blocks, each with the same mass and volume, to build the two rectangular prisms shown. If each rectangular prism is pushed by the same amount of force, which one will move more slowly? Write how the volume amounts compare using > or <.

Rectangular Prism A

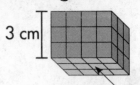

3 cm

Area of base:
12 square cm

Rectangular Prism B

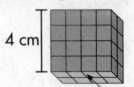

4 cm

Area of base:
8 square cm

8. **Reason** What is the height of a rectangular prism that has a volume of 192 cubic feet and a base with an area of 48 square feet? Show your work.

9. What is the perimeter of the rectangle shown?

23 yd

14 yd

10. ★ Which expression can be used to find the volume of the brick?

A 28 × 2.25
B (2.25 + 2.25) × 28
C (2.25 × 2.25) + 28
D 28 + 2.25 + 28 + 2.25

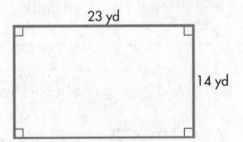

2.25 in.

Area of base:
28 square in.

11. **Extend Your Thinking** Two cereal boxes have measurements as shown. Which box has less volume? How much smaller is its volume?

Cereal Box A

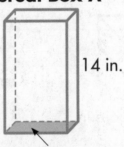

14 in.

Area of base:
16 square in.

Cereal Box B

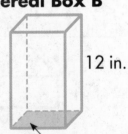

12 in.

Area of base:
21 square in.

Name _____

☆ **Solve & Share** ☆

Kevin needs a new aquarium for his fish. The aquatic store has a fish tank in the shape of a rectangular prism that measures 5 feet × 2 feet × 4 feet. Kevin needs a fish tank that has a volume of at least 35 cubic feet. Will this fish tank be big enough? *Solve this problem any way you choose.*

Formulate a Plan
You can use the formula $V = \ell \times w \times h$ to find the volume of a rectangular prism. *Show your work!*

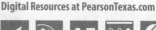

○ **TEKS 5.4G** Use concrete objects and pictorial models to develop the formulas for the volume of a rectangular prism, including the special form for a cube ($V = \ell \times w \times h$, $V = s \times s \times s$, and $V = Bh$). Also, 5.6, 5.6B. **Mathematical Process Standards** 5.1A, 5.1B, 5.1C, 5.1D, 5.1E

Digital Resources at PearsonTexas.com

Solve	Learn	Glossary	Check	Tools	Games

Look Back!

Reason Would the volume of this figure change if the dimensions were $\ell = 2$ feet, $w = 4$ feet, $h = 5$ feet? Explain.

How Can You Use a Formula to Find the Volume of a Rectangular Prism?

Volume is the number of cubic units needed to fill a solid figure.

Find the volume of the rectangular prism if each cubic unit represents 1 cubic foot.

You know that $V = B \times h$. Here is another formula to find the volume of a rectangular prism.

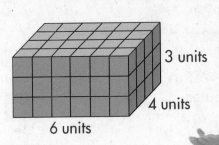

3 units

4 units

6 units

B If the measurements of a rectangular prism are given in length ℓ, width w, and height h, then use this formula to find volume V:

Volume = (length $\times$ width) $\times$ height

$V = \ell \times w \times h$

The base area is length $\times$ width.

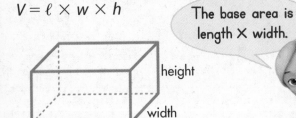

height

width

length

C Use the formula to find the volume of the rectangular prism.

$V = \ell \times w \times h$
$V = 6 \times 4 \times 3$
$V = 72$ cubic feet

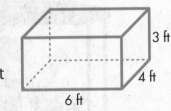

3 ft

4 ft

6 ft

The volume of the rectangular prism is 72 cubic feet.

Do You Understand?

Convince Me! Give the dimensions of a different model made out of cubes that also has a volume of 72 cubic feet. Explain how you decided.

© Pearson Education, Inc. 5

Another Example

How Can You Find the Volume of a Cube?

A cube is a type of rectangular prism. A cube has six faces that are identical squares.

$V = s \times s \times s$

$V = 7 \times 7 \times 7$

$V = 343$ cubic units

The volume of the cube is 343 cubic units.

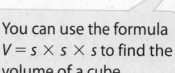

You can use the formula $V = s \times s \times s$ to find the volume of a cube.

☆Guided Practice*

In **1** and **2**, find the volume of each rectangular prism.

1.

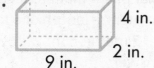

4 in.

2 in.

9 in.

2.

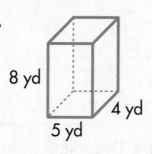

8 yd

4 yd

5 yd

3. How is this volume formula, $V = \ell \times w \times h$, similar to the volume formula, $V = B \times h$?

4. **Represent** A wooden block measures 5 centimeters long, 3 centimeters wide, and 2 centimeters tall. Draw a rectangular prism to show the block and label it. What is the volume of the block?

Independent Practice ☆

In **5** through **7**, find the volume of each rectangular prism.

5.

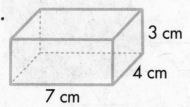

3 cm

4 cm

7 cm

6.

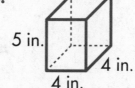

5 in.

4 in.

4 in.

7.

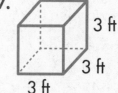

3 ft

3 ft

3 ft

Problem Solving

For **8** and **9**, use the picture of the dictionary.

9 in.

7 in.

8. Connect The dictionary is 3 inches thick. What is the volume of the dictionary?

9. Number Sense A school orders 10 dictionaries. They cost $25 each. The school also pays $15 for shipping. How much does the school pay to get the new dictionaries? Show your work.

What operations do you need to use to solve this problem?

---

10. Estimation The Outer Bay exhibit at the Monterey Bay Aquarium has a viewing window that is 56.5 feet long, 17 feet tall, and 13 inches thick. Estimate its volume in cubic feet.

Remember, 12 inches = 1 foot

11. Extend Your Thinking What is the height of a rectangular prism that has a volume of 280 cubic meters, a length of 8 meters, and a width of 7 meters? Show how you found your answer.

---

12. Nat used the expression $3s - 17$ to find the cost of 3 shirts after a discount. What is the value of the expression if $s = 20$?

13. Number Sense The height of a tree is 8.19 meters. What is the height rounded to the nearest tenth of a meter?

---

14. Which expression can be used to find the volume ⭐ of this wooden box?

    A $(6 \times 4) \times 3$
    B $(6 \times 4) + 3$
    C 6×4
    D $2 \times (6 \times 4 \times 2)$

3 in.

4 in.

6 in.

712

© Pearson Education, Inc. 5

Name _____

Another Look!

What is the volume of a rectangular prism that has a length of 2 centimeters, a width of 4 centimeters, and a height of 3 centimeters?

3 cm
4 cm
2 cm

A model with unit cubes can show the meaning of ℓ, w, and h.

$V = \ell \times w \times h$ ℓ = length w = width 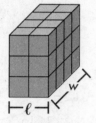 ℓ = 2 cm w = 4 cm	h = height 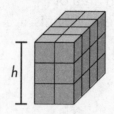 h h = 3 cm	Insert the values in the formula. $V = \ell \times w \times h$ $V = (2 \times 4) \times 3$ $V = 8 \times 3$ $V = 24$ cubic cm

In **1** through **6**, find the volume of each rectangular prism.

1.

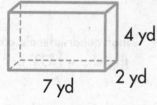

4 yd
7 yd   2 yd

2.

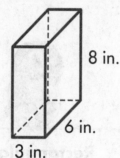

8 in.
6 in.
3 in.

3.

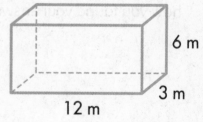

6 m
3 m
12 m

4.

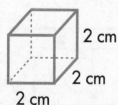

2 cm
2 cm
2 cm

5.

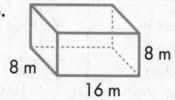

8 m
8 m
16 m

6.

7 yd
5 yd
11 yd

7. Write an expression for the volume of the bar magnet.

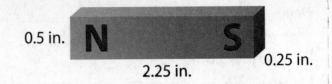

0.5 in.
2.25 in.
0.25 in.

8. Connect The front door of a house is 80 inches tall. What is the volume of the door, in cubic inches?

2 in.

36 in.

9. The living room in the house has an area of 224 square feet and a width of 14 feet. What is the length of the room?

10. Extend Your Thinking A cube has a volume of 1,000 cubic feet. What is the length of an edge of the cube? Show how you found your answer.

11. A quadrilateral has all sides the same length and no right angles. What is the name of the quadrilateral?

What quadrilaterals can this shape **NOT** be?

12. Which statement is true about the two rectangular prisms shown?

A Rectangular Prism G and Rectangular Prism H have the same volume.

B Rectangular Prism G has a greater volume than Rectangular Prism H.

C The volume of Rectangular Prism H is 10 cubic meters greater than the volume of Rectangular Prism G.

D The combined volume of Rectangular Prism G and Rectangular Prism H is 490 cubic meters.

Rectangular Prism G

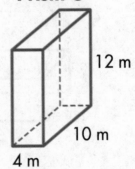

12 m
10 m
4 m

Rectangular Prism H

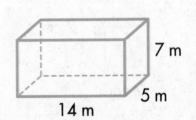

7 m
5 m
14 m

Name _____

☆ ☆
Solve & Share

Ariel is thinking of a three-dimensional figure that is made by combining two rectangular prisms. Can you find the volume of this three-dimensional figure? *Solve this problem any way you choose.*

 TEKS 5.4H Represent and solve problems related to perimeter and/or area and related to volume. Also, 5.6. Mathematical Process Standards 5.1D, 5.1E, 5.1F, 5.1G

Digital Resources at PearsonTexas.com

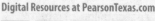

Solve   Learn   Glossary   Check   Tools   Games

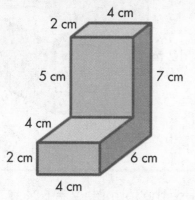

2 cm   4 cm

5 cm   7 cm

4 cm

2 cm   6 cm

4 cm

Analyze Relationships
You can find the volumes of rectangular prisms within a three-dimensional figure. *Show your work!*

Look Back!

Communicate How did you separate the solid into simpler prisms? Write the dimensions of each of the prisms.

How Can You Use Volume Formulas to Solve Problems?

The shape and size of a storage building are shown in the figure. The building supervisor wants to find the volume to determine how much storage space is available. What is the volume of the building?

You can find the volume of this figure by using the formula for a rectangular prism.

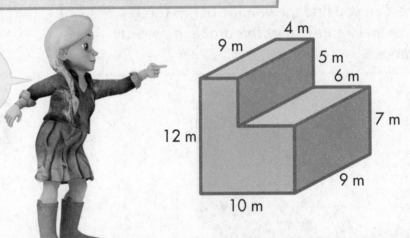

B The building can be separated into two rectangular prisms. Identify the measurements for the length, width, and height of each prism.

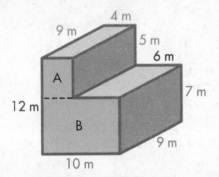

C Use the formula $V = \ell \times w \times h$ to find the volume of each rectangular prism.

Volume of Prism A	Volume of Prism B
$V = \ell \times w \times h$	$V = \ell \times w \times h$
$= 4 \times 9 \times 5$	$= 10 \times 9 \times 7$
$= 180$	$= 630$

Add to find the total volume.

$180 + 630 = 810$

The volume of the storage building is 810 cubic meters.

Do You Understand?

Convince Me! How else could you divide the solid above into two rectangular prisms? What are the dimensions of each prism?

Name _____

In **1** and **2**, find the volume of each solid figure.

In **3** and **4**, use the shape below. The dashed line separates it into two rectangular prisms, A and B.

1.

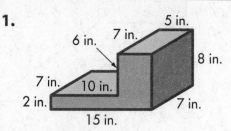

5 in.
6 in. 7 in.
8 in.
7 in. 10 in.
2 in. 7 in.
15 in.

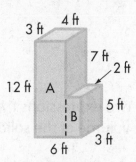

3 ft 4 ft
7 ft
2 ft
12 ft A
5 ft
B
6 ft 3 ft

3. What is the length, width, and height of Prism A? What is the length, width, and height of Prism B?

2.

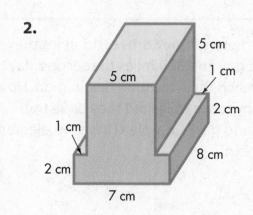

5 cm
5 cm
1 cm
2 cm
1 cm
8 cm
2 cm
7 cm

4. Reason How else could you separate the shape into two rectangular prisms?

In **5** through **7**, find the volume of each solid figure.

5.

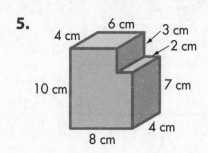

6 cm 3 cm
4 cm 2 cm
10 cm 7 cm
4 cm
8 cm

6.

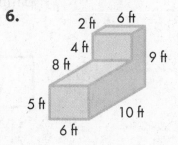

2 ft 6 ft
4 ft
8 ft 9 ft
5 ft
6 ft 10 ft

7.

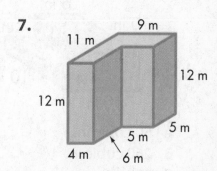

9 m
11 m
12 m
12 m
5 m
4 m 5 m
6 m

Problem Solving

For **8** and **9**, use the drawing of the solid figure.

8. Communicate How would you find the volume of the figure shown?

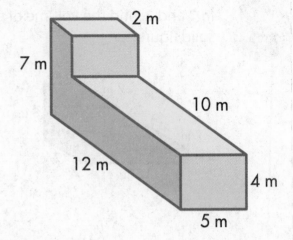

9. Represent Write two expressions that can be added to find the volume of the solid figure.

---

10. Extend Your Thinking A solid figure is separated into two rectangular prisms. The volume of Rectangular Prism A is 80 cubic feet. Rectangular Prism B has a length of 6 feet and a width of 5 feet. The total volume of the solid figure is 200 cubic feet. What is the height of Rectangular Prism B? Show your work.

11. The Peters family drove 615 miles the first day and 389 miles the second day to reach their vacation destination. How many fewer miles did they drive the second day? Complete the strip diagram to help.

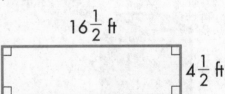

---

12. What is the volume of this solid figure?

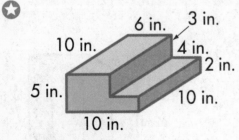

A 50 cubic in.

B 260 cubic in.

C 380 cubic in.

D 500 cubic in.

13. The rectangle shows the dimensions of Richard's patio. Find the perimeter of the patio in feet.

$16\frac{1}{2}$ ft

$4\frac{1}{2}$ ft

Name _____

Another Look!

What is the volume of the solid figure?

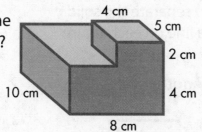

Make sure you find the ℓ, w, and h of each rectangular prism.

Separate the solid figure into rectangular prisms.	Find the volume of each rectangular prism.	Add the volumes.
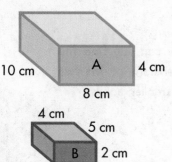	**Prism A:** $V = \ell \times w \times h$ $V = 8 \times 10 \times 4$ $V = 80 \times 4$ $V = 320$ cubic cm	$320 + 40 = 360$
	Prism B: $V = \ell \times w \times h$ $V = 4 \times 5 \times 2$ $V = 20 \times 2$ $V = 40$ cubic cm	So, the volume of the solid figure is 360 cubic cm.

In **1** through **6**, find the volume of each solid figure.

1.
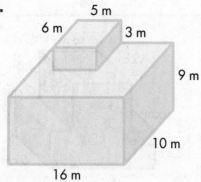

2.
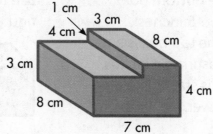

3.
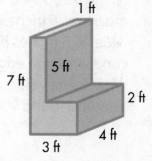

4.

5.
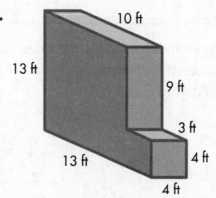

6.
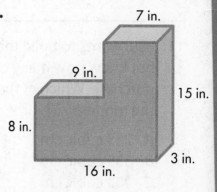

For **7** and **8**, use the drawing of the solid figure.

7. Draw a Picture Find two different ways to separate the solid figure into two rectangular prisms. Draw a line on each figure below to show each way.

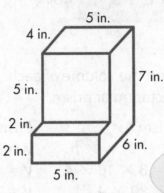

One Way

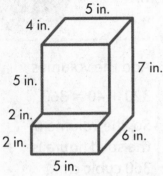

Another Way

How can you find the dimensions of the two smaller solids?

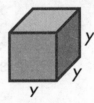

8. Represent Choose one way that you found. Write and solve an equation for the volume of each rectangular prism. Then find the volume of the solid figure.

9. Extend Your Thinking Ashley is stacking two boxes on a shelf. The bottom box measures 6 inches long × 5 inches wide × 5 inches high. The top box is a cube with one edge measuring 4 inches. What is the volume of this stack? Explain how you found your answer.

10. Represent Write an expression you can use to find the volume of the cube. Then find the volume if $y = 9$ feet.

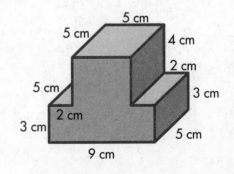

y
y
y

11. Paul wants to build this model with clay, but he does not know how many cubic centimeters of clay to purchase. Which of the following is the volume of the model?

A   235 cubic cm

B   335 cubic cm

C   405 cubic cm

D   935 cubic cm

Name _____

⭐ **Solve & Share**

Find the number of cubes needed to extend the following pattern. There is 1 cube in the top row. Each row has 1 more cube than the row above it. Find the total number of cubes in a shape with 15 cubes in the bottom row. *Solve this problem any way you choose.*

🌟 TEKS 5.1F Analyze mathematical relationships to connect and communicate mathematical ideas. Also, 5.6A. Mathematical Process Standards 5.1, 5.1B, 5.1C, 5.1D, 5.1G

Digital Resources at PearsonTexas.com

Solve   Learn   Glossary   Check   Tools   Games

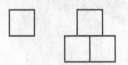

← row 1
← row 2
← row 3

You can use **number sense** to find a pattern to solve the problem. *Show your work!*

Look Back!

Reason If you know the total number of cubes in this shape when there are 15 cubes in the bottom row, how many cubes would be in the shape if there are 16 cubes in the bottom row? Explain.

How Can You Use Objects to Solve a Simpler Problem?

A Analyze

Paul has 27 cubes that are glued together to form a larger cube. He painted all 6 faces of the larger cube. How many of the 27 cubes have paint on 1 face? How many have paint on 2 faces?

You can break apart a problem into simpler ones in order to find a solution.

B Plan

How many cubes have paint on 1 face?

The center cube on each of the 6 faces of the larger cube has paint on 1 face.

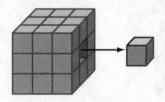

Six of these cubes have paint on 1 face.

C Solve

How many cubes have paint on 2 faces?

Only 1 cube on each of the 12 edges of the larger cube has paint on 2 faces.

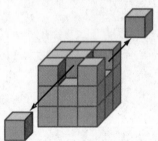

Twelve of these cubes have paint on 2 faces.

Do You Understand?

Convince Me! Wooden posts are used to build garden plots. If the garden plots are built as shown, how many posts are needed for 10 garden plots? Explain how you decided.

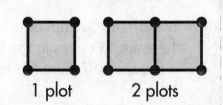

1 plot   2 plots

722

© Pearson Education, Inc. 5

Guided Practice

In **1**, use objects to solve the problem. Use a simpler problem to help.

1. Tools Use cubes to build a large cube with 4 layers. Each layer will have 4 rows of 4 cubes. How many cubes in the large cube will have exactly 1 face showing on the outside?

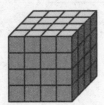

2. Think of gluing the cubes together for the 4 × 4 × 4 cube you made in Exercise 1. Then, think of painting the outside faces. How many cubes will have paint on 2 faces? On 3 faces?

3. Connect Write a real-world problem that involves using objects to help solve a simpler problem.

Independent Practice

In **4** through **6**, use objects to solve the problem. Use a simpler problem to help.

4. Tools Alicia uses timbers to build steps. The pattern is shown for 1, 2, 3, and 4 steps. How many timbers will she need to build 10 steps?

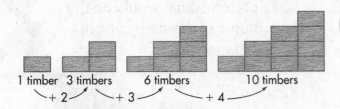

Remember to look for a pattern to help solve the problem.

5. Use the information in Exercise 4. When the 10 steps have been made, how many of the timbers that were used to make the 10 steps would not be stepped on?

6. One rectangular prism has 3 cubes in each of 5 layers. Another rectangular prism has 5 cubes in each of 3 layers. Which prism has the greater volume?

Problem Solving

7. Jeremiah wants to make a display of boxes. He wants a single box on the top layer. Layers that are below the top layer must form a square, with each layer being 1 box wider than the layer above it. The display can only be 4 layers high. What is the total number of boxes that will be in the display?

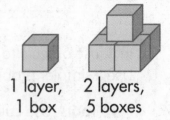

1 layer, 1 box   2 layers, 5 boxes

---

8. Katherine is constructing a patio using the design shown at the right.

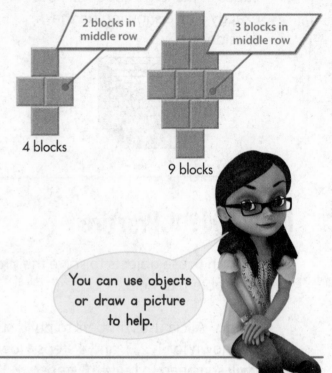

2 blocks in middle row

3 blocks in middle row

4 blocks

9 blocks

a What is the total number of blocks that she will need in order to have 5 blocks in the middle row?

b What is the total number of blocks that she will need in order to have 6 blocks in the middle row?

c Explain What do you notice about the number of blocks in the middle row compared to the total number of blocks?

You can use objects or draw a picture to help.

---

9. Extend Your Thinking Keiko made a rectangular prism using centimeter cubes. The prism had a length of 4 centimeters, a width of 3 centimeters, and a height of 3 centimeters. How many cubes in the rectangular prism are not corner cubes? Show how you found your answer.

10. Tonya used unit cubes to build a pattern. What would be the volume of the sixth cube in the pattern?

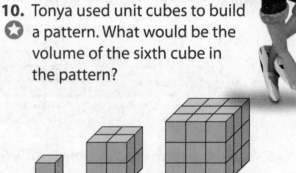

1st   2nd   3rd

A 36 cubic units

B 125 cubic units

C 216 cubic units

D 343 cubic units

Name _____

Another Look!

Lily used centimeter cubes to make a rectangular prism with a length of 5 centimeters, a width of 2 centimeters, and a height of 3 centimeters. How many cubes of the prism are not corner cubes?

Use a model if it can help show the information better than words.

Step 1

Use objects. Make a model.

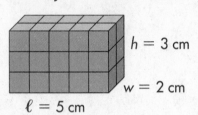

$h = 3$ cm
$w = 2$ cm
$\ell = 5$ cm

Step 2

Use a simpler problem.

How many cubes on 1 face are not corner cubes?

C	1	2	3	C
4	5	6	7	8
C	9	10	11	C

On 1 face, 11 cubes are not corner cubes.

Step 3

Use your answer from the simpler problem to solve.

There are 2 equal faces on this rectangular prism.

$2 \times 11 = 22$

So, 22 cubes on the prism are not corner cubes.

In **1** through **3**, use objects to solve the problem. Use a simpler problem to help.

1. Bo used centimeter cubes to make a rectangular prism with a length of 4 centimeters, a width of 2 centimeters, and a height of 3 centimeters. How many cubes of the prism have exactly 2 faces showing?

   Draw your model. Show your simpler problem. Solve.

2. How many cubes have exactly one face showing?

3. How many cubes have exactly three faces showing?

4. **Tools** Four people can be seated at a table. If two tables are put together, six people can be seated. How many tables are needed to make a long table that will seat 20 people?

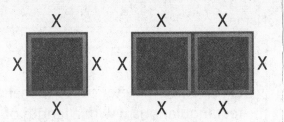

5. An artist wants to cut 1 square sheet of copper into 16 equal pieces. Before he cuts, he will draw segments on the sheet of copper showing where to make the cuts. How many horizontal and vertical segments will he need to draw?

6. There are 24 balls in a large bin. Two out of every three are basketballs. The rest are footballs. How many basketballs are in the bin?

7. **Extend Your Thinking** Dija made this solid figure by gluing together a cube and a rectangular prism. After gluing the shapes together, she painted all faces on the solid figure, except the bottom face. What is the total area of the figure that she painted?

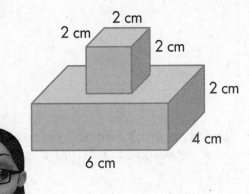

You can draw on the picture to help you find the answer.

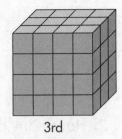

8. Don used centimeter cubes to build rectangular prisms in a pattern. What would be the volume of the fifth rectangular prism in the pattern?

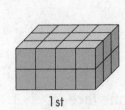
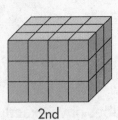

A 96 cubic cm
B 84 cubic cm
C 72 cubic cm
D 60 cubic cm

Name _____

1. **Justify** Yoshi says that $5 \times \frac{1}{10}$ is one way to find the next number in the pattern. Explain why you agree or disagree with Yoshi.

$$\frac{1}{10} \quad \frac{1}{5} \quad \frac{3}{10} \quad \frac{2}{5}$$

Applying Math Processes

- How does this problem connect to previous ones?
- What is my plan?
- How can I use tools?
- How can I use number sense?
- How can I communicate and represent my thinking?
- How can I organize and record information?
- How can I explain my work?
- How can I justify my answer?

2. **Reason** I am a triangle and I have no sides that are the same length. What kind of triangle am I?

3. **Analyze Information** From school, Luke walked 3 blocks right. Next, he walked 1 block up. Then, he walked 2 blocks left. Last, he walked 1 block up. Give the ordered pair for his starting position.

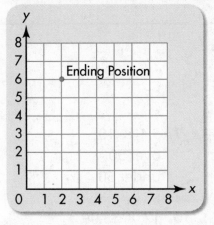

4. **Represent** A ticketing service charges a fixed amount on top of any ticket bought. Write an algebraic expression that shows the total cost including the fixed amount.

DATA	Ticket Price (*t*)	$18.25	$26.50	$29.75
	Total Charge	$22.75	$31.00	$34.25

5. **Extend Your Thinking** Sal's grape vine grew $\frac{1}{6}$ foot one week and $\frac{3}{4}$ foot the next week. Sal estimates that it grew a total of 1 foot. Is his estimate greater or less than the actual total? Explain. What numbers might he have used to estimate?

6. Mrs. Jenkins knitted $\frac{5}{6}$ of a foot of a scarf in the morning. She knitted some more of the scarf in the afternoon. She knitted $1\frac{1}{4}$ feet in all. How many feet of the scarf did she knit in the afternoon?

   A $\frac{1}{2}$ foot   C $\frac{7}{12}$ foot

   B $\frac{5}{12}$ foot   D $2\frac{1}{12}$ feet

Error Search

Find each problem that is not correct. Circle what is wrong and rewrite the problem so it is correct.

1. $24 - 12 \div 6 \times 3$
$12 \div 6 \times 3$
2×3
6

2. $20 + 16 \div 4 + 9$
$36 \div 4 + 9$
$9 + 9$
18

3. $7 \times 15 - 10 \div 2$
$105 - 10 \div 2$
$105 - 5$
100

4. $80 + (60 - 12) + 7 \times 5$
$80 + 48 + 7 \times 5$
$128 + 7 \times 5$
135×5
675

Over or Under

Estimation   Circle the better estimate.

5. 1.2×1.8
over 1
under 1

6. 3.78×100
over 400
under 400

7. 5.4×10
over 50
under 50

8. $2.6 \times 1,000$
over 2,000
under 2,000

9. 4.9×100
over 500
under 500

10. $12 \times \$3.09$
over $36
under $36

11. 31.59×0.48
over 31
under 31

12. 8.9×6.8
over 60
under 60

13. 0.26×5
over 5
under 5

14. $\$61 \times 0.12$
over $6.00
under $6.00

15. 0.5×0.4
over 1
under 1

16. $1.7 \times \$0.90$
over $2.00
under $2.00

Name _____

Set A pages 673–678

Find the perimeter.

 7 m
12 m

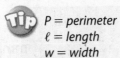 **TIP** P = perimeter
ℓ = length
w = width

Use a formula:

Perimeter = (2 × length) + (2 × width)
$P = (2 × ℓ) + (2 × w)$
$P = (2 × 12) + (2 × 7)$
$P = 24 + 14 = 38$ m

Add the side lengths:

$P = 12 + 7 + 12 + 7 = 38$ m

> For finding the perimeter of a square, use the formula $P = 4s$.

Remember that the perimeter is the distance around a figure.

Reteaching

Find each perimeter.

1.
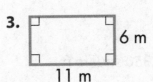 7 m
7 m

2. 23.2 in.   23.2 in.
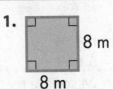
42.5 in.

3.
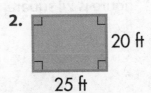 6 m
11 m

Set B pages 679–684

Use a formula to find each area.

For squares:

 7 ft

Use $A = s × s$.
$A = 7 × 7 = 49$ square ft

For rectangles:

 6 in.
8 in.

Use $A = ℓ × w$.
$A = 8 × 6 = 48$ square in.

Remember to use the correct area formula for each polygon.

Find each area.

1.
 8 m
8 m

2.
 20 ft
25 ft

Set C pages 685–690

Find the area of the figure.

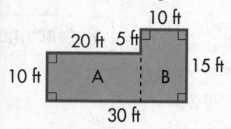

Separate the figure into two rectangles.

Use the formula $A = \ell \times w$ to find the area of each rectangle.

Rectangle A

$A = 20 \times 10$
   $= 200$ square ft

Rectangle B

$A = 10 \times 15$
   $= 150$ square ft

Add the areas of the rectangles to find the total area:

$200 + 150 = 350$

The area of the figure is 350 square ft.

Remember to try to separate a figure into familiar figures.

Find the area of each figure.

1.

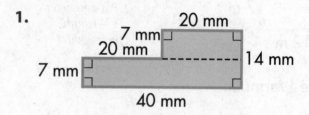

2.

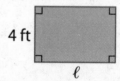

Set D pages 691–696

The perimeter of the green figure is 22 feet. What is the area of the figure?

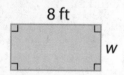

8 ft

w

$P = (2 \times \ell) + (2 \times w)$
$22 = (2 \times 8) + (2 \times w)$
$22 = 16 + 2w$
$22 - 16 = 2w$
$6 = 2w$
So, $w = 3$.

$A = \ell \times w$
   $= 8 \times 3$
   $= 24$ square feet
So, the area of the figure is 24 square feet.

Remember that area is measured in square units.

Remember that you can use the formulas that you know to help find missing dimensions.

Find the missing dimension.

1. The area of the purple figure is 28 feet. What is the perimeter of the figure?

4 ft

ℓ

2. The perimeter of the figure is 50 meters. What is the area of the figure?

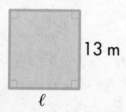

13 m

ℓ

Set E | pages 697–702

Find the number of cubes needed to make this rectangular prism.

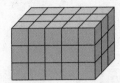

There are 3 rows of 5 cubes in the bottom layer. There are 3 layers.

Multiply to find the total number of cubes.

$3 \times 5 \times 3 = 45$

The volume is 45 cubic units.

Remember, you can multiply the numbers in any order!

Remember that you can find the number of cubes in each layer and then multiply by the number of layers.

Find each volume. You may use cubes to help.

1.

2.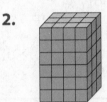

Set F | pages 703–708, 709–714

Find the volume of this rectangular prism.

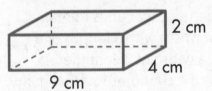
2 cm
4 cm
9 cm

Volume = length × width × height

$V = \ell \times w \times h$
$= 9\text{ cm} \times 4\text{ cm} \times 2\text{ cm}$
$V = 72$ cubic cm

The volume of the prism is 72 cubic cm.

Remember if you know the base area of a rectangular prism, use the formula $V = B \times h$, where B is the base area.

Find each volume. You may use cubes to help.

1. Base area = 42 square m, height = 3 m

2.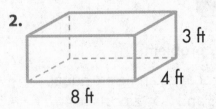
3 ft
4 ft
8 ft

Set G pages 715–720

Some solid figures can be separated into two rectangular prisms.

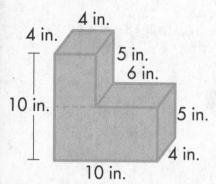

Add the volume of each prism to find the total volume of the solid figure.

$V = (4 \times 4 \times 5) + (10 \times 4 \times 5)$
$= 280$ cubic in.

Remember to identify the length, width, and height of each prism, so that you can calculate the volume of each part.

1. Find the volume.

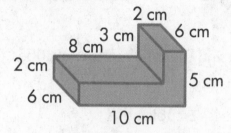

2.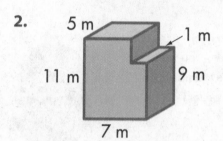

Set H pages 721–726

Ms. Lopez built a rectangular chicken pen, 8 feet long and 6 feet wide. She put 1 post on each corner. Then she put posts along the sides of the rectangle at every 2 feet between the corner posts. How many posts were not corner posts?

Make a model.

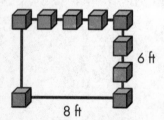

Solve a simpler problem.

Opposite sides of a rectangle are equal.
2 × 3 posts = 6 and 2 × 2 posts = 4
6 + 4 = 10 posts

Remember that you can use objects and a simpler problem to solve.

1. Casey used centimeter cubes to make a rectangular prism with a length of 6 centimeters, a width of 2 centimeters, and a height of 4 centimeters. How many cubes of the prism are not corner cubes?

2. Use the information in Problem 1. How many cubes of the prism have exactly 2 faces showing on the outside?

3. Use the information in Problem 1. How many cubes of the prism have exactly 1 face showing on the outside?

Name _____

1. Julio used unit cubes to make a rectangular prism. What is the volume of the prism?

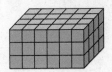

A 18 cubic units

B 54 cubic units

C 72 cubic units

D 108 cubic units

4. Jill's rectangular picture frame has the dimensions shown. Which equation shows the perimeter of the frame?

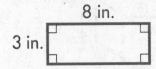

8 in.

3 in.

A 8 × 3 = 24 sq in.

B (2 × 8) + (2 × 3) = 22 in.

C 8 × 4 = 32 in.

D 2 × (8 × 3) = 48 sq in.

2. A rectangular window measures 36 inches wide by 48 inches tall. What is the area of the window?

A 1,728 square inches

B 1,488 square inches

C 864 square inches

D 168 square inches

5. Maria glued sequins around the edges of her rectangular party invitations. If an invitation is 5 inches wide and 2.5 inches tall, what is its perimeter?

A 7.5 in.

B 12.5 in.

C 15 in.

D 20 in.

3. A piece of wood has the dimensions shown. What is the area of the piece of wood?

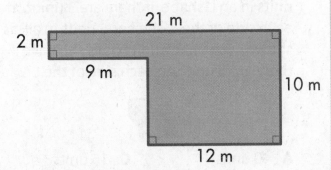

21 m

2 m

9 m

10 m

12 m

A 11 square meters

B 62 square meters

C 138 square meters

D 210 square meters

6. Donna drew the square below. Which equation can she use to find the area of her square?

A $A = 4 \times 4$

B $A = 16 \times 16$

C $A = 4 \times 16$

D $A = 2 \times 16$

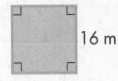

16 m

7. Madeline made the wooden steps shown. What is the volume of the steps?

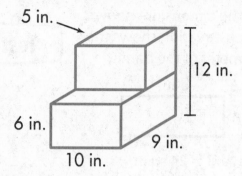

A 72 cubic in.

B 540 cubic in.

C 840 cubic in.

D 1,080 cubic in.

8. For her science project, Nija built a rectangular prism out of foam block. The block had a base area of 225 square inches and a height of 3 inches. What was the block's volume?

A 900 cubic in.

B 675 cubic in.

C 228 cubic in.

D 75 cubic in.

9. Teressa made the letter T out of paper. It has a perimeter of 46 centimeters. What is the missing side length?

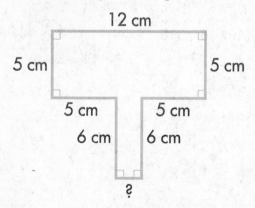

10. What is the volume of the trunk shown?

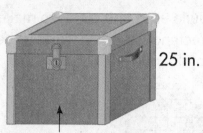

Area of base: 750 square in.

A 775 cubic in.

B 1,550 cubic in.

C 1,875 cubic in.

D 18,750 cubic in.

11. Lily's suitcase measures 9 inches wide, 13 inches long, and 21 inches high. Clara's suitcase measures 3 inches shorter on all sides. What is the combined volume of the two suitcases?

A 7,371 cubic in.

B 3,537 cubic in.

C 2,457 cubic in.

D 1,080 cubic in.

12. Todd's mother is setting up a storage unit rental business. She is arranging the units in an L-shape. If there are 3 units on each side of the L, she has 5 units in all, as shown. How many units does she have if there are 8 units on each side of the L?

A 40 units   **C** 16 units

B 24 units   **D** 15 units

13. Howie used 20 feet of fencing in designing different gardens. Which of the following is **NOT** a design Howie used?

A   6 ft
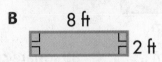
    4 ft

B   8 ft
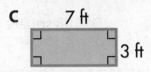
    2 ft

C   7 ft
    3 ft

D   5 ft
    4 ft

14. A table is 9 feet long and has a perimeter of 24 feet. What is the area of the top of the table?

15. A swimming pool has 6 lanes. Each lane is 50 meters long, 2.5 meters wide, and 3 meters deep. What is the volume of the pool?

   A 4,500 cubic meters

   B 2,250 cubic meters

   C 900 cubic meters

   D 750 cubic meters

16. A patio has the shape shown below. What is the area of the patio?

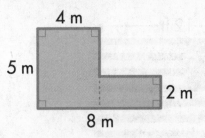

4 m

5 m

2 m

8 m

   A 20 square meters

   B 24 square meters

   C 36 square meters

   D None of these

17. A small building has the dimensions shown. What is the volume of the building?

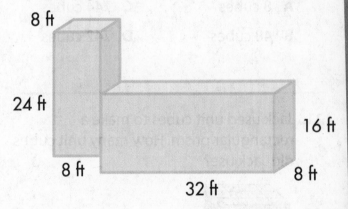

8 ft

24 ft

16 ft

8 ft

32 ft

8 ft

18. What is the volume of the bale of hay?

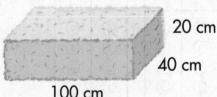

20 cm

40 cm

100 cm

   A 80,000 square cm

   B 80,000 cubic cm

   C 8,000 square cm

   D 8,000 cubic cm

19. The area of the flag is 96 square feet. What is the perimeter of the flag?

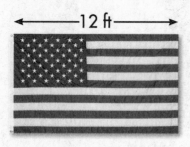

←————12 ft————→

22. Sara is using the piece of wrapping paper shown below to wrap a gift. What is the area of the paper?

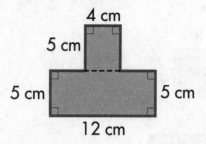

4 cm
5 cm
5 cm   5 cm
12 cm

A 20 square cm   **C** 80 square cm

B 60 square cm   **D** 108 square cm

20. A rectangular prism made of centimeter cubes has a length of 10 centimeters, a width of 15 centimeters, and a height of 5 centimeters. How many cubes of the prism are not corner cubes?

A 8 cubes   **C** 744 cubes

B 48 cubes   **D** 742 cubes

23. In the rectangular prism shown in Problem 21, how many of the unit cubes have exactly one face showing on the outside?

A 2 cubes   **C** 8 cubes

B 6 cubes   **D** 10 cubes

21. Jack used unit cubes to make a rectangular prism. How many unit cubes did Jack use?

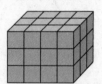

⓪	⓪	⓪	·	⓪	⓪
①	①	①		①	①
②	②	②		②	②
③	③	③		③	③
④	④	④		④	④
⑤	⑤	⑤		⑤	⑤
⑥	⑥	⑥		⑥	⑥
⑦	⑦	⑦		⑦	⑦
⑧	⑧	⑧		⑧	⑧
⑨	⑨	⑨		⑨	⑨

24. Pepper's dog pen measures 4 meters wide and has an area of 20 square meters. What is the perimeter of the pen in meters?

⓪	⓪	⓪	·	⓪	⓪
①	①	①		①	①
②	②	②		②	②
③	③	③		③	③
④	④	④		④	④
⑤	⑤	⑤		⑤	⑤
⑥	⑥	⑥		⑥	⑥
⑦	⑦	⑦		⑦	⑦
⑧	⑧	⑧		⑧	⑧
⑨	⑨	⑨		⑨	⑨

Measurement Units and Conversions

Essential Questions: What are customary measurement units and how are they related? What are metric measurement units and how are they related?

Wind and water carved out the Grand Canyon.

The flowing water of the Colorado River moved rock and soil to help form the canyon. This is called *water erosion.*

That's a lot of movement! Here's a project about the Grand Canyon.

Math and Science Project: Grand Canyon

Do Research Use the Internet and other sources to learn about the Grand Canyon and the Colorado River. Where is the Grand Canyon? How was it formed? What do the different rock layers tell us? Predict how you think the canyon dimensions will change in a million years.

Journal: Write a Report Include what you found. Also in your report:

- Describe the canyon's dimensions.
- Describe the Colorado River's dimensions.
- Define erosion.
- Make up and solve problems involving measurement units and conversions.

Name _____

Review What You Know

Vocabulary

Choose the best term from the box. Write it on the blank.

- customary
- metric
- multiplication
- subtraction

1. A meter is a unit of length in the _____ system of measurement.

2. A foot is a unit of length in the _____ system of measurement.

3. Division has an inverse relationship with _____.

Multiplication

Find each product.

4. 60×6 **5.** 24×3

6. 16×7 **7.** 12×16

8. 100×34 **9.** 10×6

Division

Find each quotient.

10. $144 \div 16$ **11.** $56 \div 7$

12. $1,000 \div 100$ **13.** $176 \div 16$

14. $3,600 \div 60$ **15.** $120 \div 24$

Measurement

Choose the more appropriate unit of measure for each item.

16. the capacity of a swimming pool: liters or milliliters

17. the length of an ear of corn: feet or inches

18. the mass of a gorilla: grams or kilograms

19. the weight of a tennis ball: ounces or pounds

20. Explain Would you use more centimeters or meters to measure the length of car? Explain.

My Word Cards

Use the examples for each word on the front of the card to help complete the definitions on the back.

A-Z

inch (in.)

12 inches (in.) = 1 foot

foot (ft)

1 foot (ft) = 12 inches

yard (yd)

1 yard (yd) = 3 ft = 36 in.

mile (mi)

1 mile (mi) = 1,760 yd = 5,280 ft

capacity

Cups, fluid ounces, pints, quarts, and gallons are all customary units of capacity.

cup (c)

1 cup (c)

1 cup (c) = 8 fluid ounces

fluid ounce (fl oz)

8 fluid ounces (fl oz) = 1 cup

pint (pt)

1 pint (pt) = 2 cups

Complete the definition. Extend learning by writing your own definitions.

A customary unit of length equal to 12 inches is a _____.

A customary unit of length less than 1 foot is an _____.

A customary unit of length equal to 5,280 feet is a _____.

A customary unit of length equal to 3 feet is a _____.

A customary unit of capacity equal to 8 fluid ounces is a _____.

_____ is the volume of a container measured in liquid units.

A customary unit of capacity equal to 2 cups is a _____.

A customary unit of capacity equal to 2 tablespoons is a _____.

My Word Cards

Use the examples for each word on the front of the card to help complete the definitions on the back.

quart (qt)

1 quart (qt) = 2 pints

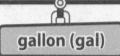

gallon (gal)

1 gallon (gal) = 4 quarts

weight

The weight of the peach is 7 ounces.

ton (T)

1 ton (T) = 2,000 pounds

pound (lb)

1 pound (lb) = 16 ounces

ounce (oz)

16 ounces (oz) = 1 pound

kilometer (km)

1 kilometer (km) = 1,000 meters

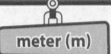

meter (m)

1 meter (m) = 100 centimeters

My Word Cards

Complete the definition. Extend learning by writing your own definitions.

A customary unit of capacity equal to 4 quarts is a _____.

A customary unit of capacity equal to 2 pints is a _____.

A customary unit of weight equal to 2,000 pounds is a _____.

_____ is a measure of how light or heavy something is.

A customary unit of weight less than 1 pound is an _____.

A customary unit of weight equal to 16 ounces is a _____.

A metric unit of length equal to 100 centimeters is a _____.

A metric unit of length equal to 1,000 meters is a _____.

My Word Cards

Use the examples for each word on the front of the card to help complete the definitions on the back.

A-Z

centimeter (cm)

1 centimeter (cm) = 10 milimeters

millimeter (mm)

1,000 millimeters (mm) = 1 meter

liter (L)

1 liter (L) = 1,000 milliliters

milliliter (mL)

1,000 milliliters (mL) = 1 liter

mass

The brick has a mass of 3 kilograms.

milligram (mg)

1,000 milligrams (mg) = 1 gram

gram (g)

1 gram (g) = 1,000 milligrams

kilogram

1 kilogram (kg) = 1,000 grams

My Word Cards

Complete the definition. Extend learning by writing your own definitions.

A metric unit of length less than a centimeter is a _____.

A metric unit of length equal to 10 millimeters is a _____.

A metric unit of capacity less than a liter is a _____.

A metric unit of capacity equal to 1,000 milliliters is a _____.

A metric unit of mass less than a gram is a _____.

_____ is the measure of the quantity of matter in an object.

A metric unit of mass equal to 1,000 grams is a _____.

A metric unit of mass equal to 1,000 milligrams is a _____.

Name _____

Solve & Share

William has a piece of wire that measures 1 yard long. He will use wire to fix several electrical outlets around the house that need repairing. Can you find how many inches of wire he has from this piece? **Solve this problem by using a strip diagram.**

⭐ TEKS 5.7 Select appropriate units, strategies, and tools to solve problems involving measurement. Solve problems by calculating conversions within a measurement system, customary or metric. Mathematical Process Standards 5.1A, 5.1C, 5.1D, 5.1F, 5.1G

Digital Resources at PearsonTexas.com

Solve   Learn   Glossary   Check   Tools   Games

Connect You can show the relationship between yards and inches. **Show your work!**

Look Back!

Connect Ideas How can you convert inches to yards? Would you multiply or divide when converting from a smaller unit to a larger unit? Explain.

A

Some frogs can jump 11 feet. What are some other ways to describe the same distance?

You can convert one unit of measurement to another.

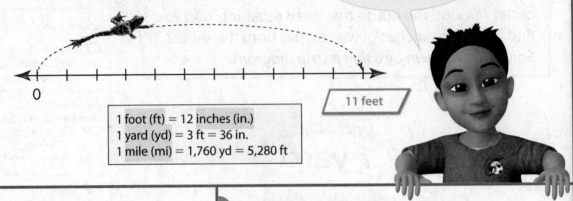

11 feet

1 foot (ft) = 12 inches (in.)
1 yard (yd) = 3 ft = 36 in.
1 mile (mi) = 1,760 yd = 5,280 ft

B **To change larger units to smaller units, multiply.**

11 ft = ☐ in.

You know
1 foot = 12 inches.

11 ft

| 12 in. | 12 in. | 12 in. | 12 in. | 12 in. | 12 in. | 12 in. | 12 in. | 12 in. | 12 in. | 12 in. |

↑
1 ft

Find 11 × 12.

11 × 12 = 132   So, 11 feet = 132 inches.

C **To change smaller units to larger units, divide.**

11 ft = ☐ yd ☐ ft

You know
3 feet = 1 yard.

1 ft
↓

| 1 | 1 | 1 | 1 | 1 | 1 | 1 | 1 | 1 | 1 | 1 |

1 yd   1 yd   1 yd   2 ft left

Find 11 ÷ 3.

11 ÷ 3 = 3 R2   So, 11 feet = 3 yards, 2 feet.

Do You Understand?

Convince Me! In the example above, explain how you could use a mixed number to write 11 feet as an equivalent measure in yards.

Guided Practice

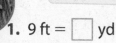

In **1** through **5**, convert each unit of length.

1. 9 ft = ☐ yd   **2.** 288 in. = ☐ yd

3. 5 ft = ☐ in.   **4.** 8 ft 7 in. = ☐ in.

5. 219 in. = ☐ ft ☐ in. or ☐ ft

6. If you want to convert yards to feet, what operation would you use?

7. If you want to convert feet to miles, what operation would you use?

8. Candice drives from Houston, TX, to Crowley, LA. Which customary unit would be appropriate to measure the length of her drive?

Independent Practice

In **9** through **14**, convert each unit of length.

Will your answer be greater than or less than the given measurement?

9. 3 yd = ☐ in.   **10.** 24 ft = ☐ yd   **11.** 2 mi = ☐ ft

12. 56 ft = ☐ yd ☐ ft   **13.** 12 ft 6 in. = ☐ in.   **14.** 6 in. = ☐ ft

In **15** through **17**, compare lengths. Write >, <, or = for each ◯.

15. 100 ft ◯ 3 yd   **16.** 74 in. ◯ 2 yd 2 in.   **17.** 5,200 ft 145 in. ◯ 1 mi 40 in.

In **18** through **20**, write the customary unit that would be appropriate to measure each length.

18. basketball court   **19.** river   **20.** grasshopper

Problem Solving

21. Number Sense Which number would be greater, the height of a tree in feet or the height of a tree in yards?

22. Estimation What is a good estimate for the length of a desk, 1 yard or 12 inches?

23. Personal Financial Literacy Roger earns $24 a week mowing lawns. He shares $\frac{1}{6}$ of his earnings, spends $\frac{2}{3}$, and saves the rest. How many dollars does Roger save? Tell how you found the answer.

24. Reason The dimensions of the nation's smallest post office are 8 feet 4 inches by 7 feet 3 inches. Why would you use the measurement 8 feet 4 inches instead of 7 feet 16 inches?

25. Ariana has 144 peaches. She has to pack 9 boxes with an equal number of peaches. How many peaches should she pack in each box?

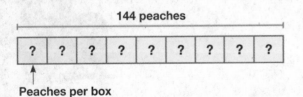

144 peaches

| ? | ? | ? | ? | ? | ? | ? | ? | ? |

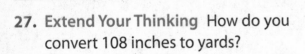

Peaches per box

26. Which measure is less than 435 inches?

- **A** 37 feet
- **B** 36 feet 10 inches
- **C** 12 yards 3 inches
- **D** 12 feet 3 inches

Divide to change smaller units to larger units.

27. Extend Your Thinking How do you convert 108 inches to yards?

28. Justify What is an appropriate customary unit to use to measure the length of a driveway? Justify your answer.

Name _____

Another Look!

Remember:
1 ft = 12 in.
1 yd = 3 ft = 36 in.
1 mi = 1,760 yd = 5,280 ft

How to change from one customary unit of length to another:

Converting from a smaller unit to a larger unit:

6 feet = _____ yards

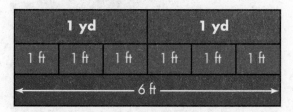

You know 3 ft = 1 yd. **Divide** 6 ÷ 3.

So, 6 ft = 2 yd.

Converting from a larger unit to a smaller unit:

2 feet = _____ inches

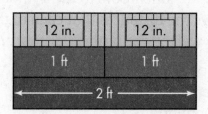

You know 1 ft = 12 in. **Multiply** 2 × 12.

So, 2 ft = 24 in.

In **1** through **9**, convert each unit of length.

1. 12 ft = _____ yd

2. 2 mi = _____ yd

3. 46 in. = _____ ft _____ in.

4. 7 ft = _____ in.

5. 3 mi = _____ ft

6. 108 in. = _____ ft

7. 72 in. = _____ yd

8. 2 ft 3 in. = _____ in.

9. 45 in. = _____ yd _____ in.

In **10** through **12**, compare lengths. Write >, <, or = for each ◯.

10. 64 in. ◯ 5 ft

11. 2 mi ◯ 3,333 yd

12. 36 yd 2 ft ◯ 114 ft 2 in.

In **13** through **15**, write the customary unit that would be appropriate to measure each length.

13. computer screen

14. coastline

15. skyscraper

16. Connect Find the perimeter of the rectangle in yards.

33 in. [rectangle] 75 in.

17. Number Sense Which is greater, 5,280 yards or 1 mile? Would you use yards or miles to measure the distance between two cities?

For **18** and **19**, use the table.

18. Four friends each took a different path walking from the lunchroom to the gymnasium. The table shows the distances that each of them walked. Who walked the farthest distance?

A Rowan
B Janelle
C Domingo
D Lydia

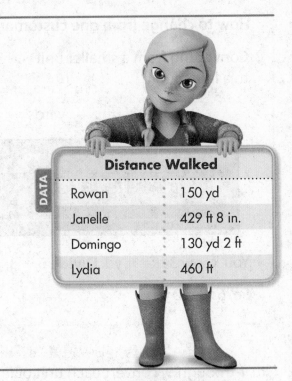

DATA	Distance Walked	
	Rowan	150 yd
	Janelle	429 ft 8 in.
	Domingo	130 yd 2 ft
	Lydia	460 ft

19. Write the distance Domingo walked in feet and in inches.

20. Lucy wants to make different types of cheesecake. Each cheesecake uses $\frac{2}{3}$ pound of cream cheese. She has 2 pounds of cream cheese. How many cheesecakes can she make?

21. Extend Your Thinking The New York City Marathon is 26 miles 385 yards long. How long is it in feet?

Remember:
1 mi = 5,280 ft

22. Explain Jordan is 4 feet 8 inches tall. Her mother is 5 feet 10 inches tall. How much taller is Jordan's mother than Jordan? Give your answer in feet and inches.

23. Extend Your Thinking How can you find the number of inches in 1 mile? Show your work.

Name _____

☆ Solve & Share ☆

A recipe makes 16 cups of soup. How many quarts does the recipe make? *Solve this problem any way you choose!*

 TEKS 5.7 Select appropriate units, strategies, and tools to solve problems involving measurement. Solve problems by calculating conversions within a measurement system, customary or metric.
Mathematical Process Standards 5.1B, 5.1C, 5.1D, 5.1F, 5.1G

Digital Resources at PearsonTexas.com

Solve   Learn   Glossary   Check   Tools   Games

You can formulate a plan to help you convert between different units.

Look Back!

Analyze Relationships Is the number of cups greater than or less than the number of quarts? Why do you think that is?

How Do You Change Units of Capacity?

A

Sue is making punch. She needs 3 cups of orange juice and 6 pints of lemonade. How many fluid ounces of orange juice and how many quarts of lemonade does she need?

1 gallon (gal) = 4 quarts (qt)
1 quart = 2 pints (pt)
1 pint = 2 cups (c)
1 cup = 8 fluid ounces (fl oz)

You can multiply or divide to get from one unit of capacity to a different one.

1 cup   1 pint   1 quart

B **To change a larger unit to a smaller unit, multiply.**

3 c

$3 c = \boxed{} \text{ fl oz}$

| 8 fl oz | 8 fl oz | 8 fl oz |

Find 3 × 8.

3 × 8 = 24

So, 3 c = 24 fl oz.

C **To change a smaller unit to a larger unit, divide.**

$6 \text{ pt} = \boxed{} \text{ qt}$

2 pt = 1 qt

1 pt

| 1 | 1 | 1 | 1 | 1 | 1 |

1 qt   1 qt   1 qt

Find 6 ÷ 2.

6 ÷ 2 = 3

So, 6 pt = 3 qt.

Do You Understand?

Convince Me! Which unit of capacity would be appropriate for measuring each object? How did you decide?

Bathtub _____

Pot for cooking _____

Can of juice _____

Container of milk _____

☆ Guided Practice *

In **1** through **6**, convert each unit of capacity.

1. 32 c = ☐ gal   **2.** 16 qt = ☐ c

3. 48 qt = ☐ pt   **4.** 40 qt = ☐ gal

5. 3 qt 1 pt = ☐ pt

6. 5 pt = ☐ qt ☐ pt

7. Reason Why would you change 4 gallons 5 quarts to 5 gallons 1 quart?

8. Explain Why is $\frac{1}{8}$ cup equal to one fluid ounce?

☆ Independent Practice ☆

In **9** through **20**, convert each unit of capacity.

You may need to convert more than once.

9. 10 pt = ☐ qt   **10.** 48 fl oz = ☐ c   **11.** 70 c = ☐ pt

12. 15 pt = ☐ c   **13.** 36 pt = ☐ qt   **14.** 30 qt = ☐ gal ☐ qt

15. 1 qt = ☐ gal   **16.** 5 gal = ☐ c   **17.** 1 gal 1 c = ☐ fl oz

18. 7 c = ☐ fl oz   **19.** 72 pt = ☐ gal   **20.** 4 pt 3 c = ☐ c

In **21** through **23**, write the unit that would be appropriate to measure each capacity.

21. drinking glass   **22.** gas tank of car   **23.** medicine bottle

Problem Solving

For **24** through **26**, use the aquarium.

24. **Connect** The class aquarium holds 2 gallons of water. How many cups is this? How many fluid ounces is this?

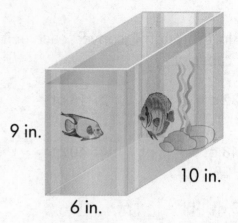

9 in.

10 in.

6 in.

25. Susan finds that 2 pints, 1 cup of water has evaporated from the class aquarium. How much water, in pints, is left in the aquarium?

26. If all of the dimensions of the aquarium were doubled, what would be the volume of the new aquarium?

27. How many 1-cup servings can be ☆ poured from 1 gallon of milk?

A 2
B 4
C 8
D 16

Which operation should you use to solve this problem?

28. **Explain** Lorelei filled her 5-gallon jug with water. How many times could she fill her 2-quart canteen with water from the jug?

29. Carrie has 3 gallons of paint. Bryan has 10 quarts of paint. How many more pints of paint does Carrie have than Bryan?

30. What is an equivalent measurement for 2 cups of oil used in a recipe?

31. **Extend Your Thinking** Use the information in the table. A recipe calls for 3 tablespoons of pineapple juice. A can of pineapple juice is 12 fluid ounces. How many teaspoons of juice are in the can?

DATA

| 1 tablespoon (tbsp) = 3 teaspoons (tsp) |
| 1 fluid ounce (fl oz) = 2 tablespoons (tbsp) |

Name _____

Another Look!

Remember:
1 gal = 4 qt
1 qt = 2 pt
1 pt = 2 c
1 c = 8 fl oz

How to change from one customary unit of capacity to another:

Converting from a smaller unit to a larger unit:

4 pints = _____ quarts

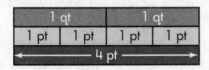

Operation: Divide.

You know 2 pt = 1 qt.

Find 4 ÷ 2; 4 pt = 2 qt

Converting from a larger unit to a smaller unit:

2 gallons = _____ quarts

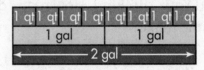

Operation: Multiply.

You know 1 gal = 4 qt.

Find 2 × 4; 2 gal = 8 qt

In **1** through **12**, convert each unit of capacity.

1. 16 fl oz = _____ c

2. 8 gal = _____ qt

3. 3 pt = _____ fl oz

4. 10 c = _____ pt

5. 6 qt = _____ pt

6. 28 c = _____ qt

7. 2 qt = _____ pt

8. 5 c = _____ pt _____ c

9. 3 gal = _____ pt

10. 96 fl oz = _____ c

11. 4 qt = _____ c

12. 9 pt = _____ c

In **13** through **15**, write the unit that would be appropriate to measure each capacity.

13. bathtub

14. cooking pot

15. cereal bowl

16. Estimation Estimate the number of pints in 445 fluid ounces. Explain your work.

17. If you needed only 1 cup of milk, what is your best choice at the grocery store—a quart container, a pint container, or a $\frac{1}{2}$-gallon container?

For **18** and **19**, use the recipe.

18. Sadie is making punch. How many more quarts of lemon-lime juice will she use than orange juice?

19. Extend Your Thinking How many gallons of punch will Sadie make?

Ingredients for Punch
8 quarts lemon-lime juice
4 pints vanilla ice cream
8 cups orange juice

20. Jeremy made 2 quarts of lemonade. Which expression can be used to find the number of fluid ounces of lemonade Jeremy made?

A $2 \times 2 \times 2$
B $2 \times 2 \times 8$
C $2 \times 2 \times 2 \times 2$
D $2 \times 2 \times 2 \times 8$

21. Explain How would you convert a measurement given in fluid ounces into pints?

Which operation would you use?

22. Personal Financial Literacy Callie bought 2 gallons of juice for $2.58 per gallon. She sold the juice in 1-cup servings for $0.75 each. Each serving is $\frac{1}{16}$ gallon. How much more did she get for selling the juice than she paid to buy it? Tell how you found the answer.

23. Which of the following is **NOT** true?

A 7 pints > 2 quarts
B 4 pints 1 cup < 10 cups
C 1 quart > 40 fl oz
D 1 gallon < 8 pints 1 cup

Name _____

☆ ☆
Solve & Share

Maria adopted 4 dogs. All together they eat 1 pound of food a day. If 1 pound is equal to 16 ounces, how many ounces of food will the dogs eat in 4 days? *Solve this problem any way you choose.*

Select and Use Tools
You can use drawings or equations to solve the problem. *Show your work!*

TEKS 5.7 Select appropriate units, strategies, and tools to solve problems involving measurement. Solve problems by calculating conversions within a measurement system, customary or metric. Mathematical Process Standards 5.1C, 5.1D, 5.1F, 5.1G

Digital Resources at PearsonTexas.com

Solve   Learn   Glossary   Check   Tools   Games

Look Back!

Analyze Relationships Which is the larger unit of weight, an ounce or a pound? How can you use this relationship to find the number of ounces in 5 pounds?

How Can You Convert Units of Weight?

An adult African elephant weighs about 5 tons. A baby African elephant weighs about 250 pounds. How many pounds does the adult elephant weigh? How can you convert 250 pounds to tons?

1 ton (T) = 2,000 pounds (lb)
1 pound (lb) = 16 ounces (oz)

To convert from one unit of weight to another, you can use multiplication or division.

about 250 pounds

about 5 tons

B **To convert from larger units to smaller units, multiply.**

5 T = ☐ lb   1 T = 2,000 lb

2,000 lb	2,000 lb	2,000 lb	2,000 lb	2,000 lb

5 T

Find 5 × 2,000.

5 × 2,000 = 10,000

So, 5 T = 10,000 lb.

C **To convert from smaller units to larger units, divide.**

250 lb = ☐ T   2,000 lb = 1 T

? T → [250 lb]

1 T → [2,000 lb]

Find $\frac{250}{2,000}$.

$\frac{250 \div 250}{2,000 \div 250} = \frac{1}{8}$ So, 250 lb = $\frac{1}{8}$ T.

Do You Understand?

Convince Me! When you convert 16 pounds to ounces, do you multiply or divide? Explain.

Name _____

In **1** through **4**, convert each unit of weight.

1. 2,000 lb = ☐ T   **2.** 48 oz = ☐ lb

3. $\frac{1}{2}$ lb = ☐ oz   **4.** 16,000 lb = ☐ T

In **5** and **6**, compare. Write >, <, or = for each ◯.

5. 2 T ◯ 45,000 lb   **6.** 4 lb ◯ 64 oz

7. Explain Would it be best to measure the weight of an egg in tons, pounds, or ounces?

8. Estimate the number of tons in 10,145 pounds.

9. An adult giraffe can weigh up to 3,000 pounds. Does an adult giraffe or an adult elephant weigh more?

☆ **Independent Practice** ☆

In **10** through **15**, convert each unit of weight.

10. 240 oz = ☐ lb   **11.** 8 T = ☐ lb   **12.** 8 lb = ☐ oz

13. 8 oz = ☐ lb   **14.** 1,000 lb = ☐ T   **15.** 1 T = ☐ oz

Will your answer be greater than or less than the number you started with?

In **16** through **18**, compare. Write >, <, or = for each ◯.

16. 5,000 lb ◯ 3 T   **17.** 24 lb ◯ 124 oz   **18.** 64,000 oz ◯ 2 T

For **19** through **21**, write the unit that would be appropriate to measure the weight of each object.

19. honeydew melon   **20.** bar of soap   **21.** truck

Problem Solving

22. Reason The perimeter of the rectangular playground shown below is 160 feet. What is the area of the playground?

50 ft

23. Kelly's family has a very large dog that weighs $92\frac{1}{2}$ pounds. Which of the following is equivalent to $92\frac{1}{2}$ pounds?

A 1,472 ounces

B 1,480 ounces

C 1,479 ounces

D 1,488 ounces

In **24** through **27**, use the table.

24. What would be the most appropriate unit to measure the weight of 4 horses?

25. How much do 4 horses weigh? Write the weight two different ways.

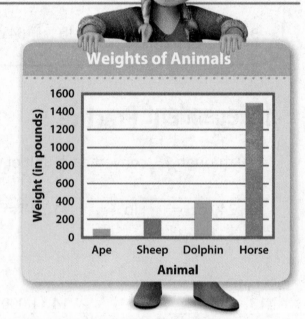

Weights of Animals

26. How many more ounces does a sheep weigh than an ape?

27. Extend Your Thinking What is the difference in weight between a horse and the combined weight of a dolphin and an ape? Write your answer in tons.

28. Communicate The world's heaviest lobster weighed 44 pounds 6 ounces. How many ounces did the lobster weigh? Describe the steps you took to find your answer.

29. Humans exploring space have left behind bags of trash, bolts, gloves, and pieces of satellites. There are currently about 4,000,000 pounds of litter in orbit around Earth. About how many tons of space litter is this?

Name _____

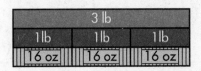

Homework 14-3
Converting Customary Units of Weight

Another Look!

> **Remember:**
> 1 T = 2,000 lb
> 1 lb = 16 oz

How to change from one unit of weight to another:

Converting from a smaller unit to a larger unit:	Converting from a larger unit to a smaller unit:
32 ounces = _____ pounds	3 pounds = _____ ounces
You know 16 oz = 1 lb, so divide.	You know 1 lb = 16 oz, so multiply.
Find 32 ÷ 16; 32 oz = 2 lb	Find 3 × 16; 3 lb = 48 oz

In **1** through **6**, convert each unit of weight.

1. 4 T = _____ lb

2. 5 lb = _____ oz

3. 6,000 lb = _____ T

4. $2\frac{1}{2}$ lb = _____ oz

5. 90 lb = _____ oz

6. 224 oz = _____ lb

In **7** through **12**, compare. Write >, <, or = for each ◯.

7. 16 lb ◯ 16 oz

8. 1,500 lb ◯ 2 T

9. 3 T ◯ 5,999 lb

10. 1,600 oz ◯ 10 lb

11. 19 lb ◯ 300 oz

12. 8 oz ◯ $\frac{1}{2}$ lb

In **13** through **15**, write the unit that would be appropriate to measure the weight of each object.

13. sack of potatoes

14. pencil

15. puppy

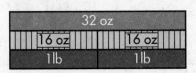

For **16** and **17**, use the recipe.

16. Aaron bought these ingredients to make the trail mix recipe. How many pounds of trail mix will he make?

17. Aaron wants to divide the trail mix equally into 6 bags to give to his friends. How much trail mix will be in each bag? Draw a strip diagram and write an equation to help you find the answer.

Trail Mix Recipe
10 ounces dried bananas
20 ounces raisins
18 ounces nuts

DATA

18. Estimation A candy maker buys a bar of chocolate weighing 162 ounces. About how many pounds does the bar weigh?

19. How many ounces are equal to $1\frac{1}{2}$ pounds?

20. Students visited a zoo where they learned that a large white rhinoceros could weigh as much as 6,000 pounds. Which measurement is greater than 6,000 pounds?

  A 6 tons
  B 3 tons
  C 2 tons
  D 1 ton

21. Complete the table. Which expression can be used to find the missing value in the second row?

n	12	15	21	28
$n +$ ☐	18	21	27	☐

22. Communicate Paula's kitten weighs $3\frac{1}{2}$ pounds. Write this weight using pounds and ounces. Explain how you found your answer.

23. Extend Your Thinking Karla bought 2 pounds of broccoli, $1\frac{3}{4}$ pounds of green beans, and 10 ounces of kale. How much do Karla's vegetables weigh in all? Write your answer two different ways.

Name _____

☆ ☆
Solve & Share
Measure the length of your book in centimeters. Then measure it in millimeters. What do you notice about the two measurements?

⭐ **TEKS 5.7** Select appropriate units, strategies, and tools to solve problems involving measurement. Solve problems by calculating conversions within a measurement system, customary or metric.
Mathematical Process Standards 5.1C, 5.1D, 5.1F, 5.1G

Digital Resources at PearsonTexas.com

Solve   Learn   Glossary   Check   Tools   Games

You can **select and use tools** to measure objects!

Look Back!

Connect Ideas How many meters long is your textbook? How do you know?

How Do You Convert Metric Units of Length?

A

The most commonly used units of length are the kilometer (km), meter (m), centimeter (cm), and millimeter (mm).

1 km = 1,000 m
1 m = 100 cm
1 m = 1,000 mm
1 cm = 10 mm

1 kilometer 1,000 m	1 hectometer 100 m	1 dekameter 10 m	1 meter 1 m	1 decimeter 0.1 m	1 centimeter 0.01 m	1 millimeter 0.001 m

Every metric unit is 10 times as much as the next smaller unit.

B The distance between two highway markers is 3 kilometers. How many meters is this?

3 km = ☐ m

To change from larger units to smaller units, multiply.

1 km = 1,000 m

Find 3 × 1,000.
3 km = 3,000 m

C The distance between a kitchen and living room is 1,200 centimeters. How many meters is this?

1,200 cm = ☐ m

To change from smaller units to larger units, divide.

Find 1,200 ÷ 100.
1,200 cm = 12 m

Do You Understand?

Convince Me! Which unit of length would be appropriate for measuring each object? How did you decide?

Classroom length _____

Height of a milk carton _____

Distance from your school to the next closest school _____

Length of a paperclip _____

☆ Guided Practice*

> In **1** through **4**, convert each unit of length.

1. 1,000 cm = ____ m

2. 58 m = _____ mm

3. 1,000 mm = ____ cm

4. 3 km = _____ m

> In **5** and **6**, compare lengths. Write >, <, or = for each ◯.

5. 9,000 m ◯ 20 km

6. 400 cm ◯ 4 m

7. Explain To find the number of meters in one kilometer, why do you multiply 1 × 1,000?

8. Reason Convert 12.5 centimeters to millimeters. Explain.

Independent Practice ☆

> In **9** through **14**, convert each unit of length.

9. 7.5 cm = ____ mm

10. 120,000,000 mm = ____ km

11. 121 km = _____ cm

12. 17,000 m = ____ km

13. 48,000 mm = ____ m

14. 4 km = _____ m

> In **15** through **20**, compare lengths. Write >, <, or = for each ◯.

15. 25,365 cm ◯ 30 m

16. 3.6 km ◯ 3,600 m

17. 1,200 mm ◯ 12 m

18. 52,800 cm ◯ 1 km

19. 7,500,000 m ◯ 750 km

20. 800 m ◯ 799,999 mm

> For **21** through **23**, write the metric unit that would be appropriate to measure the length of each object.

21. computer keyboard

22. button

23. boardwalk

Problem Solving

24. Number Sense Which number is smaller, the length of an object in meters or the length of the same object in millimeters?

25. Extend Your Thinking How many millimeters are equal to one kilometer? Show your work.

26. Eileen plants a tree that is 2 meters tall ⭐ in her yard. Which of the following is equal to 2 meters?

   A 200 mm   **C** 200 km

   B 20 cm   **D** 2,000 mm

What do you know about millimeters, centimeters, meters, and kilometers that can help you?

27. A week ago, Trudy bought the pencil shown. Now the pencil measures 12.7 centimeters.

How many centimeters of the pencil have been used?

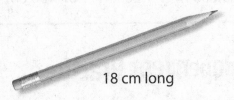

18 cm long

28. Explain Which fraction is greater: $\frac{7}{8}$ or $\frac{9}{12}$? Explain how you know.

How do you compare fractions?

29. Estimation As of 2008, the longest car ever built was 30.5 meters long. A meter is a little longer than a yard. Estimate the length of this car in feet.

30. Math and Science Mount St. Helens, located in Washington, erupted on May 18, 1980. Before the eruption, the volcano was 2.95 kilometers high. After the eruption, the volcano was 2.55 kilometers high. Use the strip diagram to find the difference in height of Mount St. Helens before and after the eruption, in meters.

2.95 km	
2.55 km	?

Name _____

Another Look!

Remember:
1 km = 1,000 m
1 m = 100 cm
1 m = 1,000 mm
1 cm = 10 mm

How to change from one metric unit of length to another:

Converting a length from a smaller to a larger metric unit:

200 centimeters = _____ meters

1 m	1 m
100 cm	100 cm

←———— 200 cm ————→

You know 100 cm = 1 m, so divide.

Find 200 ÷ 100; 200 cm = 2 m

Converting a length from a larger to a smaller metric unit:

2 kilometers = _____ meters

1,000 m	1,000 m
1 km	1 km

←———— 2 km ————→

You know 1 km = 1,000 m, so multiply.

Find 2 × 1,000; 2 km = 2,000 m

In **1** through **6**, convert each unit of length.

How can you double check that your answers are correct?

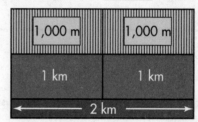

1. 25 m = _____ cm

2. 345 cm = _____ m

3. 4.5 m = _____ cm

4. 10 m = _____ mm

5. 987 mm = _____ cm

6. 5 km = _____ m

In **7** through **9**, compare lengths. Write >, <, or = for each ◯.

7. 3 km ◯ 5,000 m

8. 800 cm ◯ 8 m

9. 38.5 mm ◯ 10 cm

In **10** through **12**, write the metric unit that would be appropriate to measure the length of each object.

10. city block

11. baseball bat

12. cell phone

13. Extend Your Thinking Park rangers at the North Rim of the Grand Canyon recorded the amounts of rainfall over 12 months. What was the total amount of rainfall in centimeters?

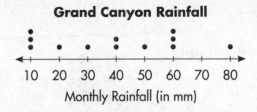

Grand Canyon Rainfall

10 20 30 40 50 60 70 80
Monthly Rainfall (in mm)

---

14. Explain Explain how you would convert 4 meters to millimeters.

15. Number Sense List three measurements with different units that are equal to 5 meters.

What other metric units of length are there?

---

16. Which of these number sentences is **NOT** true?

A 4,000,000 millimeters = 4 kilometers

B 300 millimeters > 3 centimeters

C 5 meters > 5,000 millimeters

D 2,000 meters < 20 kilometers

17. Communicate Explain how you can move the decimal point to convert 3,200 meters to kilometers.

---

18. There are 16 seats in each row of a theater. There are 32 rows in all. Which expression would you use to find the number of seats in the theater?

A 16 + 32   **C** 32 × 16

B 32 ÷ 16   **D** 32 − 16

19. The lengths of three trails at Cedar Woods Park are shown in the table. If you walked all three trails in one day, how far would you walk? Write the answer in meters and in kilometers.

Trail	Length
Spring Hollow	2 km
Brookside	2,400 m
Oak Ridge	1 km 600 m

DATA

Which answer choices can you eliminate?

Name _____

☆ ☆
Solve & Share

A pitcher holds 4 liters of water. How many milliliters does the pitcher hold? *Solve this problem any way you choose.*

Analyze Relationships
You can convert metric units of capacity using multiplication or division. *Show your work!*

⭐ **TEKS 5.7** Select appropriate units, strategies, and tools to solve problems involving measurement. Solve problems by calculating conversions within a measurement system, customary or metric. **Mathematical Process Standards 5.1D, 5.1F, 5.1G**

Digital Resources at PearsonTexas.com

Solve   Learn   Glossary   Check   Tools   Games

Look Back!

Reason Which is the larger unit of capacity, milliliters or liters? Explain how you know.

How Do You Convert Metric Units of Capacity?

A

The most commonly used units of capacity in the metric system are the liter (L) and the milliliter (mL).

Can you find a liter or milliliter in the real world?

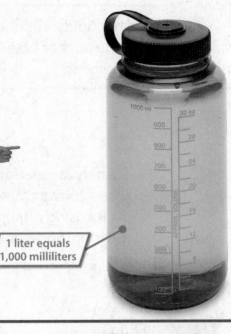

1 liter equals 1,000 milliliters

B **From Liters to Milliliters**

$$2 \text{ L} = \boxed{} \text{ mL}$$

To change a larger unit to a smaller unit, multiply.

1 L = 1,000 mL

Find 2 × 1,000.
2 L = 2,000 mL

C **From Milliliters to Liters**

$$3{,}000 \text{ mL} = \boxed{} \text{ L}$$

To change a smaller unit to a larger unit, divide.

1,000 mL = 1 L

Find 3,000 ÷ 1,000.
3,000 mL = 3 L

Do You Understand?

Convince Me! Order these measurements from greatest to least. Explain how you decided.

2,300 L   500 mL   3,000 mL   2 L   22 L

Name _____

In **1** through **6**, convert each unit of capacity.

1. 275 L = ☐ mL

2. 34,000 mL = ☐ L

3. 5 L = ☐ mL

4. 25,000 mL = ☐ L

5. 227 L = ☐ mL

6. 40 L = ☐ mL

7. Communicate Explain how you can convert milliliters to liters.

8. The relationship between kiloliters and liters is the same as between liters and milliliters. If there are 2,250 kiloliters of water in a pond, how many liters are in the pond? Explain how you found your answer.

Independent Practice ☆

In **9** through **20**, convert each unit of capacity.

9. 5,000 mL = ☐ L **10.** 45,000 mL = ☐ L **11.** 427 L = ☐ mL **12.** 13 L = ☐ mL

13. 37,000 mL = ☐ L **14.** 25 L = ☐ mL **15.** 17,000 mL = ☐ L **16.** 314,000 mL = ☐ L

17. 6 L = ☐ mL **18.** 2,000 mL = ☐ L **19.** 8,000 mL = ☐ L **20.** 9 L = ☐ mL

In **21** through **24**, circle the capacity that is more appropriate for each container.

21. test tube
9 L or 200 mL

22. canteen
1 L or 100 mL

23. bird bath
4 L or 450 mL

24. teacup
325 L or 325 mL

Problem Solving

25. You are filling a 2-liter bottle with liquid from full 80-milliliter containers. How many containers will it take to fill the 2-liter bottle?

Which operation will you use to find the answer?

- **A** 400
- **B** 250
- **C** 40
- **D** 25

26. Bobby filled the jug shown here with water for soccer practice. If each member of the team gets 250 milliliters of water per serving, how many team members will the water jug serve?

holds 5 L

27. Reason Carla's famous punch calls for 3 liters of mango juice. The only mango juice she can find is sold in 500-milliliter cartons. How many cartons of mango juice does Carla need to buy?

28. Which capacity is the most appropriate for a pitcher of lemonade?

- **A** 3 mL
- **B** 3 L
- **C** 30 mL
- **D** 30 L

29. Connect One cubic centimeter will hold 1 milliliter of water. How many milliliters will the aquarium below hold? How many liters will it hold?

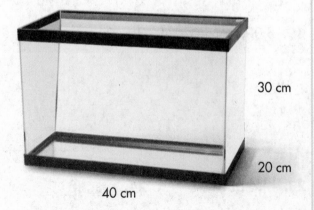

30 cm

20 cm

40 cm

30. Extend Your Thinking Terry is buying juice. He needs 3 liters. A half-liter of juice costs $2.39. A 250-milliliter container of juice costs $1.69. What should Terry buy so he gets 3 liters at the lowest price? Explain.

What steps do you need to do to solve this problem?

Name _____

Another Look!

> **Remember:**
> To change from L to mL, multiply by 1,000.
> To change from mL to L, divide by 1,000.

How to change from one metric unit of capacity to another:

Converting a capacity from a smaller to a larger metric unit:

2,000 milliliters = _____ liters

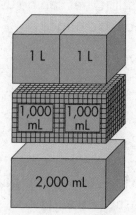

You know 1,000 mL = 1L, so divide.

Find 2,000 ÷ 1,000; 2,000 mL = 2 L

Converting a capacity from a larger to a smaller metric unit:

3 liters = _____ milliliters

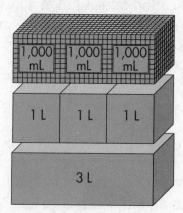

You know 1 L = 1,000 mL, so multiply.

Find 3 × 1,000; 3 L = 3,000 mL

In **1** through **9**, convert each unit of capacity.

1. 5 L = _____ mL

2. 13,000 mL = _____ L

3. 16 L = _____ mL

4. 4,000 mL = _____ L

5. 9,000 mL = _____ L

6. 40 L = _____ mL

7. 2.7 L = _____ mL

8. 8,400 mL = _____ L

9. 71 L = _____ mL

In **10** through **12**, circle the capacity that is more appropriate for each container.

10. soup bowl

    2 L or 300 mL

11. bathtub

    200 L or 34,000 mL

12. can of soup

    500 mL or 10 L

13. A community center has the swimming pool shown here. How many liters of water can the pool hold?

    A 290,000,000 liters
    B 2,900,000 liters
    C 290,000 liters
    D 29,000 liters

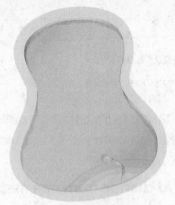

holds 29,000,000 mL

---

14. Explain Tell whether you would use multiplication or division to convert milliliters to liters. Explain your answer.

15. Complete the following table. Then write an equation that can be used to convert *p* pounds to *o* ounces.

Pounds	3	4	5	6	7
Ounces	48	☐	☐	☐	☐

---

16. The length of a rectangular garden is 10 yards and its width is 10 feet. What is the perimeter of the garden?

    A 20 feet
    B 20 yards
    C 80 feet
    D 100 feet

Are both dimensions given in the same unit?

17. Estimation You are preparing for a breakfast party and need enough milk for 20 people. Each person will drink about 200 milliliters of milk. Which is the better estimate of the amount of milk you should prepare: 400 milliliters or 4 liters? Why?

---

18. Extend Your Thinking Suppose you have the 3 cups shown at the right. List two different ways you can measure exactly 1 liter.

100-mL cup   300-mL cup   500-mL cup

Name _____

Solve & Share

In Chemistry class, Rhonda measured 10,000 milligrams of a substance. How many grams is this? *Solve this problem any way you choose.*

⭐ TEKS 5.7 Select appropriate units, strategies, and tools to solve problems involving measurement. Solve problems by calculating conversions within a measurement system, customary or metric.
Mathematical Process Standards 5.1C, 5.1D, 5.1F, 5.1G

You can use **number sense** to help you see a relationship between the units.

Digital Resources at PearsonTexas.com

Solve   Learn   Glossary   Check   Tools   Games

Look Back!

Analyze Relationships How many kilograms did Rhonda measure? Write two equations to show your work.

How Do You Convert Metric Units of Mass?

A

The three most commonly used units of mass are the milligram (mg), the gram (g), and the kilogram (kg).

about 5 g

Converting metric units of mass is like converting other metric units:

1,000 mg = 1 g
1,000 g = 1 kg

about 100 kg

From Grams to Milligrams

B

$$600 \text{ g} = \boxed{} \text{ mg}$$

To change from a larger unit to a smaller unit, multiply.

1 g = 1,000 mg

Find 600 × 1,000.
600 g = 600,000 mg

From Grams to Kilograms

C

$$13,000 \text{ g} = \boxed{} \text{ kg}$$

To change from a smaller unit to a larger unit, divide.

1,000 g = 1 kg

Find 13,000 ÷ 1,000.
13,000 g = 13 kg

Do You Understand?

Convince Me! If you need to convert kilograms to milligrams, what operation would you use? Explain.

Name _____

In **1** through **3**, convert each unit of mass.

1. 925 g = ☐ mg **2.** 19,000 g = ☐ kg

3. 1,000,000 mg = ☐ kg

In **4** and **5**, compare. Write >, <, or = for each ◯.

4. 7,000 mg ◯ 7,000 g

5. 100 kg ◯ 10,000 g

6. Connect How does the relationship between meters and millimeters help you understand the relationship between grams and milligrams?

7. Explain Which has the greater mass: 1 kilogram or 137,000 milligrams? Explain how you made your comparison.

Independent Practice ☆

In **8** through **13**, convert each unit of mass.

8. 17,000 g = ☐ kg

9. 18 kg = ☐ g

10. 420,000 mg = ☐ g

11. 276 g = ☐ mg

12. 438 kg = ☐ g

13. 43,000 mg = ☐ g

In **14** through **19**, compare. Write >, <, or = for each ◯.

14. 2,000 g ◯ 3 kg

15. 4 kg ◯ 4,000 g

16. 10,000 mg ◯ 13 g

17. 7 kg ◯ 7,000 g

18. 9,000 g ◯ 8 kg

19. 8,000 g ◯ 5 kg

In **20** through **22**, circle the mass that is more appropriate for each object.

20. cantaloupe

1 kg or 1 mg

21. laptop computer

3,000 g or 3,000 mg

22. mug

5 kg or 5 g

Problem Solving

23. Sheryl has a recipe for pasta with vegetables. The recipe calls for 130 grams of vegetables and twice as much pasta as vegetables. What is the total mass in grams of the recipe?

What is the hidden question?

24. Terri is beginning a science experiment in the lab. The instructions call for 227 milligrams of potassium. What is the difference between this amount and 1 gram?

25. **Number Sense** One of the world's heaviest hailstones weighed 2.2 pounds. Which is more appropriate to express its mass, 1 kilogram or 1 gram?

26. Order the following masses from least to greatest.
500 g   50 kg   5,000 mg

For **27** and **28**, use the given information and the picture.

If a man weighs 198 pounds on Earth, his mass on Earth is 90 kilograms.

27. What is this man's weight on the Moon?

28. What is his mass on the Moon? Explain.

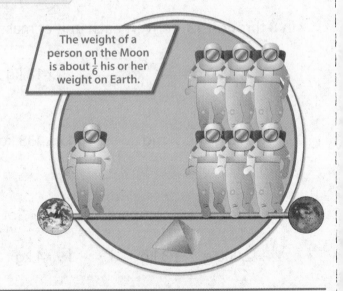

The weight of a person on the Moon is about $\frac{1}{6}$ his or her weight on Earth.

29. Which object would most likely have a mass of 2 kilograms?

A a car
B a strawberry
C an ant
D a watermelon

30. **Extend Your Thinking** If 6 onions have a mass of 900 grams and 8 apples have a mass of 1 kilogram, which food has the greater mass, an onion or an apple? Explain.

Name _____

Another Look!

Remember:
1,000 mg = 1 g
1,000 g = 1 kg

How to convert from one metric unit of mass to another:

Smaller metric unit to a larger unit:

6,000 grams = _____ kilograms

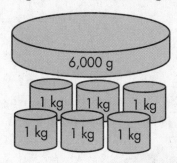

You know 1,000 g = 1 kg, so divide.

Find 6,000 ÷ 1,000; 6,000 g = 6 kg

Larger metric unit to a smaller unit:

2 grams = _____ milligrams

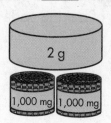

You know 1 g = 1,000 mg, so multiply.

Find 2 × 1,000; 2 g = 2,000 mg

In **1** through **6**, convert each unit of mass.

1. 72 g = _____ mg

2. 8,000 g = _____ kg

3. 2,000,000 mg = _____ kg

4. 490,000 g = _____ kg

5. 648 g = _____ mg

6. 61 kg = _____ g

In **7** through **12**, compare. Write >, <, or = for each ◯.

7. 4,000 mg ◯ 5 g

8. 64 kg ◯ 64,000 g

9. 3 kg ◯ 40,000 mg

10. 6,000 g ◯ 6 kg

11. 93 g ◯ 92,000 mg

12. 90 kg ◯ 90,000 mg

In **13** through **15**, circle the mass that is more appropriate for each object.

13. pear

250 kg or 250 g

14. walrus

1,000 mg or 1,000 kg

15. book

1 kg or 1 g

16. What is the value of x?
⭐ $40{,}000 \text{ mg} = 10x \text{ g}$

   A 400   **C** 4

   B 40   **D** 0.4

17. Reason How many centigrams are there in 50 grams?

Use what you know about metric prefixes to solve.

---

18. A recipe that serves two people calls for 1,600 milligrams of baking soda. You want to make enough for 10 people. How many grams of baking soda will you need?

19. Communicate What steps would you take to compare 2 kilograms and 3,200 grams?

Is there more than one way to compare them?

---

20. It is recommended that people eat 25,000 milligrams of fiber each day. The table shows the amount of fiber Jodi has eaten today. How many more grams of fiber does she need to get the recommended daily amount of fiber?

DATA

Food	Amount of Fiber
1 cup raspberries	8 grams
1 cup oatmeal	4 grams
2 cups orange juice	1 gram

---

21. Classify the triangle by its sides and its angles.

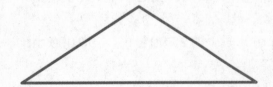

22. Extend Your Thinking How is converting grams to milligrams similar to converting pounds to ounces? How is it different?

© Pearson Education, Inc. 5

Name _____

☆ ☆
Solve & Share

Amy wants to frame a poster that has a width of 8 inches and a length of 1 foot. What is the perimeter of the poster? *Solve this problem any way you choose.*

Connect
You can use measurement conversions in real-world situations. *Show your work!*

⭐ TEKS 5.1A Apply mathematics to problems arising in everyday life, society, and the workplace. Also, 5.4H, 5.7. Mathematical Process Standards 5.1B, 5.1C, 5.1D, 5.1F, 5.1G

Digital Resources at PearsonTexas.com

 Solve   Learn   A-Z Glossary   Check   Tools   Games

Look Back!

Justify Which measurement did you convert? Can you find the perimeter by converting to the other unit of measurement?

How Can You Convert Units of Measurement to Solve a Problem?

A-Z

A city pool is in the shape of a rectangle with the dimensions shown. What is the perimeter of the pool?

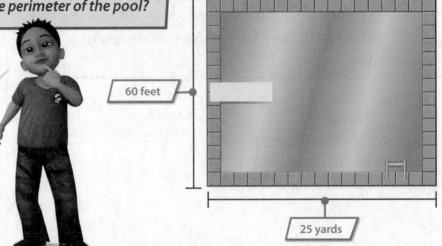

60 feet

25 yards

> You can convert one of the measures so that you are adding like units.

B Plan

What do you know?

The dimensions of the pool:
$\ell = 25$ yards
$w = 60$ feet

What are you asked to find?

The perimeter of the pool

> You can use feet for perimeter.

C Plan and Solve

Find the hidden question:

How many feet are in 25 yards?

1 yard = 3 feet

From larger units to smaller units: multiply

25 × 3 feet = 75 feet

D Solve

Now you can find the perimeter.

Perimeter = (2 × length) + (2 × width)

$P = (2 \times \ell) + (2 \times w)$

$P = (2 \times 75) + (2 \times 60)$

$P = 150 + 120$

$P = 270$ feet

The perimeter of the pool is 270 feet.

Do You Understand?

Convince Me! What is the area of the surface of the swimming pool above? Show how you found the answer.

Name _____

Guided Practice

1. Stacia needs enough ribbon to wrap around the length (ℓ) and height (h) of a box. If the box length is 2 feet and the height is 4 inches, how much ribbon will she need?

h

ℓ

2. If ribbon is sold in whole number yards and costs $1.50 per yard, how much will it cost Stacia to buy the ribbon?

3. What are the hidden questions and answers in Exercise 1?

4. **Connect** Write a real-world multiple-step problem that involves measurement.

Independent Practice

In **5** and **6**, write and answer the hidden question or questions. Then solve.

5. Becca wants to edge her hexagonal garden with brick. All sides are equal. The brick costs $2 per foot. How much will it cost to buy the edging she needs?

Edging means she will put bricks around the perimeter of the hexagon.

Becca's Garden

12 feet

6. If Isaac buys 12 tickets, how much money will he save by buying in groups of 4 tickets instead of individually?

$1 per ticket $3 for 4 tickets

Problem Solving

7. Reason Matt's family is thinking about buying a family pass to the city pool. The pass is $80 for a family of 4. Individual passes are $25 each. How much money can Matt's family save by purchasing a family pass instead of 4 individual passes?

8. Marcia is attending the annual library book sale. Paperback books are $0.50 each and hardcover books are $1.00 each. Marcia buys 8 paperback books and 7 hardcover books. If she pays with one $10 bill and one $5 bill, how much change should she receive?

9. Extend Your Thinking Raul wants to put wood shavings in his rabbit's cage. The floor of the cage measures 3 feet wide by 5 feet long. One bag of shavings covers 10 square feet.

How many bags will Raul have to buy to cover the floor of the cage? Explain.

10. Cheryl's fish tank is 2 yards long by 24 inches wide by 3 feet high. What is the volume of Cheryl's tank in cubic inches?

Remember,
Volume = $\ell \times w \times h$

11. Analyze Information Joann wants to put a ⭐ wallpaper border around her room. The border costs $3 per foot. The diagram shows Joann's room. How much money will the border cost?

A $114   C $120

B $118   D $125

```
|— 6 feet —|


                        
8 feet

|——— 11 feet ———|
```

12. Analyze Information Some statistics about a typical adult Royal antelope are shown in the data table.

a   What is a typical Royal antelope's tail length in millimeters?

b   How many centimeters high can a typical Royal antelope jump?

c   What is the mass of a typical Royal antelope in grams?

DATA

An Adult Royal Antelope	
Head and body length	43 cm
Tail length	6 cm
Mass	2.4 kg
Vertical leap	2 m

Name _____

Another Look!

Kyle hiked 10 miles on Saturday. He hiked half as many miles on Sunday. How many total yards did Kyle hike?

Read the problem. Underline what you know. Circle what you are asked to find.

What is the hidden question?
How many miles did Kyle hike on Sunday?

Answer the hidden question.
$10 \div 2 = 5$ miles

What is the total number of miles hiked?
$10 + 5 = 15$ miles

Convert the answer to yards.
1 mi = 1,760 yd, so 15 miles is $15 \times 1,760 = 26,400$ yd

1. Kendra biked 10 kilometers on Monday. She biked twice as many kilometers on Tuesday. How many total meters did she bike?

   Underline what you know. Circle what you need to find.

   What hidden question do you need to answer?

   _____

   How many meters did Kendra bike in all?

2. Wilson made fruit punch. He used 2 quarts of orange juice and 1 pint of cranberry juice. He used one quart more ginger ale than orange juice. How many cups of fruit punch did Wilson make?

Remember to check your calculations and make sure you answered the correct question.

3. Claire's backyard is in the shape of a rectangle and has a length of 19.5 feet. It cost her $945 to fence in the yard. If fencing costs $15 per foot, what is the width of Claire's backyard?

4. Communicate Isabel ran around the track 6 times at the same rate of speed. It took her 24 minutes to run. John took 3 minutes to run around the track once. Which student ran faster? Explain.

5. ⭐ For every 3 cans of vegetables purchased, you get 1 free can. Tessie went home with 32 cans of vegetables. How many cans did she have to pay for?

    A 32 cans   **C** 16 cans

    B 24 cans   **D** 8 cans

6. Mental Math Ann is putting carpet in a room that is 12 feet long and 10 feet wide. The carpet costs $3.00 per square foot. How much will the carpet for the room cost?

7. Explain Badal has 120 cubic centimeters of water. He wants to pour it into a rectangular vase that is 4 centimeters high, 4 centimeters wide, and 5 centimeters long. Will all the water fit into the vase? Explain.

8. ⭐ Darin wants to put a fence around his garden. How much fencing should he buy?

    A 26 yards

    B 40 yards

    C 46 feet

    D 120 feet

What are the steps you need to do to solve this problem?

8 ft

5 yd

9. Extend Your Thinking Nancy is saving $2 from her allowance every week. Marco is saving $1 the first week, $2 the second week, $3 the third week, and so on. At the end of 10 weeks, who will have saved more money? How much more?

10. Jose is painting a backdrop for the school play. The rectangular backdrop is 60 inches by 45 inches. If Jose's container of paint can cover 25 square feet, does he have enough to paint the backdrop?

HINT: Convert the dimensions from inches to feet.

Name _____

1. **Mental Math** On Monday, Jared swam 2 kilometers. On Wednesday he swam 2,600 meters, and on Friday, he swam 1 kilometer 400 meters. How many kilometers did he swim in all?

Applying Math Processes
- How does this problem connect to previous ones?
- What is my plan?
- How can I use tools?
- How can I use number sense?
- How can I communicate and represent my thinking?
- How can I organize and record information?
- How can I explain my work?
- How can I justify my answer?

2. **Reason** A bushel of apples weighs about 42 pounds. There are 4 pecks in a bushel. It takes 2 pounds of apples to make a 9-inch pie. How many pies can you make with one peck of apples?

3. **Explain** A 5-foot piece of ribbon costs $2. A 2-yard piece of ribbon costs $3. Which is the better buy?

4. **Estimation** The Indian rhinoceros eats about 100 pounds of food per day. There are about 2.2 pounds in 1 kilogram. About how many kilograms of food does an Indian rhinoceros eat in one week?

5. **Extend Your Thinking** What will be the volume of the 5th cube?

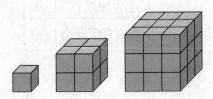

6. **Check for Reasonableness** Marco is buying drinks for a study group with 16 members. He estimates that each person will drink two 8-ounce drinks. Is one gallon of drinks enough? Explain.

Error Search

Find each number sentence that is not correct.
Change the symbol to make the sentence correct.

1. 10 ft > 34 yd

2. 340,000 mm = 34 km

3. 5 L < 5,000 mL

4. 800 kg > 8,000 g

5. 2 mi > 3,000 yd

6. 12 pt > 2 gal

7. 12 lb > 120 oz

8. 9,000 cm > 6.5 km

9. 2 qt > 64 fl oz

Target Number

Mental Math Using any numbers from the box as factors, list as many products equivalent to the Target Number as you can. Numbers in the box may be used more than once.

10.

72

2	3	4
6	8	9
12	24	36

11.

120

2	3	4
5	6	10
12	30	40

12.

300

2	3	5	6
10	30	50	60

Name _____

Set A pages 745–750

Convert 3 yards to inches.

1 foot (ft) = 12 inches (in.)
1 yard (yd) = 3 ft = 36 in.
1 mile (mi) = 1,760 yd = 5,280 ft

1 yard = 36 inches. To change larger units to smaller units, multiply.

$3 \times 36 = 108$

So, 3 yards = 108 inches.

Remember to multiply when changing larger units to smaller units and to divide when changing smaller units to larger units.

Convert.

1. 2 ft = ☐ in.   **2.** 2 mi = ☐ ft

3. 5 yd = ☐ ft   **4.** 54 in. = ☐ ft

Compare. Write >, <, or = for each ◯.

5. 7 yd ◯ 50 ft   **6.** 212 in. ◯ 2 yd

Set B pages 751–756

Convert 16 cups to pints.

2 cups = 1 pint. To change smaller units to larger units, divide.

$16 \div 2 = 8$

So, 16 cups = 8 pints.

Remember that 1 gal = 4 qt, 1 qt = 2 pt, and 1 pt = 2 cups.

Convert.

1. 32 c = ☐ gal   **2.** 6 pt = ☐ qt
3. 2 gal = ☐ pt   **4.** 6 pt = ☐ c

5. List 12 pt, 3 gal, and 16 cups in order from least to greatest.

Set C pages 757–762

Convert 6 pounds to ounces.

1 pound = 16 ounces. To change larger units to smaller units, multiply.

$6 \times 16 = 96$

So, 6 pounds = 96 ounces.

To compare customary units, convert one of the units first, so that you can compare like units.

Remember that there are 16 ounces in one pound, and there are 2,000 pounds in one ton.

Convert.

1. 2 lb = ☐ oz   **2.** 48 oz = ☐ lb

3. 4,000 lb = ☐ T   **4.** 6 T = ☐ lb

Compare. Write >, <, or = for each ◯.

5. 7 lb ◯ 70 oz   **6.** 6,000 oz ◯ 3 T

7. How many ounces are equivalent to one fourth of one ton?

Convert 2 meters to centimeters.

1 km = 1,000 m   1 m = 100 cm
1 m = 1,000 mm   1 cm = 10 mm

1 meter = 100 centimeters. To change larger units to smaller units, multiply.

2 × 100 = 200

So, 2 meters = 200 centimeters.

Remember to convert to the same unit of measure before comparing two lengths.

Convert.

1. 5 m = ☐ cm   2. 2 km = ☐ m

3. 2 km = ☐ cm   4. 20 m = ☐ mm

5. 10 cm = ☐ mm   6. 2,000 mm = ☐ m

7. 9,000 m = ☐ km   8. 7,000 cm = ☐ m

Convert 6,000 milliliters to liters.

1,000 milliliters = 1 liter. To change smaller units to larger units, divide.

6,000 ÷ 1,000 = 6

So, 6,000 milliliters = 6 liters.

Remember that the most commonly used metric units of capacity are the liter and milliliter.

Convert.

1. 6 L = ☐ mL   2. 15 L = ☐ mL

3. 2,000 mL = ☐ L   4. 9,000 mL = ☐ L

Convert 6 kilograms (kg) to grams (g).

1 kilogram = 1,000 grams. To change larger units to smaller units, multiply.

6 × 1,000 = 6,000

So, 6 kg = 6,000 g.

Remember that to compare metric units, convert one of the units first, so that you can compare like units.

Convert.

1. 30 kg = ☐ g   2. 3,000 mg = ☐ g

3. 5,000 g = ☐ kg   4. 17 g = ☐ mg

In a contest, Lina jumped 3 yards and Ed jumped 8 feet. Who jumped farther?

Identify the hidden question or questions.
How many feet are in 3 yards?

1 yd = 3 ft, so 3 yd = 9 ft.

Compare the two distances.
Lina jumped 9 feet, Ed jumped 8 feet. So, Lina jumped farther.

Remember to check if the units in the problem are the same.

1. Max wants to put a fence around his triangular garden. If each side is 6 yards, how many feet of fencing does Max need?

Name _____

 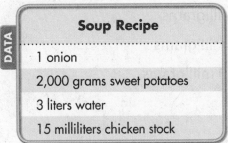

1. During a science experiment, students were asked to compare different masses. Which comparison is **NOT** true?

A 100 mg < 10 g

B 2,000 kg > 2,000 g

C 1,000,500 mg > 1 kg

D 600 g > 6 kg

4. Which of the following can be used to find how many kilograms of sweet potatoes are needed for the recipe?

DATA	**Soup Recipe**
	1 onion
	2,000 grams sweet potatoes
	3 liters water
	15 milliliters chicken stock

A 1,000 ÷ 2,000

B 2,000 ÷ 1,000

C 2,000 × 1,000

D 2,000 × 100

2. Veena's baseball bat has a length of 100 centimeters. Which of the following is true?

A 100 cm < 500 mm

B 100 cm > 3 m

C 100 cm > 1 km

D 100 cm = 1 m

5. Ten bales of cotton weigh about 5,000 pounds. Which comparison is true?

A 5,000 pounds < 10,000 ounces

B 5,000 pounds = 3 tons

C 5,000 pounds < 3 tons

D 5,000 pounds > 3 tons

3. The dimensions of Justin's garden are shown below. What is the perimeter of the garden in inches?

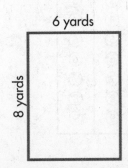

6 yards

8 yards

6. Tyrell bought 4 liters of fruit punch for a party. He will serve the punch in glasses that can hold 200 milliliters. How many glasses of fruit punch can he serve?

7. The nutrition label on a carton of soy milk says that one glass contains 7 grams of protein. How many milligrams of protein does one glass contain?

A 7 milligrams

B 70 milligrams

C 700 milligrams

D 7,000 milligrams

8. Marc says he needs more than 1 yard 9 feet of chicken wire to make a pen for his rabbits. Which length will **NOT** be long enough for Marc to use?

A 54 inches

B 2 ft 25 inches

C 4 yards

D All of these

9. Juanita has a pail with a capacity of 96 fluid ounces. How many pints will the pail hold?

10. Mason made 5 quarts of salsa. Which of the following can be used to find the number of cups of salsa Mason made?

A $5 \times 2 \times 2$

B $5 \times 4 \times 4$

C $5 \div 2 \div 2$

D $5 \times 4 \div 2$

11. Alicia bought 5 pounds of potting soil. She wants to put 10 ounces of soil in each of her flower pots. How many flower pots can she fill?

A 6 flower pots

B 8 flower pots

C 10 flower pots

D 12 flower pots

12. The tail of a Boeing 747 is 63 feet 8 inches tall. How many inches tall is the tail?

Data Analysis

Essential Questions: What are ways to display and compare data? How can graphs be used to display data and answer questions?

Wildfires help nature by burning away dead plant material.

Lightning can cause wildfires. But did you know human activities cause 9 out of 10 wildfires?

I'm shocked! It's time for some trailblazing research! Here's a project about wildfires.

Math and Science Project: Wildfires

Do Research Use the Internet and other sources to learn more about wildfires. Investigate how wildfires affect ecosystems. Explore the costs and benefits of wildfires. List five living things in an ecosystem. Research how long it takes each one to recover from a wildfire.

Journal: Write a Report Include what you found. Also in your report:

• Make a pamphlet to show how wildfires affect ecosystems.

• Suggest ways to prevent wildfires.

• Display your data using a graph of your choice.

• Make up and solve problems using data analysis.

Name _____

Review What You Know

Vocabulary

Choose the best term from the box.
Write it on the blank.

> • bar
>
> • point
>
> • x-axis
>
> • y-axis

1. The first number of an ordered pair describes the distance to the right or left of the origin along the
_____ .

2. An exact location on a coordinate grid is shown with a(n)
_____ .

3. A _____ on a graph uses length to show data.

Number Line

Use the number line to answer
4 through **6**.

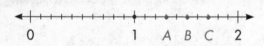

4. Which point is halfway between 1 and 2?

5. Which point is closer to 1 than to 2?

6. Which point is closer to 2 than to 1?

Comparing and Ordering

Order each group of numbers from least to greatest.

7. 18,837, 15,465, 101,702, 9,821

8. 1,500,000, 1,150,000, 15,000,000, 150,000

9. 0.78, 1.0, 0.91, 0.09

10. Some tall waterfalls include: Browne at 2,744 feet, Wishbone at 1,968 feet, Tugela at 3,110 feet, and Kerepakupai at 3,212 feet. What is the difference in height between the tallest and shortest waterfalls listed?

   A 1,142 ft
   B 1,244 ft
   C 5,078 ft
   D 5,180 ft

Graphing Points

11. Explain the digital tool you would use to solve this problem. Then graph the points.

   Graph the points (3, 5), (2, 7), and (5, 4) on a coordinate grid.

My Word Cards

Use the examples for each word on the front of the card to help complete the definitions on the back.

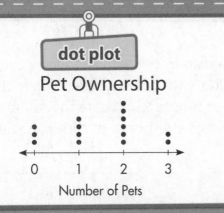

dot plot

Pet Ownership

Number of Pets

---

data

Number of Pets:

0, 3, 2, 2, 1, 0, 3, 2, 2,

0, 1, 1, 2, 2, 1

---

outlier

2, 3, 3, 1, 4, 15, 4, 1, 2, 2

15 is an outlier.

---

frequency table

Number of Pets	0	1	2	3
Frequency	3	4	6	2

---

numerical data

Amount of Rainfall:

$\frac{1}{4}, \frac{1}{2}, 1, 1\frac{1}{2}, \frac{3}{4}, 0, \frac{5}{8}, 0$

$0, 1\frac{1}{4}, \frac{7}{8}, \frac{1}{2}, 1$

---

bar graph

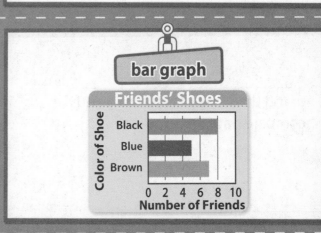

---

scale

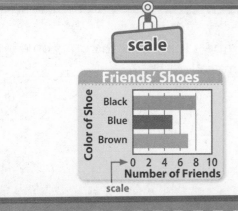

---

interval

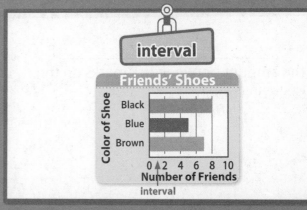

Complete the definition. Extend learning by writing your own definitions.

Collected information is called

_____.

A display of responses along a number line, with dots recorded above the responses to indicate the number of times a response occurred, is called a

_____.

A _____
is used to show the number of times something occurs.

An _____ is a value that is much greater or much less than the other values in a data set.

A _____ is a graph that uses bars to show and compare data.

_____
are data involving numbers, including measurement data.

An _____ is the amount between tick marks on the scale of a graph.

The numbers that show the units on a graph are called the _____.

My Word Cards

Use the examples for each word on the front of the card to help complete the definitions on the back.

categorical data

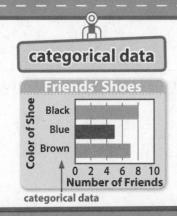

categorical data

survey

How many pets do you have?

What is your favorite sport?

sample

Sample Population:
Every 5th student in the
lunch line

stem-and-leaf plot

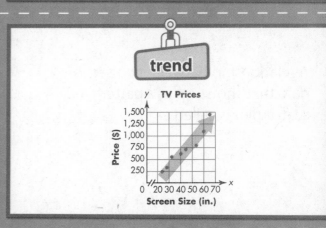

scatterplot

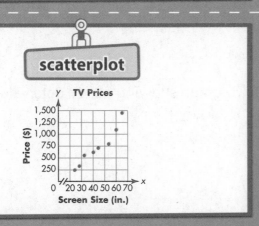

trend

discrete data

Number of Students

Drama: 25

Band: 15

Chorus: 34

My Word Cards

Complete the definition. Extend learning by writing your own definitions.

A _____ is a question or questions used to gather information.

_____ are data that can be divided into groups.

A _____ is a convenient way to organize numerical data using place value.

A representative part of a larger group is called a _____.

A relationship between two sets of data that shows up as a pattern in a scatterplot is called a _____.

A _____ is a graph showing paired data values.

Data where only whole numbers are possible are called _____.

Name _____

Solve & Share

A fifth-grade class recorded the height of each student. How could you organize the data? *Make a dot plot to solve this problem.*

TEKS 5.9A Represent categorical data with bar graphs or frequency tables and numerical data, including data sets of measurements in fractions or decimals, with dot plots or stem-and-leaf plots. Also, 5.9, 5.9C.
Mathematical Process Standards 5.1B, 5.1D, 5.1E, 5.1F

Digital Resources at PearsonTexas.com

| Solve | Learn | Glossary | Check | Tools | Games |

> **Heights of Students in Grade 5**
> (to the nearest $\frac{1}{2}$ inch):
>
> 55, 52, $50\frac{1}{2}$, $50\frac{1}{2}$, 55, $50\frac{1}{2}$,
>
> 50, 55, $50\frac{1}{2}$, 55, $58\frac{1}{2}$, 60, 52,
>
> $50\frac{1}{2}$, $50\frac{1}{2}$, 50, 55, 55, $58\frac{1}{2}$, 60

You can **create and use representations** to organize data. *Show your work!*

Look Back!

Connect Ideas How does organizing the data help you see the height that occurs most often? Explain.

How Can You Use a Dot Plot to Organize and Represent Measurement Data?

A

Measurement data
can be organized so
it is easier to see.

The dogs in Paulina's Pet Shop have the following weights. The weights are in pounds.

How can you organize this information in a dot plot?

Weights of Dogs (in pounds)					
8.50	12.25	6	11.50	7.25	12.25
8.50	12.25	8.50	12.25	12.25	6

DATA

B Organize the data.

Order the weights from least to greatest.

6, 6, 7.25, 8.50, 8.50, 8.50, 11.50, 12.25, 12.25, 12.25, 12.25, 12.25

A frequency table uses numbers to show how many times a given response occurs.

Make a frequency table to show the data.

DATA

Dog Weight (pounds)	Tally	Frequency
6	||	2
7.25	|	1
8.50	|||	3
11.50	|	1
12.25	╫╫	5

C Make a dot plot.

First draw the number line. Then make a dot for each value in the data set. Then write a title.

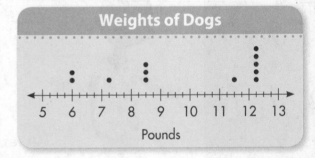

Weights of Dogs

Pounds

Do You Understand?

Convince Me! Which weight for the dogs occurs most often? Which weight occurs least often? How can you tell from the dot plot?

806

© Pearson Education, Inc. 5

Name _____

☆ Guided Practice*

1. Draw a dot plot to represent the data for weights of pumpkins in a crate.

DATA	Weights of Pumpkins (to the nearest $\frac{1}{8}$ pound)	Tally	Frequency
	$3\frac{1}{2}$	||	2
	$5\frac{1}{4}$	|||	3
	7	||||	4
	$8\frac{1}{8}$	|	1

2. How many pumpkins are in the crate?

3. What values do you need to show on the number line?

4. Communicate What observations can you make about the crate of pumpkins?

Independent Practice ☆

In **5** and **6**, organize the data into a frequency table. Then complete the dot plot for each data set.

> Double check that you have a tally mark and a dot for each value.

5. 11.25, 12.5, 11.25, 14.125, 10.5, 11.25, 12

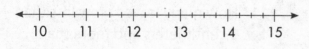

6. $1\frac{1}{8}$, 2, $1\frac{1}{2}$, $1\frac{1}{4}$, $1\frac{1}{8}$, 1, 2, $1\frac{1}{2}$, $1\frac{1}{4}$

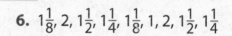

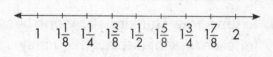

Problem Solving

For **7** through **9**, use the data set.

Marvin's Tree Service purchased several spruce tree saplings. The heights of the saplings are shown in the table.

7. Make a frequency table to organize the data.

Heights of Saplings (in.)				
$26\frac{1}{2}$	27	$26\frac{3}{4}$	$27\frac{1}{2}$	$26\frac{3}{4}$
$27\frac{1}{2}$	$27\frac{3}{4}$	$27\frac{1}{4}$	$27\frac{1}{2}$	$27\frac{1}{4}$
$27\frac{3}{4}$	$27\frac{1}{2}$	$26\frac{1}{2}$	$26\frac{1}{2}$	$27\frac{1}{2}$
$27\frac{1}{4}$	$27\frac{1}{4}$	$27\frac{1}{2}$	27	$26\frac{3}{4}$

8. **Make a Graph** Draw a dot plot of the

9. **Analyze Information** How many more trees with a height of $27\frac{1}{?}$ inches or less were there than trees with a height of $27\frac{1}{2}$ inches or greater?

---

10. **Extend Your Thinking** Give one benefit for each type of display: frequency table and dot plot.

11. How many leaves grew less than 5 centimeters and more than 3 centimeters in July?

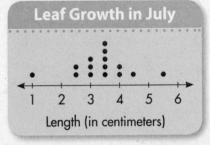

Leaf Growth in July

Length (in centimeters)

- A 11 leaves
- B 10 leaves
- C 8 leaves
- D 5 leaves

Name _____

Another Look!

Mick recorded data of the lengths of 10 Steller sea lions. Which length occurs most often?

Steller Sea Lion Lengths (in feet)				
$9\frac{1}{4}$	$9\frac{1}{8}$	$8\frac{3}{4}$	$9\frac{1}{4}$	$9\frac{1}{4}$
$9\frac{3}{8}$	$9\frac{1}{4}$	$9\frac{1}{8}$	$9\frac{1}{4}$	$9\frac{1}{8}$

Step 1

Make a frequency table.

Value	Tally	Frequency
$8\frac{3}{4}$	I	1
$9\frac{1}{8}$	III	3
$9\frac{1}{4}$	HHI	5
$9\frac{3}{8}$	I	1

Step 2

Make a dot plot. Draw a dot for each value. Stack dots for values that occur more than once.

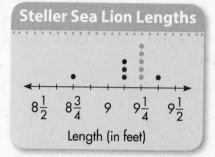

Steller Sea Lion Lengths

Length (in feet)

The length $9\frac{1}{4}$ feet occurs most often.

In **1** through **4**, organize the data into a frequency table. Then construct a dot plot for each data set.

1.

Math Quiz Scores				
24	12	25	19	21
24	21	18	25	24
21	21	9	21	21
13	10	17	20	20

2.

Haircut Prices (in dollars)					
13	12	9	9	9	12
31	25	25	11	12	15
20	20	25	20	12	12
15	13	15	20	25	17

3.

Scrap Wood Lengths (in inches)					
$4\frac{1}{2}$	4	5	$4\frac{1}{4}$	$4\frac{1}{2}$	$4\frac{3}{8}$
$4\frac{1}{8}$	$4\frac{1}{2}$	$4\frac{1}{4}$	$4\frac{3}{4}$	$4\frac{1}{2}$	$4\frac{1}{2}$
$4\frac{5}{8}$	$4\frac{3}{4}$	$4\frac{1}{4}$	$4\frac{1}{8}$	$4\frac{1}{2}$	4

4.

Fish Lengths (in cm)			
10.25	10.50	11.75	12.00
10.75	11.00	11.25	11.50
11.25	11.25	11.	11.00

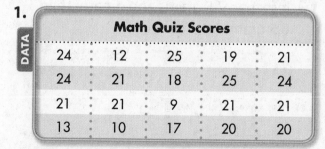

For **5** through **8**, use the table showing data from recipes used in a chili cooking contest.

5. Organize the data in a frequency table.

Amount of Beans (in cups)				
5	$5\frac{1}{2}$	$4\frac{1}{2}$	$4\frac{1}{2}$	$4\frac{1}{2}$
$4\frac{1}{2}$	$4\frac{1}{2}$	$4\frac{1}{2}$	$4\frac{3}{4}$	$4\frac{1}{2}$

6. Make a Graph Draw a dot plot of the data.

7. Reason Using the data, what conclusion can you draw about the chili recipes?

8. Extend Your Thinking Suppose the contestants were asked to make two batches of their recipe instead of one batch. Would the value that occurred most often be different? Explain.

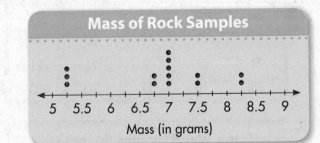

Would the data values change in both the frequency table and the dot plot?

9. How many rock samples have masses less than 7.5 grams and greater than 6.5 grams?

Mass of Rock Samples

Mass (in grams)

A 1 sample C 5 samples
B 2 samples D 7 samples

Name _____

Solve & Share

Rainfall for the Amazon was measured and recorded for 30 days and displayed in a dot plot. What can you tell about the differences in the amounts of rainfall? *Use the dot plot to solve this problem.*

⊕ **TEKS 5.9A** Represent categorical data with bar graphs or frequency tables and numerical data, including data sets of measurements in fractions or decimals, with dot plots or stem-and-leaf plots. Also, 5.9, 5.9C.
Mathematical Process Standards 5.1B, 5.1D, 5.1E, 5.1F, 5.1G

Amazon Rainfall

```
                        .
                        .
                    .   .
                    .   .
              .     .   .
          .   .     .       .
      .   .   .     .   .   .
  ←———|———|———|———|———|———|———→
      0   ½   1   1½  2
              Inches
```

Digital Resources at PearsonTexas.com

Solve   Learn   Glossary   Check   Tools   Games

Analyze Relationships You can use a data representation to analyze information. *Show your work!*

Look Back!

Communicate What was the difference between the greatest amount of rain in a day and the least amount of rain in a day? How can you tell?

How Can You Use Measurement Data Represented in a Dot Plot to Solve Problems?

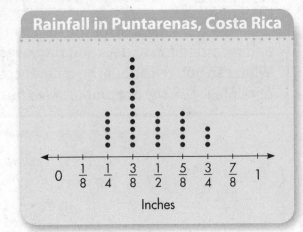

Rainfall in Puntarenas, Costa Rica

Bruce measured the daily rainfall while working in Costa Rica. His dot plot shows the rainfall for each day in September.

You can make a frequency table to find the total rainfall for the month.

B Multiply each data value by the frequency to find the amount of rain for that value. Then add all of the products to find the total amount of rain for the month.

The table helps you organize the numerical data so you can multiply. Then you can add to find the total rainfall.

DATA

Rainfall (inches)	Frequency	Multiplication
$\frac{1}{4}$	5	$\frac{1}{4} \times 5 = 1\frac{1}{4}$
$\frac{3}{8}$	12	$\frac{3}{8} \times 12 = 4\frac{1}{2}$
$\frac{1}{2}$	5	$\frac{1}{2} \times 5 = 2\frac{1}{2}$
$\frac{5}{8}$	5	$\frac{5}{8} \times 5 = 3\frac{1}{8}$
$\frac{3}{4}$	3	$\frac{3}{4} \times 3 = 2\frac{1}{4}$

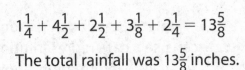

$$1\frac{1}{4} + 4\frac{1}{2} + 2\frac{1}{2} + 3\frac{1}{8} + 2\frac{1}{4} = 13\frac{5}{8}$$

The total rainfall was $13\frac{5}{8}$ inches.

Do You Understand?

Convince Me! Rosie says she can find the total rainfall in the example above without multiplying. Do you agree? Explain.

Name _____

☆ Guided Practice*

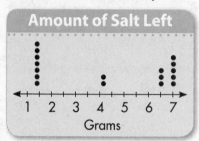

In **1** through **3**, use the dot plot and frequency table.

Bella's experiment showed how many grams of salt were left after containers of various liquids evaporated. The results are shown in the dot plot.

Amount of Salt Left

Amount of Salt (grams)	Frequency	Multiplication
1.4	7	$1.4 \times 7 = 9.8$
4.2	2	$4.2 \times 2 = 8.4$
6.5		
7.0		

1. What is the total amount of salt left? Complete the frequency table to help.

2. **Represent** Write an equation that shows how to find the total grams of salt left.

3. **Reason** What would be the total grams of salt left if Bella used two of each container?

Which operation(s) could you use to find the answer?

☆ Independent Practice ☆

In **4** through **6**, use the dot plot Allie made to show the lengths of strings she cut for her art project.

4. What is the total length of the strings that Allie cut for her art project?

5. Write an equation for the total amount of string.

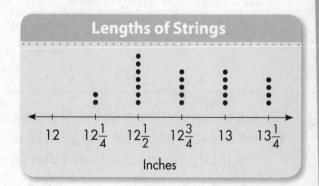

Lengths of Strings

Inches

6. What is the difference in length between the longest and the shortest lengths of string?

Problem Solving

For **7** and **8**, use the dot plot Susannah made to show the distances she hiked each day in the past two weeks.

7. Write and solve an equation for the total number of miles Susannah hiked.

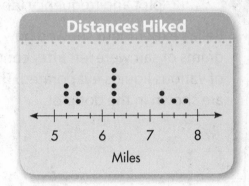

8. **Analyze Information** What distance did Susannah hike most often? least often?

---

9. A square deck has an area of 81 square feet. How long is each side of the deck?

How does knowing the shape of the deck help you?

10. In a survey of 100 people, $\frac{3}{5}$ of the people answered that their favorite meal is lunch. How many people chose lunch as their favorite meal?

---

11. **Extend Your Thinking** Althea recorded the amount she earned from T-shirt sales each day for 14 days. She organized the data into the frequency table shown. Write a problem that can be answered by using the frequency table.

Total Amount of Sales in a Day (in $)	Frequency	Multiplication
7.50	3	7.50 × 3 = 22.50
15.00	4	15.00 × 4 = 60.00
22.50	5	22.50 × 5 = 112.50
30.00	1	30.00 × 1 = 30.00
37.50	1	37.50 × 1 = 37.50

---

12. Kurt recorded the amount of snow that fell in each month for one year. What was the total amount of snowfall that year?

   A 3.95 in.   **C** 12.0 in.

   B 4.1 in.   **D** 18.6 in.

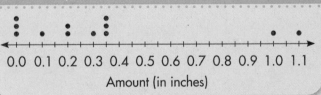

© Pearson Education, Inc. 5

Name _____

Another Look!

Cora sells seed packets. She made a dot plot to show the amount of sales for the first 12 weeks. What was the total amount of sales for the 12 weeks?

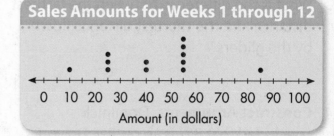

Sales Amounts for Weeks 1 through 12

Amount (in dollars)

Step 1

Use the dot plot to make a frequency table.

Multiply each amount by its frequency to find the total amount for that value.

Weekly Sales (in $)	Frequency	Multiplication
10	1	$10 \times 1 = 10$
25	3	$25 \times 3 = 75$
40	2	$40 \times 2 = 80$
55	5	$55 \times 5 = 275$
85	1	$85 \times 1 = 85$

Step 2

Add the total amounts for each value.

$10 + 75 + 80 + 275 + 85 = 525$

The total amount of sales in 12 weeks was $525.

In **1** and **2**, make a frequency table for each dot plot to answer the question.

1. Wai recorded the length of each wire needed for a science project. What is the total length of wire needed?

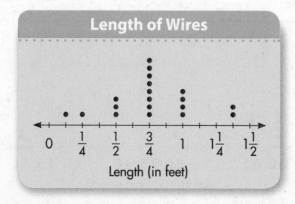

Length of Wires

Length (in feet)

2. Trey measured the mass of some pebbles. What is the combined mass of the pebbles that are 4.5 grams or more?

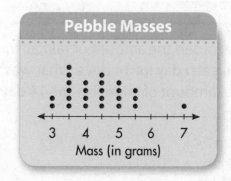

Pebble Masses

Mass (in grams)

For **3** and **4**, Dominick's class flew toy gliders. He recorded the distances in a dot plot.

3. What is the difference between the farthest distance and the shortest distance flown by the gliders?

4. Construct Arguments Dominick concluded that $32\frac{1}{2}$ is an outlier. Do you agree with him or not? Explain.

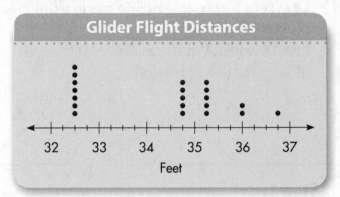

Glider Flight Distances

Feet

5. Molly runs 3 miles on Monday, Wednesday, and Friday. She runs twice as far on Saturday as she does on Monday. What is the total number of miles she runs each week?

6. Personal Financial Literacy Carl spent $9.52 of his $15 allowance. He divided the rest equally between saving and sharing. How much did he save? Tell how you found the answer.

7. Extend Your Thinking Nolan listed the weights of oranges in a carton in the frequency table shown. Which is greater, the total weight of the 6.25-ounce oranges or the total weight of the 7.25-ounce oranges? Explain.

Weight (in ounces)	Frequency	Multiplication
6.25	13	
6.5	16	$6.5 \times 16 = 104$
6.75	20	$6.75 \times 20 = 135$
7.0	14	$7.0 \times 14 = 98$
7.25	9	

8. Anita recorded the amount of rainfall in her area each day for 14 days. What was the total amount of rainfall in the 14 days?

   A   40 cm
   B   36 cm
   C   13.5 cm
   D   12.5 cm

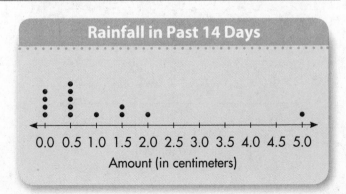

Rainfall in Past 14 Days

Amount (in centimeters)

Name _____

Solve & Share

A zoologist recorded the heights of four different types of land mammals. The graph shows heights in feet. Can you tell how much taller an African elephant is than a rhinoceros? *Use the graph to solve this problem.*

 TEKS 5.9C Solve one- and two-step problems using data from a frequency table, dot plot, bar graph, stem-and-leaf plot, or scatterplot. Also, 5.9. Mathematical Process Standards 5.1A, 5.1B, 5.1C, 5.1G

Digital Resources at PearsonTexas.com

Solve   Learn   Glossary   Check   Tools   Games

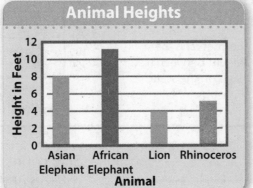

Animal Heights

Height in Feet (y-axis: 0, 2, 4, 6, 8, 10, 12)

Animal (x-axis): Asian Elephant, African Elephant, Lion, Rhinoceros

Select and Use Tools
You can compare data using a bar graph. *Show your work!*

Look Back!

Construct Arguments Why does it make sense to use a bar graph for this set of data?

What Do Bar Graphs Show?

A bar graph uses bars to show and compare data. About how many more species of animals are in the Minnesota Zoo than the Phoenix Zoo?

The scale consists of numbers that show the units used on a graph.

Bar graphs are useful for comparing data.

The interval is the amount between tick marks on the scale.

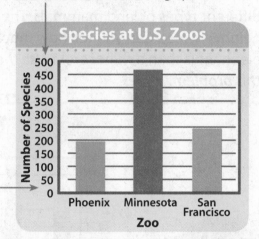

Species at U.S. Zoos

B

The purple bar is just above the number 450. The Minnesota Zoo has about 450 species of animals.

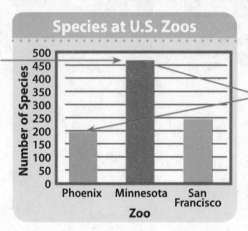

Species at U.S. Zoos

Skip count by 50s from the top of the green bar (Phoenix Zoo) until you are even with the top of the purple bar (Minnesota Zoo). Count: 50, 100, 150, 200, 250.

The Minnesota Zoo has about 250 more species than the Phoenix Zoo.

Do You Understand?

Convince Me! The Miami Metro Zoo has about 300 species of animals. In the example above, which zoos have fewer species than the Miami Metro Zoo?

Name _____

In **1** through **4**, use the bar graph.

1. About how many more counties does North Carolina have than Arizona?

2. Which state has about the same number of counties as Georgia and North Carolina combined?

3. What is the interval of the bar graph?

4. **Connect** Write a problem involving comparing data in the bar graph.

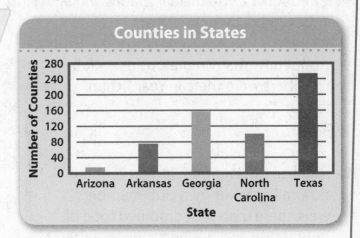

Counties in States

☆ **Independent Practice** ☆

In **5** through **8**, use the bar graph.

5. About how much less does a giant octopus weigh than a pig?

6. About how much more does a giraffe weigh than all the other animals combined?

7. A black bear weighs about 250 pounds. Which animals in the graph weigh more than a black bear?

8. A walrus weighs about 2,200 pounds. How would you change the graph to add a bar for a walrus?

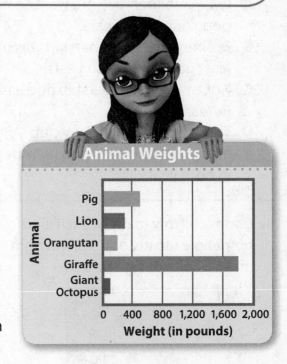

Animal Weights

Problem Solving

In **9** through **12**, use the bar graphs showing club membership data for two years.

9. About how many more business club members were there in Year 1 than in Year 2?

10. **Analyze Information** In Year 2, about how many fewer gym club members were there than the combined total of hobby club and business club members?

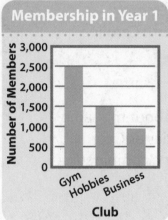

11. Which of these is **NOT** true about the data in the bar graphs?

    A Gym club membership was the most popular in both years.

    B Business club membership was the least popular in both years.

    C Hobby club membership decreased in Year 2.

    D There were fewer hobby club members than gym club members in both years.

12. **Extend Your Thinking** How could you change the bar graphs to make it easier to compare the membership data in the two years?

13. **Connect** How many of each kind of triangle (acute, obtuse, and right) make up the design below?

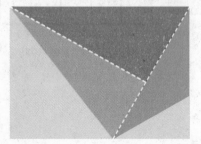

14. **Explain** If the interval in a bar graph becomes greater, do the values of the bars change? Explain.

820

Name _____

Another Look!

Cy graphed the number of people taking part in different health studies at his college. About how many more people are in the health study on fruits than in the studies on sleep and vegetables combined?

Step 1

Read the labels of the bar graph.
The **categories** show kinds of information.
The **scale** shows the units used.
A **bar's length** shows its value.

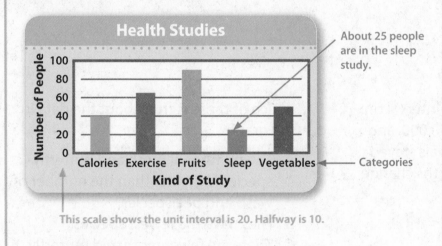

About 25 people are in the sleep study.

Categories

This scale shows the unit interval is 20. Halfway is 10.

Step 2

You can use a strip diagram to help solve.

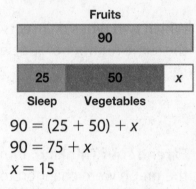

$90 = (25 + 50) + x$
$90 = 75 + x$
$x = 15$

So, the study on fruits has about 15 more people than the studies on sleep and vegetables combined.

In **1** through **3**, use the bar graph.

1. About how many fewer ants are there in Ant Farms A and C combined than in Ant Farm E?

2. Which two ant farms combined have about the same number of ants as Ant Farm E?

3. Suppose Ant Farm F has 25 ants. Which ant farms have more ants than Ant Farm F?

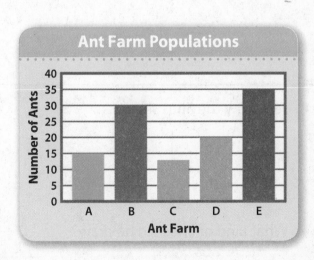

In **4** through **7**, use the bar graph.

4. Analyze Information There are over 350,000 species of beetles. How does this compare to the number of species of moths and butterflies?

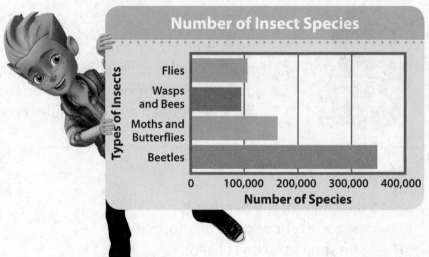

Number of Insect Species

5. Which two types of insects have about the same number of species?

6. Extend Your Thinking If the interval on the graph were changed to 50,000, and the space between the intervals stayed the same, would the bar lengths change or stay the same? Explain.

7. Which of these is true about the data in the graph?

   A The number of moth and butterfly species is greater than the number of wasp and bee species.

   B Flies have the fewest species.

   C There are fewer moth and butterfly species than fly species.

   D The number of fly species is about 400,000 less than the number of beetle species.

8. Jeff drew the lines shown.

What kind of lines did he draw?

9. Ms. Jensen wants to buy enough brown rice to feed 25 campers for 2 weeks. She needs 2 ounces of rice for each camper per day. How many whole pounds of rice does Ms. Jensen need to buy?

Name _____

Solve & Share

Students were surveyed to see which fruit is their favorite. Out of all the students surveyed, 10 students chose apples, 3 students chose bananas, and 4 students chose grapes. Make a bar graph of the data. *Use the grid to solve this problem.*

⭐ **TEKS 5.9A** Represent categorical data with bar graphs or frequency tables and numerical data, including data sets of measurements in fractions or decimals, with dot plots or stem-and-leaf plots. Also, 5.9, 5.9C.
Mathematical Process Standards 5.1A, 5.1B, 5.1C, 5.1D, 5.1E, 5.1F, 5.1G

Digital Resources at PearsonTexas.com

Solve   Learn   Glossary   Check   Tools   Games

Favorite Snack Fruit

Number of Students

Apples   Bananas   Grapes

Create and Use Representations
You can create a bar graph to organize data from a survey. *Show your work!*

Look Back!

Connect Ideas How many students were surveyed? How can you tell?

How Do You Display Data Collected From a Survey?

A survey is a question, or questions, used to gather information called data. When people surveyed represent a larger group, the people are a sample of the larger group. The sample should be selected randomly.

A sample group of students was surveyed about what they do after school. The results were displayed in a tally chart.

Categorical data are data that can be divided into groups.

DATA

After-School Activities

Sports	𝍢𝍢𝍢 𝍢𝍢𝍢 𝍢𝍢𝍢
Homework	𝍢𝍢𝍢 IIII
Chorus	𝍢𝍢𝍢 I
Other	𝍢𝍢𝍢 𝍢𝍢𝍢 II

B **Use the Data to Create a Graph**

Step 1 List the survey answers along one axis.

Step 2 Along the other axis, choose an interval and scale. Make sure your scale includes the least and greatest numbers in the survey results. Label both axes.

Step 3 Graph the data by drawing bars of the correct length or height.

Step 4 Title the graph.

C **Interpret the Graph**

A bar graph uses rectangles (bars) to show how many or how much.

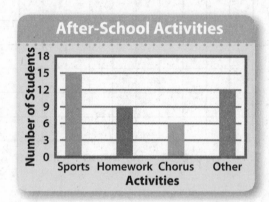

After-School Activities

The activity chosen by the most students is sports. Fewer students participate in chorus than do homework.

Do You Understand?

Convince Me! What is the interval on the graph above?
Would the graph look different if the interval was 1? Explain.

Name _____

☆ Guided Practice*

In **1** through **3**, use the table and bar graph.

City	Number of People
Chicago	3,000,000
Houston	2,000,000
Los Angeles	4,000,000
New York	8,000,000
Philadelphia	1,500,000

Largest U.S. Cities by Population

1. **Make a Graph** Complete the numbers on the scale of the bar graph.

2. Draw the bars showing the values for the last two cities.

3. **Analyze Information** What is the difference in population between the second most populated city and the fifth most populated city?

☆ Independent Practice ☆

In **4** through **6**, use the table and bar graph.

Lake Depths	
Lake	**Depth (in meters)**
Great Salt	7.6
Kyoga	9.1
Manitoba	6.7
Urmia	14.9

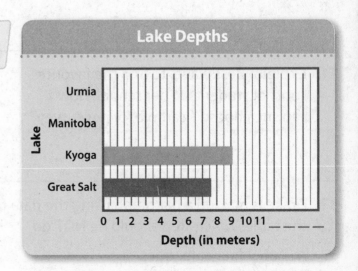

Lake Depths

4. Complete the numbers on the scale of the bar graph.

5. Draw the bars showing the values for the last two lakes.

6. What is the approximate difference in depth between the lake with the greatest depth and the lake with the least depth?

Problem Solving

In **7** through **10**, use the table and bar graph.

Estimated Bald Eagle Population

Year	Number of Pairs
1995	4,712
1996	5,094
1997	5,295
1998	5,748
1999	6,404
2000	6,471

Estimated Number of Bald Eagle Pairs in Lower 48 U.S. States

7. **Make a Graph** Complete the categorical data on the *x*-axis and draw the missing bars.

8. **Analyze Information** Between which two years did the number of eagle pairs increase the least?

9. **Estimation** About how many fewer eagle pairs were there in 1996 than in 2000?

10. **Extend Your Thinking** Do you think the number of eagle pairs increased or decreased in the following years? Explain.

---

11. **Explain** Bess wants to find the favorite sport of students at her school. How can she choose a sample for her survey?

12. **Connect** Vin bought 2 quarts of juice. How many 1-cup servings can he make from 2 quarts of juice?

---

13. Drake is making a bar graph using the data from ⭐ the table. Which step should he **NOT** do?

   A Label four categories.
   B Use an interval of 1,000.
   C Use values on the scale up to 7,000.
   D Match the bar lengths to an interval unit.

Cement Required for Home Projects

Project	Cement Amount (in kg)
Garage Floor	6,680
Porch Floor	2,225
Garden Path	3,500
Backyard Deck	4,200

Name _____

Another Look!

Students were asked to choose their favorite computer activity from a list. How can the data be shown in a bar graph?

DATA

Favorite Computer Activity	
Activity	**Number of Votes**
Games	23
News	8
Research	19

Step 1

Label each axis. Use the data values to choose intervals for the scale.

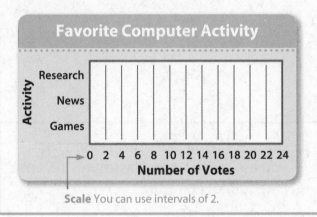

Scale You can use intervals of 2.

Step 2

Draw a bar for each category. Match the bar length to the value on the scale.

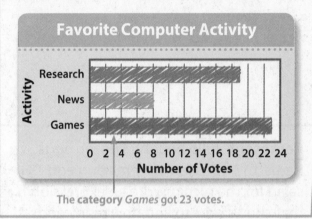

The **category** *Games* got 23 votes.

In **1** and **2**, use the table and bar graph.

DATA

License Plates	
State	**Number of Plates**
Texas	32
Oklahoma	26
Louisiana	17
New Mexico	9

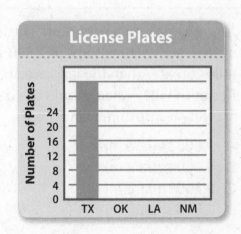

1. Complete the bar graph.

2. How many more license plates were from Texas than from New Mexico?

In **3** through **6**, use the table.

3. If you were to draw a bar graph for this table, what scale and interval would you use?

Top 5 Destinations of U.S. Residents, 2011	
Destination	**Number of Travelers**
Mexico	20,084,000
Canada	11,595,000
United Kingdom	2,405,000
France	1,756,000
Italy	1,702,000

4. How many more U.S. residents visited France than Italy in 2011?

5. **Communicate** Describe how the bars would look in a bar graph of this data.

6. **Extend Your Thinking** Why do you think more residents went to Mexico and Canada than the other destinations?

7. **Represent** Julio bought 3 dozen eggs. He had 13 eggs left after making egg salad for the picnic. Write an expression that shows how to find how many eggs Julio used.

8. **Connect** What survey question can you ask to find your classmates' favorite category of literature?

9. Jenny is making a bar graph. The land area of New Hampshire is about 2,500 square miles greater than the land area of Hawaii. At about what value should the bar end for New Hampshire's land area?

A 9,500 square mi
B 9,000 square mi
C 8,250 square mi
D 7,000 square mi

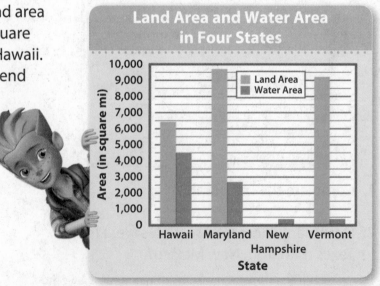

Land Area and Water Area in Four States

© Pearson Education, Inc. 5

Solve & Share

For ten weeks, Joseph washes cars after school. He washes a different number of cars each week: 23, 2, 30, 12, 41, 13, 17, 42, 4, and 24. He created this stem-and-leaf plot to organize the data. What is the difference between the greatest and least values? Can you explain what this means? *Solve this problem any way you choose.*

Lesson 15-6
Reading Stem-and-Leaf Plots

 TEKS 5.9C Solve one- and two-step problems using data from a frequency table, dot plot, bar graph, stem-and-leaf plot, or scatterplot. Also, 5.9. Mathematical Process Standards 5.1B, 5.1C, 5.1D, 5.1G

Digital Resources at PearsonTexas.com

 Solve Learn Glossary Check | Tools | Games

DATA

Number of Cars Washed	
Stem	**Leaf**
0	2 4
1	2 3 7
2	3 4
3	0
4	1 2

KEY: 1 | 2 = 12

Number Sense
You can organize numerical data using place value. *Show your work!*

Look Back!

Justify Does the stem-and-leaf plot make it easy to identify which data values are more common? Explain.

How Do You Read a Stem-and-Leaf Plot?

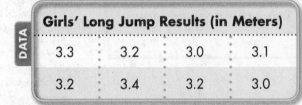

The girls' track team coach wants to display the results of the long jump competition. The distances are displayed in the table below.

Do you know another way you can organize the data?

Girls' Long Jump Results (in Meters)			
3.3	3.2	3.0	3.1
3.2	3.4	3.2	3.0

B

A stem-and-leaf plot is a convenient way to organize data using numerical order and place value.

The ones digit of each data value forms a stem.

The key shows how to read the stems and leaves.

Girls' Long Jump Results (m)

Stem	Leaf
3	0 0
3	1
3	2 2 2
3	3
3	4

KEY: 3│0 = 3.0

The tenths digit of each data value forms a leaf.

This represents the data value of 3 ones and 4 tenths, or 3.4.

Do You Understand?

Convince Me! Write two conclusions about the data shown in the stem-and-leaf plot above.

☆ **Guided Practice**

For **1** and **2**, use the stem-and-leaf plot.

1. What is the least number of points scored? the greatest?

12   45
L   G

Points Scored

Stem	Leaf
1	2 5 8 9
2	0 4 7
3	0 4 6 6 8
4	3 5

KEY: 1|2 = 12

2. How many data values are displayed in the stem-and-leaf plot?

14

3. Explain What is the meaning of this key at the bottom of a stem-and-leaf plot?

KEY: 1|7 = 17

4. Why should the data from a table be written in numerical order before making a stem-and-leaf plot?

☆ **Independent Practice** ☆

Leveled Practice For **5** through **10**, use the stem-and-leaf plot. It shows the number of points scored by a basketball player in each game.

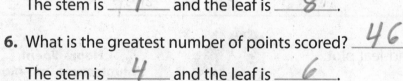

5. What is the least number of points scored? __18__

The stem is __1__ and the leaf is __8__.

6. What is the greatest number of points scored? __46__

The stem is __4__ and the leaf is __6__.

7. How many games were played? __12__

There are __12__ data values in the plot.

8. Which score occurred most often?

35

9. How many scores are less than 29 points?

5

10. How many scores are greater than 35 points?

3

Points Scored Per Game

Stem	Leaf
1	8
2	1 6 7 8 9
3	0 5 5
4	1 4 6

KEY: 1|8 = 18

Problem Solving

11. Reasoning Suppose there are 15 leaves on a stem-and-leaf plot. How many values are in the data set?

12. Terri makes flower bouquets with exactly 3 roses and 5 daisies in each bouquet. She has 72 roses. How many daisies will she need to make the bouquets?

13. Communicate How do you find the least and greatest data values on a stem-and-leaf plot?

14. Extend Your Thinking Some values from a stem-and-leaf plot are 2.1, 2.4, 3.6, and 4.9. Write a key for this plot and explain what the stems and leaves represent.

For **15** and **16**, use the strip diagram.

15. At a discount store, all DVDs have the same price. Chan bought 6 DVDs and paid a total of $62.87, which includes $2.99 in sales tax. What is the first step in finding the cost of one DVD? Complete the strip diagram to solve the first step.

2.99	x

16. What is the cost of one DVD? Draw a strip diagram to help you solve.

For **17** and **18**, use the stem-and-leaf plot.

17. Manny spent 19 hours volunteering last month. What is the difference between this value and the greatest value recorded in the stem-and-leaf plot?

A 7 hours

B 16 hours

C 18 hours

D 37 hours

Hours Spent Volunteering Last Month

Stem	Leaf
1	6 7 9
2	0 6 6 7 9
3	1 5 6 7

KEY: 1|6 = 16

18. Analyze Information How many people volunteered more than 25 hours last month?

Name _____

☆ ☆
Solve & Share

The table shows the cost of ten different concert tickets. Make a stem-and-leaf plot for the data. What conclusions can you make about the ticket prices? *Solve this problem any way you choose.*

⭐ TEKS 5.9A Represent categorical data with bar graphs or frequency tables and numerical data, including data sets of measurements in fractions or decimals, with dot plots or stem-and-leaf plots. Also, 5.9.
Mathematical Process Standards 5.1B, 5.1D, 5.1E, 5.1G

DATA

Cost of Concert Tickets ($)				
42	39	50	38	46
47	44	46	45	51

Digital Resources at PearsonTexas.com

Solve   Learn   Glossary   Check   Tools   Games

Create and Use Representations
You can organize data in a stem-and-leaf plot. *Show your work!*

Look Back!

Justify Is there an outlier in the data set? Explain your answer.

How Can You Make and Use a Stem-and-Leaf Plot?

A stem-and-leaf plot is a chart that uses place value to organize and show individual values in a set of numerical data. The table shows a data set for the mass of ten different rock samples.

You can make a stem-and-leaf plot from the data in the table.

DATA

Mass of Rock Samples (kg)				
0.25	0.32	0.29	0.36	0.08
0.27	0.40	0.34	0.40	0.33

How do you organize the data in a stem-and-leaf plot?

B Order the data from least to greatest:
0.08, 0.25, 0.27, 0.29, 0.32, 0.33, 0.34, 0.36, 0.40, 0.40

A stem-and-leaf plot makes it easy to see how the data values are distributed.

1. Write a title.

3. Write the tenths digits in order as stems.

Mass of Rock Samples (kg)

Stem	Leaf
0	8
1	
2	5 7 9
3	2 3 4 6
4	0 0

KEY: 4|0 = 0.40

2. Draw and label Stem and Leaf.

4. Write the hundredths digits for each stem in order as leaves.

5. Write a key.

Do You Understand?

Convince Me! How would the stem-and-leaf plot above change if 0.49 replaced 0.36?

☆ Guided Practice *

For **1** through **3**, use the table that shows costs of several candles.

Cost of Candles ($)				
5	10	12	8	2
8	15	20	15	6

1. Order the data from least to greatest.

2. If you made a stem-and-leaf plot of the data, what numbers would you use for the stems?

3. Write a key for the stem-and-leaf plot.

4. A stem-and-leaf plot has a key 2|6 = 2.6. How would you add 3.8 to the plot?

5. **Reason** Jackson wants to make a stem-and-leaf plot for 10 data values ranging from 10 to 39. Will there be 10 stems? Will there be 10 leaves? Explain.

☆ Independent Practice ☆

Leveled Practice For **6** and **7**, complete the stem-and-leaf plot of the data.

6. **Prices of Sweaters (dollars)**

33 18 26 37 22
42 26 30 19 27

Prices of Sweaters ($)	
Stem	Leaf
1	
2	
3	
4	
KEY: 1|8 = ☐	

7. **Weights of Pumpkins (pounds)**

35 29 50 49 32 16 55 38
57 43 21 72 56 44 49 40

Weights of Pumpkins (lb)	
Stem	Leaf
1	
2	
3	
4	
5	
6	
7	
KEY: 1|6 = ☐	

Problem Solving

8. **Represent** In a timed race, 10 students took the following times to solve a math puzzle. Represent the data in a stem-and-leaf plot.

Time to Solve (min)

20	14	18	23	15
16	17	16	18	19

DATA

For **9** and **10**, use the plot you made in **8**.

9. **Analyze Information** Write a statement to describe the data.

10. **Extend Your Thinking** An absent student later solved the math puzzle in 9 minutes. How would you add this data value to the plot?

11. **Reason** Shelby scored 85, 84, 77, and 87 on four math tests. She says that a stem-and-leaf plot of her scores would have 3 leaves. Is she correct? Explain.

12. **Explain** How do you determine what key to use in a stem-and-leaf plot when the data values are two-digit numbers?

13. The stem-and-leaf plot shows the side lengths of a ⭐ pentagon. What is the perimeter of the pentagon?

A 147 cm
B 75 cm
C 14.7 cm
D 7.5 cm

Side Lengths (cm)

Stem	Leaf
0	8
1	1 5 9
2	2

KEY: 1|5 = 1.5

DATA

Name _____

Another Look!

The list shows the number of minutes it took each person to complete a crossword puzzle.

Crossword Puzzle Times (min)

35, 23, 27, 31, 25, 24, 19, 41

To represent the data in a stem-and-leaf plot:

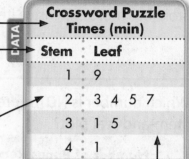

Crossword Puzzle Times (min)

Stem	Leaf
1	9
2	3 4 5 7
3	1 5
4	1

KEY: 1|9 = 19

1. Write a title.

2. Draw two columns. Label one column **Stem** and one column **Leaf**.

3. Write the numbers in order from least to greatest:
   19, 23, 24, 25, 27, 31, 35, 41

4. Write the tens digits from the data in order from least to greatest in the stem column.

5. Next to each stem, write the ones digit from each data value from least to greatest.

6. Include a key for the data values.

---

1. Order the data from least to greatest.

Number of Pages Read

49, 57, 48, 54, 53, 72, 68, 62, 64, 51, 62, 71, 78

2. Complete the stem-and-leaf plot for the data in **1**.

Pages Read

Stem	Leaf

---

3. Order the data from least to greatest.

Hours Worked in 10 Days

28, 30, 35, 40, 28, 32, 41, 34, 38, 33

Remember that the number of leaves should be the same as the number of data values.

4. Complete the stem-and-leaf plot for the data in **3**.

Hours Worked

Stem	Leaf

KEY: 2|8 = 28

For **5** and **6**, use the stem-and-leaf plots that show the prices in dollars of items in two stores.

5. **Analyze Information** What is the difference between the lowest price in Store 1 and the lowest price in Store 2? the highest prices?

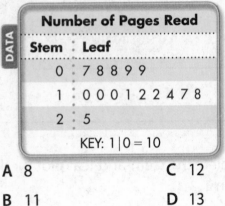

Store 1

DATA	Stem	Leaf
	1	0 1 2 4
	2	1 3 6 7 8
	3	0 1 2 2 2 4 8
	4	0 1 2 5

KEY: 1|0 = 10

Store 2

DATA	Stem	Leaf
	2	0 1 8 9 9
	3	1 3 7 8
	4	0 1 2 3 4 6 7 9
	5	5 7 8

KEY: 2|0 = 20

6. **Extend Your Thinking** Overall, which store has more expensive items? Explain.

7. Which number is **NOT** represented in the stem-and-leaf plot?

Number of Pages Read

DATA	Stem	Leaf
	0	7 8 8 9 9
	1	0 0 0 1 2 2 4 7 8
	2	5

KEY: 1|0 = 10

A 8

B 11

C 12

D 13

8. **Explain** Why is it helpful to write the data from a table in numerical order before making a stem-and-leaf plot?

Make sure your explanation is clear and simple.

9. **Represent** The list shows the mass of several textbooks. Complete the stem-and-leaf plot of the data.

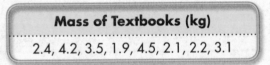

Mass of Textbooks (kg)

2.4, 4.2, 3.5, 1.9, 4.5, 2.1, 2.2, 3.1

Mass of Textbooks (kg)

Stem	Leaf

KEY: 1|9 = 1.9

10. **Explain** What steps did you use to make the stem-and-leaf plot in Problem 9?

11. **Extend Your Thinking** The weights of different televisions range between 10.2 pounds and 15.3 pounds. Write a key that could be used in a stem-and-leaf plot of this data. What stems might be in the plot?

Name_____

☆ ☆
Solve & Share

The graph below shows the ages and prices of 15 used cars at Sam's Wheels and Deals. Describe how the prices of the older cars compare to the prices of the newer cars. *Show your work in the space below!*

⭐ **TEKS 5.9C** Solve one- and two-step problems using data from a frequency table, dot plot, bar graph, stem-and-leaf plot, or scatterplot. Also, 5.9. Mathematical Process Standards 5.1A, 5.1B, 5.1C, 5.1F, 5.1G

Digital Resources at PearsonTexas.com

| Solve | Learn | Glossary | Check | Tools | Games |

You can **connect** what you know about ordered pairs to read the age and price of each car. The point at (3, 14,000) on the graph represents a 3-year-old car whose price is $14,000.

Used Car Prices

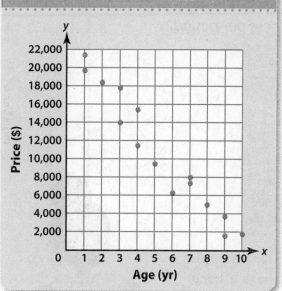

Look Back!

Analyze Information According to the graph, how does the price of a 6-year-old car compare to the price of a 2-year-old car? Explain how you found your answer.

How Can You Read a Scatterplot?

A scatterplot is a coordinate graph that shows paired data. This scatterplot shows the heights and weights of some 5th grade students.

Notice that in general, as the value along one axis increases, the value along the other axis also increases. This suggests that the taller a student is, the more he or she weighs.

When the points lie in a pattern, the two sets of values have a relationship called a trend.

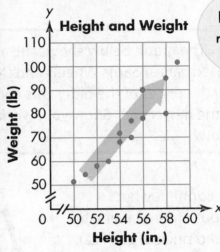

Height and Weight

The marks between 0 and 50 mean that the scale skips some values.

B In this scatterplot, as the value along one axis increases, the value along the other axis decreases. This suggests that a larger bag costs less per pound.

Dog Food

This scatterplot shows a trend.

C In this scatterplot, there is no relationship between the age of a student and the number of sisters he or she has.

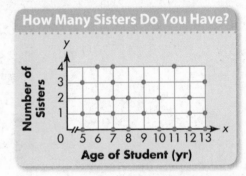

How Many Sisters Do You Have?

Data where only whole numbers are possible are called discrete data. This scatterplot does not show a trend.

Do You Understand?

Convince Me! Which scatterplot on this page shows a trend similar to the trend shown in the scatterplot about used cars on page 841? How are the trends similar?

Name _____

 Guided Practice

For **1** through **4**, use the scatterplot.

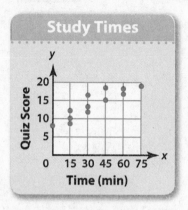

1. What information is shown on the horizontal axis?

2. What information is shown on the vertical axis?

3. What does the point (15, 10) represent?

4. Analyze Information Is there a trend shown in the scatterplot? If so, what does the trend suggest?

Remember that a trend shows a pattern.

Independent Practice

For **5** through **9**, use the scatterplot.

5. What information is shown on the horizontal axis?

6. What information is shown on the vertical axis?

7. How many mistakes did the student who practiced 10 hours make?

8. How long did the student who made 3 mistakes practice?

9. How many fewer mistakes were made by the student who practiced 12 hours than the student who practiced 3 hours?

Problem Solving

10. Gregory needs to apply lawn fertilizer to a lawn with the dimensions shown. Each small bag of fertilizer covers 90 square feet. How many bags of fertilizer will Gregory need?

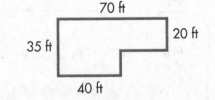

    A 20 bag   C 22 bags
    B 21 bags   D 23 bags

For **11** and **12**, use the scatterplot that shows the prices and screen sizes of TVs at an electronics store.

11. What is the most likely cost of a 50-inch TV?

    A $500   C $1,000
    B $750   D $1,250

12. **Explain** What do the points (52, 800) and (60, 1,100) represent? What conclusion can you draw from these 2 points? Explain.

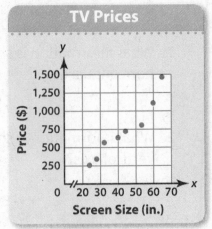

For **13** and **14**, use the scatterplot that shows the number of hours that several students spent watching TV and exercising last Saturday.

13. **Analyze Information** Is there a trend shown in the scatterplot? If so, what does the trend suggest?

14. **Extend Your Thinking** Suppose Jason spent 4 hours exercising last Saturday. How many hours do you suppose he spent watching TV? Explain how you found your answer.

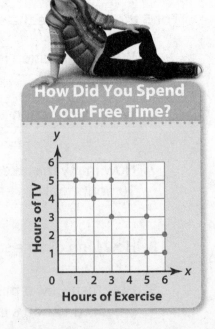

Another Look!

Try to draw a line that is close to most of the data points to see if a relationship exists.

In this scatterplot, there is no relationship between the age of a student and how many miles from school the student lives.

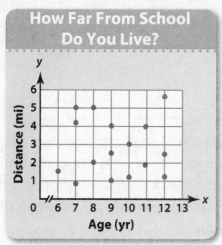

How Far From School Do You Live?

In this scatterplot, as the temperature increases, the attendance at the amusement park increases.

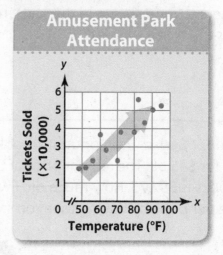

Amusement Park Attendance

For **1** through **5**, use the scatterplot.

1. What quantity is shown on the horizontal axis?

2. What quantity is shown on the vertical axis?

3. What does the point (5, 55) represent?

4. How tall is the student who was born in December?

5. Is there a trend shown in the scatterplot? If so, what does the trend suggest?

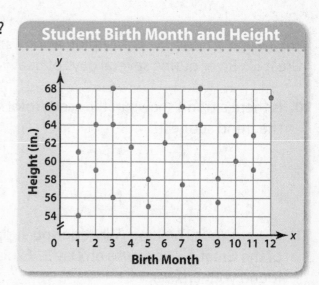

Student Birth Month and Height

For **6** and **7**, use the scatterplot. It shows the number of turnovers made by a basketball team during each of their first 8 games.

6. What does the point (7, 5) represent?

A In game 5, the team had 7 turnovers.
B In game 7, the team had 5 turnovers.
C In game 7, the team had 7 turnovers.
D In game 5, the team had 5 turnovers.

7. Is there a trend shown in the scatterplot? If so, what does the trend suggest?

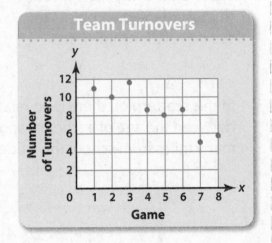

8. **Number Sense** Evan bought 7 books on sale for $45.50. The regular price of the 7 books is $57.75. How much did Evan save per book by buying them on sale?

What operation will you use first?

9. **Reason** A scatterplot shows a laptop computer's age on the *x*-axis and its price on the *y*-axis. What relationship do you think there would be between the data values?

For **10** and **11**, use the scatterplot. It shows the level of the Great Elk River during several days of heavy rain.

10. Is there a trend shown in the scatterplot? If so, what does the trend suggest?

11. **Extend Your Thinking** What do you suppose the depth of the Great Elk River was on Day 3? Explain how you found your answer.

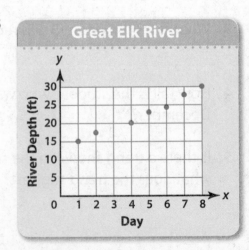

Name _____

Solve & Share

The table shows the distance to a shopping mall and the number of trips made last month by 10 shoppers. Determine if there is a relationship between the distance and the number of trips. *Show your work in the space below!*

⭐ TEKS 5.9B Represent discrete paired data on a scatterplot. Also, 5.9, 5.9C. Mathematical Process Standards 5.1B, 5.1C, 5.1D, 5.1E, 5.1F, 5.1G

Digital Resources at PearsonTexas.com

Solve Learn Glossary Check Tools Games

DATA

Shopping Mall Trips

Distance (mi)	Number of Trips
3	5
4	6
16	1
8	5
13	2
12	2
1	8
3	6
10	4
4	4

Select Tools
What kind of graph would help you see if there is a relationship between the data?

Look Back!

Reason What information can you see in the scatterplot of the data that you might not see in the table?

How Do You Make a Scatterplot?

A

On Sundays, Vivian works at the food stand at the zoo. The table shows data she collected for each Sunday in June and July. Make a scatterplot and describe the relationship, if there is one, between the two sets of values.

Daily High Temperature (°F)	Number of Pints of Water Sold
78°	218
84°	240
87°	248
71°	204
77°	196
80°	211
84°	258
91°	250
81°	241

B Step 1

On a coordinate grid, label the axes. Let *x* represent the first column of data, and let *y* represent the second column of data. Choose a reasonable scale and interval. Give the graph a title.

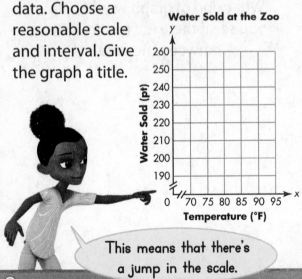

This means that there's a jump in the scale.

C Step 2

Plot the points. Each row of the table represents an ordered pair.

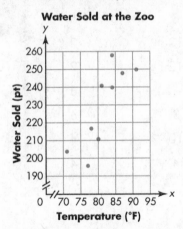

The trend appears to be that as the temperature increases, the water sales also increase.

Do You Understand?

Convince Me! Travis is making a table like the one at the right to record data about the books his classmates read over the summer. If he makes a scatterplot of his data, how should he label the axes? What information can he use to determine the scale on each axis? What would be a good title?

Number of Pages	Weeks Spent Reading

☆ **Guided Practice**

For **1** through **3**, use the table that shows Ben's heart rate, in beats per minute, after different lengths of time exercising.

Minutes of Exercise	Heart Rate (bpm)
0	82
6	103
10	109
15	116
22	132
29	140

1. How should Ben label the axes for a scatterplot of the data?

2. What would be a good title for the scatterplot?

3. Explain How can you determine the scale on each axis of the scatterplot?

4. Communicate How can a scatterplot help you see a trend in data?

Independent Practice

For **5** and **6**, make a scatterplot of the data in each table. Describe the relationship, if there is one, between the two sets of values.

5.

Movie Ticket Sales	Concessions Sales
$150	$45
$375	$110
$300	$90
$450	$125
$275	$100
$200	$75

6.

Weeks of Training	1-Mile Times (min)
1	10.25
4	9.5
6	8.75
9	8.5
11	8
12	7.5

Problem Solving

7. **Represent** Make a scatterplot of the data. Describe the relationship, if there is one, between the two sets of values.

Student's Shoe Size	6	10	8	7	11	8	4
Pairs of Shoes Owned	4	3	2	1	5	6	7

8. **Represent** Make a scatterplot of the data for 8 different snacks. Describe the relationship, if there is one, between the two sets of values.

Number of Fat Grams	17	25	22	18	29	21	23	14
Number of Calories	240	290	300	290	340	275	325	180

9. The scatterplot shows the value of a car after each year it is driven. Describe the relationship between the two sets of values.

   A As the time a car is driven decreases, the value of the car decreases.

   B As the time a car is driven decreases, the value of the car stays the same.

   C As the time a car is driven increases, the value of the car decreases.

   D As the time a car is driven increases, the value of the car increases.

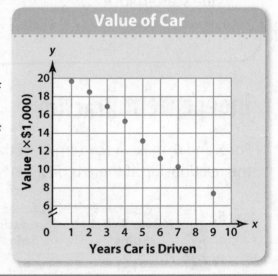

10. **Extend Your Thinking** Draw a straight line on the scatterplot in Problem 9 that is close to most of the data points. Use this line to predict the value of the car after 10 years.

11. **Number Sense** There are 29 students learning to speak a foreign language. Of those, 5 students are studying German. There are twice as many students studying Spanish as there are studying French. How many students are studying each language?

850

Name _____

Homework 15-9
Making Scatterplots

Another Look!

Make a scatterplot and describe the relationship, if there is one, between the two sets of values.

Temperature (°F)	28	27	32	41	36	35	22	38	25
Ski Lift Tickets Sold	62	75	40	19	52	45	77	31	66

Step 1 Label the axes. Let *x* represent the top row of data, and let *y* represent the bottom row.

Step 2 Choose a reasonable scale and interval. The range of *x*-values is 22–41. A good scale is 20–45 with an interval of 5. The range of *y*-values is 19 to 77. A good scale is 10–80 with an interval of 10.

Step 3 Plot the points. Each column of the table represents an ordered pair. Give the graph a title.

The trend appears to be that as the temperature increases, the lift ticket sales decrease.

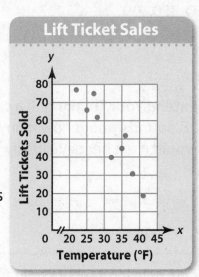

For **1** through **3**, make a scatterplot of the data in each table. Describe the relationship, if there is one, between the two sets of values.

1.

Age (yr)	10	16	21	18	15	9	11	12
Time to Complete Maze (min)	18	20	15	16	25	24	18	20

2.

Tire Size (in.)	15	18	17	16	22	20	19
Cost ($)	110	165	149	135	225	210	180

3.

Amount of Farmland (acres)	18	32	57	63	70	79	84
Number of Cows	15	33	51	60	69	82	85

For **4** through **6**, use the scatterplot that shows the amount of food eaten per day for cats of varying weights.

4. Which ordered pair is **NOT** included in the scatterplot?

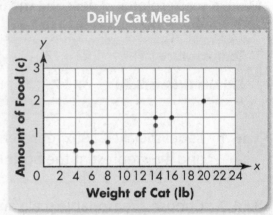

Daily Cat Meals

A (6, 0.5)
B (14, 1)
C (16, 1.5)
D (20, 2)

5. **Extend Your Thinking** If a cat weighed 18 pounds, about how many cups of food would it eat per day? Justify your answer.

6. **Connect** Write an ordered pair for a cat that weighs 10 pounds that would be an outlier for the data.

7. One mile is approximately 1.6 kilometers. How many meters are in one mile?

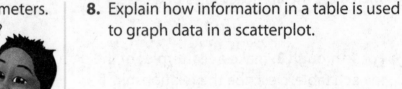

How many meters are in one kilometer?

8. Explain how information in a table is used to graph data in a scatterplot.

9. **Analyze Information** Graph the data from both tables on the same scatterplot. Describe the relationship between the values. Then write a statement that compares the data.

DATA	Dry Pavement	
	Speed (mph)	**Stopping Distance (ft)**
	30	75
	40	120
	50	175
	60	240

DATA	Wet Pavement	
	Speed (mph)	**Stopping Distance (ft)**
	30	120
	40	200
	50	300
	60	420

Name_____

☆ *Solve & Share* ☆

The graph shows Jenna's reading time in minutes. Can you use the information in this graph to describe a real-world situation? *Solve this problem any way you choose.*

⭐ TEKS 5.1E Create and use representations to organize, record, and communicate mathematical ideas. Mathematical Process Standards 5.1A, 5.1B, 5.1D, 5.1F, 5.1G

Digital Resources at PearsonTexas.com

Solve   Learn   Glossary   Check   Tools   Games

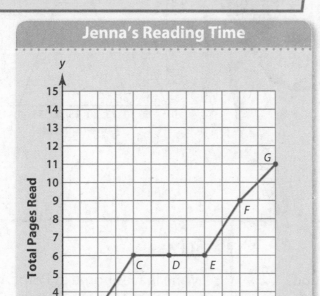

Jenna's Reading Time

Total Pages Read (y-axis)
Time (minutes) (x-axis)

Connect What does the information in this graph tell you? *Show your work!*

Look Back!

Analyze Relationships How would the graph be different if Jenna had finished 9 pages in 15 minutes?

The graph shows a trip that Lynne took to the grocery store. Write a story about Lynne's trip that fits the data on the graph.

Can you explain what happens at each point shown on the graph?

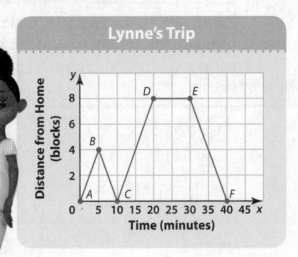

Lynne's Trip

B Plan

Points *A*, *C*, and *F* all have a *y*-value of 0.

So, Lynne must have returned home once during her trip.

Your explanation should be correct, simple, complete, and easy to understand.

C Solve

Lynne leaves home at Point *A* to go to the store. At Point *B*, she is halfway to the store but realizes she has forgotten her wallet. She walks back home to Point *C*. After getting her wallet, Lynne walks to the store at Point *D*. She shops for 10 minutes, to Point *E*. Then Lynne walks home, arriving at Point *F*.

Do You Understand?

Convince Me! After Point *C*, did it take Lynne more time to get to the store or more time to go home? How can you tell from the graph?

☆ **Guided Practice** *

For **1** through **4**, use the graph on page 854.

1. What ordered pair locates Point *B* on the graph? What do these coordinates represent?

2. What does Point *C* tell you about Lynne's location?

3. How can you explain what happened between Points *A* and *C*?

4. Why can you say that Lynne was at the store for 10 minutes?

☆ **Independent Practice** ☆

For **5** through **8**, use the graph that shows what happened when Jim went biking.

5. What might have happened between Points *C* and *D*?

6. Between which two points did Jim bike the fastest?

7. Between which two points did Jim bike the slowest?

8. Write a story to fit the data on the graph. Tell what Jim might have been doing between each pair of data points.

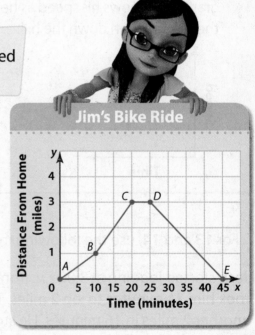

Jim's Bike Ride

Problem Solving

For **9** and **10**, use the graph that shows the route Monique walked her dog. There is a dog park 5 blocks from her home.

9. **Reason** Between which two points did Monique stop at the dog park?

10. How long did Monique stay at the dog park?

   A 5 min
   B 20 min
   C 25 min
   D 60 min

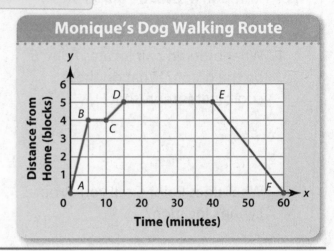

Monique's Dog Walking Route

11. **Extend Your Thinking** Hector is riding his bike on a bike trail when he comes to a large hill. Sketch and describe a graph that shows his speed as he rides up the hill and then down the hill.

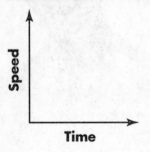

12. **Math and Science** In July 2008, a wildfire near Yosemite National Park burned about 53 square miles of forest. If one square mile equals 640 acres, about how many acres of forest were burned?

For **13** and **14**, use the following information.

Josh started jogging at 3:00 P.M. from his home. It took him 24 minutes to jog 2 miles. Then he jogged another 2 miles in 16 minutes. He stopped to rest for 8 minutes before turning around to jog home. He got home at 4:36 P.M.

13. Complete the graph of Josh's jogging route.

14. How many miles did Josh jog all together? How many minutes did it take him to complete his route?

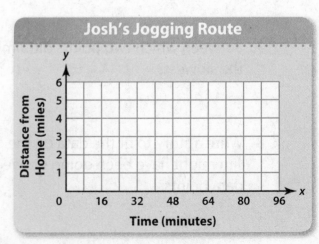

Josh's Jogging Route

856
© Pearson Education, Inc. 5

Another Look!

Della comes home and sits down to have a snack for 15 minutes. Then she gets a 15-minute ride to her violin lesson, which is 3 miles away. Della spends 45 minutes at the lesson. She gets another ride home that lasts for 30 minutes.

A horizontal line tells you that Della has stopped at a location.

The graph shows the events of the story.

Between Points A and B, Della is having a snack at home for 15 minutes.

Between Points B and C, Della gets a ride to violin practice. The car ride lasts 15 minutes.

Between Points C and D, Della is at practice for 45 minutes.

Between Points D and E, Della gets a ride home.

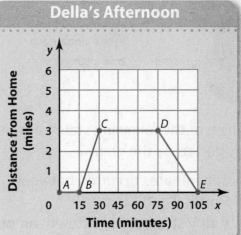

Della's Afternoon

For **1** through **4**, use the following information and the graph.

Students at Larkin High School had a car wash to raise funds for the music club. The car wash began at 11:00 A.M.

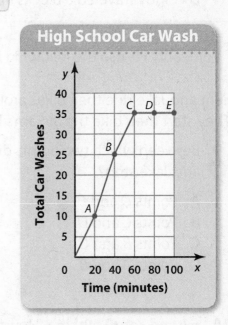

High School Car Wash

1. Look at Point A. How many cars were washed after 20 minutes?

2. Look at Point B. How many more cars were washed in the next 20 minutes?

3. What might have happened between Points C and D?

4. **Explain** Write a story to fit the data on the graph.

In **5** through **8**, use the graph that shows Cindy's errands.

5. Look at the coordinates at Point *A*. What does Point *A* represent?

6. **Analyze Information** What do you think happened between Points *B* and *C*?

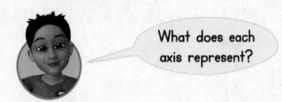

What does each axis represent?

Cindy's Errands

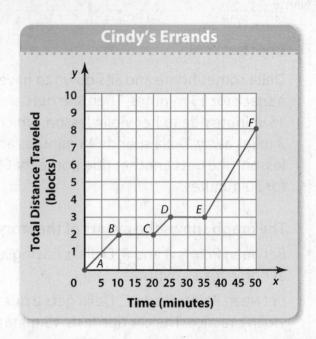

7. Which of the following statements is supported by the graph?

   A Ten minutes occurred between Points *B* and *C*.

   B Cindy stopped for different amounts of time.

   C Cindy spent more time stopping than walking.

   D Cindy traveled 8 blocks in 30 minutes.

8. Write a complete story to match the data from the graph.

For **9** and **10**, use the following information and the graph.

Sam and Jake ride their bikes around the neighborhood. They start their bike trip at Sam's house.

9. Between which two points did Sam and Jake stop?

   A Points *D* and *E*

   B Points *C* and *D*

   C Points *B* and *C*

   D Points *A* and *B*

Sam and Jake's Bike Trip

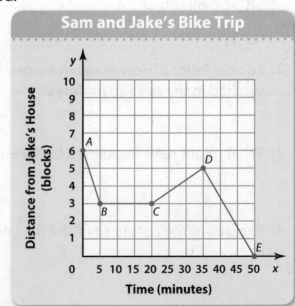

10. **Extend Your Thinking** How far does Jake live from Sam?

© Pearson Education, Inc. 5

Name _____

1. **Connect** The average car length is 200 inches. How many feet and inches long is the average car?

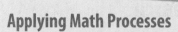

Applying Math Processes

- How does this problem connect to previous ones?
- What is my plan?
- How can I use tools?
- How can I use number sense?
- How can I communicate and represent my thinking?
- How can I organize and record information?
- How can I explain my work?
- How can I justify my answer?

2. **Number Sense** Rosa spent $\frac{2}{7}$ of each ⭐ week, for 5 weeks, training for a swim meet. What was the total amount of time, in weeks, she spent training for the swim meet?

   A $5\frac{2}{7}$ weeks   **C** $\frac{5}{7}$ week

   B $1\frac{3}{7}$ weeks   **D** $\frac{10}{35}$ week

3. Which figure does **NOT** have 2 pairs of parallel sides?

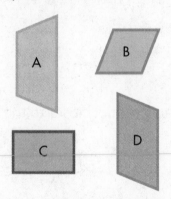

4. **Extend Your Thinking** Mr. Li made a necktie with an area of 120 square inches. What is a possible length and width, in whole numbers, for the necktie? Explain.

5. Fran measured the growth of the fleece on her angora goat for 6 months. The goat began with 1 inch of fleece. She saw that the goat's fleece grew by the same amount each month. What was the total length of the goat's fleece in Month 5?

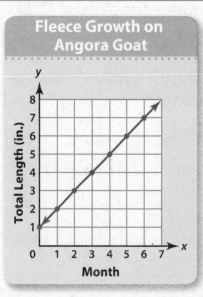

Error Search

Find each problem that is not correct. Circle what is wrong and rewrite the problem so it is correct.

1. $\frac{1}{7} \div 4 = \frac{1}{7} \times \frac{4}{1} = \frac{4}{7}$

2. $18 \times \frac{5}{6} = \frac{18 \times 5}{1 \times 6} = \frac{90}{6} = 15$

3. $54 \div \frac{1}{8} = 54 \times \frac{8}{1} = 432$

4. $\frac{7}{9} \times 36 = \frac{7 \times 36}{9 \times 9} = \frac{252}{81} = 3\frac{9}{81} = 3\frac{1}{9}$

Reasoning

Write whether each statement is true or false. If you write false, change the numbers or words so that the statement is true.

5. Estimating the product of 380 and 12 by using 400 × 10 will give a product closer to the exact answer than by using 350 × 10.

6. Estimating the quotient of 4,318 ÷ 67 by using 4,800 ÷ 60 will give a quotient closer to the exact answer than by using 4,200 ÷ 70.

7. Estimating the quotient of $764.18 ÷ 24 by using 750 ÷ 25 will give a quotient closer to the exact answer than by using 780 ÷ 20.

8. When you multiply 0.65 by 72, the product is greater than 72.

9. When you divide 9 wholes into equal $\frac{1}{8}$ pieces, the quotient is less than 1.

Name _____

Set A | pages 799–804

The data set below shows the number of goals scored by 20 teams in a soccer tournament.

4, 8, 7, 0, 3, 3, 7, 4, 6, 1,

2, 7, 6, 4, 2, 7, 2, 6, 7, 4

Team Soccer Goals

Number of Soccer Goals

The dot plot shows how often each data value occurs.

Reteaching

Remember that an outlier is a number that is very different from the rest of the numbers in a dot plot.

Use the dot plot at the left.

1. How many soccer teams scored 3 goals?

2. How many teams scored more than 5 goals?

3. What was the greatest number of goals scored by a team?

4. How many teams scored only 2 goals?

5. What is the difference between the greatest and least number of goals scored?

Set B | pages 805–810

Twenty people were surveyed about the amount of time they watch TV on a Saturday. Make a dot plot and frequency table to display the data.

2, 3, 1, 4, 3, 5, 1, 0, 1, 1

1, 3, 0, 3, 3, 4, 5, 0, 0, 1

Number of Hours	Tally	Frequency
0	IIII	4
1	⧞⧞⧞ I	6
2	I	1
3	⧞⧞⧞	5
4	II	2
5	II	2

DATA

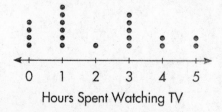

Hours Spent Watching TV

Remember that you can make a dot plot to show the frequency of the data.

Use the dot plot at the left.

1. What was the longest amount of time spent watching TV?

2. How many people in the survey did not watch TV?

3. How many hours of TV did the most people watch?

4. What fraction of the 20 people watched TV for 3 hours or more on Saturday? What fraction of people watched an hour or less of TV?

Set C pages 811–816

The dot plot shows the amount of flour Cheyenne needs for each batch of baked goods. She organizes the data in a frequency table to calculate the total amount of flour she needs.

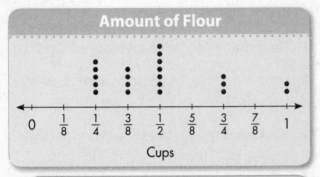

Amount of Flour (cups)	Frequency	Multiplication
$\frac{1}{4}$	5	$\frac{1}{4} \times 5 = 1\frac{1}{4}$
$\frac{3}{8}$	4	$\frac{3}{8} \times 4 = 1\frac{1}{2}$
$\frac{1}{2}$	7	$\frac{1}{2} \times 7 = 3\frac{1}{2}$
$\frac{3}{4}$	3	$\frac{3}{4} \times 3 = 2\frac{1}{4}$
1	2	$1 \times 2 = 2$

Remember that you can multiply each data value by its frequency to find the total amount.

Use the dot plot and frequency table at the left.

1. What values are multiplied in the third column of the table?

2. How many cups of flour does Cheyenne need in all?

3. Write an equation to find the total amount of flour Cheyenne needs.

Set D pages 817–822

A bar graph uses bars to show data. The bars can then be used to compare the data. Which animal has about 34 teeth?

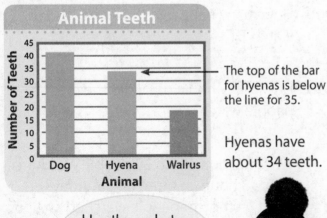

The top of the bar for hyenas is below the line for 35.

Hyenas have about 34 teeth.

Use the scale to find how much each bar represents.

Remember that a bar graph can be a good way to compare categorical data.

Use the bar graph at the left.

1. What is the graph about?

2. What is the scale of the graph?

3. What is the interval?

4. Which animal has 18 teeth?

5. About how many more teeth does a dog have than a walrus?

© Pearson Education, Inc. 5

TOPIC
15

You can show the results of a survey in a bar graph. The height of each bar matches the number of votes in the frequency table.

Favorite Sport

DATA

Activity	Number of Votes
Football	15
Soccer	7
Volleyball	12
Basketball	20

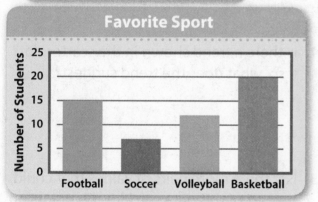

Favorite Sport

Remember that the bar graph uses bars to show how many or how much.

Reteaching
Continued

Use the bar graph and frequency table at the left.

1. Which activity had the most votes?

2. Which activity had the fewest votes?

3. Describe the scale and interval.

4. If 3 more students voted for soccer, how would the bar graph change?

5. How many more students voted for football than for volleyball?

A stem-and-leaf plot can display data.

Jean Sizes (in.):

31, 32, 41, 44, 33, 21, 22, 32, 36, 37, 42, 29

1. List the numbers in order from least to greatest: 21, 22, 29, 31, 32, 32, 33, 36, 37, 41, 42, 44

Jean Sizes (in.)

DATA

Stem	Leaf
2	1 2 9
3	1 2 2 3 6 7
4	1 2 4

KEY: 2|1 = 21

2. For the stems, list the tens digits in order.

3. For each tens digit, record the ones digits in order as the leaves.

Remember to write the data in order from least to greatest before making your plot.

Use the stem-and-leaf plot at the left.

1. How many pairs of jeans had sizes greater than 30 inches?

Use each set of data to make a stem-and-leaf plot.

2. Math scores: 75, 86, 92, 90, 88, 79, 95, 98, and 85.

3. Daily high temperatures: 28, 32, 27, 34, 38, 48, 50, 47, 34, 38, 49

You can plot data in a table in a scatterplot. A scatterplot can show relationships between two sets of data values.

DATA	Daily High Temperature (°F)	70	86	85	95	87	90	84
	Number of People	70	90	80	104	95	98	74

1. Label the axes.

2. Choose a reasonable scale and interval.

3. Plot the ordered pairs on the scatterplot.

The scatterplot shows a trend in the data since the points seem to lie in a pattern.

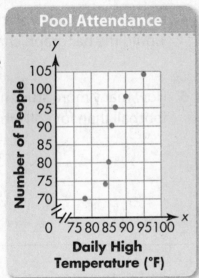

Pool Attendance

Number of People (vertical axis); Daily High Temperature (°F) (horizontal axis)

Remember that if the points in a scatterplot lie in a pattern, there is a relationship between the data values. If the points do not lie in a pattern, there is no relationship.

Use the scatterplot at the left.

1. What quantity is shown on the horizontal axis?

2. What quantity is shown on the vertical axis?

3. What does the point (85, 80) represent?

4. Is there a trend shown in the scatterplot? If so, what does the trend suggest?

5. List three more pairs of values that could be part of this data set. Plot the points on the scatterplot.

The graph shows sales of a new video game. Write a story about the first 3 days of the sale.

New Video Game

Number Sold (vertical axis); Days of Sale (horizontal axis)

Sales of a new video game rise during the first 3 days. Sales increase from 4 games on Day 1 to 12 games on Day 3.

Remember that a written explanation should be correct, simple, complete, and easy to understand.

Use the graph at the left.

1. What happens to sales on Days 4 and 5?

2. What happens on Day 6?

3. How might you explain what happened on Day 7?

© Pearson Education, Inc. 5

Name_____

1. Which dot plot shows the data?

8	$7\frac{1}{2}$	$8\frac{3}{4}$	$7\frac{1}{4}$	$7\frac{1}{4}$	$8\frac{3}{4}$	$8\frac{3}{4}$
$8\frac{3}{4}$	$8\frac{3}{4}$	8	$8\frac{3}{4}$	$9\frac{1}{4}$	$9\frac{1}{4}$	$7\frac{1}{4}$

A

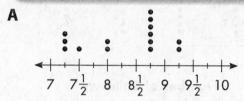

7 $7\frac{1}{2}$ 8 $8\frac{1}{2}$ 9 $9\frac{1}{2}$ 10

B

7 $7\frac{1}{2}$ 8 $8\frac{1}{2}$ 9 $9\frac{1}{2}$ 10

C

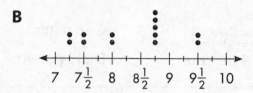

7 $7\frac{1}{2}$ 8 $8\frac{1}{2}$ 9 $9\frac{1}{2}$ 10

D

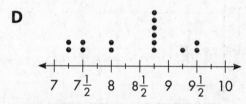

7 $7\frac{1}{2}$ 8 $8\frac{1}{2}$ 9 $9\frac{1}{2}$ 10

2. How many students scored between 80 and 90 points?

Student Test Scores	
Stem	**Leaf**
7	2 4 8 8
8	1 1 3 5 6 8 9
9	1 3 3 6 7
KEY: 7|2 = 72	

A 16 students   **C** 8 students

B 12 students   **D** 7 students

3. Use the stem-and-leaf plot in Problem **2**. What is the difference between the highest score and the lowest score?

4. Which statement best describes the trend in the data?

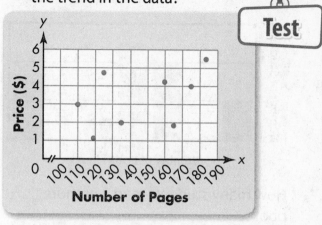

A As the number of pages decreases, the price decreases.

B As the number of pages increases, the price decreases.

C As the number of pages increases, the price increases.

D There is no trend in the data.

5. Which data point is **NOT** on the scatterplot in Problem **4**?

A (125, 4.75)   **C** (160, 4.25)

B (150, 5)   **D** (175, 4)

6. The graph shows the flight of a red-tailed hawk. Explain what could have happened between Point *C* and Point *D*.

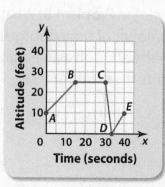

7. Mrs. Chi made a bar graph of the number of books her students read.

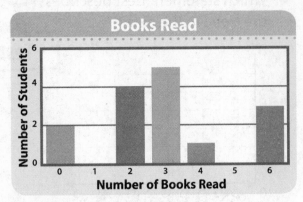

Books Read

How many students read 3 or more books?

A 5 students   **C** 9 students

B 8 students   **D** 10 students

8. Georgiana made a dot plot of her violin practice schedule for the past two weeks.

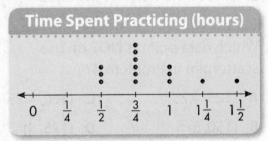

Time Spent Practicing (hours)

What is the difference between the greatest and least times spent practicing?

A $\frac{1}{2}$ hour   **C** 1 hour

B $\frac{3}{4}$ hour   **D** $1\frac{1}{2}$ hour

9. Use the dot plot in Problem **8**. What is the total amount of time Georgiana practiced? Write and solve an equation that represents the total amount of time.

10. The dot plot shows the results from a survey asking parents how many children they have in the school. How many parents have two children in the school?

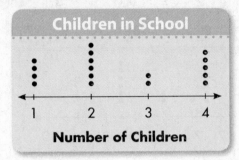

Children in School

A 2 parents   **C** 6 parents

B 4 parents   **D** 12 parents

11. What is the interval used on the y-axis?

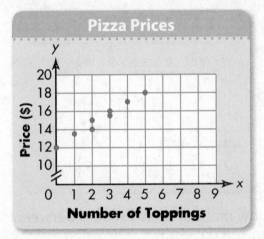

Pizza Prices

A 1

B 10

C 20

D Not here

12. In the scatterplot in Problem **11**, what does the point (2, 14) represent?

Name _____

13. Which is the total length of rope represented by the data in the dot plot?

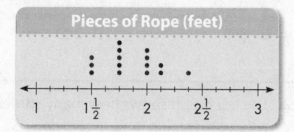

Pieces of Rope (feet)

1   1½   2   2½   3

A $25\frac{1}{8}$ feet   C $27\frac{7}{8}$ feet

B $27\frac{5}{8}$ feet   D 28 feet

14. Which statement is true?

Students per Class	
Stem	**Leaf**
1	7 8 8 9
2	0 2 2 3 4 4 4 8
3	0

KEY: 1 | 7 = 17

A The smallest class has 19 students.

B Most classes have fewer than 25 students.

C The biggest class has 28 students.

D Most of the classes have between 10 and 19 students.

15. In Problem **14**, how many students are in the most common class size?

A 18 students

B 19 students

C 22 students

D 24 students

16. If you made a stem-and-leaf plot of the data in the table, how many stems and how many leaves would you use?

Ages of People Taking Guitar Lessons
15, 18, 16, 22, 15, 17, 30, 25, 14, 19

A 2 stems, 10 leaves

B 3 stems, 10 leaves

C 10 stems, 3 leaves

D 10 stems, 10 leaves

17. How many students are included in the stem-and-leaf plot?

Heights of Students (in.)	
Stem	**Leaf**
4	8 9 9
5	2 4 4 4 5 8
6	0 1 2

KEY: 4 | 8 = 48

A 10 students   C 12 students

B 11 students   D 15 students

18. In Problem **17**, how many students are taller than 50 inches?

A 9 students

B 8 students

C 6 students

D 3 students

19. Jason left his house at 12:30 P.M. First he stopped at the bank. Then he went to the library before going back home. The graph shows Jason's trip.

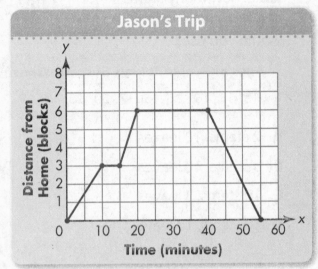

Jason's Trip

How long was Jason at the library?

A 6 min   **C** 20 min

B 15 min   **D** 25 min

20. Use the graph in Problem **19**. What time did Jason get home?

A 1:25 P.M.   **C** 1:35 P.M.

B 1:30 P.M.   **D** 1:55 P.M.

21. In Problem **19**, how many blocks did Jason walk in all?

22. A key on a scatterplot reads $5 \mid 2 = 0.52$. What number is represented with a stem of 3 and a leaf of 4?

A 0.34   **C** 34

B 3.4   **D** 340

23. The bar graph shows how many students take each foreign language class. How many more students take Spanish than Latin?

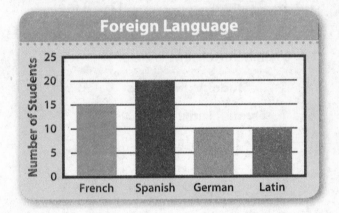

Foreign Language

A 5 students   **C** 15 students

B 10 students   **D** 30 students

24. Use the bar graph in Problem **23**. How many students are taking a foreign language in all?

Personal Financial Literacy

Essential Question: How can understanding taxes, income, methods of payment, and budgets help you make decisions about saving and spending?

Most fossils form when living things die and get buried in sediment.

Scientists dig up and study fossils. They help to show a picture of Earth's past environments.

Dig it! So finding fossils of mammals and plants in Antarctica tells us that the environment there has changed. Here's a project about fossils and environment.

Math and Science Project: Fossils and Environment

Do Research Use the Internet or other sources to find out more about what fossils tell us about past environments. Research and make a booklet of fossils found in your state. Find at least 5 fossils and use one page for each fossil. Include where each fossil was found and what type of environment each location is now.

Write a Report: Journal Include what you found. Also in your report:

- List the types of food each of the five creatures ate when they were alive.

- Determine whether each of the 5 creatures on your list could live in today's environment. Why or why not?

- Make up and solve problems about buying fossils. How much do you budget to save and spend?

Review What You Know

Vocabulary

Choose the best term from the box. Write it on the blank.

> - decimal number
> - decimal point
> - fraction
> - whole number

1. To round 7.2 to the nearest _____, drop the digits in the decimal part of the number.

2. A number with digits in the tenths and hundredths places is a _____.

3. To place the _____ in a product, count the decimal places in both factors.

Add and Subtract Decimals

Find each sum or difference.

4. $80.3 + 0.79$ **5.** $6.18 - 4.25$

6. $3.2 - 3.094$ **7.** $49.702 + 12.6$

8. $962.05 + 26.18$ **9.** $71.80 - 15.064$

Multiply with Decimals

Find each amount.

10. The cost of 1.8 pounds of macadamia nuts with a price of $14 for each pound

11. The cost of a 4-kilogram pumpkin with a price of $1.20 for each kilogram

12. The cost of 0.6 meter of electrical wire with a price of $2.30 for each meter

13. The price of a bicycle increased by 0.13 times the amount of last year's price. If last year's price was $74, how much is the increase?

   A $9.62
   B $13.00
   C $83.62
   D $96.20

---

14. **Writing to Explain** It cost Ali $2 for materials to make a ring. Her selling price is the cost of materials increased by $1.50. What is the selling price? Explain how you found your answer.

My Word Cards

Use the examples for each word on the front of the card to help complete the definitions on the back.

A-Z

taxes

Sales tax
Property tax
Income tax

gross income
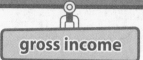

$1,000   Gross Income
− 350   Deduction
$ 650   Net Income

net income

$1,000   Gross Income
− 350   Deduction
$ 650   Net Income

deposit
$20(+)

BANK

debit
$20(−)

BANK

balance
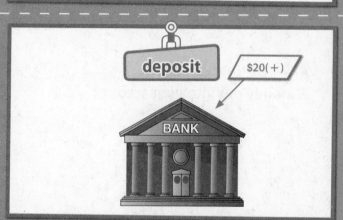

Bank Statement	
Deposit	+ $125.50
Withdrawal	− $50.00
Deposit	+ $87.00
Balance	$162.50

DATA

budget

Mia's Monthly Budget
Income: $800
Expenses: $725
Savings: $75

balanced budget

Total Income = Total Expenses

My Word Cards

Complete the definition. Extend learning by writing your own definitions.

Gross income
is the total amount of money you earn.

Money people pay to support the government is called _taxes_.

A _deposit_
is money put into your account.

Net income is the amount of money you receive after deductions are subtracted from your gross income.

The _balance_ is the money in your account.

A _debit_
is money taken out of your account.

A _balanced budget_
occurs when the total amount of money spent, saved, and shared equals total income.

A plan for how much income will be received and how it will be spent is called a _budget_.

Name _____

☆ **Solve & Share** ☆

Your county needs $100,000 to finish work on a new park. List at least three different ways county officials might get this money.

⊕ TEKS 5.10A Define income tax, payroll tax, sales tax, and property tax. Also, 5.10. Mathematical Process Standards 5.1A, 5.1B, 5.1C, 5.1D, 5.1G

Digital Resources at PearsonTexas.com

Solve   Learn   Glossary   Check   Tools   Games

You can **connect** to the real world by thinking about when your family pays money to your county or state.

Look Back!

Check for Reasonableness Explain why your answers are reasonable.

What Are Taxes?

A

Taxes are money people pay to support governments.

Sales tax is paid whenever you buy things.

Property tax is paid when you own property, such as a home.

Income tax is paid when you have income.

Tina bought the jeans shown in a county where the sales tax is 7%, which means 0.07 times the price. What is the cost of the jeans with sales tax?

SALE $15

Governments use tax money to pay for things like roads and schools.

B Step 1

Multiply to find the amount of sales tax.

$$\begin{array}{r} \overset{3}{\$15} \\ \times\ \ 0.07 \\ \hline \$1.05 \end{array}$$

7% = 0.07

The sales tax is $1.05.

C Step 2

Add to find the cost with sales tax.

$$\begin{array}{r} \$15.00 \\ +\ \ \ 1.05 \\ \hline \$16.05 \end{array}$$

Remember:
$15 = $15.00

The cost with tax is $16.05.

Do You Understand?

Convince Me! What would Tina pay with sales tax for a $25 pair of shoes in the same mall? Show how you found the answer.

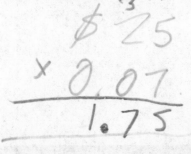

$$\begin{array}{r} \overset{3}{\$25} \\ \times\ 0.07 \\ \hline 1.75 \end{array}$$

$$\begin{array}{r} 25.00 \\ 1.75 \\ \hline 26.75 \end{array}$$

Name _____

Another Look!

Emma's employer deducts 20% from her wages in payroll taxes. How much is deducted when Emma earns $460?

Remember: 20% means 0.2.

$$\begin{array}{r} \overset{1}{\$460} \leftarrow \text{0 decimal places} \\ \times\ 0.2 \leftarrow +\text{1 decimal place} \\ \hline 92.0 \leftarrow \text{1 decimal place} \end{array}$$

$92 is deducted in payroll taxes.

For **1** through **6**, find the cost with sales tax for each purchase price. Assume that the sales tax is 7%, or 0.07 times the price.

1. $17

2. $63

3. $37

4. $59

5. $82

6. $44

---

7. Janie's employer deducts 20%, 0.2 times her wages, in payroll taxes. How much is deducted when Janie earns $675?

8. Val's employer deducts 20%, 0.2 times his wages, in payroll taxes. How much is deducted when Val earns $421?

---

9. How much property tax must be paid each month when the property tax is $1,176 a year?

10. How much property tax must be paid each month when the property tax is $1,644 a year?

Remember: There are 12 months in one year.

11. The Keskin family pays $1,503 a year in property tax and $874 a month for their house payment. How much do they pay each month for the property tax and the house payment combined?

A $999.25   C $1,014.30

B $962.25   D $1,024.30

12. **Estimation** Harry bought a saxophone for $109 in a county where the sales tax is 7%, or 0.07 times the purchase price. Should the sales tax be more or less than $7? Use estimation to explain your answer.

13. Gordon earned $268 last week. Complete the table by finding the amount of each deduction taken out of his paycheck. Then find his total payroll deductions.

Deduction	Multiply Earnings By	Amount
Federal income tax	0.10	
Social security	0.06	
Medicare	0.02	
Total		

For **14** and **15**, use the picture. Assume that the sales tax is 8%, or 0.08 times the price.

14. What is the cost with sales tax for the package of glitter pens shown? Show your work.

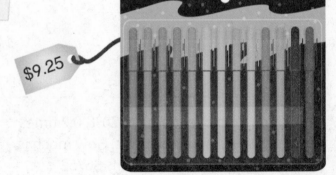

$9.25

15. **Number Sense** Les bought glitter pens, paper, and an easel. If he paid $2.74 in sales tax for the easel, did the easel or the glitter pens cost more?

16. **Explain** How many half-pint servings are in a gallon of lemonade? Explain your answer.

How many pints are in a gallon?

17. **Extend Your Thinking** Jacky used the equation below to show the amount she paid in sales tax for an item that cost $80.

$$80 \times s = 4$$

Explain how you would solve the equation for s, the sales tax.

Remember: Another way to write 4 is 4.00.

Name _____

☆ ☆
Solve & Share

Marcus worked 40 hours last week. He makes $10 an hour. His paycheck for the week was $320. Why do you think he did not receive all the money he earned?

TEKS 5.10B Explain the difference between gross income and net income Also, 5.10, 5.10A.
Mathematical Process Standards 5.1B, 5.1C, 5.1F, 5.1G

Digital Resources at PearsonTexas.com

Solve   Learn   Glossary   Check   Tools   Games

You can use **mental math** to find the total amount Marcus earned and compare it to what he got.

Look Back!

Number Sense If Marcus worked 20 hours another week, how much do you think his paycheck will be? Explain why.

How Can You Find Gross Income and Net Income?

A

Gross income is the total amount of money you earn.

Net income is the amount of money you receive after deductions are subtracted from your gross income.

Jasmine worked 35 hours last week at Quick Burgers. She makes $8 an hour. What is Jasmine's gross income? What is her net income?

> Deductions include payroll taxes, health insurance, and other things.

B Paychecks usually come with a pay stub, like the one shown. Here is how amounts on the pay stub are calculated.

Quick Burgers 324 Main St.			Jasmine Sanchez 156 3rd St.	Week of March 2
	Rate	Hrs	Deductions	Amount
	$8	35	Federal Income Tax	33.60
			Social Security	16.80
Gross Income	$280.00		Medicare	5.60
Deductions	$81.50		Health Insurance	25.50
Net income	$198.50		Total Deductions	$81.50

Multiply to find gross income: $8 x 35

Subtract deductions to find net income: $280.00 - 81.50

Add to find total deductions: 33.60 + 16.80 + 5.60 + 25.50

Jasmine's gross income is $280.00 and her net income is $198.50.

Do You Understand?

Convince Me!
Complete Arnold's pay stub.
What is Arnold's gross income?
What is his net income?

Pump and Go 647 Main St.			Arnold Katz 523 Vine St.	March 4
	Rate	Hours	Deductions	Amount
	$12	32	Federal Income Tax	46.08
			Social Security Tax	23.04
Gross Income			Medicare Tax	7.68
Deductions			Health Insurance	$45.00
Net income			Total Deductions	

© Pearson Education, Inc. 5

Name _____

In **1** and **2**, find each net income.

1. Gross income: $126.35
   Deductions: $35.30

2. Gross income: $603
   Deductions: $151.12

3. **Explain** Madelyn's gross income is $410. The deductions are 0.2 times her gross income. What is her net income? How did you find the answer?

Independent Practice *

In **4** and **5**, find each net income.

4. Gross income: $500.50
   Deductions: $25.27

5. Gross income: $326
   Deductions: 0.2 times gross income

For **6** through **8**, use the pay stub.

6. Complete Wendy's pay stub.

7. How did you find Wendy's gross income?

8. How did you calculate Wendy's total deductions?

Wendy Stevens		T & G Bookstore	February 25
Rate: $11/ hour Hours: 26		Deductions	Amount
Gross Income		Federal Income Tax	$42.90
		Social Security	$17.73
Deductions		Medicare	$4.15
		Community Charity	$10.00
Net Income		Total Deductions	

Problem Solving

9. Analyze Information Janine's gross income was $450. What was her net income if the deductions were $90 for payroll taxes and $32.75 for health insurance?

10. Tyrone's gross income was $388.40. His net income was $299.07. What was the total amount of his deductions?

A $89.33

B $99.30

C $209.74

D $687.47

For **11** and **12**, use the picture.

11. What is the cost with sales tax for the scooter? Assume sales tax is 8%, or 0.08 times the cost of the purchase.

12. Monty is buying a scooter and a helmet. The cashier finds his total for the purchase, including sales tax. If Monty gives the cashier six $20 bills, how much change should he receive?

$57

$40

13. The Chinns pay $2,568 a year in property taxes on their home. If they make monthly payments, how much do they pay each month? Complete the strip diagram.

| ? | ? | ? | ? | ? | ? | ? | ? | ? | ? | ? | ? |

↑
? monthly payment

14. Extend Your Thinking Ms. Lynch's gross income for the year is $31,920. Every month, the deductions total $611. What is Ms. Lynch's net income for the year?

What operation will you use first?

Name _____

Another Look!

Brian earns $8.75 an hour. Last month, he worked 34 hours. The deductions are shown in the box. Find Brian's gross income and net income.

Remember:

gross income − deductions = net income

DATA		
Federal Income Tax	$35.70
Social Security	$18.45
Medicare	$4.32
Neighbor's Aid Charity	$5.00

Step 1

Multiply.

```
  2 1
  3 2
  8.75
× 34
 3500
26250
297.50
```

Brian's gross income is $297.50.

Step 2

Find the total deductions.

```
  2 1
 35.70
 18.45
  4.32
+ 5.00
 63.47
```

The total deductions are $63.47.

Step 3

Subtract.

```
      4 10
297.50
− 63.47
234.03
```

Brian's net income is $234.03.

In **1** and **2**, find each net income.

1. Gross income: $408.68
   Deductions: $98.98

2. Gross income: $252.00
   Deductions: $70.75

3. Complete George's pay stub.

George Brown		Signature Software	February 25
Rate: $16/ hour Hours: 25		Deductions	Amount
Gross Income		Federal Income Tax	$48.00
		Social Security	$24.80
Deductions		Medicare	$5.80
		Dental Insurance	$24.00
Net Income		Total Deductions	

For **4** and **5**, use the yearly property tax bill.

4. The Ericsons have a house payment each month of $1,436 before taxes. They make a monthly payment for their property tax that gets added to their house payment. What is the total amount of their monthly payment with taxes?

Yearly Property Tax Bill

Jacob Ericson and Sonya Ericson
1925 Springfield Avenue

Please pay this amount:	$1,632

5. The Ericsons' monthly net income is $7,500. How much of this amount is left after they pay their monthly house payment with taxes?

6. **Connect** Nina's net income was $423.65, and her gross income was $558. What was the total amount of deductions?

7. Ricky's net income was $258.17. What was his gross income if the total amount of the deductions was $69.83?

   A $188.34
   B $327.00
   C $328.00
   D $397.83

8. **Construct Arguments** Otis bought a flashlight for $8 and a sleeping bag for $55. The sales tax was 7%, which means 0.07 times the price. Find the amount of sales tax Otis paid on his purchases. Explain two different ways to solve the problem.

9. **Extend Your Thinking** Mr. Pardo's gross income each month is $3,092. He spends $\frac{1}{3}$ of his net income on rent. How much rent does he pay if the deductions from his gross income total $692 a month?

What amount must you find first in order to solve this problem?

Name _____

Solve & Share

When you buy something, what are different ways you can pay? Which one do you like best?

TEKS 5.10C Identify the advantages and disadvantages of different methods of payment, including check, credit card, debit card, and electronic payments. Also, 5.10. Mathematical Process Standards 5.1A, 5.1B, 5.1D, 5.1G

You can **connect** math to the real world by thinking about how people pay for things different ways.

Digital Resources at PearsonTexas.com

 Solve   Learn   Glossary   Check   Tools   Games

Look Back!

Reason How would you pay for a book you bought at a bookstore?

What Are Different Ways to Pay?

A

Tammy's mom, Joan, wants to buy the gift shown for Tammy. She is trying to decide whether to pay with a check, a credit card, or a debit card. What are some advantages and disadvantages of each way to pay?

$8.97

Of course, Tammy's mom could also use cash.

B

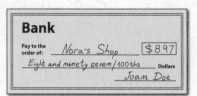

Bank

Pay to the order of: *Nora's Shop* $8.97

Eight and ninety seven/100ths **Dollars**

Joan Doe

Advantages
- Get a record of money spent
- Safe way to mail a payment

Disadvantages
- Takes time to fill out while other people are waiting
- May not be accepted
- Can spend more than you have
- May have bank fees

C

Credit Card

1234 5678 9876 5432

JOAN DOE

Advantages
- Fast and easy
- Get a record of money spent
- Accepted most places
- Works like a loan

Disadvantages
- May have to pay interest
- Can spend more than you have
- May have to pay fees

D

Debit

1234 5678 9876 5432

JOAN DOE

Advantages
- Fast and easy
- Get a record of money spent
- Works like an electronic check

Disadvantages
- May not be accepted
- Can spend more than you have

Do You Understand?

Convince Me! Which method would you use if you had the choice of all 3 ways? Explain.

Another Example

When you use electronic payment, you use the Internet to tell your bank to pay your bills with money from your checking account. Tammy's dad pays the bills with electronic payment.

Advantages of Electronic Payment
- Easy and fast to use
- Safe
- Get a record of money spent

Disadvantages of Electronic Payment
- Must have Internet access

Guided Practice

1. Mr. Ford bought a new car battery for $179. He paid with a debit card. Tell one advantage and one disadvantage of paying with a debit card.

2. **Reason** In the problem on the previous page, what are advantages of using cash to buy Tammy's gift? What are disadvantages?

Independent Practice

In **3** through **5**, tell one advantage and one disadvantage of each way to pay.

3. Check

4. Credit card

5. Electronic payment

6. **Explain** Kevin's brother is paying his cell phone bill. He wants the money to come out of his checking account. What are some ways he can pay his cell phone bill?

Problem Solving

7. Reason Jordan's dad mailed a check to pay for Jordan's basketball camp. What is a good reason for writing and mailing a check?

8. Which method of payment does **NOT** take money from your checking account?

   A Electronic payment

   B Debit card

   C Cash

   D Check

9. Analyze Information Complete Linda's pay stub.

Linda Bergen		Westside Pet Clinic	May 14
Rate: $13/ hour		**Deductions**	**Amount**
Hours: 36		Federal Income Tax	68.70
		Social Security	29.02
Gross Income		Medicare	6.79
Deductions		Health Insurance	$52.00
Net Income		Total Deductions	

10. Marcy bought an umbrella priced at $12. The sales tax is 7%, which means 0.07 times the price. What was the cost of the umbrella with sales tax? If Marcy paid with a $20 bill, how much change should she receive?

11. Extend Your Thinking Ms. Thillens had $157.19 in her checking account. She wrote a check for $98.16 for groceries and another check for $64.43 for a new coat. Is there enough money in her checking account to cover these two checks? Explain.

© Pearson Education, Inc. 5

Name _____

Another Look!

Here are some ways you can pay for things:

• Cash
• Check
• Credit card
• Debit card
• Electronic payment

Each method of payment has advantages and disadvantages.

Here are some advantages.

Fast and easy:
    Cash, credit card, debit card

Statement shows your spending:
    Credit card, debit card, electronic payment

Accepted almost everywhere:
    Cash, credit card

Here are some disadvantages.

Could spend more money than you really have:
    Check, credit card, debit card

May have to pay fees or interest:
    Check, credit card, debit card

Need Internet access:
    Electronic payment

In **1** through **8**, tell which method of payment an adult might use for each purchase. Explain why.

1. $12 for sunglasses

2. $4.50 for a sandwich

3. $440.16 for an airplane ticket

4. $83.26 for an electric bill

5. $11.88 for music downloads

6. $150 for soccer camp

7. $0.75 for a pack of gum

8. $1,089 for a refrigerator

9. For which method of payment do you need to have Internet access?

Which form would you need a computer for?

A Debit card
B Electronic payment
C Check
D Credit card

10. **Analyze Information** Charlotte earned $519 last week. Her employer deducted $77.85 from her check for federal income tax, $32.18 for Social Security, and $7.53 for Medicare. How much did Charlotte's employer deduct in payroll taxes?

11. The Levines pay $2,100 a year in property taxes on their home. If they make monthly payments, how much do they have to pay each month?

12. **Reason** Jack's mom used a credit card to pay for a new sofa. What is a disadvantage of using a credit card?

13. Perry drew a design for a number cube and marked it with the given dimensions. Find the surface area of the design.

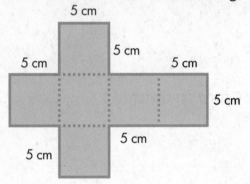

5 cm
5 cm
5 cm
5 cm
5 cm
5 cm
5 cm

14. Evangeline has a pad of paper that weighs 7.50 ounces and a book that weighs 3 pounds. Which weight is greater? Write >, <, or =.

7.50 oz ◯ 3 lb

15. **Extend Your Thinking** Oscar's mom wants to purchase 3 yards of ribbon and a spool of thread. Sales tax is $0.51. Will her credit card be accepted? Explain.

16. How much change will Oscar's mom receive if she pays for her purchases with a $5 bill, two $1 bills, two quarters, and three dimes? Show your work.

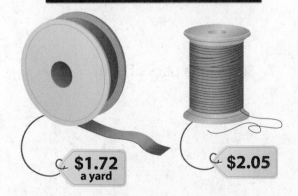

Store policy:
Credit cards accepted for purchases over $10

$1.72
a yard

$2.05

Name _____

Solve & Share

Anthony made the deposits and wrote the checks shown. How can he keep a record of this information?

Bank of Eastland
DEPOSIT

Date: 4/9   Total: **$200**
15348

Bank of Eastland
DEPOSIT

Date: 4/25   Total: **$30**
15348

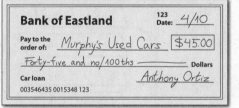

Bank of Eastland   123 Date: 4/10

Pay to the order of: Murphy's Used Cars $45.00

Forty-five and no/100ths ———— Dollars

Car loan   Anthony Ortiz
003546435 0015348 123

Cindy's Market
Receipt
4/27

Milk   2.99
Bread

Total due: **$16.78**

Paid by debit card: xxx 0354

⭐ TEKS 5.10D Develop a system for keeping and using financial records. Also, 5.10.
Mathematical Process Standards 5.1B, 5.1C, 5.1D, 5.1E

Digital Resources at PearsonTexas.com

Solve   Learn   Glossary   Check   Tools   Games

You can **create and use a representation**, such as a table, to organize information.

Look Back!

Reason Why do you think it is important to keep a record of your money?

How Can You Keep Financial Records?

A

A deposit is money put into your account.

A debit is money taken out of your account such as when you write a check, use a debit card, get cash, or transfer money to another account.

The balance is the money in your account. It changes whenever you make a deposit or have a debit.

Suzy kept track of the money she spent and earned. How much did Suzy have at the end of the month?

$36.72

Guest Check
345567

1 SLICE CAKE	$4.50
1 SODA	$1.00
Tax	.35
Total	$5.85

Thank You
345567

Remember: You add deposits to the balance and subtract debits.

B

Date	Activity	Deposits	Debits	Balance
2/9	Balance			$100.00
2/15	Eat out with friends		$5.85	$94.15
2/17	Shopping for clothes		$36.72	$57.43
2/21	Deposit (babysitting)	$35.00		$92.43
2/25	Pay back mom for loan		$25.00	$67.43
2/26	Donate to charity		$15.00	$52.43

$100 − $5.85
$94.15 − $36.72
$57.43 + $35.00
$92.43 − $25.00
$67.43 − $15.00

Suzy had $52.43 at the end of the month.

You can keep a record of your money like the one shown.

Do You Understand?

Convince Me! Find the balance after each activity shown in the financial record.

Date	Activity	Deposits	Debits	Balance
3/2	Balance			$200.00
3/5	Deposit	$40.00		
3/15	School supplies		$6.43	
3/17	Transfer to savings		$35.00	
3/22	Deposit	$40.00		
3/25	Payment on loan		$25.80	

☆ **Guided Practice** ☆

1. On the previous page, if Suzy earned $25 babysitting and put that in her account, would she record it in the deposits or debits column?

What other columns are there?

2. **Check for Reasonableness** Explain why a final balance of $52.43 is reasonable for the record on the previous page.

☆ **Independent Practice** ☆

For **3** and **4**, find the balance after each activity in the financial records.

3.

Date	Activity	Deposits	Debits	Balance
5/1	Balance			$123.47
5/5	Deposit	$31.22		
5/14	Debit Taco! Taco!		$4.09	
5/16	Transfer to savings		$35.00	
5/20	Deposit	$54.19		
5/28	Debit Buddy's Books		$25.80	

4.

Date	Activity	Deposits	Debits	Balance
5/1	Balance			$56.00
5/5	Deposit	$42.28		
5/14	Debit Buster's Burgers		$5.16	
5/16	Check for soccer		$25.00	
5/20	Debit Soccer socks		$9.57	
5/28	Debit Buster's Burgers		$5.16	

Remember to add deposits to the balance and subtract debits.

Problem Solving

5. Jenna's older sister, Hayley, had $78.42 in her account at the beginning of the month. Complete the record for the deposits, debits, and checks shown.

Third Bank of Jenkins
DEPOSIT

Date: 5/5   Total: **$372.45**
0014359

Third Bank of Jenkins   248
Date: 5/9

Pay to the order of: Sky Apartments $109.00

One hundred mine and no/100ths   Dollars

Rent   Hayley Riley
003576219 0014359 248

Shoe Place
Receipt
5/6

Shoes   35.99
Tax

Total due: **$38.51**

Paid by debit card: xxx 1427

> Make sure you put the amounts in the correct column.

Date	Activity	Deposits	Debits	Balance
5/1	Balance			$78.42
				$303.36

6. Check for Reasonableness Explain why a final balance of $303.36 is reasonable for the record in Exercise 5.

7. Formulate a Plan The Chou family must pay $504 a year in property tax on their home. Their house payment is $628 a month before the tax. What is their payment each month with the tax?

A $568
B $586
C $668
D $670

8. Which quadrilateral always has perpendicular sides?

A Rectangle
B Trapezoid
C Parallelogram
D Rhombus

9. Extend Your Thinking Candy's employer deducts 20% of her wages in payroll taxes. How much is her net income when her gross income is $409?

> Remember, 20% means multiply by 0.2.

Name _____

Another Look!

You can keep records of your money like the one shown.
Add each deposit and subtract each debit.

Date	Activity	Deposits	Debits	Balance	
3/1	Balance			$65.00	
3/5	Debit Sandwich Stop		$6.95	$58.05	← $65.00 − 6.95
3/7	Debit Book House		$8.46	$49.59	← $58.05 − $8.46
3/10	Deposit	$25.00		$74.59	← $49.59 + $25.00
3/10	Get cash		$12.00	$62.59	← $74.59 − $12.00
3/15	Donate to charity		$10.00	$52.59	← $62.59 − 10.00

For **1** and **2**, find the balance after each activity in
the financial records.

1.

Date	Activity	Deposits	Debits	Balance
6/1	Balance			$248.25
6/5	Deposit	$198.68		
6/6	Transfer to savings		$25.00	
6/6	Payment on loan check 125		$36.00	
6/19	Debit Quick Gas		$32.47	
6/27	Debit Sandwich Place		$7.22	

2.

Date	Activity	Deposits	Debits	Balance
12/8	Balance			$174.62
12/9	Debit Cell phone bill		$38.91	
12/13	Deposit	$19.10		
12/17	Check 219 for car payment		$97.55	
12/18	Gift from Aunt Lil	$30.00		
12/29	Debit Corner Store		$4.99	

3. Number Sense In the financial record in Another Look, which was greater, the total money debited or the total money deposited? Explain your answer.

4. ⭐ Which method of payment could end up costing interest?

A Debit card

B Cash

C Check

D Credit card

---

5. Justin had $56.73 in his account at the beginning of the month. Complete the record for the deposits and debits shown.

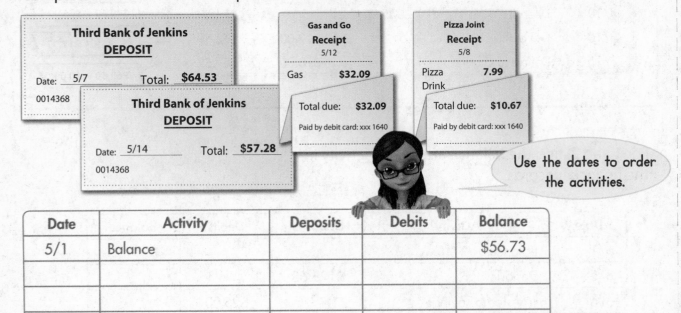

Third Bank of Jenkins
DEPOSIT

Date: 5/7   Total: **$64.53**

0014368

Third Bank of Jenkins
DEPOSIT

Date: 5/14   Total: **$57.28**

0014368

Gas and Go
Receipt
5/12

Gas $32.09

Total due: $32.09

Paid by debit card: xxx 1640

Pizza Joint
Receipt
5/8

Pizza   7.99
Drink

Total due: $10.67

Paid by debit card: xxx 1640

Use the dates to order the activities.

Date	Activity	Deposits	Debits	Balance
5/1	Balance			$56.73

For **6** and **7**, use the picture.

6. What is the cost with sales tax for the lounge pillow? Assume sales tax is 7%, or 0.07 times the price.

7. Extend Your Thinking Becca bought a lounge pillow and a blanket for a total of $78.11, including sales tax. For which item did Becca pay more in sales tax? Explain how you know.

$39

Name _____

☆ Solve & Share ☆

You earn $20 babysitting and $12 raking leaves. Make a plan that describes how you can spend, save, and share your income. Tell why your plan is a good plan.

⬆ TEKS 5.10F Balance a simple budget. Also, 5.10. Mathematical Process Standards 5.1B, 5.1C, 5.1D

Digital Resources at PearsonTexas.com

Solve   Learn   Glossary   Check   Tools   Games

You can use **number sense** to check that the total amount that you spend, save, and share equals your income.

Look Back!

Reason Suppose you want to give $5 to your friend. What can you do to change your plan? Explain.

How Can You Balance a Budget?

A

Drew's money plan is shown. How much money can Drew spend at the fair? Explain how you found your answer.

A budget is a plan for how much income will be received and how it will be spent, saved, and shared.

A balanced budget occurs when the total amount of money spent, saved, and shared equals total income.

Drew's Budget

Income:
$24 dog walking
$16.75 raking leaves

Expenses:
$5 to charity
Save $10 for Summer trip
$12.95 for apps
Spend rest at fair

B Find Drew's total income and the total of the expenses listed.

Total income	Expenses
	$5.00
$24.00	$10.00
+ $16.75	+ $12.95
$40.75	$27.95

C Subtract to see how much money is left.

$$\begin{array}{r} 3\ 9\ 17 \\ \$4\cancel{0}.7\cancel{5} \\ -\ \$27.95 \\ \hline \$12.80 \end{array}$$

If Drew spends exactly $12.80 at the fair, then his budget will be balanced. That is, his total expenses will equal his total income.

Do You Understand?

Convince Me! Suppose Drew only spends $10.90 at the fair. What can he do to balance his budget? Explain.

☆ Guided Practice *

For **1**, find the missing amount so the budget is balanced.

1. Allowance: $10
   Earn: $14
   Spend: $5.67, $2.58, and $4.56
   Save: ?

2. **Reason** In the problem on the previous page, suppose Drew earned an extra $6 walking dogs. How could he balance his budget?

☆ Independent Practice ☆

For **3** through **6**, find the missing amount so the budget is balanced.

3. Allowance: $12
   Earn: $15
   Spend: $2.98, $5.29, and $8.43
   Save: ?

4. Earn: $21
   Spend: $3.22 and $9.16
   Save: $5
   Share: ?

5. Allowance: $15
   Spend: $3.28, $2.17, and $4.79
   Share: $2
   Save: ?

6. Earn: $24
   Spend: $11.54 and $2.98
   Save: $8
   Share: ?

For **7** and **8**, use Rosie's budget.

7. How much can Rosie share and still balance her budget?

8. Suppose Rosie earned some extra money doing chores, making her total income $32. How could Rosie balance her budget?

Rosie's Budget

Earn $20 cleaning house
Save $5
$4.75 to rent video game
$6.50 for bowling

Problem Solving

9. **Formulate a Plan** How much can Art save and
⭐ still balance his budget?

   A $8.27

   B $8.73

   C $9.27

   D $12.73

Art's Budget

Earn $24 giving drum lessons

$4 to charity

$7.29 for shoes on sale

$3.98 for lunch

For **10** and **11**, use the picture.

10. What is the cost with sales tax for the wall
    decoration shown? Assume sales tax is 8%, or
    0.08 times the price of the purchase. Show
    your work.

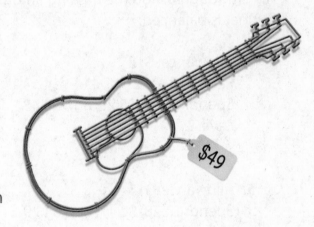

$49

11. **Number Sense** Henry can save $8 each week.
    How many weeks will it take him to save enough
    money to buy the wall decoration? Use number
    sense to explain your answer.

---

12. Find the balance after each activity shown in the financial record.

Date	Activity	Deposits	Debits	Balance
6/1	Balance			$98.43
6/5	Deposit	$57.32		
6/6	Transfer to savings		$20.00	
6/12	Deposit	$57.32		
6/14	Debit Juicy Burgers		$6.25	
6/15	Debit Craft Supplies		$17.38	

© Pearson Education, Inc. 5

Name _____

Another Look!

Marsha earned $28 giving trombone lessons. She spent $15.78 and $5.56. She shared $3.50 with her little brother. How much can she save and still balance her budget?

Step 1	**Step 2**	**Step 3**
$\begin{array}{r} {\tiny 1\ 1\ 1} \\ \$15.78 \\ +\ \ \ \ 5.56 \\ \hline \$21.34 \end{array}$	$\begin{array}{r} \$21.34 \\ +\ \$3.50 \\ \hline \$24.84 \end{array}$	$\begin{array}{r} {\tiny 7\ 9\ 10} \\ \$28.0\!\!\!\!0 \\ -\ 24.84 \\ \hline \$3.16 \end{array}$
She spent $21.34.	She spent and shared $24.84.	She can save $3.16.

For **1** through **4**, find the missing amount so the budget is balanced.

1. Allowance: $10
   Earn: $18
   Spend: $3.28, $7.15, and $9.54
   Save: ?

2. Earn: $23
   Spend: $2.46 and $7.96
   Save: $10
   Share: ?

3. Allowance: $14
   Spend: $2.28, $2.78, and $1.79
   Share: $3
   Save: ?

4. Earn: $24
   Spend: $11.54 and $2.98
   Save: $8
   Share: ?

For **5** and **6**, use Paul's budget.

5. How much can Paul save and still balance his budget?

6. Suppose Paul spent an additional $2.99 for pens. How much could Paul save and still balance his budget? Show your work.

Paul's Budget

Earn $22 raking leaves
$6.75 on pizza
$7.95 for paintball
$3.48 for paper

7. **Extend Your Thinking** How can Ellen balance her budget? Explain your answer. Include a way Ellen could earn more money.

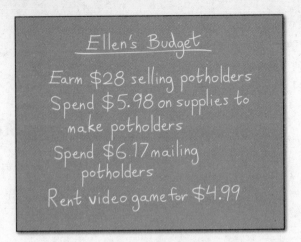

Ellen's Budget

Earn $28 selling potholders

Spend $5.98 on supplies to make potholders

Spend $6.17 mailing potholders

Rent video game for $4.99

8. **Reason** Toby's mom paid for groceries with a debit card. What are advantages and disadvantages of using a debit card?

9. **Formulate a Plan** Cameron's employer deducts 0.2 times his wages in payroll taxes. How much is his net income when his gross income is $347? Show how you found your answer.

For **10** through **12**, use the stem-and-leaf plot.

Marcie's family has a fruit and vegetable stand. The stem-and-leaf plot shows the amount of sales tax they collected on 10 sales.

10. How much sales tax did they collect in all?

11. How much more was the greatest amount of sales tax they collected than the least amount?

12. What is the most common amount of sales tax that was collected at the stand?

Sales Tax Collected

Stem	Leaf
0	07 08 08 14 28 67 89
1	16 18 25

Key: 0|07 = $0.07

Name _____

☆ ☆
Solve & Share

Alan has an income of $20 a week. He usually spends $15 and saves $5. He wants to buy the skateboard shown. Describe ways he can buy the skateboard and still balance his weekly budget.

⊕ **TEKS 5.1G** Display, explain, and justify mathematical ideas and arguments using precise mathematical language in written or oral communication.
⊕ **TEKS 5.10E** Describe actions that might be taken to balance a budget when expenses exceed income. Also, 5.10. Mathematical Process Standards 5.1B, 5.1C, 5.1D, 5.1E, 5.1G

Digital Resources at PearsonTexas.com

Solve   Learn   Glossary   Check   Tools   Games

How can what you know about balancing a budget help you **formulate a plan**?

~$39.50

Look Back!

Construct Arguments If Alan buys the skateboard on credit, he has to pay a total of $47.79 with tax and interest. How could he pay that amount in a maximum of 9 payments? How would this change his weekly budget?

A Analyze

How Can You Balance a Budget When Expenses Are More Than Income?

Mona wants to buy the soccer equipment shown. How can she get what she wants and balance her budget?

$28.88 with tax

$160.50 with tax

Mona's Weekly Budget

Income:
$35 tutoring (5 hours)
$17.50 walking dogs
Total: $52.50
Expenses:
$4.55 to charity
Save $5 for soccer camp
$12.60 for sunglasses
$11.25 for movies with Lisa
Total: $33.40

$52.50 − 33.40 = $19.10

B Plan

Mona could cut expenses.

If Mona does not go to the movies, she would have $30.35, which is enough to buy the soccer ball with some left.

$$\begin{array}{r} \overset{1}{\$19.10} \\ + \ 11.25 \\ \hline \$30.35 \end{array}$$

C Mona could increase her income.

If Mona can earn $9.78 more, she can buy the soccer ball.

$$\begin{array}{r} \overset{118}{\$28.88} \\ - \ 19.10 \\ \hline \$9.78 \end{array}$$

D Solve

Mona could save.

If Mona saves $19.10 for 2 weeks, she can buy the soccer ball. If she saves for 9 weeks, she can buy the cleats.

$$\begin{array}{r} \overset{1}{\$19.10} \\ \times \qquad 2 \\ \hline \$38.20 \end{array} \qquad \begin{array}{r} \overset{8}{\$19.10} \\ \times \qquad 9 \\ \hline \$171.90 \end{array}$$

Mona might be able to borrow the money to buy the ball and the cleats if none of the other options work.

Do You Understand?

Convince Me! How could you estimate how many weeks Mona needs to save to buy the cleats?

904 © Pearson Education, Inc. 5

☆ Guided Practice *

1. Clint earns $45 a week. He has $18 in fixed expenses, and he usually spends $7.50 a week bowling. He also had to get his car fixed for $138. How can Clint balance his budget and pay for the car repair? Give specific money amounts in your explanation.

2. **Estimation** In the problem on the previous page, if Mona doesn't go to the movies, how many weeks would it take her to save enough money to buy the cleats? Explain how estimation can help you solve.

☆ Independent Practice ☆

For **3** through **5**, use Corey's weekly budget.

3. If Corey saves the rest of his money, how much can he save each week and balance his budget? Show your work.

4. Corey wants a wall decoration which costs $39. How many weeks does he need to save in order to buy it? Explain how estimation can help you solve.

Corey's Weekly Budget

Income:
$35 newspaper delivery

Expenses:
$5 gas to pick up newspapers
$12 for snacks with friends
$7.50 for tennis lessons

5. How can Corey afford to buy the $39 wall decoration sooner and still balance his budget? Give specific money amounts in your explanation.

Problem Solving

6. **Justify** Ophelia has $25 a week in income and $25 a week in fixed expenses. How can she buy a terrarium and still balance her budget?

7. ★ Kevin's mom is buying him some shoes through a website. Which of the following is the best way for her to pay for the shoes?

   A In person
   B Check
   C Cash
   D Credit card

8. **Extend Your Thinking** The ceramic plate shown is packed in the box and then the box is filled with packing peanuts. How many cubic centimeters of packing peanuts are needed to finish filling the box? Show how you found your answer.

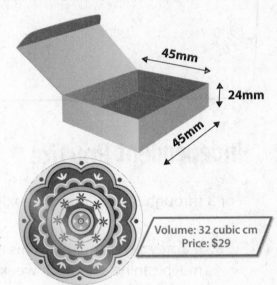

45mm

24mm

45mm

Volume: 32 cubic cm
Price: $29

9. What is the cost of one ceramic plate shown with tax and shipping? Tax is 7%, or 0.07 times the price, and shipping is $8.95.

10. **Formulate a Plan** Brendon's employer deducts 20%, or 0.2 times his wages, in payroll taxes. How much is his net income when his gross income is $537? Show your work.

11. **Create and Use Representations** Penny had $3\frac{1}{2}$ yards of cloth and used $2\frac{1}{4}$ yards. How much did she have left? Draw a strip diagram and write an equation to help you solve.

Name _____

Another Look!

Lenny has the budget shown. He wants to buy a necklace, which costs $112.56. How can he buy the necklace and balance his budget?

Option 1: Save

Lenny can save $40.25 for 3 weeks and buy the necklace. 3 × $40.25 = $120.75

Option 2: Cut Expenses and Save

If Lenny doesn't go to dinner and a movie, he could save $63.75 each week. He could buy the necklace after two weeks. 2 × $63.75 = $127.50

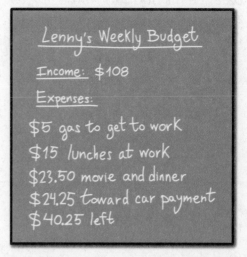

Lenny's Weekly Budget

Income: $108

Expenses:

$5 gas to get to work
$15 lunches at work
$23.50 movie and dinner
$24.25 toward car payment
$40.25 left

For **1** through **3**, use Patty's monthly budget and the given information.

Peter's older sister Patty works part-time and drives a car. Her monthly budget is shown. She wants to buy a car that costs $575.

1. If Patty borrows the money to buy the car, she must pay $73 interest and pay the car off in a year. How much would she need to pay each month? Show how you found your answer.

2. How can Patty afford to make the car payments and still balance her budget?

Patty's Monthly Budget

Income: $136
Fixed expenses: $54
Give to charity: $12
Entertainment: $25
$45 left

3. Could Patty pay for the car sooner by saving instead of borrowing? Explain.

4. Extend Your Thinking Ted has a monthly income of $129 and $104 a month of fixed expenses. How can he buy a game system for $299 and still balance his budget? Name at least 4 ways.

5. Check for Reasonableness The Yeldin family must pay $956 a month for their house payment and $1,536 a year in property tax. They pay the tax in equal monthly payments. Is it reasonable that their house payment and tax combined equals $1,048? Explain your answer.

6. ⭐ How many feet of wood would it take to frame the poster?

A 8 ft

B $8\frac{5}{12}$ ft

C $9\frac{1}{3}$ ft

D $9\frac{5}{6}$ ft

$2\frac{1}{4}$ ft

$2\frac{2}{3}$ ft

For **7** through **9**, use the pay stub.

7. Complete Sophie's pay stub.

Buddy's Pets **792 Longhorn Blvd.**			Sophie Ming 45 Twin Oaks Apts	June 1
	Rate	**Hours**	**Deductions**	**Amount**
	$9.45	18	Federal Income Tax	20.41
			Social Security	10.55
Gross Income			Medicare	2.47
Deductions			Health Insurance	24.00
Net Income			Total Deductions	

8. What is Sophie's gross income?

9. What is her net income?

Name _____

For **1** through **3**, identify the disadvantages of each payment method.

1. Check payment

2. Credit payment

3. Debit card payment

Applying Math Processes

- How does this problem connect to previous ones?
- What is my plan?
- How can I use tools?
- How can I use number sense?
- How can I communicate and represent my thinking?
- How can I organize and record information?
- How can I explain my work?
- How can I justify my answer?

Define each of the following types of tax.

4. Income tax

5. Payroll tax

6. Sales tax

7. Property tax

8. Analyze Information How many pencils have a price that is $0.60 or less?

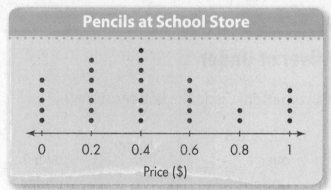

Pencils at School Store

Price ($)

A 52 pencils   **C** 25 pencils

B 65 pencils   **D** 27 pencils

---

9. Which figure appears to be a regular polygon?

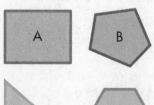

10. Extend Your Thinking A rectangular parking lot has a length of *x* meters and a width of *y* meters. Explain how you can use multiplication or addition to find the perimeter of the parking lot.

Error Search

Find each problem that is not correct. Circle what is wrong and rewrite the problem so it is correct.

1. $3\frac{1}{3} = 3\frac{4}{12} = 2\frac{16}{12}$
    $-1\frac{3}{4} = 1\frac{9}{12} = 1\frac{9}{12}$
    _____
    $1\frac{7}{12}$

2. $5\frac{7}{8} = 5\frac{7}{8} = 5\frac{7}{8}$
    $-2\frac{1}{4} = 2\frac{4}{8} = 2\frac{4}{8}$
    _____
    $3\frac{3}{8}$

3. $6\frac{2}{3} = 6\frac{14}{24}$
    $+3\frac{3}{8} = 3\frac{9}{24}$
    _____
    $9\frac{23}{24} = 9\frac{23}{24}$

4. $1\frac{3}{5} = 1\frac{6}{10}$
    $+4\frac{1}{2} = 4\frac{5}{10}$
    _____
    $5\frac{11}{10} = 6\frac{1}{10}$

Over or Under

Estimation Circle the better estimate.

5. 0.2×0.8
    over 1
    under 1

6. 1.6×1.3
    over 1
    under 1

7. $\$28 \times 0.59$
    over $14.00
    under $14.00

8. 4.23×100
    over 400
    under 400

9. 0.36×4
    over 12
    under 12

10. 9.9×100
    over 1,000
    under 1,000

11. 6.2×4.3
    over 30
    under 30

12. $8.4 \times 1,000$
    over 10,000
    under 10,000

13. 72.39×0.96
    over 72
    under 72

14. 12.5×10
    over 100
    under 100

15. $19.5 \times \$0.40$
    over $8.00
    under $8.00

16. $15 \times \$2.19$
    over $30
    under $30

© Pearson Education, Inc. 5

Name _____

Set A pages 873–878

Debbie bought a pair of inline skates priced at $41. The sales tax was 8%, which means 0.08 times the price. What was the cost of the skates with sales tax?

Multiply to find the sales tax.	Add the sales tax to the price.
$41	$41.00
× 0.08	+ $ 3.28
$3.28	$44.28

The cost with sales tax was $44.28.

Remember that people support government by paying taxes such as sales tax, payroll taxes, and property tax.

Find the cost with sales tax for each purchase price. Assume sales tax is 8%, or 0.08 times the price.

1. $28   2. $60

3. Roscoe bought a tent priced at $75. What was the cost of the tent with sales tax?

Set B pages 879–884

Aidan's gross income is $388. The total amount of the deductions from his gross income is $85.36. What is his net income?

Subtract.

$$
\begin{array}{r}
\overset{9}{\cancel{7}}\,\overset{10}{\cancel{10}}\,\overset{10}{\cancel{0}} \\
\$38\,8.0\,0 \\
-\ \$\ \ 85.36 \\
\hline
\$302.64
\end{array}
$$

Aidan's net income is $302.64.

Remember that gross income minus deductions equals net income.

1. What is the total amount of these deductions?

Federal Income Tax	$34.92
Social Security	$18.04
Medicare	$ 4.22
Health insurance	$17.30

2. Kate's gross income is $291. The deductions are shown in Exercise 1. What is her net income?

Set C pages 885–890

Mrs. Hale used a credit card to buy a rug priced at $86. What is one advantage and one disadvantage of using a credit card?

An advantage is that a credit card is fast and easy to use. A disadvantage is that you might have to pay interest.

Remember that some methods of payment are cash, check, credit card, debit card, and electronic payment.

1. Mr. Reynolds used an electronic payment to pay his water bill. What is one advantage and one disadvantage of electronic payments?

Set D pages 891–896

Mrs. Schneider had a balance of $714.39 in her checking account. She used her debit card to buy a fishing pole for $34.25. Then she deposited her paycheck of $304.03. What was the new balance?

Subtract the debit.   Add the deposit.

$$\begin{array}{r} \overset{6\,11}{\$7\cancel{1}4.39} \\ -\ \$\ \ 34.25 \\ \hline \$680.14 \end{array} \qquad \begin{array}{r} \$680.14 \\ +\ \$304.03 \\ \hline \$984.17 \end{array}$$

The new balance is $984.17.

Remember that a deposit is money you put into your account, and a debit is money taken out of your account. The amount of money in the account is the balance.

1. Dwight is keeping track of his money.

   7/14 Balance: $66.45
   7/18 Deposit: $18 for mowing lawns
   7/20 Debit: $10.55 for Fun Fair

   What is the new balance after the debit for Fun Fair?

Set E pages 897–902, 903–908

Donald is working on the budget shown here.

> Allowance: $7.50
> Earn: $12
> Spend: $1.49, $4.80, and $6.02
> Save: ?

How much can Donald save and still balance his budget?

1. Find his total income.

   $7.50 + $12 = $19.50

2. Find his total expenses so far.

   $1.49 + $4.80 + 6.02 = $12.31

3. Subtract the expenses from total income.

   $19.50 − $12.31 = $7.19

Donald can save $7.19.

Keeping a record of all income and expenses is important to maintaining a balanced budget.

Remember that a balanced budget occurs when the total amount of money spent, saved, and shared equals total income.

1. Renee is working on the budget shown here.

   Income:
      $40 paycheck
      $32 walking Mr. Fay's dog
      $20 doing yard work

   Expenses:
      $12.40 for picture frame
      $8.71 for water bottle

   Left: ?

   How much money does Renee have left?

2. Renee wants to go camping for a weekend. It will cost $77. Describe 2 ways that Renee can pay for the camping trip and still balance the budget shown in Exercise 1.

1. Justin bought a shirt for $6. Sales tax is 7%, or 0.07 times the purchase price. How much did the shirt cost with sales tax?

   A $6.07

   B $6.42

   C $7.06

   D $10.42

2. Julie makes $9.26 an hour. This week she worked 20 hours and had $32.62 deducted for payroll taxes. What was her net income?

   A $185.20

   B $153.68

   C $153.42

   D Not here

3. Which method of payment does **NOT** give you a record of money spent?

   A Cash

   B Credit card

   C Debit card

   D Check

Use the financial record for **4** and **5**.

DATA	Date	Activity	Deposits	Debits	Balance
	5/1	Balance			$18.43
	5/10	Debit		$5.98	
	5/14	Deposit	$15.00		
	5/16	Debit		$4.98	

4. In the financial record shown, what is the balance on 5/10?

   A $12.45   C $23.31

   B $13.55   D $24.41

5. In the financial record shown, what is the balance on 5/16? Explain how you found your answer.

6. Vince has a weekly income of $26 and weekly expenses of $18. He saves the rest. How can he buy a tablet that costs $99 including tax and still balance his budget?

   A He can save for 11 weeks.

   B He can cut expenses by $4 a week and save for 8 weeks.

   C He can cut expenses by $3 a week and save for 9 weeks.

   D He can increase his income by $2 a week and save for 9 weeks.

7. Which of the following is a disadvantage of using electronic payment for bills?

   A It takes a lot of time.

   B You don't get a record of money spent.

   C You may have to pay interest.

   D You must have Internet access.

---

8. Ken's employer deducts 0.2 times his gross income in payroll taxes. What is his net income if his gross income is $271?

   A $206.80

   B $216.80

   C $265.58

   D $270.80

---

9. The Garofalo family pays $2,496 a year in property taxes. They pay in equal monthly payments. How many dollars do they pay in property taxes each month?

			.		
⓪	⓪	⓪		⓪	⓪
①	①	①		①	①
②	②	②		②	②
③	③	③		③	③
④	④	④		④	④
⑤	⑤	⑤		⑤	⑤
⑥	⑥	⑥		⑥	⑥
⑦	⑦	⑦		⑦	⑦
⑧	⑧	⑧		⑧	⑧
⑨	⑨	⑨		⑨	⑨

Use Dorothy's budget for **10** through **12**.

Dorothy's Weekly Budget

Income:
$25 babysitting

Expenses:
$12 banjo lesson
$6.75 for skating
$2.50 for snacks

10. How much can Dorothy save and still balance her budget?

   A $2.75   **C** $3.75

   B $3.25   **D** $4.75

11. How can Dorothy buy a jacket which costs $37.45 including tax and still balance her budget? Give money amounts in your explanation.

---

12. Instead of going skating, Dorothy goes to a movie and spends $5.50. How many dollars could she save that week and still balance her budget?

			.		
⓪	⓪	⓪		⓪	⓪
①	①	①		①	①
②	②	②		②	②
③	③	③		③	③
④	④	④		④	④
⑤	⑤	⑤		⑤	⑤
⑥	⑥	⑥		⑥	⑥
⑦	⑦	⑦		⑦	⑦
⑧	⑧	⑧		⑧	⑧
⑨	⑨	⑨		⑨	⑨

914

Here's a preview of next year. These lessons help you step up to Grade 6.

Step Up to Grade 6

Lessons

1 Understanding Integers **917**

2 Comparing and Ordering Integers **921**

3 Understanding Division of Fractions **925**

4 Dividing a Whole Number by a Fraction **929**

5 Understanding Ratios **933**

6 Understanding Percents **937**

7 Fractions, Decimals, and Percents **941**

8 Rates and Unit Rates **945**

9 Area of Parallelograms and Triangles **949**

10 Graphing Points on a Coordinate Plane **953**

TEKS 6.2B Identify a number, its opposite, and its absolute value.

TEKS 6.2C Locate, compare, and order integers and rational numbers using a number line.

TEKS 6.3A Recognize that dividing by a rational number and multiplying by its reciprocal result in equivalent values.

TEKS 6.4C Give examples of ratios as multiplicative comparisons of two quantities describing the same attribute.

TEKS 6.4E Represent ratios and percents with concrete models, fractions, and decimals.

TEKS 6.4G Generate equivalent forms of fractions, decimals, and percents using real-world problems, including problems that involve money.

TEKS 6.5A Represent mathematical and real-world problems involving ratios and rates using scale factors, tables, graphs, and proportions.

TEKS 6.8B Model area formulas for parallelograms, trapezoids, and triangles by decomposing and rearranging parts of these shapes.

TEKS 6.11 Use coordinate geometry to identify locations on a plane. Graph points in all four quadrants using ordered pairs of rational numbers.

The following Grade 6 TEKS are introduced in the Step-Up Lessons.

Name _____

☆ ☆
Solve & Share

Leila and Erik recorded these temperatures during an experiment: 10°C, 4°C, 0°C, −4°C, and −10°C. Make a mark on the thermometer at each of these temperatures. Tell how you decided where to place each mark. *Solve this problem any way you choose.*

Lesson 1
Understanding Integers

⭐ TEKS 6.2B Identify a number, its opposite, and its absolute value. Mathematical Process Standards 6.1A, 6.1D, 6.1F

Digital Resources at PearsonTexas.com

Solve   Learn   Glossary   Tools   Games

0

°C

You can **analyze relationships** to help you solve a problem. *Show your work!*

Look Back!

Connect Ideas In what other situations have you seen negative numbers used?

A

You can compare integers to degrees of temperature measured on a thermometer. When the temperature goes below zero, it is written with a negative sign.

6°C is 6°C warmer than 0°C.
– 6°C is 6°C colder than 0°C.
The distance from 0°C is the same.

Negative numbers are written using a negative sign.

Use a number line.

B A number line can also show numbers greater than and less than 0.

Numbers that are the same distance from 0 are called opposites: −6 and 6 are opposites.

Integers are the set of numbers that includes the counting numbers, their opposites, and zero.

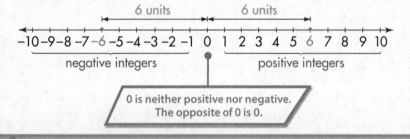

6 units   6 units

−10 −9 −8 −7 −6 −5 −4 −3 −2 −1 0 1 2 3 4 5 6 7 8 9 10

negative integers   positive integers

0 is neither positive nor negative.
The opposite of 0 is 0.

C The absolute value of an integer is its distance from 0.

Distance is always positive.

The absolute value of 6 is written $|6| = 6$.

The absolute value of −6 is written $|-6| = 6$.

Do You Understand?

Convince Me! The absolute value of a number is 12. What are the possible numbers? How do you know?

© Pearson Education, Inc. 5

Name _____

Another Example

You have learned how to read the counting numbers. This chart shows how to read negative integers.

Integer	How to Read It
−3	Negative three
−(−3)	The opposite of negative three
|−3|	The absolute value of negative three

☆ Guided Practice*

In **1** through **6**, use the number line below. Give the integer that each point represents. Then write its opposite and absolute value.

1. A   **2.** B   **3.** C

4. D   **5.** E   **6.** F

7. Reason What do you know about two different integers that have the same absolute value?

8. Connect Which integers do you use for counting?

9. Communicate How would you read the number −17?

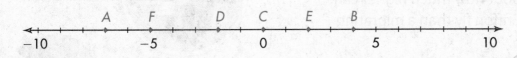

> Remember:
> Absolute value is
> always positive.

☆ Independent Practice ☆

In **10** through **21**, write the opposite and absolute value of each integer.

10. 5   **11.** −13   **12.** 22   **13.** −31

14. −50   **15.** 66   **16.** 45   **17.** −70

18. 80   **19.** −21   **20.** 125   **21.** −5,846

Problem Solving

22. Ella picked the polygon with the greatest perimeter. Which of the following polygons did she pick?

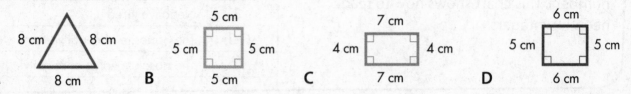

A 8 cm, 8 cm, 8 cm

B 5 cm, 5 cm, 5 cm, 5 cm

C 7 cm, 4 cm, 4 cm, 7 cm

D 6 cm, 5 cm, 5 cm, 6 cm

---

23. Construct Arguments Sam said the absolute value of 14 is −14. Kai said the absolute value of 14 is 14. Who is correct? Explain.

24. Explain If the opposite of a non-zero number is equal to its absolute value, is the number positive or negative? Explain your answer.

In **25** through **27**, use the pictures at the right.

25. Connect About how much higher can a Ruppell's Griffon fly than a migrating bird?

  A About 32,000 feet
  B About 25,000 feet
  C About 12,000 feet
  D About 10,000 feet

26. Extend Your Thinking Write a negative integer to represent the depth to which a dolphin may dive.

27. Reason Which animal can fly or swim at a greater distance from sea level, a dolphin or a migrating bird?

Ruppell's Griffons fly up to 37,000 feet.

Mexican free-tailed bats fly up to 10,000 feet.

A migrating bird flies up to 5,000 feet.

A dolphin can swim to 150 feet below sea level.

Name _____

Lesson 2
Comparing and Ordering Integers

Solve & Share   Place the integers −7, 4, −2, and 5 in order from least to greatest. Write and explain how you decided. *Solve this problem any way you choose.*

⭐ TEKS 6.2C Locate, compare, and order integers and rational numbers using a number line.
Mathematical Process Standards 6.1B, 6.1C, 6.1D

You can use **tools**. How can you use a number line or thermometer to solve this problem? *Show your work!*

Digital Resources at PearsonTexas.com

Solve   Learn   Glossary   Tools   Games

Look Back!

Number Sense How can you use a number line to tell if an integer is greater than or less than another integer?

A

The table shows the low temperatures during a cold week. Find which day had the lowest temperature. Then order the temperatures from least to greatest.

You can use a number line to help compare and order integers.

DATA	Day	Temperature
	Monday	3°C
	Tuesday	−6°C
	Wednesday	5°C
	Thursday	1°C
	Friday	−5°C

Compare.

B First, locate the integers on a number line.

−8 −7 −6 −5 −4 −3 −2 −1 0 1 2 3 4 5 6 7 8

When comparing integers on a number line, the integer that is farthest to the left is the least.

−6 is farther to the left than −5, so −6 is less.

It was colder on Tuesday than on Friday.

You can use symbols to compare integers. Write:

$$-6 < -5 \text{ or } -5 > -6$$

Order.

C Integer values on a number line decrease as you move left and increase as you move right.

The temperature farthest to the left is −6.

Moving left to right, you can write the temperatures from least to greatest.

−6, −5, 1, 3, 5

Tuesday was the coldest day.

Do You Understand?

Convince Me! The temperature on Saturday was −8°C. Was the temperature colder on Saturday or on Tuesday? How do you know?

Name _____

In **1** through **4**, use <, >, or = to compare.

1. 7 ◯ −12   **2.** −3 ◯ −9

3. −8 ◯ 0   **4.** |−2| ◯ −2

In **5** through **8**, order the numbers from least to greatest.

5. −6, 5, −7   **6.** 8, −6, −2

7. −21, |−15|, −12   **8.** |3|, −3, −19, 11

9. Reason Is −7 to the right or to the left of −2 on a number line? What does that tell you about their values?

10. Number Sense From warmest to coldest, what were the three lowest temperatures in the table on the previous page?

11. Which day listed in the table had the warmest temperature?

☆ **Independent Practice** ☆

In **12** through **19**, use <, >, or = to compare.

12. 5 ◯ −18   **13.** |−7| ◯ 7   **14.** 0 ◯ 9   **15.** 18 ◯ 9

16. −19 ◯ −23   **17.** 4 ◯ −6   **18.** |−32| ◯ |7| **19.** −1 ◯ 3

You can use a number line to help.

In **20** through **25**, order the numbers from least to greatest.

20. −6, 8, −9, 13   **21.** |−19|, 12, |−21|, −3   **22.** 17, 14, −10, 4, −2, −4

23. 4.5, −4.66, −5, 7   **24.** −37, |15|, 11, −3, 8, |−12| **25.** 57, −21, 43, −6, 7, 23

Problem Solving

In **26** and **27**, use the table.

26. Analyze Information In miniature golf, the lowest score wins. Scores can be compared to par, which is the number of strokes set for the course. List the top five finishers in order from first place to fifth place.

27. Number Sense Which students' scores are opposites?

Player	Par Score
Martha	0 (par)
Madison	−2
Tom	−3
Emma	4
Ben	1
Quincy	−4
Jackson	6

28. Shayla has 4 roses, 7 tulips, and 3 daffodils. Fred has 5 roses, 3 morning-glories, and 3 tulips. Nick has 7 roses and 5 tulips. Who has the most flowers? Who has the least?

29. Avery wrote her friends' game scores in order from least to greatest. What did she write?

A −4, −7, −9, 6, 10
B −4, 6, −7, −9, 10
C −4, −7, −9, 6, 10
D −9, −7, −4, 6, 10

For **30** and **31**, use the number line.

30. Tools The variables on the number line represent integers. Order the variables from least to greatest.

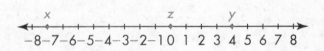

31. Explain why this statement is true: The absolute value of any integer, *n*, is equal to the absolute value of the opposite of *n*.

Replace *n* with any integer to help solve this problem.

Name _____

Solve & Share

A square flower garden has a perimeter of 10 feet. Duncan uses stones to edge the garden. Each stone is $\frac{1}{2}$-foot long. How many stones will Duncan need to edge the garden? *Solve this problem any way you choose.*

 TEKS 6.3A Recognize that dividing by a rational number and multiplying by its reciprocal result in equivalent values. Mathematical Process Standards 6.1C, 6.1D, 6.1G

Digital Resources at PearsonTexas.com

 Solve Learn A-Z Glossary Tools Games

You can use a **representation** to show the edge of the garden. *Show your work!*

Look Back!

Mental Math How could you use basic math facts to solve this problem?

How Can You Model Division of Fractions?

Mr. Roberts uses pieces of wood that are each $\frac{3}{4}$ foot long for a set of shelves he is making. How many pieces of wood can he get from a board that is 3 feet long?

There are different ways to model division of fractions.

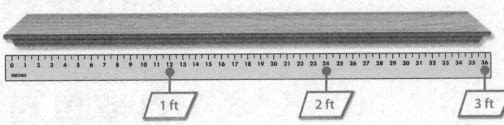

| 1 ft | 2 ft | 3 ft |

Use a number line.

B How many $\frac{3}{4}$s are in 3?

Use a number line to show 3 feet. Divide each foot into 4 equal parts.

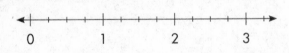

C Divide 3 feet into $\frac{3}{4}$-foot parts.

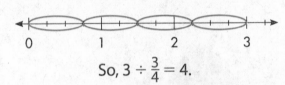

So, $3 \div \frac{3}{4} = 4$.

The divisor, $\frac{3}{4}$, is less than 1, so the quotient, 4, is greater than the dividend, 3.

Do You Understand?

Convince Me! Mr. Roberts has another piece of wood that is 5 feet long. How many $\frac{3}{4}$-foot long shelves can he get from the board? Explain.

926

Name _____

Another Example

Dividing a Fraction by a Whole Number

Find $\frac{1}{2} \div 3$.
Use a picture to show $\frac{1}{2}$.

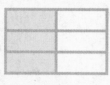

Divide $\frac{1}{2}$ into 3 equal parts.
$\frac{1}{2} \div 3$

Each part contains $\frac{1}{6}$ of the whole.
So, $\frac{1}{2} \div 3 = \frac{1}{6}$.

Dividing a Fraction by a Fraction

Find $\frac{3}{4} \div \frac{1}{4}$.

Use a number line to show $\frac{3}{4}$.

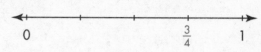

Divide $\frac{3}{4}$ into $\frac{1}{4}$ parts. There are 3 parts.

So, $\frac{3}{4} \div \frac{1}{4} = 3$.

☆ Guided Practice *

In **1** and **2**, write a division sentence to represent each diagram.

1.

2.

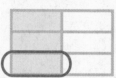

3. Reason When you divide a whole number by a fraction less than 1, will the quotient be greater than or less than the whole number?

4. Number Sense How many $\frac{2}{3}$-foot pieces can you cut from a 10-foot-long board?

Independent Practice ☆

Leveled Practice In **5** through **10**, divide.

Draw a model to help you visualize.

5. $6 \div \frac{1}{2} =$ _____

6. $\frac{2}{3} \div 3 =$ _____

7. $\frac{6}{7} \div \frac{3}{7}$

8. $\frac{7}{8} \div 3$

9. $8 \div \frac{4}{5}$

10. $\frac{5}{9} \div 10$

Problem Solving

11. Draw a Picture Keiko divided $\frac{3}{8}$ gallon of milk equally into 5 glasses. Draw a picture to find what fraction of a gallon is in each glass.

12. Explain Without solving, explain how you can compare the quotient of $7 \div \frac{1}{2}$ to 7.

Is $\frac{1}{2}$ greater than or less than 1?

13. Use a Strip Diagram A car trip takes 6 hours. Every $\frac{2}{3}$ of an hour, Brian changes the radio station. Use a strip diagram to find how many times Brian changes the station during the trip.

14. Extend Your Thinking. A regular polygon has a perimeter of 8 centimeters. If each side measures $\frac{4}{5}$ centimeter, how many sides does the polygon have?

Hint: Divide to find the number of sides.

15. Mental Math In a relay race, each runner on a team runs one part of a 1-mile racecourse.

  a If each runner runs $\frac{1}{4}$ mile, how many relay runners must be on a team?

  b If each runner runs $\frac{1}{3}$ mile, how many runners must be on a team?

16. Which division sentence is shown by this model?

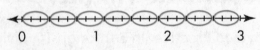

0   1   2   3

A $\frac{3}{8} \div 3$ **C** $8 \div \frac{3}{5}$

B $3 \div \frac{3}{8}$ **D** $\frac{3}{5} \div 8$

Name _____

☆ ⚡ ☆
Solve & Share

Nigel has a 6-pound bag of mixed nuts. He wants to put $\frac{1}{4}$ pound of nuts in each bowl. How many bowls will Nigel be able to fill? *Solve this problem any way you choose.*

Lesson 4
Dividing a Whole Number by a Fraction

 TEKS 6.3A Recognize that dividing by a rational number and multiplying by its reciprocal result in equivalent values. Mathematical Process Standards 6.1A, 6.1B, 6.1C, 6.1D, 6.1F, 6.1G

Digital Resources at PearsonTexas.com

Solve   Learn   Glossary   Tools   Games

You can **draw a picture** to show how many bowls can be filled. *Show your work!*

Mixed Nuts 6 lbs.

Look Back!

Analyze Information How can you use the number of $\frac{1}{4}$s in 1 pound to help solve the problem?

How Are Division and Multiplication of Fractions Related?

A

Look at the division and multiplication sentences. What is the pattern?

Use the pattern to find the quotient for $4 \div \frac{2}{3}$.

$8 \div \frac{4}{1} = 2$	$8 \times \frac{1}{4} = 2$
$6 \div \frac{2}{1} = 3$	$6 \times \frac{1}{2} = 3$
$5 \div \frac{1}{2} = 10$	$5 \times \frac{2}{1} = 10$
$3 \div \frac{3}{4} = 4$	$3 \times \frac{4}{3} = 4$

The pattern in the table shows a rule for dividing by a fraction.

B Step 1

First, find the reciprocal of $\frac{2}{3}$.

Dividing by a fraction is the same as multiplying by its reciprocal.

Two numbers whose product is 1 are called reciprocals.

For example, the reciprocal of $\frac{2}{3}$ is $\frac{3}{2}$ because $\frac{2}{3} \times \frac{3}{2} = \frac{6}{6}$, and $\frac{6}{6} = 1$.

C Step 2

Then, rewrite $4 \div \frac{2}{3}$ as a multiplication problem.

$$4 \div \frac{2}{3} = 4 \times \frac{3}{2}$$
$$= \frac{{}^2 4}{1} \times \frac{3}{2^1}$$
$$= \frac{6}{1} = 6$$

$$4 \div \frac{2}{3} = 6$$

Simplify, then multiply.

Do You Understand?

Convince Me! Explain how you would find the reciprocal of a whole number.

Name _____

In **1** through **4**, find the reciprocal of each fraction or whole number.

1. $\frac{3}{5}$ **2.** $\frac{1}{6}$

3. 9 **4.** $\frac{7}{4}$

In **5** and **6**, find each quotient. Simplify, if possible.

5. $6 \div \frac{2}{3}$ **6.** $12 \div \frac{3}{8}$

7. Connect Is $4 \div \frac{3}{2}$ the same as $4 \div \frac{2}{3}$? Explain.

8. Reason When a whole number is divided by a fraction less than 1, what do you know about the quotient?

☆**Independent Practice**☆

In **9** through **16**, find the reciprocal of each number.

Remember: The product of a number and its reciprocal is 1.

9. $\frac{3}{10}$ **10.** 6 **11.** $\frac{1}{15}$ **12.** 3

13. $\frac{7}{12}$ **14.** $\frac{11}{5}$ **15.** 12 **16.** $\frac{22}{5}$

In **17** through **28**, find each quotient. Simplify if possible.

17. $4 \div \frac{4}{7}$ **18.** $2 \div \frac{3}{8}$ **19.** $5 \div \frac{2}{3}$ **20.** $9 \div \frac{4}{5}$

21. $36 \div \frac{3}{4}$ **22.** $7 \div \frac{3}{4}$ **23.** $18 \div \frac{2}{3}$ **24.** $20 \div \frac{1}{2}$

25. $9 \div \frac{3}{5}$ **26.** $5 \div \frac{2}{7}$ **27.** $12 \div \frac{1}{3}$ **28.** $8 \div \frac{3}{8}$

Problem Solving

In **29** and **30**, use the pictures to the right.

29. **Connect** About how far could each animal move in one hour?

30. Which animal would move the farthest in 3 hours traveling at its maximum speed?

A tortoise can move 300 ft in $\frac{1}{3}$ h.

A snail can move 40 ft in $\frac{1}{4}$ h.

A sloth can move 50 ft in $\frac{1}{8}$ h.

31. **Explain** A bowl of soup holds 7 ounces. If a spoonful holds $\frac{1}{6}$ ounce, how many spoonfuls are in 3 bowls of soup? Explain.

32. **Number Sense.** A recording of the current weather conditions lasts $\frac{3}{4}$ minute. If the recording is repeated continuously for 1 hour, how many times will the recording be played?

33. How many $\frac{1}{4}$-pound burgers can Danny ★ make with 12 pounds of ground turkey?

   A 56 burgers
   B 48 burgers
   C 12 burgers
   D 3 burgers

34. **Draw a Picture** Kerry has 3 apples. She divides each of the apples into $\frac{1}{3}$ sections. Draw a number line to show $3 \div \frac{1}{3}$.

35. **Extend Your Thinking** Valeria bought a 9-foot length of ribbon from which she wants to cut $\frac{2}{3}$ foot pieces. How many pieces can she cut? What will be the length of the leftover piece of ribbon?

36. **Formulate a Plan** Each health book is $\frac{3}{4}$ inch thick. If Mrs. Menes's bookshelf is 2 feet wide, how many books can she fit on the shelf?

Name _____

Step Up to Grade 6

Lesson 5
Understanding Ratios

TEKS 6.4C Give examples of ratios as multiplicative comparisons of two quantities describing the same attribute. Mathematical Process Standards 6.1A, 6.1B, 6.1D, 6.1G

☆ ☆
Solve & Share

There are 15 laptop computers in the computer lab. There are 45 students in the lab. Write an expression that represents the relationship between the number of students and the number of computers. *Solve this problem any way you choose.*

Digital Resources at PearsonTexas.com

Solve   Learn   Glossary   Tools   Games

You can **communicate** the relationship using words, symbols, and numbers. *Show your work!*

Look Back!

Explain How would your expression be different if you are comparing the number of computers to the number of students?

What Is a Mathematical Way to Compare Quantities?

Ratios can be used to compare quantities.

Tom's Pet Service takes care of cats and dogs. Currently, there are more dogs than cats. Compare the number of cats to the number of dogs. Then compare the number of cats to the total number of pets at Tom's Pet Service.

17 dogs

14 cats

B A **ratio** is a relationship where for every *x* units of one quantity, there are *y* units of another quantity.

A ratio can be written three ways: *x* to *y*, *x* : *y*, or $\frac{x}{y}$.

The quantities *x* and *y* in a ratio are called **terms**.

C Use a ratio to compare the number of cats to the number of dogs:

14 to 17,

14:17, or

$\frac{14}{17}$

This ratio compares one part to another part.

D Use a ratio to compare the number of cats to the total number of pets:

14 to 31,

14:31, or

$\frac{14}{31}$

This ratio compares one part to the whole.

Do You Understand?

Convince Me! Is the ratio of dogs to cats the same as the ratio of cats to dogs? Explain.

Name _____

In **1** through **3**, use the information below to write a ratio for each comparison in three different ways.

A sixth-grade basketball team has 3 centers, 5 forwards, and 6 guards.

1. Forwards to guards

2. Centers to total

3. Centers to guards

4. **Reason** What are two different types of comparisons a ratio can be used to make? How is this different from a fraction?

5. In the example on the previous page, compare the number of dogs to the total number of pets.

☆ Independent Practice ☆

In **6** through **13**, use the data table to write a ratio for each comparison in three different ways.

A person's blood type is denoted with the letters A, B, and O, and the symbols $+$ and $-$. The blood type A$+$ is read as *A positive*. The blood type B $-$ is read as *B negative*.

6. O$+$ donors to A$+$ donors

7. AB$-$ donors to AB$+$ donors

8. B$+$ donors to total donors

9. O$-$ donors to A$-$ donors

10. B$-$ donors to B$+$ donors

11. O$-$ donors to total donors

12. A$+$ and B$+$ donors to AB$+$ donors

13. A$-$ and B$-$ donors to AB$-$ donors

Blood Donors	
Type	**Donors**
A+	45
B+	20
AB+	6
O+	90
A−	21
B−	0
AB−	4
O−	9
Total	195

14. Which comparison does the ratio $\frac{90}{9}$ represent?

Problem Solving

15. Analyze Information A math class surveyed the musical preferences of 42 students. Use their data table to write a ratio for each comparison in three different ways for **a**, **b**, and **c**.

  a Students who prefer jazz to students who prefer country

  b Students who prefer classic rock to the total number of students surveyed

  c Students who prefer rock or classic rock to students who prefer all other types of music

Favorite Music Type	Number of Students
Rock	12
Classic rock	4
Country	18
Jazz	2
Heavy metal	6

16. Extend Your Thinking Use the data table for Problem 15. Write two equivalent ratios using four different types of music. How do you know the ratios are equivalent?

17. On average, about 45,000,000 gallons of water flow over the Niagara Falls in 60 seconds. About how much water flows over the Niagara Falls in one second?

18. There are 12 girls and 18 boys in Martine's class. There are 24 computers in the computer lab. What ratio represents the total number of students compared to the number of computers?

  A 12:18

  B 12:24

  C 18:24

  D 30:24

19. Explain Rita's class has 14 girls and 16 boys. How do the ratios 14:16 and 14:30 describe Rita's class?

936

Name _____

☆ ☆
Solve & Share

For every group of 20 students, 5 bring their lunch from home and 15 buy their lunch. How many students out of 100 bring their lunch? *Solve this problem any way you choose.*

⊕ TEKS 6.4E Represent ratios and percents with concrete models, fractions, and decimals.
Mathematical Process Standards 6.1A, 6.1C, 6.1D, 6.1E, 6.1G

Digital Resources at PearsonTexas.com

Solve   Learn   Glossary   Tools   Games

You can **connect** what you have learned about equivalent fractions to find the solution. *Show your work!*

Look Back!

Represent Model your solution another way. Explain your strategy.

What Is a Percent?

A

A *percent* is a special kind of ratio in which the first term is compared to 100.

What percent of people prefer Bright White Toothpaste?

Seven out of ten people prefer Bright White Toothpaste.

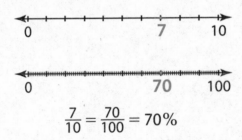

The percent is the number of hundredths that represents the part of the whole.

There are different ways to show a percent.

B Use a grid to model the percent.

$$\frac{7}{10} = \frac{70}{100} = 70\%$$

C Use number lines to model the percent.

```
←——+——+——+——+——+——+——+——+——+——+——→
   0               7        10
```

```
←—+++++++++++++++++++++++++++++++++——→
  0             70        100
```

$$\frac{7}{10} = \frac{70}{100} = 70\%$$

D Use equivalent fractions to find the percent.

$$\frac{7}{10} = \frac{x}{100}$$

$$\frac{7}{10} = \frac{70}{100}$$

$$\frac{7}{10} = \frac{70}{100} = 70\%$$

70% of people prefer Bright White Toothpaste.

Do You Understand?

Convince Me! What percent of people do not prefer Bright White Toothpaste? How do you know?

Name _____

☆ Guided Practice*

In **1** through **3**, write the percent of each figure that is shaded.

1.   **2.**

3.

4. Communicate What is the whole to which a percent is compared?

5. Explain Why are tenths, fifths, and fourths easy to convert to percents?

6. Connect Suppose that 4 out of 5 people prefer Bright White Toothpaste. What percent of people prefer that toothpaste?

Independent Practice ☆

Leveled Practice In **7** through **11**, write the percent of each figure or line segment that is shaded.

7.   **8.**   **9.**

10.
```
0        6    10
```

11.
```
0          14   20
```

In **12** through **16**, draw a picture or use equivalent fractions to find each percent.

12. $\frac{2}{5}$ **13.** $\frac{1}{2}$ **14.** $\frac{8}{10}$ **15.** $\frac{17}{20}$ **16.** $\frac{22}{25}$

Problem Solving

17. Estimation Each line segment below represents 100%. Estimate the percents that points *A, B,* and *C* represent.

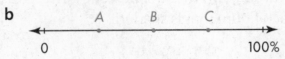

18. Reason Easton won Best in Show in 60% of the shows he entered. In how many shows was Easton entered if he won Best in Show 15 times last year?

19. Suppose that a diamond weighs 0.0182 carat. What is that number in expanded form?

20. Explain Is 25% always the same amount? Explain your answer and provide examples.

21. Connect Sixteen lizards have white stripes on their tails. The ratio of lizards with white stripes to those with yellow stripes is 1:2. How many lizards have yellow stripes?

22. Represent One side of a school building has 10 windows. Four windows have the blinds down. Which model represents the percent of windows with the blinds down?

A   B   C   D

In **23** and **24**, use line segment *AB*.

A •———————————————————• B

3 in.

23. Reason If line segment *AB* represents 50%, what is the length of a line segment that is 100%?

24. Extend Your Thinking If line segment *AB* is 300%, what is the length of a line segment that is 100%?

Name _____

Solve & Share

40% of the people who live in Oak City commute more than 30 minutes to and from work each day. Write this number in as many different ways as you can. *Solve this problem any way you choose.*

⭐ TEKS 6.4G Generate equivalent forms of fractions, decimals, and percents using real-world problems, including problems that involve money.
Mathematical Process Standards 6.1B, 6.1C, 6.1D, 6.1E, 6.1G

Digital Resources at PearsonTexas.com

Solve   Learn   Glossary   Tools   Games

You can **represent** parts of a whole in different ways. Use equivalent fractions to help you solve the problem. *Show your work!*

Look Back!

Communicate What is the same about each different way of writing 40%? What is different?

How Are Fractions, Decimals, and Percents Related?

The circle graph shows each part in a different form. Write 30% as a fraction and a decimal. Write 0.10 as a fraction and a percent.

Fractions, decimals, and percents are three ways to show the same amount.

Fractions, Decimals, and Percents

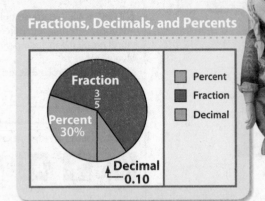

Fraction $\frac{3}{5}$

Percent 30%

Decimal 0.10

☐ Percent
☐ Fraction
☐ Decimal

You can use each of them to represent portions of a whole.

B A percent compares a number to 100. You can write 30% as a decimal and a fraction.

$$30\% = \frac{30}{100}$$

Simplify the fraction:

$$\frac{30 \div 10}{100 \div 10} = \frac{3}{10}$$

30% can be written as 0.30 or $\frac{3}{10}$.

C Use decimal place value to write the decimal 0.10 as a fraction and a percent.

Fraction: $0.10 = \frac{10}{100} = \frac{1}{10}$

Percent: $0.10 = \frac{10}{100} = 10\%$

0.10 can be written as $\frac{1}{10}$ or 10%.

Do You Understand?

Convince Me! Write $\frac{3}{5}$ as a decimal and a percent.

Name _____

In **1** through **6**, write each number in two other ways.

1. 27%   **2.** 0.91   **3.** $\frac{6}{100}$

4. 0.465   **5.** 49%   **6.** $\frac{5}{8}$

7. Reason Why are you able to change between fractions, decimals, and percents?

8. Communicate How is the decimal point moved when changing from a decimal to a percent?

Independent Practice ☆

Leveled Practice In **9** through **11**, write the value of the shaded portion as a fraction, decimal, and percent.

9.   **10.**   **11.**

In **12** through **20**, write each number in two other ways.

12. 38%   **13.** $\frac{7}{8}$ **14.** 0.04

15. $\frac{3}{4}$ **16.** 65%   **17.** 0.46

18. 29%   **19.** 0.01   **20.** $\frac{5}{100}$

Problem Solving

21. **Analyze Information** Many chemical elements can be found in Earth's atmosphere. Use the circle graph to answer the following questions.

a What fraction of Earth's atmosphere is made up of nitrogen?

b What part of Earth's atmosphere is made up of oxygen? Write the part as a decimal.

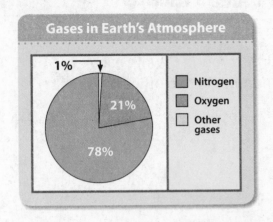

Gases in Earth's Atmosphere

1%
21%
78%

Nitrogen
Oxygen
Other gases

---

22. **Estimation** Mrs. Nellon's class sold 18 rolls of wrapping paper. In all, the school sold 82 rolls. About what percent of the sales came from Mrs. Nellon's class?

23. **Explain** Explain how you would use mental math to express $\frac{16}{25}$ as a percent.

---

24. Which list shows the following values in order from least to greatest?

$\frac{1}{3}$, 0.25, 16%

A $\frac{1}{3}$, 0.25, 16%   **C** 16%, 0.25, $\frac{1}{3}$

B 0.25, 16%, $\frac{1}{3}$ **D** 16%, $\frac{1}{3}$, 0.25

25. **Extend Your Thinking** In a stock market game, Sergio bought 150 shares of stock at a price of $\frac{5}{8}$ a game dollar per share. How much game money did 150 shares cost?

In **26** and **27**, use the table at the right.

The table shows the number of states in the United States at different times in history. There are currently 50 states in the United States.

26. **Analyze Information** What percent of the current number of states had joined the United States by the year 1863?

27. **Reason** In what year were there $\frac{2}{3}$ as many states as in 1896?

Year	States
1792	15
1817	20
1836	25
1848	30
1863	35
1889	42
1896	45
1959	50

Name _____

☆ **Solve & Share** ☆

Suppose that you walk 3,540 feet in 20 minutes. How many feet do you walk in 1 minute? *Solve this problem any way you choose.*

You can **use a strip diagram** to help you solve the problem. *Show your work!*

⊕ **TEKS 6.5A** Represent mathematical and real-world problems involving ratios and rates using scale factors, tables, graphs, and proportions.
Mathematical Process Standards 6.1A, 6.1B, 6.1D, 6.1F, 6.1G

Digital Resources at PearsonTexas.com

Solve   Learn   Glossary   Tools   Games

Look Back!

Check for Reasonableness How do you know your answer is reasonable?

Are There Special Types of Ratios?

A

A rate is a special type of ratio that compares quantities with unlike units of measure.

How far does the car travel in 1 minute?

7 km in
4 minutes

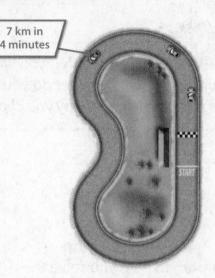

If the comparison is to 1 unit, the rate is called a **unit rate**.

Divide to find the unit rate.

B First, write how fast the car travels as a rate.

Write 7 km in 4 minutes as $\frac{7 \text{ km}}{4 \text{ min}}$.

Remember, fractions represent division.

Divide 7 kilometers by 4 minutes.

$$
\begin{array}{r}
1.75 \\
4\overline{)7.00} \\
-4 \\
\hline
30 \\
-28 \\
\hline
20 \\
-20 \\
\hline
0
\end{array}
$$

C To understand why it works, remember that you can divide the terms of any ratio by the same number to find an equal ratio.

$$\frac{7 \div 4}{4 \div 4} = \frac{1.75}{1}$$

The unit rate is $\frac{1.75 \text{ km}}{1 \text{ min}}$.

The car travels 1.75 kilometers in 1 minute.

Do You Understand?

Convince Me! What is the car's rate for 1 hour? Explain.

Name _____

In **1** through **4**, write each as a rate and as a unit rate.

1. 60 km in 12 hours

2. 26 cm in 13 s

3. 230 miles on 10 gallons

4. $12.50 for 5 lb

5. Explain What makes a unit rate different from another rate?

6. Communicate Explain the difference in meaning between these two rates: $\frac{5 \text{ trees}}{1 \text{ chimpanzee}}$ and $\frac{1 \text{ tree}}{5 \text{ chimpanzees}}$.

Independent Practice ☆

In **7** through **18**, write each as a rate and a unit rate.

How are each rate and unit rate related?

7. 35 minutes to run 5 laps

8. 36 butterflies on 12 flowers

9. 252 days for 9 full moons

10. 18 eggs laid in 3 days

11. 56 points scored in 8 games

12. 216 apples growing on 9 trees

13. 125 giraffes on 50 hectares

14. 84 mm in 4 seconds

15. 123 miles driven in 3 hours

16. 210 miles in 7 hours

17. 250 calories in 10 crackers

18. 15 countries visited in 12 days

Problem Solving

In **19** through **21**, use the bar graph at the right.

19. Reason Give three equivalent rates that describe the top speed of a tuna.

20. Connect At top speeds how much faster can a swordfish swim than a killer whale?

21. Explain Which animal swims at a top speed of about 0.33 mile per minute? Explain how you found your answer.

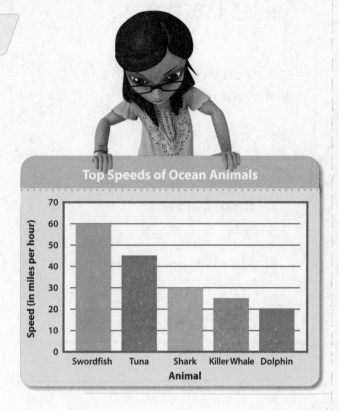

Top Speeds of Ocean Animals

22. Reason The *X-43 Hyper-X* is the fastest aircraft in the world. It can reach a maximum speed of 6,750 mph. What is its maximum rate of speed in miles per minute?

23. Connect Ava found that 5 cars passed her house in 10 minutes. At this rate, how many cars would you expect to pass her house in 2 hours?

24. Doug caught 10 fish over a period of ⭐ 4 hours. Which of the following is a unit rate per hour for this situation?

   A 2.5 fish per hour
   B 5 fish per 2 hours
   C 2 hours per 5 fish
   D 4 hours per 10 fish

25. Extend Your Thinking Make a list of three rates that describe things that you do. For example, you could describe how many classes you attend in a day. For each example, explain why it is a rate.

Name _____

☆ ☆
Solve & Share

Can a parallelogram with a height of 3 units have the same area as a rectangle with a width of 3 units? How do you know? *Solve this problem any way you choose.*

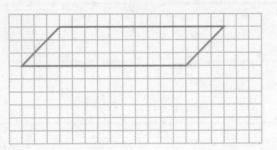

⭐ **TEKS 6.8B** Model area formulas for parallelograms, trapezoids, and triangles by decomposing and rearranging parts of these shapes.
Mathematical Process Standards 6.1D, 6.1G

Digital Resources at PearsonTexas.com

Solve Learn Glossary Tools Games

A picture can help you compare the figures and **justify** your reasoning. *Show your work!*

Look Back!

Explain How are the two figures alike? How are they different?

How Can You Use the Formula for the Area of a Rectangle to Find the Area of a Parallelogram?

Look at the parallelogram below. If you move the triangle to the opposite side, you form a rectangle with the same area as the parallelogram.

> Recall that the formula for the area of a rectangle is $A = \ell \times w$.

B The base of the parallelogram (b) equals the length of the rectangle (ℓ).

The height of the parallelogram (h), which is perpendicular to the base, equals the width of the rectangle (w).

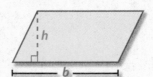 

> Rectangles are special kinds of parallelograms.

C The area of the parallelogram equals the area of the rectangle.

Area of a Rectangle → $A = \ell \times w$

⇅

Area of a Parallelogram → $A = b \times h$

$A = bh$

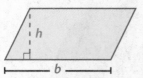

Do You Understand?

Convince Me! How can the formula for the area of a rectangle be used to find the area of a parallelogram?

Another Example

Since two identical triangles can form a parallelogram, the area of one triangle must be half the area of the parallelogram that has the same base and height.

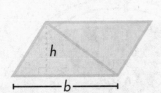

Area of a Parallelogram
$A = bh$

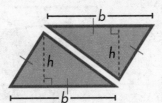

Two identical triangles

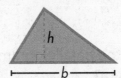

Area of a Triangle
$A = \frac{1}{2} bh$

☆ Guided Practice*

In **1** through **4**, use a formula to find the area of each parallelogram or triangle.

1.
21.5 in.
20 in.

2.
2 ft
4 ft

3. Triangle: *b*: 14 cm; *h*: 23 cm

4. Parallelogram: *b*: 27 ft; *h*: 32 ft

5. Tools The base of a parallelogram is 8 meters, and its height is twice the base. What is the area of the parallelogram?

6. Construct Arguments A triangle and a parallelogram have the same base and height. How are their areas related?

☆ Independent Practice ☆

Leveled Practice In **7** though **12**, find the area of each parallelogram or triangle.

7.
6 yd
2 yd

8.
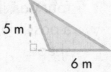
5 m
6 m

9.

10 in.
10 in.

10.

14 cm
31 cm

11. Parallelogram: *b*: 42 m; *h*: 33 m

12. Triangle: *b*: 32 in.; *h*: 2 yd

Problem Solving

In **13** and **14**, use the origami figures.

13. What is the area in square centimeters of the triangle outlined on the figure?

14. ⭐ What is the area of the parallelogram outlined on the figure?

    A 4.44 square centimeters

    B 10.44 square centimeters

    C 9.44 square centimeters

    D Need more information

$b = 3$ cm
$h = 1.76$ cm

$b = 4$ cm
$h = 2.36$ cm

---

15. Explain If you know both the area and height of a triangle, how can you find the base?

16. Extend Your Thinking The base of a parallelogram is 12 meters and its height is 5 meters. Two congruent triangles can form this parallelogram. What is the area of one of these triangles?

---

17. ⭐ Emma wanted to make an origami fish for each of her 22 classmates. It takes 30 minutes to make one fish. How long will it take Emma to make all the fish?

    A 320 minutes   **C** 600 minutes

    B 11 hours   **D** 660 hours

18. Reason Ms. Lopez drew parallelogram *M* with a height of 6 inches and a base of 6 inches, and parallelogram *N* with a height of 4 inches and a base of 8 inches. Which parallelogram has the greater area, *M* or *N*?

---

19. Explain The area of a triangle is 42 square inches. The triangle's base is 6 inches. Find the height of the triangle. Explain how you found the height.

20. Extend Your Thinking The area of a figure is 36 square centimeters. Give four possible shapes of the figure and a possible set of dimensions for each shape.

Name _____

☆ ☆
Solve & Share
A grid map of Washington, D.C., is shown below. Kayla wants to visit the White House and the FBI Building. What ordered pairs represent these two locations? *Solve this problem any way you choose.*

⭐ TEKS 6.11 Use coordinate geometry to identify locations on a plane. Graph points in all four quadrants using ordered pairs of rational numbers.
Mathematical Process Standards 6.1A, 6.1B, 6.1D, 6.1G

Digital Resources at PearsonTexas.com

Solve   Learn   Glossary   Tools   Games

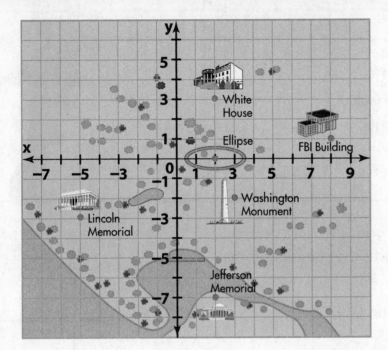

You can **formulate a plan** to help you solve this problem. *Show your work!*

Look Back!

Communicate Using the grid, give directions on how to move from the Jefferson Memorial to the Washington Monument.

How Can You Graph a Point on a Coordinate Plane?

A

Graph the points Q (2, −3), R(−1, 1), and S (0, 2) on a coordinate plane.

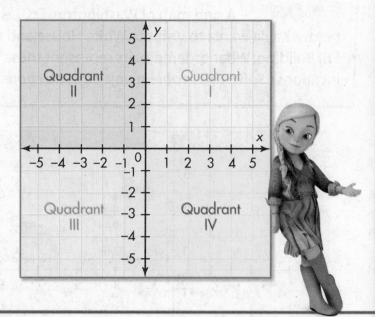

A coordinate plane is a grid containing two number lines that intersect at a right angle at zero. The number lines, called the *x*- and *y*-axes, divide the plane into four quadrants.

B

Graphing points on a coordinate grid:

An ordered pair (*x*, *y*) of numbers gives the coordinates that locate a point relative to each axis.

To graph any point *P* with coordinates (*x*, *y*):

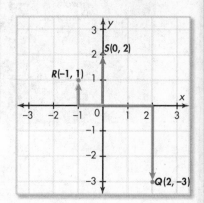

- Start at the origin, (0, 0).
- Use the *x*-coordinate to move right (if positive) or left (if negative) along the *x*-axis.
- Then use the *y*-coordinate to move up (if positive) or down (if negative) along the *y*-axis.
- Plot a point on the coordinate grid and label the point.

Do You Understand?

Convince Me! Kayla says that the Lincoln Memorial is located at (−3, −5) on the grid map of Washington D.C. Do you agree? Explain.

Name _____

☆ Guided Practice *

In **1** through **3**, graph and label the points given.

1. $W(-5, 1)$

2. $X(4, 3)$

3. $Z(-2, 0)$

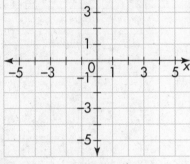

4. In which quadrant does a point lie if its *x*- and *y*- coordinates are negative?

5. Communicate Do (4, 5) and (5, 4) locate the same point? Explain.

☆ Independent Practice ☆

In **6** through **13**, graph and label the points given.

6. $A(1, -1)$ **7.** $B(5, 3)$

8. $C(-3, 2)$ **9.** $D(5, -2)$

10. $E\left(-4\frac{1}{2}, -4\right)$ **11.** $F\left(1, 3\frac{1}{4}\right)$

12. $G\left(-5\frac{1}{3}, 0\right)$ **13.** $H(5, -5)$

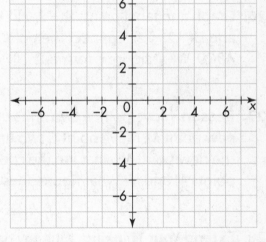

In **14** through **21**, give the ordered pair of each point.

14. P   **15.** Q

16. R   **17.** S

18. H   **19.** J

20. K   **21.** L

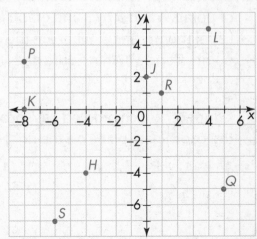

Problem Solving

In **22** through **25**, use the map at the right. The Market Square is at the origin.

Use the red dots to locate the coordinates of the buildings.

22. Give the coordinates of the Library.

23. What building is located in Quadrant III?

24. **Analyze Information** $\frac{3}{4}$ of the quadrants have buildings in them. Which quadrants are they?

25. **Explain** If you were at the Market Square and you wanted to get to the Doctor's Office, according to the map, how would you get there?

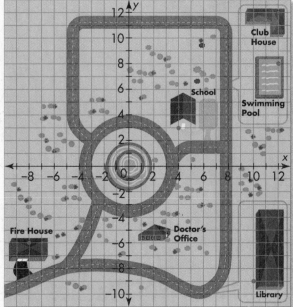

In **26** through **28**, use the grid to the right.

26. Graph and label points $A(-2, 2)$, $B(2, 2)$, $C(2, -2)$, and $D(-2, -2)$. Connect the points to form figure ABCD. What figure is formed?

27. **Reason** Move point B two units up and label the new point M. Move point C two units up and label the new point N. What are the coordinates of points M and N? What figure does AMND form?

28. **Extend Your Thinking** Multiply the x-coordinates of points A and B by 3 and graph the new points. Label them R and S. What are the coordinates of points R and S? What figure does RSCD form?

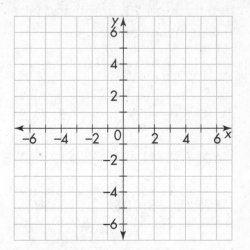

29. **Connect** Which ordered pair locates point P on the coordinate plane on the right?

    A $(-4, -4)$ **C** $(4, 3)$

    B $(-4, 4)$ **D** $(-3, 4)$

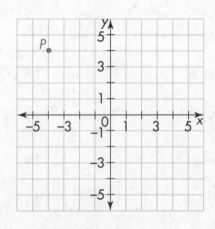

Glossary

A

acute angle An angle whose measure is between 0° and 90°.

acute triangle A triangle whose angles are all acute angles.

Addition Property of Equality The same number can be added to both sides of an equation and the sides remain equal.

additive pattern A pattern in which corresponding values are related by addition.

algebraic expression A mathematical phrase involving a variable or variables, numbers, and operations.
Example: $x - 3$

angle A figure formed by two rays that have the same endpoint.

area The number of square units needed to cover a surface or figure.

array A way of displaying objects in rows and columns.

Associative Property of Addition Addends can be regrouped and the sum remains the same.
Example: $1 + (3 + 5) = (1 + 3) + 5$

Associative Property of Multiplication Factors can be regrouped and the product remains the same.
Example: $2 \times (4 \times 10) = (2 \times 4) \times 10$

attribute A characteristic of a shape.

axis (plural: axes) Either of two lines drawn perpendicular to each other in a graph.

B

balance The amount of money in a person's account.

balanced budget A budget in which the total amount of money spent, saved, and shared equals total income.

bar graph A graph that uses bars to show and compare data.

base (of a polygon) The side of a polygon to which the height is perpendicular.

base (of a solid) The face of a solid that is used to name the solid.
Base

benchmark fraction Common fractions used for estimating, such as $\frac{1}{4}, \frac{1}{3}, \frac{1}{2}, \frac{2}{3}$, and $\frac{3}{4}$.

brackets The symbols [and] that are used to group numbers or variables in mathematical expressions.

breaking apart A mental math method used to rewrite a number as the sum of numbers to form an easier problem.

budget A plan for how much income will be received and how it will be spent.

capacity The volume of a container measured in liquid units.

categorical data Data that can be divided into groups.

Celsius (°C) A unit of measure for temperature in the metric system.

centimeter (cm) A metric unit of length. 100 centimeters equal 1 meter.

circle A closed plane figure made up of all the points that are the same distance from a given point.

common denominator A number that is the denominator of two or more fractions.

common multiple A number that is a multiple of two or more numbers.

Commutative Property of Addition The order of addends can be changed and the sum remains the same. *Example:* $3 + 7 = 7 + 3$

Commutative Property of Multiplication The order of factors can be changed and the product remains the same. *Example:* $3 \times 5 = 5 \times 3$

compatible numbers Numbers that are easy to compute with mentally.

compensation Adjusting a number to make a computation easier and balancing the adjustment by changing another number.

composite number A whole number greater than 1 with more than two factors.

composite shape A figure made up to two or more shapes.

coordinate grid A grid that is used to plot and name points in a plane using an ordered pair of numbers.

coordinates The two numbers in an ordered pair.

corresponding Matching terms in a pattern.

credit **a.** Money put into a person's account. **b.** Buying something now, but paying for it later.

cube A solid figure with six identical squares as its faces.

cubic unit The volume of a cube that measures 1 unit on each edge.

cup (c) A customary unit of capacity. 1 cup = 8 fluid ounces

customary units of measure Units of measure that are used in the United States.

data Collected information.

debit Money taken out of a person's account.

decimal A number with one or more places to the right of a decimal point.

degree (°) A unit of measure for angles. Also, a unit of measure for temperature.

denominator The number below the fraction bar in a fraction.

deposit Money put into a person's account.

difference The result of subtracting one number from another.

digits The symbols used to show numbers: 0, 1, 2, 3, 4, 5, 6, 7, 8, 9.

discrete data Data where only whole numbers are possible.

Distributive Property Multiplying a sum (or difference) by a number is the same as multiplying each number in the sum (or difference) by the number and adding (or subtracting) the products. *Example:* $3 \times (10 + 4) = (3 \times 10) + (3 \times 4)$

dividend The number to be divided.

divisible A number is divisible by another number if there is no remainder after dividing.

Division Property of Equality Both sides of an equation can be divided by the same nonzero number and the sides remain equal.

divisor The number by which another number is divided. *Example:* In $32 \div 4 = 8$, 4 is the divisor.

dot plot A display of responses along a number line with dots used to indicate the number of times a response occurred.

edge A line segment where two faces meet in a solid figure.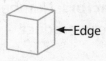

elapsed time The amount of time between the beginning of an event and the end of the event.

equation A number sentence that uses an equal sign to show that two expressions have the same value. *Example:* $9 + 3 = 12$

equilateral triangle A triangle whose sides all have the same length.

equivalent decimals Decimals that name the same amount. *Example:* $0.7 = 0.70$

equivalent fractions Fractions that name the same part of a whole region, length, or set.

estimate To give an approximate value rather than an exact answer.

evaluate To find the value of an expression when a variable is replaced by a number.

expanded form A way to write a number that shows the place value of each digit. *Example:* 3,000 + 500 + 60 + 2

expenses The amount of money spent.

face A flat surface of a solid figure.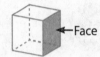

factors Numbers that are multiplied to get a product.

Fahrenheit (°F) A unit of measure for temperature in the customary system.

fluid ounce (fl oz) A customary unit of capacity equal to 2 tablespoons.

foot (ft) A customary unit of length equal to 12 inches.

formula A rule that uses symbols to relate two or more quantities.

fraction A symbol, such as $\frac{2}{3}$, $\frac{5}{1}$, or $\frac{8}{5}$, used to describe one or more parts of a whole that is divided into equal parts. A fraction can name a part of a whole, a part of a set, a location on a number line, or a division of whole numbers.

frequency table A table used to show the number of times each response occurs in a set of data.

gallon (gal) A unit for measuring capacity in the customary system. 1 gallon = 4 quarts.

gram (g) A metric unit of mass. One gram is equal to 1,000 milligrams.

greater than symbol (>) A symbol that points away from a greater number or expression. *Example:* 450 > 449

gross income The total amount of money a person earns.

height of a polygon The length of a segment from one vertex of a polygon perpendicular to its base.

height of a solid In a prism the perpendicular distance between the top and bottom bases of the figure.

hexagon A polygon with 6 sides.

hundredth One part of 100 equal parts of a whole.

Identity Property of Addition The sum of any number and zero is that number.

Identity Property of Multiplication
The product of any number and 1 is that number.

improper fraction A fraction whose numerator is greater than or equal to its denominator.

income Money earned from doing work.

inch (in.) A customary unit of length. 12 inches = 1 foot

input-output table A table that uses a rule to relate one set of numbers to another set of numbers.

intersecting lines Lines that pass through the same point.

interval (on a graph) The difference between consecutive numbers on an axis of a graph.

inverse operations Operations that undo each other. *Example:* Adding 6 and subtracting 6 are inverse operations.

isosceles triangle A triangle with two sides of the same length.

kilogram (kg) A metric unit of mass. One kilogram is equal to 1,000 grams.

kilometer (km) A metric unit of length. One kilometer is equal to 1,000 meters.

less than symbol (<) A symbol that points towards a lesser number or expression.
Example: 305 < 320

line A straight path of points that goes on forever in two directions.

line graph A graph that connects points to show how data change over time.

line of symmetry The line on which a figure can be folded so that both halves are the same.

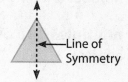

line segment Part of a line having two endpoints.

liter (L) A metric unit of capacity. One liter is equal to 1,000 milliliters.

mass The measure of the quantity of matter in an object.

meter (m) A metric unit of length. One meter is equal to 1,000 millimeters.

metric units of measure Units of measure commonly used by scientists.

mile (mi) A customary unit of length equal to 5,280 feet.

milligram (mg) A metric unit of mass. 1,000 milligrams equal 1 gram.

milliliter (mL) A metric unit of capacity. 1,000 milliliters equal 1 liter.

millimeter (mm) A metric unit of length. 1,000 millimeters equal 1 meter.

mixed number A number that has a whole-number part and a fraction part.

multiple The product of a given whole number and any other whole number.

multiple of 10 A number that has 10 as a factor.

Multiplication Property of Equality Both sides of an equation can be multiplied by the same nonzero number and the sides remain equal.

multiplicative inverse (reciprocal) Two numbers whose product is one.

multiplicative pattern A pattern in which corresponding values are related by multiplication.

net income The amount of money a person receives after deductions are taken from gross income.

numerator The number above the fraction bar in a fraction.

numerical data Data involving numbers including measurement data.

numerical expression A mathematical phrase that contains numbers and at least one operation. *Example:* 325 + 50

obtuse angle An angle whose measure is between 90° and 180°.

135°

obtuse triangle A triangle in which one angle is an obtuse angle.

octagon A polygon with 8 sides.

order of operations The order in which operations are done in calculations. Work inside parentheses and brackets is done first. Then multiplication and division are done in order from left to right, and finally addition and subtraction are done in order from left to right.

ordered pair A pair of numbers used to locate a point on a coordinate grid.

origin The point where the two axes of a coordinate plane intersect. The origin is represented by the ordered pair (0, 0).

ounce (oz) A customary unit of weight. 16 ounces equal 1 pound.

outlier A value that is much greater or much less than the other values in a data set.

overestimate An estimate that is greater than the actual answer.

parallel lines In a plane, lines that never cross and stay the same distance apart.

parallel sides Sides in a polygon that are the same distance apart at every point.

parallelogram A quadrilateral with both pairs of opposite sides parallel.

parentheses The symbols (and) used to group numbers or variables in mathematical expressions.
Example: $3(15 - 7)$

partial products Products found by breaking one of two factors into ones, tens, hundreds, and so on, and then multiplying each of these by the other factor.

pentagon A polygon with 5 sides.

perfect square A number that is the product of a counting number multiplied by itself.

perimeter The distance around a figure.

period In a number, a group of three digits, separated by commas, starting from the right.

perpendicular lines Two lines that intersect to form square corners or right angles.

pint (pt) A customary unit of capacity equal to 2 cups.

place value The position of a digit in a number that is used to determine the value of the digit.
Example: In 5,318, the 3 is in the hundreds place. So, the 3 has a value of 300.

plane An endless flat surface.

point An exact location in space.

polygon A closed plane figure made up of line segments.

pound (lb) A customary unit of weight equal to 16 ounces.

prime number A whole number greater than 1 that has exactly two factors, itself and 1.

prism A solid figure with two identical parallel bases and faces that are parallelograms.

product The number that is the result of multiplying two or more factors.

proper fraction A fraction less than 1; its numerator is less than its denominator.

protractor A tool used to measure and draw angles.

pyramid A solid figure with a base that is a polygon whose faces are triangles with a common vertex.

quadrilateral A polygon with 4 sides.

quart (qt) A customary unit of capacity equal to 2 pints.

quotient The answer to a division problem.

ray Part of a line that has one endpoint and extends forever in one direction.

reciprocal A given number is a reciprocal of another number if the product of the numbers is one. *Example:* The numbers $\frac{1}{8}$ and $\frac{8}{1}$ are reciprocals because $\frac{1}{8} \times \frac{8}{1} = 1$.

rectangle A parallelogram with four right angles.

rectangular prism A solid figure with 6 rectangular faces.

regular polygon A polygon that has sides of equal length and angles of equal measure.

remainder The amount that is left after dividing a number into equal parts.

rhombus A parallelogram with all sides the same length.

right angle An angle whose measure is 90°.

right triangle A triangle in which one angle is a right angle.

rounding A process that determines which multiple of 10, 100, 1,000, and so on, a number is closest to.

sample A representative part of a larger group.

scale (in a graph) A series of numbers at equal intervals along an axis on a graph.

scalene triangle A triangle in which no sides have the same length.

scatterplot A graph that shows paired data values.

sequence A set of numbers that follows a pattern.

sides (of an angle) The two rays that form an angle.

sides of a polygon The line segments that form a polygon.

simplest form A fraction in which the only common factor of the numerator and denominator is one.

solid figure (also: solid) A figure that has three dimensions (length, width, and height).

solution The value of the variable that makes the equation true.

square A rectangle with all sides the same length.

square unit A square with sides one unit long used to measure area.

standard form A common way of writing a number with commas separating groups of three digits starting from the right. *Example:* 3,458,901

stem-and-leaf plot A way to organize numerical data using place value.

straight angle An angle measuring 180°.

strip diagram A tool used to help understand and solve word problems. It is also known as a bar diagram or a tape diagram.

Subtraction Property of Equality The same number can be subtracted from both sides of an equation and the sides remain equal.

sum The result of adding two or more addends.

survey A question or questions used to gather information.

symmetric A figure is symmetric if it can be folded on a line to form two halves that fit exactly on top of each other.

tablespoon (tbsp) A customary unit of capacity. 2 tablespoons = 1 fluid ounce

taxes Money people pay to support the government.

tenth One of ten equal parts of a whole.

terms Numbers in a sequence or variables, such as x and y, in an algebraic expression.

thousandth One of 1,000 equal parts of a whole.

three-dimensional shape A solid with three dimensions that has volume, such as a rectangular prism.

ton (T) A customary unit of weight equal to 2,000 pounds.

trapezoid A quadrilateral that has exactly one pair of parallel sides.

trend A relationship between two sets of data that shows up as a pattern in a graph, including scatterplots.

triangle A polygon with 3 sides.

underestimate An estimate that is less than the actual answer.

unknown A symbol or letter, such as x, that represents a number in an expression or equation.

unit fraction A fraction with a numerator of 1.

value (of a digit) The number a digit represents, which is determined by the position of the digit. See also *place value*.

variable A letter, such as *n*, that represents a number in an expression or an equation.

vertex (plural: vertices) a. The common endpoint of the two rays in an angle. **b.** A point at which two sides of a polygon meet. **c.** The point at which three or more edges meet in a solid figure.

volume The number of cubic units needed to fill a solid figure.

weight A measure of how light or how heavy something is.

whole numbers The numbers 0, 1, 2, 3, 4, and so on.

word form A way to write a number using words.

x-axis A horizontal number line on a coordinate grid.

x-coordinate The first number in an ordered pair, which names the distance to the right or left from the origin along the *x*-axis.

y-axis A vertical number line on a coordinate grid.

y-coordinate The second number in an ordered pair, which names the distance up or down from the origin along the *y*-axis.

yard (yd) A customary unit of length equal to 3 feet.

Zero Property of Multiplication The product of any number and 0 is 0.

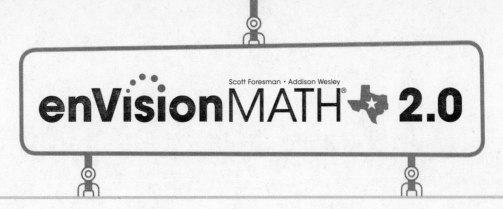

Scott Foresman · Addison Wesley

enVisionMATH® ★ 2.0

Photographs

Every effort has been made to secure permission and provide appropriate credit for photographic material. The publisher deeply regrets any omission and pledges to correct errors called to its attention in subsequent editions.

Unless otherwise acknowledged, all photographs are the property of Pearson Education, Inc.

Photo locators denoted as follows: Top (T), Center (C), Bottom (B), Left (L), Right (R), Background (Bkgd)

003 Daniel Prudek/Shutterstock;**010** Stockbyte/ Thinkstock;**014** Vladislav Gajic/Fotolia;**020BL** James Steidl/Fotolia;**020BR** Hemera Technologies/ PhotoObjects.net/Getty Images/Thinkstock;**020T** Ivelin Radkov/Fotolia;**043B** Nicolas Larento/Fotolia;**043BC** Ivan kmit/Fotolia;**043T** Gewoldi/Fotolia;**043TC** Formiktopus/Fotolia;**072L** Robert Marien/Spirit/ Corbis;**072R** Frank Burek/Spirit/Corbis;**095** Smileus/ Shutterstock;**112** Cphoto/Fotolia;**153** Viacheslav Krylov/Fotolia;**165** Alisonhancock/Fotolia;**176** PhotostoGo;**177** Tatiana Popova/Shutterstock;**193** Tom Wang/Shutterstock;**216** Joe Sohm/Visions of America.LLC/Alamy;**233** Lisastrachan/Fotolia;**260** Sommai/Shutterstock;**271** Zest_marina/Fotolia;**321** Mandy Godbehear/Shutterstock;**385** Paul B. Moore/Shutterstock;**385** Paul Moore/Fotolia;**408R** Esanbanhao/Fotolia;**420** Image Source/Jupiter Images ;**341** Barbara Helgason/Fotolia

447 Mat Hayward/Fotolia;**482** Bev/Fotolia;**499** Natalia Pavlova/Fotolia;**567** Solarseven/Shutterstock;**619** Michael J Thompson/Shutterstock;**628L** Photodisc/ Getty Images;**628R** Corbis;**630B** Ingram Publishing/ Fotosearch;**636** 2010/Photostogo;**669** Morgan Lane Photography/Shutterstock;**737** Iktomi/ Fotolia;**739L** Photolibrary/PhotostoGo;**758** Photodisc/Getty Images;**776L** Marianne de Jong/ Shutterstock ;**776R** Brocreative/Fotolia;**793** Jon Beard/Shutterstock;**817** Patryk Kosmider/Fotolia;**869**

B.G.Smith/Shutterstock;**920BL** Sebastian French/ Fotolia;**920C** Steve Nagy/Design Pics/Corbis;**920BR** DLILLC/Cardinal/Corbis;**920TL** Nicola G/Fotolia;**920TR** Photolibrary/PhotostoGo;**932B** Hotshotsworldwide/ Fotolia;**932TL** Jupiter Images;**932TR** Jupiter Images;**952** Getty Images